AF580441

Renaissance and Baroque Treasury Art

The Green Vault in Dresden

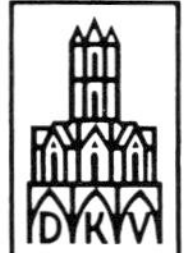

Dirk Syndram

Renaissance and Baroque Treasury Art The Green Vault in Dresden

Translation
Daniel Kletke

STAATLICHE
KUNSTSAMMLUNGEN
DRESDEN

Deutscher Kunstverlag

Hall of Precious Objects, The Green Vault
Southwest corner with door to Silver Gilt Room
Appearance in 1904

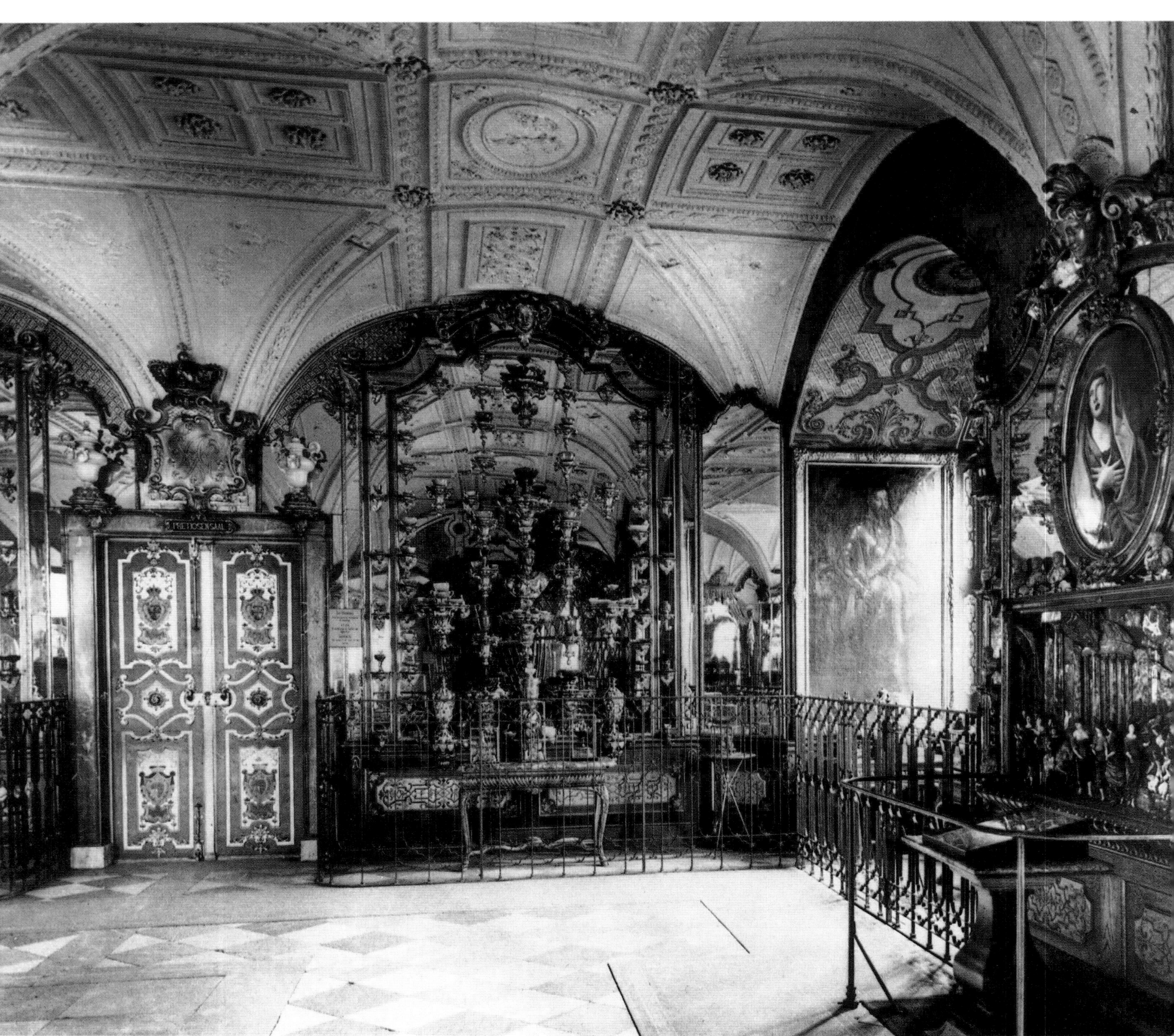

From the *Kunstkammer* and the Treasure Vault – the Green Vault and Treasury Art

Dresden's Green Vault is one of the few European Treasuries that preserves its former inventory almost completely intact. This art collection, gathered during the late Baroque period under Augustus the Strong, who contributed his own purchases and inherited portions to the collection, offers an exceptionally special perspective into the nature of Treasury Art and the changes it underwent during the early modern period. Treasury Art of the Renaissance and Baroque epochs is a particularly splendid segment of European courtly culture. Although the production of artworks made of precious materials such as gold, silver, or precious stones is as old as the history of seigniorial collecting, Treasury Art experienced a notable flourishing from the mid-16th until the 18th century. It developed autocratic forms, its own fashions, and individual collection traditions, and alongside the fine arts, the applied arts and ornamentation evolved into independent types of artistic expression. At the same time, Treasury Art maintained a differentiated connection with other creative genres.

About the Nature of Treasury Art

The most prominent characteristic of Treasury Art is its virtuosic treatment of precious materials. While the real material value and preciousness attributed to the natural products, their rarity, or even their supernatural powers are indispensable for a work of Treasury Art, they are by no means its main attributes. The deliberate renunciation of any practical utilitarian merit is the most important criterion. The emphasis on sensuous appearance dominates the aesthetic attributes of pieces of Treasury Art, making all functionality obsolete.

A comparable phenomenon in modern art is aptly described by the term Object Art. Interestingly, in order to define the latter, documents regarding Treasury Art created since the Renaissance are frequently cited as pivotal sources of inspiration. This is justified insofar as objects from both past Treasury Art and present-day Object Art are sculptural, quoting basic naturalistic shapes and extracting them from their actual functional context. Material collages encountered in contemporary art and works of Treasury Art transmute into art objects by virtue of tempered copies, aesthetic alterations, and stunning combinations of artistic shapes combined with natural products, while their form and decoration are exclusively based on artistic intentions. Such a purposeless art object was often termed »kunststuckh« (art piece) according to the language of the 16th and 17th centuries.

Whereas Object Art – beginning with classical modernity – places real objects into a new context that changes the viewer's perception of them, the most any Treasury Art object does is to playfully pretend that it has a practical aspect. Treasury Art pieces were collector's items, created for the beholder's skilled eye and the touch of one's hand. They could also serve as the source of inspiration for cultured conversations. In this way, they clearly differed from other Renaissance and Baroque luxury articles of the applied arts. The Treasury Art created in the 16th to 18th centuries was – much more so than contemporary paintings, sculptures, and prints – conceived for »interesseloses Wohlgefallen« (interest-free pleasure), which the philosopher Immanuel Kant defined as a criterion of pure art pleasure. Its aesthetics were determined by the sensuous delight of the material's beauty, its physical make-up, and its masterly treatment. In its function within society, however, Treasury Art was a statement of power and affluence.

The objectified character of such an artwork can be illuminated by an example from the Green Vault: A goblet whose cup is made from an iridescent nautilus shell bowl (ill. 1). A broad-lipped edge with Baroque scrollwork ornamentation is set on top of the exotic mother-of-pearl bowl and is reminiscent of a customary form at the time, adapted from the realm of applied arts. The inner chamber of the squid's shell has been cut open and serves as a dragon-like monster's toothed gullet as it greedily stretches its scaled head. A rising serpent in the shape of a handle was positioned above the terrifying beast. Without harming the substance of the invaluable nautilus shell, the fragile bowl is carefully attached to the shaft by clasps, with the necessary joints seemingly dissolved in fantastic grotesques made of scrollwork based on Netherlandish models. The lower portion of the goblet stems from Italian inspirations. Contemporary Venetian prototypes may be found for the shaft's vase shape. The naturalistic foot from a cast eagle's claw reveals the influence of Paduan bronze statuettes that were inspired by Humanist thought prevalent around 1500. Since the mid-16th century, an increasing number of nature casts, supplied by the Nuremberg based goldsmith Wenzel Jamnitzer, were used. The latter incorporated them much more intricately into his ornamental structures. In the goldsmith's art, nature casts are only infrequently encountered as independent vessel parts.

It appears that this »*curiose*« artwork, i.e. one that arouses curiosity and thirst for knowledge, was probably created in circa 1580 in Southern Germany under the influence of Jamnitzer. The first description appears in a Dresden listing of 1587: »I Trinckgeschirr von Perle mutter, mit vorgultem silber beschagen, wie ein Trachen kopf gemacht, stehet vf einem fuß, wie ein Attlers klauen.«[1] (One drinking service made of mother-of-pearl with gilt silver mounts, made like a dragon's head, stands on a foot like an eagle's claw). The princely court official's term drinking service follows everyday language more than it suggests the actual usefulness of the vessel. Although the fragile nautilus bowls could be filled with liquid, their susceptibility to damage, their natural shape that did not facilitate actual use, as well as the challenge of cleaning them without harming them after use, make such utilization unlikely.

On the other hand, the nautilus goblet unites a number of attributes, making it a pure collector's item: Its bowl originates from the tropics. The squid to which the *nautilus pompilius* belongs and from whom the shell originates, lives in an area between the eastern Indian Ocean and the Fidshi Islands, between 50 and 500 m deep (approximately 150 to 1500 feet).[2] While the nautilus bowls were held in particu-

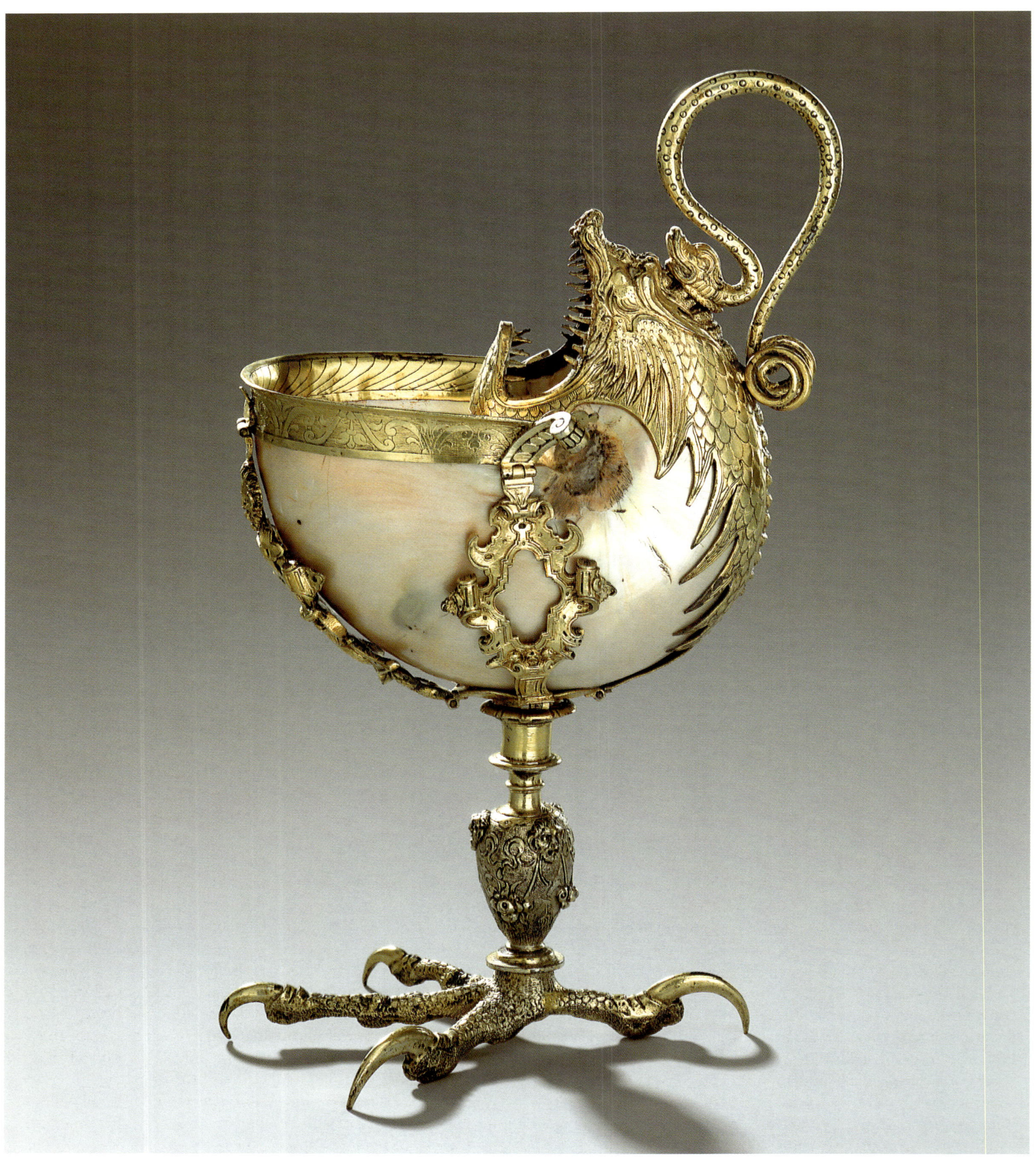

Left side:
Ill. 1 Nautilus Goblet on an Eagle's Claw
Nautilus shell, gilt silver
Probably Nuremberg, before 1587
H. 31 cm
Green Vault, Dresden, Inv.-no. III 197

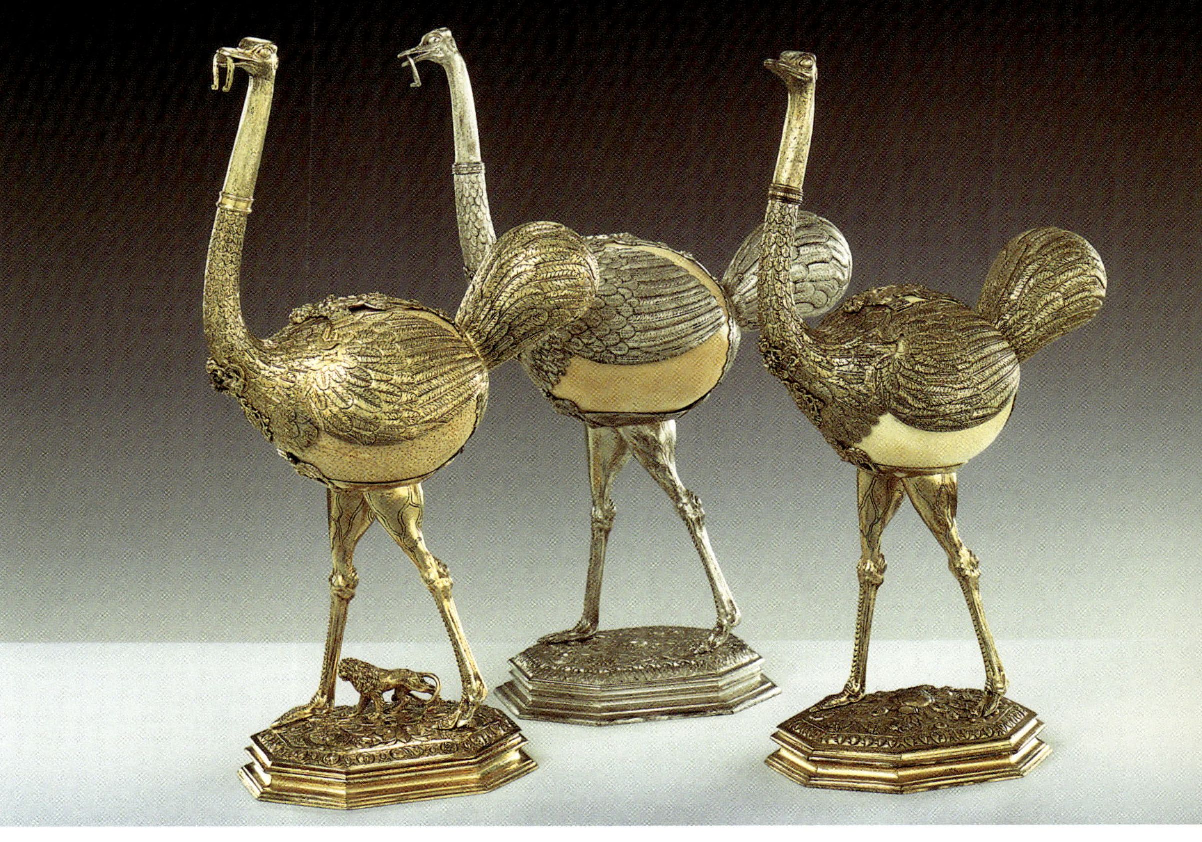

Ill. 2 Three Ostriches
Ostrich eggs, gilt silver
Elias Geyer
Leipzig, before 1595
(from left to right) H. 46,3 cm, 46,2 cm, 47,6 cm
Green Vault, Dresden, Inv.-nos. III 228, III 115, III 227

larly high esteem among princely collectors during the last quarter of the 16th century, they were initially considered rare flotsam on exotic beeches. No one knew what the animal looked like to whom the shell belonged or how it lived. The delicate shells were brought to Europe on commercial ships. In order to lend them their magical radiance, the flaming orange-brown outer skin and the whitish prism coating, similar to porcelain, had to be mechanically removed; then, the thus exposed layer of mother-of-pearl was polished. After this, the nautilus bowl was further ennobled by cutting open the regularly formed inner chambers.

In rendering his bizarre sea monster, the goldsmith also used the nautilus shell because it permitted a direct association with exotic, far-away continents. The roots of such »Naturwunder« (wonders of nature) could only be reached by traversing the expanses of the oceans, then believed to be populated by such chimera, on dangerous sea voyages. This is why the dragon's head lingers like a mighty predatory fish over the water's surface, hinted at by virtue of the broad lipped edge. Consequently, the squid's large living chamber, seemingly made of mother-of-pearl, appeared like the bottomless depths of the ocean. The slender and elegant, serpent-shaped handle makes a striking contrast with the mighty cup. The handgrip, devoid of any function, was only attached to the beast's head for the composition's sake. The base-like foot group of this goldsmith's article is also indebted to a Mannerist concept. The narrow shaft rings, diminishing towards the bottom and connecting the cup with the vase shaft, appear particularly frail. At the same time, the aggressive bird of prey's claw barely manages to retain an optical balance with the dynamics of the bowl.

Although works of Treasury Art are customarily devoid of any utilitarian function, they have a great deal more to tell us. As artistic expressions of their era, they are not merely brilliant artisanal works intended to stupefy the viewer. Instead, they illustrate, on various levels, the predominant views of the world. The nautilus goblet is not only a work of Treasury Art according to our contemporary views; it was destined to become an integral part of the electoral Saxon Treasury in whose inventory it received its first archival mention in 1587.

Beside the treasure vault, the *Kunstkammer* was a customary place to gather such art objects. Thus, the 1595 inventory of the Dresden *Kunstkammer* lists seven goldsmith sculptures in the shape of striding ostriches.[3] Apparently made between 1587 and 1591 by the Leipzig goldsmith Elias Geyer, five of these birds have survived in the Green Vault (ill. 2). Despite superficial similarities, they reveal significant differences based on their material rendering and their forms. This proves that all Treasury Art pieces, even if conceived as groups or variants of a certain type, were always unique, handmade items.

It is part of the intellectual stimulus of the »Strauß Eyer in silber eingefast, Poßirt wie ein Strauß« (ostrich egg mounted in silver, posing like an ostrich) to imagine what it would be like to drink from it. This would theoretically be conceivable, since the birds' heads can be removed. Yet, a libation would gush through the narrow neck and spew out in an uncontrolled manner. This would lead to as much gaiety as the surprise effects of the sudden stroke of the moveable silver wings, connected to the body by hinges. But such a practice is ultimately only imaginary – the ostrich eggs do not have silver liners that would permit for them to be used. In addition, the feet, tails, and head portions are only glued to the egg and drill holes are revealed in those spots. Consequently, liquid would inevitably pour out of the egg.

The ostriches are pure art objects whose particular appeal lies in the viewer's playful imagination regarding their use. They are thus, even more so than the nautilus goblet, independent sculptures. They are statues a goldsmith created, and the real bird's eggs became their bulging bodies. Elias Geyer's fascinating and artistically compelling transformation of the running bird's natural shape permits the assumption that he saw the live bird himself.

Around 1600, the Saxon prince electors naturally owned a large number of »Trinkspiele« (drinking games) formed as animals or bizarre objects. A wide variety of them have survived to this day in the Green Vault. But their repository was once the Silver Chamber, where the court's utilitarian silver was stored. The *Kunstkammer* and the Treasury, on the other hand, were almost exclusively reserved for Treasury Art items that either had no direct purpose or whose practical application had been removed from them.

The *Kunstkammers* in the Late Renaissance

Kunstkammers and Treasuries served, each in their own way, for the »fürstliche Reputation und Zier« (princely reputation and decoration) and thus promoted competition among the princely courts. The intellectual fascination of *Kunstkammers* that attempted, thanks to their universal collecting claims, to gather and to explicate the terrestrial world, is at least as high today as it was during the Renaissance.

Prince Elector August founded the *Kunstkammer* in the Dresden Residential Palace around 1560, erecting it in the attic of the west wing, then serving as the family's living quarters. For a quarter of a century, August used his »Kunststuben,« (art chambers) that extended over seven spaces, as his personal collection of *artes mechanicae* (mechanical arts). This was a technological wonder chamber, filled with artistically decorated and embellished crafting tools and instruments. The first *Kunstkammer* inventory, dated 1587 (thus eighteen months after the prince elector's demise), lists exactly 9,586 individual items and groups, among them more than 7,000 functional craftsman's gadgets and machines, over 400 scholarly instruments and clocks, as well as almost 300 specialty books.[4] For the collection's founder, the Dresden *Kunstkammer* was a place of *vita activa* (active life), a princely studio concealed from the public.

The collection contained only random and very few items then typical of a *Kunstkammer*, such as rare natural products (*naturalia*) or artifacts from far away countries (*ethnographica*).[5] Until 1586, there were only occasional paintings and sculptures kept in the electoral Saxon *Kunstkammer*. *Artificialia*: miraculous objects made with expert artistry, as well as priceless articles where the artistic hand formed rare natural products into objects were likewise largely absent. The Residential Palace foresaw other places to keep such artworks. But it can be argued, that the Dresden *Kunstkammer* was ultimately less atypical than it appears at first sight.

Emperor Ferdinand I founded the first collection entitled »*khunstcamer*« before 1550 in Vienna's *Hofburg*, for which he created an independent »Kunsthaus« (art house) in 1558.[6] A few years thereafter, between 1563 and 1567, Duke Albrecht V of Bavaria built a special *Kunstkammer* and stable edifice for his universal collection in his Munich residence, whose exhibition space was largely complete by 1578. The *Kunstkammer* of Ambras was one of the oldest collections of its type. As his father's Bohemian viceroy in Prague, Archduke Ferdinand II began to procure works of art after 1547. Thus, it was long before 1560, the year the Dresden *Kunstkammer* was founded, that an encyclopedic collection of great magnitude was being gathered and further enhanced in the most exemplary fashion by the sovereign of the Tyrol in Schloss Ambras (near Innsbruck) between 1576 and 1580. The archducal »Kunst- und Wunderkammer,« as it was entitled in its own 1596 inventory, was far more influential for the *Kunstkammers*' first phase than were theoretical 16th-century writings. Located near Innsbruck and thereby on the direct way to the Brenner Pass, Ambras was an area where Italian and German lands met; it became well known throughout the entire empire.

Initially, there were only a few princely *Kunstkammers*, predominantly private aristocratic collections. Within only a few decades, the *Kunstkammer* assumed the air of a medium that expressed the rulers' worldview. The *Kunstkammers* of Ambras and Munich, and the slightly later one created by Emperor Rudolf II in Prague's Hradshin, chiefly determined what the Renaissance and the Baroque vision was for this type of collecting.

There was no binding norm for the princely founder of a *Kunstkammer*. Theoretical writings such as the 1565 manifesto published by Samuel Quiccheberg in Munich concerning encyclopedic collecting remained almost inconsequential for further development.[7] A contemporary document illuminates to what degree the princely lifestyle contributed to the development of the *Kunstkammers*. It is an evaluation by the Bavarian counsel concerning their ruler Albrecht V's financial conduct: »Whatever precious or alien items one sees one must have! Two or three goldsmiths work full-time for the prince alone. Whatever they produce during one year gets broken or sold the next. The painters and portraitists can almost never leave the new building during the entire year! In addition the sculptors, turners, stone masons, the extraordinary expenditure for clothes, decorators, masquerades, the detrimental excess food and drink, banquets, and landscapes...«[8]

For Albrecht V of Bavaria, the *Kunstkammer* became a place of princely display and was accessible to a certain circle of people. The same is true for the *Kunstkammer* of Archduke Ferdinand II in Schloss Ambras. Both collections became magnets, even during their founder's lifetimes, to interested nobles and learned travelers who would plan a concrete visit there.[9] The Schloss Ambras *Kunstkammer* with its convincing combination of *naturalia*, *artificialia*, *mirabilia*, and *scientifica* represented the programmatic model for all princely collecting until well into the 17th century.

Concerning their quality and quantity, the holdings contained in the *Kunstkammers* founded within the Holy Roman Empire were incredibly varied. Their content as well as the form of their presentation were largely coined by the personal preferences, the financial means, and the super-regional relations of the collector. Pursuant to the classical prototypes of Munich, Ambras, and Prague, other princely collectors endeavored, starting in the late 16th century, to represent the entirety of the known and the unknown world. Thereby they attempted to show the order of the universe, as undertaken by God, in microcosm. The individual visitors or the descriptions of known collections from different courts influenced the competitive collecting aspirations by princes. The history of single *Kunstkammer*s shows to what degree their development and even their sheer existence depended on the respective sovereign's opinion of this particular collection type.

Objects that were especially brought or produced for the *Kunstkammer*s aroused curiosity and a thirst for knowledge. This attribute was used in the Latin sense of the original word as »curious.« Curiosities of this genre could be abnormal natural creations as well as admirable human achievements in the design field; objects could range from a monstrous set of antlers to a microscopic, finely carved cherry pit.

The multilayered type of a *Kunstkammer* collection united especially three large groups of objects, first classified in the inventory of the Rudolfian *Kunstkammer* as *naturalia*, *artificialia*, and *scientifica*. *Naturalia* entailed untreated products of living nature, such as taxidermized animals, coral branches, mother-of-pearl shells, antlers, feathers, bones, horns, tusks, or parts of plants. The following also qualified as *naturalia*: Rare and especially precious mineral resources such as marble, serpentine, alabaster, large minerals and crystals, but also metals in the extravagant shape of the seldom encountered ore steps.

The second large segment of a *Kunstkammer* collection was represented by *artificialia*, products resulting from humankind's creative powers. The *ethnographica* was a subgroup, reflecting the global expansion of European trade and military power during the 16th and 17th centuries. As purchases or gift, original »Indian,« »Turkish,« or »Moresque« objects – among them feather images, containers, boxes, furniture, clothing and jewelry – were incorporated into *Kunstkammer*s. The Green Vault's extraordinary collection of Indian mother-of-pearl works set in European goldsmiths' mounts is tied to this latter aspect of collecting.

The majority of *artificialia* were witty items attributed to the genre of Treasury Art. Created by court artists or artisans belonging to a guild, such *Kunstkammer* pieces are distinguished by their skillful rendering, intelligent design, and subtle artistic execution. Artworks that transformed exotic or singular natural occurrences in an artistically compelling manner – such as the Dresden *Kunstkammer*'s ostriches or the nautilus goblet in the electoral Saxon Treasury – were held in particularly high esteem. But technical innovations were also preferred if they came to the *Kunstkammer*s as curious artworks. Contemporary visitors to a *Kunstkammer* were fully aware that subtle technical innovations could easily be concealed behind the playful and extravagant forms. Turned ivories are examples from the latter category: They were expressly created with specifically invented machines and turning tools that revealed a profound knowledge of geometry combined with artisanal precision and masterful artistry. This, however, also holds true for the automatons, where the maker attempted to give man-made matter the appearance of life. Objects turned, carved, or embossed by people of high rank were termed *memorabilia*. In addition, a *Kunstkammer* preserved souvenirs such as historic jewelry or goldsmith's work in order to honor their former owners.

Around the year 1600, the special category of *scientifica* united astronomical table clocks, scientific instruments, time measuring devices, terrestrial and celestial globes, and mathematical-astronomical gadgets. Just like the *artis mechanicae* – artistically ennobled and at the same time utilitarian tools – they were part of the collecting realm of a princely *Kunstkammer*. In the generation of princes to which August belonged, the interest in imaginative, carefully executed contrivances was fairly widespread. The Saxon prince elector shared his enthusiasm with the landgrave of Hesse, the duke of Brunswick, the prince elector of Brandenburg, the Danish king, the duke of Savoy, and the Archduke of the Tyrol.[10] In Dresden's *Kunstkammer*, instruments and mechanical devices were the predominant elements for an entire generation. This changed drastically in 1586.

The Interplay between *Kunstkammer*s and Treasuries

After the death of Prince Elector August, his son Christian I assumed the rule. The new prince elector, a well-prepared man with an awareness of power, was willing and able to display princely splendor in order to reach his political goals. This was aptly expressed in his ambitious building activities in his residential city of Dresden and in the way he transformed the electoral collections. During his only five-year reign, Christian I established the measure according to which the Dresden *Kunstkammer* would evolve in the following generations. In memory of his father, the young prince elector was determined to retain the collections' technological orientation. The accumulated inventory was nonetheless adapted to the more generally accepted appearance of a *Kunstkammer* by adding invaluable new accessions of *naturalia* and *artificialia*.[11] Contemporaneous with the imperial *Kunstkammer* of Rudolf II in Prague, a new collection was created that henceforth represented the competitive standard for any collecting German prince. Christian I had the large ore step, a gift from Rudolf II to his father, moved from the Treasury to the *Kunstkammer*'s central space and declared it a possession of the noble house that could never be sold. Also in this new location, the unicorn's horn, surrounded by mythical symbolism, was suspended from the ceiling on a golden chain. Further »Naturwunder« (wonders of nature) – among them various rhinoceros' horns presented by the grand duke of Tuscany – came to the *Kunstkammer* as well. In the case of the *artificialia*, Christian I initially referred to items he already owned. For example, he displayed his father's turned artworks in the *Kunstkammer*, as well as those by the two Dresden court turners Georg Wecker and Egidius Lobenigk. Christian I granted commissions that led to the continual growth of the turned ivories collection (p. 40 – 43). These objects documented the high standard of art technology within the electorate and bestowed a singular rank to Dresden's *Kunstkammer* within the princely collections. At the same time, the prince elector bought Treasury Art objects such as the above-mentioned ostriches (p. 7), a particularly rare Seychelles' nut with Portuguese mount (p. 26), two large display caskets by south German goldsmiths (p. 38), and the sculpture of a unicorn (p. 26/27). While gifts to the sovereign were more random additions to the *Kunstkammer*, they were equally integrated into the collection. Among the latter category was the cherry pit with 185 faces carved into

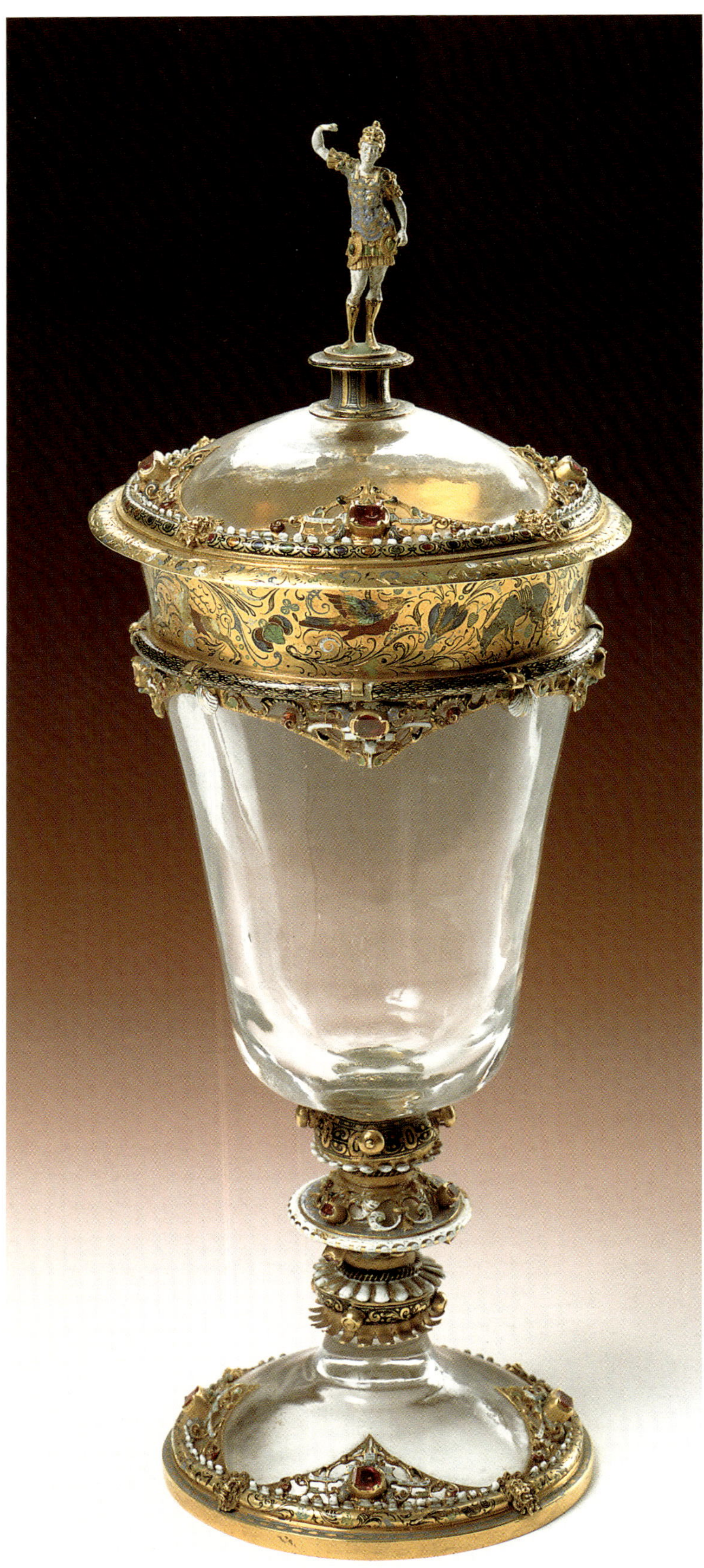

Ill. 3 Lidded Goblet with Crowning Figure in Form of a Roman Warrior
Rock crystal, gold, enamel, rubies
Stonecutting: Freiburg im Breisgau
Mounts: in the manner of David Altenstetter
Augsburg, before 1587
H. 27 cm
Green Vault, Dresden, Inv.-no. V 172

it (p. 48), as well as the sculptures by the Florentine sculptor Giambologna, with whose help Grand Duke Francesco I conferred a new rank onto the Dresden *Kunstkammer*.

It is thanks to the new order of Dresden's collections around 1586/87 that not only the *Kunstkammer* holdings but also the ones then kept in the electoral Treasury were documented in the archives. After his father's death, Christian I initially only had the contents of the Silver Chamber listed in 1586. In those days, the latter contained, apart from the utilitarian silver treasure, uncommon *naturalia* and in all likelihood Treasury Art objects as well. Later, the new ruler conceivably decided to re-dedicate a self-contained suite of rooms on the ground floor of the Residential Palace's west wing as his »Geheime Verwahrung« (secret vault) – until then the space had been used for dining, as a summer garden hall, and banquet room. The »neue Schatz Cammer« (new treasure chamber) – at this point inaccessible to the court – was colloquially entitled the Green Vault (*Grunnen Gewelb*). This term is first archivally reported for November 1586.[12] Around this time, and certainly before the early autumn of 1587, a Treasury register in the form of a list was drawn up that mentions the contents of six large cabinets as a total of 1,144 items.[13] A considerable portion of the articles listed belongs in the *artificialia* category, according *Kunstkammer* terminology. The Treasury also accommodated eccentric and exceptional *naturalia* such as a »Hasengehörn« (rabbit's antlers), skin of a bird of paradise, and different sea snail shells. According to the register, in those days the first cabinet contained the ore steps, much sought after by princely collectors at the time, a total of fifty-five handstones, among them particularly precious ones, for example one made of pure gold in the shape of a little Mount of Calvary (p. 48/49). The second cabinet contained »silbern und gulden kestiche, Auch die Corallen Zincken und andere schonne Sachen« (silver and gold boxes, also coral branches and other nice things). One of the entries probably refers to Jamnitzer's famous casket with the image of philosophy (p. 22/23). Rock crystal works were also kept in this cabinet, among them the lidded goblet embellished with a sumptuous and refined enamel ornament by David Altenstetter (ill. 3) and the Daphne crowned with a large coral branch (p. 38). In the third cabinet, the »Cristallen gleßer, Sampt andern schönen gulden und silbern Sachen« (crystal glasses together with other golden and silver things) were stored. Apart from the Orpheus sphere (p. 28/29) the almost two hundred pieces stored in this piece of furniture also noted the famous large rock crystal sphere and the rock crystal flask (p. 30/31) from the Saracchi workshop. In total, the cabinet contained thirty-three large rock crystal vessels, but also numerous sea snail and nautilus goblets (ill. 1). Agate objects, altogether 350 pieces, as well as two double-walled goblets with glass painting (p. 36) were stored in the fourth cabinet. The register allotted the »volgulde Silber Geschirr« (gilt silver service) to the fifth cabinet. This must have been a rather large piece of furniture, because 310 objects are listed, among them 140 containers. They were primarily goldsmith's works, among them the silver statuette in the shape of a wheel barrel group (p. 24/25), and not precisely identifiable coconut and ostrich egg goblets. This cabinet also held six serpentine display vessels (p. 32/33), early examples of objects designed without a purpose. The last cabinet served as the repository for particularly loved silver dishes, gifts from the duke of Savoy.

The Treasury index describes a colorful array of different objects, silver plate, as well as works of Treasury Art in a vaguely systematic way. Beside contemporary things – some of them had only been produced shortly before the list was drawn up (such as the portrait of Prince Elector August with the Saxon coat-of-arms in glass painting technique (p. 36/37) – there are diverse medieval precious stone vessels described as »Aldt vetterisch« (ancient), but also larger quantities of jewels. Yet not all Treasury Art items in electoral possession were kept in the cabinets of the »neue Schatz Cammer« or in the *Kunstkammer*. There must have been other places for safekeeping in the Dresden Residential Palace. Contemporaneous documents disclose that in March 1587 Electress Sophia, Christian I's wife, for instance, stored a number of her artifacts »in den neuen Schränkchen, darinnen allerlei geheime und seltsame Sachen verwahrt wurden« (in the new cabinets, that contained multiple secret and wondrous things.)[14] located outside her bedroom. It is highly probable that the prince elector also had – in accordance with current conventions – one or more such private safes.

The 1587 register is the only one from the 16th century to have survived. Until the end of the 17th century, no further reports are known allowing us to infer knowledge of the Treasury's possessions. It is not until the reign of Augustus the Strong that the state of the sources changes.

For Dresden's *Kunstkammer*, the situation is different. The first inventory of 1587 is followed by subsequent ones dated 1595, 1610, 1619, and 1640 with printed descriptions dating to 1653 and 1671. They enable us to trace the historic development. What becomes clear is that the evolution, initiated by Christian I (who had already passed away in 1591) was continued, after an almost ten year interruption, by his sons Christian II and Johann Georg I.

Under the influence of Prague's Rudolfian *Kunstkammer*, the Dresden *Kunstkammer* was expanded into an effective means of electoral display. To this end, it was mandatory to continue to buy spectacular objects that would distinguish Dresden's *Kunstkammer* and place it above the others in the Holy Roman Empire. The purchases of Sophia for her sons in 1601 (p. 56/57 and 58/59), but also the large number of mother-of-pearl works Christian II bought in 1602 (p. 52/53) must be seen in this light. The acquisition of the Centaur automaton in Prague underscores the direct influence the imperial collection exerted on the electoral one in Dresden. The prince elector must have seen the slightly older counterpart in Prague (ill. 4). When it was purchased in 1610, some of the imperial *Kunstkammer*'s aura was transferred to Dresden.

Only a few years thereafter, the otherwise frugal Johann Georg I was persuaded to considerably enlarge the holdings of his *Kunstkammer*. During the first few years of his rule, he bought, for more than 1,000 guilders each, the *Kunstkammer* cabinet of Hans Kellerthaler (p. 44/45), Christoph Jamnitzer's pouring garnitures (p. 64/65), and the ivory frigate of Jacob Zeller (p. 60/61). When Johann Georg I bought the pouring garniture of Christoph Kellerthaler in 1629 (p. 64/65) for the hefty sum of 2,700 guilders, the prince elector's finances – due to the Thirty Years War and the ensuing times of misery – were already considerably strained. Moreover, Johann Georg I was likewise the one who improved the architectural situation of the substantially enlarged *Kunstkammer* and thus heightened its representational function. In almost two decades, he expanded the spaces located in the attic, thereby successively adding stately chambers to the *Kunstkammer* and lending it, by virtue of cabinetry as well as wall and ceiling paintings, a festive mood. In the first half of the 17th century, the Dresden *Kunstkammer* thus presented itself in a very charming, modernized manner that turned it into a magnet for »tourism.« The printed descriptions of the *Kunstkammer* not only relate a growing sense of order to the inventory but also its – at least in the short run – increased value thanks to works derived from the field of stonecutting and goldsmith's works from the Treasury.

Whereas during the 17th century, the Dresden *Kunstkammer* was increasingly aggrandized, the historic evolution of the classical three *Kunstkammer*s in Munich, Ambras, and Prague came to a swift end. By 1597, the possibility of viewing the Bavarian dukes' *Kunstkammer* was severely restricted as a consequence of numerous thefts. One year later, Maximilian I had his grandfather's and father's collection listed in an inventory that accounted, distributed on sixty tables and tablets, for 3,407 positions with over 6,000 individual objects.[15] In about 1606, the duke of Bavaria decided to found a »Galeria negst Sr. Churfrtl. Drtl. Leibzimmer« (gallery near his electoral highness' personal chamber), the so-called *Kammergalerie*. It was furnished with particularly high quality items and precious works from Munich's *Kunstkammer*, but also with pieces from the residence's *Schatzturm*.[16] Although the ducal *Kunstkammer* continued to appear attractive for visitors, thanks to the removal of its state items, it sank back to the rank of a confined collection of historic and ethnographic objects. By integrating *Kunstkammer* artworks into the *Kammergalerie*, the latter reverted, also from an administrative viewpoint, into a collection of Treasury objects. As in Dresden, there must have been a Treasury in Munich predating the foundation of the *Kammergalerie*. It appears that this Treasury was also the place where close to three-dozen Milanese rock crystal works that Duke Albrecht VI bought between 1567 and 1579 were gathered. The place that likely served as a Treasury was the *Schatzgewölbe* (Treasure Vault) in the *Silberturm*, where the *Hausschatz* (House Treasure) entailed in 1565 and 1579, was also kept.[17] In Maximilian's personal Treasury, precious objects were preserved in wall cabinets; it was just as tied to his person as his ancestors' *Kunstkammer*s were.[18] After his death, it was dissolved in 1651 and then newly organized.

Ultimately, it was the emperor who safeguarded Archduke Ferdinand II's *Kunstkammer* in Schloss Ambras. One year after the founder's passing, his *Kunstkammer* was recorded in an estate inventory dated

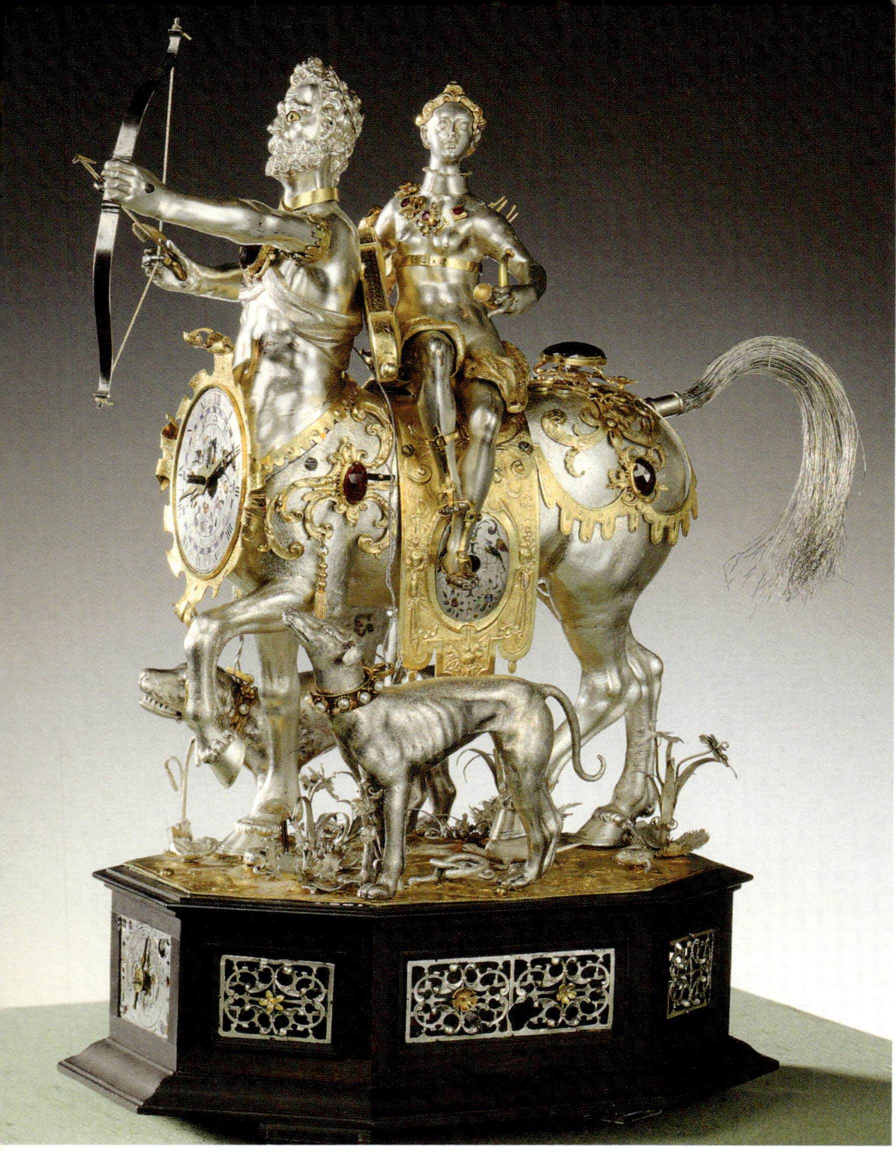

Ill. 4 Centaur Automaton with Diana
Silver, partially gilt, enamel, precious stones, ebony, iron
Hans Jacob I Bachmann
Augsburg, ca. 1605
H. 39,5 cm
Kunsthistorisches Museum, Vienna, Inv.-no. KK 1166

1596. In 1605, Rudolf II bought all collections kept in Ambras for 170,000 guilders: »die Liberey, Rüst- und Kunst- und Wunderkämmern lautt des Inventarii ganz und unverruckht« (the library, armory, *Kunstkammer*, and wonder chamber). The Kunstkammer alone was quoted at 100,000 guilders.[19] The emperor managed to convince his estranged brothers to agree to the purchase. As a consequence, the Ambras *Kunstkammer* went to the arch-house of Austria and thus remained – as a museum ensemble and an admirable collecting achievement – an important tourist destination on one's way to Italy until the early 19th century.

The existence of the Rudolfian *Kunstkammer* on the Hradshin was – like most other large princely *Kunstkammer*s – directly tied to the life and the personality of its collector. Rudolf II, creator of the largest and best *Kunstkammer* of his time, conferred his understanding of himself as Europe's first ruler onto his collecting activities. Almost all objects that entered the imperial *Kunstkammer*, were made during his lifetime. They belong to the finest objects created by any European goldsmith, stonecutter, or toolmaker at the time. The emperor called numerous distinguished artists to Prague, among them champions of their field, such as the precious stonecutter Ottavio Miseroni, or the chamber goldsmith Jan Vermeyen who worked almost exclusively for Rudolf II.

Treasury Art's symbolic function and its relationship to magic held a special place in the Prague *Kunstkammer*. Rudolf II felt himself to be a ruler by God's grace as well as his representative on earth. In his *Kunstkammer*, the emperor united the wondrous, inestimable, and precious products emerging from nature's divine creation. Thus, the emperor's *Kunstkammer* became an elitist power tool. An invitation to visit it was a sign of great benevolence, and those admitted were mostly restricted to important ambassadors or princes.[20] As a token of special imperial goodwill, in June 1607, Christian II was granted a private audience in the *Kunstkammer*.[21]

Between 1607 and 1610, the imperial antiquarian Daniel Fröschl assembled a »Verzaichnus, was in der Röm: Kay: May: Kunstcammer gefunden worden« (a record of what was found in the Roman Imperial Majesty's Kunstkammer), enabling the reconstruction of the imperial collection's content, abundance, and quality, which would be impossible today without this written statement. In September 1612, eight months after the death of Rudolf II, Emperor Matthias determined to keep his collection intact and undivided. The Rudolfian art treasures were thus spared the fate of other imperial collections, such as those formerly owned by Emperors Ferdinand II and Maximilian II, divided among the male heirs in 1564 and 1576 respectively. Instead, Matthias decided to establish a central Hapsburg *Kunstkammer* and Treasury in Vienna.[22] He put this plan into practice between 1612 and 1619, removing the especially valuable items from the Prague *Kunstkammer*. The Vienna Treasury, future center of the Hapsburg collections, did not follow any encyclopedic goals but only served to further the glory of the arch-house. In 1621, Emperor Ferdinand II founded the so-called *Majoratsstiftung*, establishing a family law that entailed the family's jewelry and its entire art treasures, including the material from Ambras and Prague, ensuring that they would always be handed over to the oldest son as possessions of the House of Hapsburg and could never be sold.[23] From 1640 to 1642, the Hapsburg Treasury in Vienna's Hofburg received a new interior design and its holdings were newly arranged.

This was the end phase of the Thirty Years War, which left many *Kunstkammer*s badly blemished. The destruction of princely collections began in 1622 with the conquest of the electoral Palatine residence in Heidelberg by imperial forces under General Tilly. Shortly after 1626, the holdings of the electoral Brandenburg *Kunstkammer* were lost when they were supposed to be evacuated. In 1632, imperial troops plundered the Coburg *Kunstkammer*, and Swedes pillaged the Munich *Kunstkammer* the same year. After the battle near Nördlingen in 1635, the house gems as well as most of the Stuttgart *Kunstkammer*'s treasures and the entire silver treasure of the ducal House of Württemberg experienced the same fate. In 1648, the last year of the war, Swedish troops occupied Prague's Small Side with the Hradshin and plundered the remaining portions of the Rudolfian *Kunstkammer*.

Treasury Art during the Baroque

It was not until decades after the end of the detrimental war that new *Kunstkammer*s were founded in many of the imperial courts. Taste had changed. The subtle shape of the virtuoso masterpiece and the seemingly carefree rendering of natural substances by the artist's hand no longer took center stage. The new generation of princely collectors was fascinated by the expensive Treasury Art works, often studded with colored, especially large and sometimes coarse precious stones. Augsburg was the center of an industry specializing in luxury goods. Meanwhile, French art exerted an increasing influence on the princely collections.

Thanks to its immense fortifications, the Dresden collection in the Residential Palace survived the war largely without losses. The *Kunstkammer* reaches the climax of its representational function during the last decades of the 17th century. As the heart of Dresden's art collections, the Residential Palace became an international travel destination. Johann Georg I began to systematize the inherited over-abundance of his art collection. The third of the eight rooms housing the core of his collection was largely different from all the others in that way that its character was similar to a Treasury. The 1640 *Kunstkammer* inventory allocates the »Kostbare Trinck-Geschirre« (precious drinking vessels) to it. Since the holdings' new installation in the 1630s, it served to present publicly the state vessels made of precious stones, rock crystal, or exotic materials, with the combination of the items – displayed on decorative shelves or on expensively inlaid tables – consistently changing. In addition, the Saxon rulers made it their custom always to show their newest acquisitions of Treasury Art here. In 1683, art chamberlain Tobias Beutel described four open shelves in this room containing plenty of valuable works.[24] One of the decorative shelves contained precious stone vessels made of rock crystal, topaz, and agate, as well as Venetian glasses, in part bought by Johann Georg II and Johann Georg III, in part given to the electoral Saxon collection as gifts from the Emperors Leopold I and Ferdinand III. Another shelf accommodated coral-adorned goldsmith's works, while the third was reserved for mother-of-pearl works, nautilus shell, and sea snail shell goblets. The last shelf held works made of ostrich eggs and »Indianische Nuss-Schalen Geschirre« (Indian nut-bowl dishes.) Beside the coconut shell containers, Beutel makes special mention of the priceless Seychelles nut ewer. Arranged on a free-standing, long table, pouring garnitures could be encountered that were made of gilt silver, mother-of-pearl, and precious stones. Two further tables with mother-of-pearl inlays housed additional goblets and basins. An »Indianischer Tresor,« apparently a little cabinet in Japanese lacquer work, was reserved for the then still very rare Far Eastern porcelain. Works with historic or dynastic connections were placed in the furniture attached to the walls. Under Johann Georg III, the monogram of the ruling prince elector, made of »Landdiamanten« (rock crystal) was installed over the first shelf, the »crystallinen Tresor.« A number of paintings attributed to famous artists further enhanced the luxury of the furnishings. The painters listed include Dürer, Lucas Cranach, Tintoretto, Titian, and Rubens. In this location, Dresden's *Kunstkammer* thus also absorbed the function of a public Treasury that documented both the wealth and the venerable age of the electoral House of Wettin. Apart from this public treasury space, there were also places for safekeeping that were inaccessible to the public in the late 17th century, namely the »Grüne Schatz Gewölbe« (Green Treasure Vault) and the »beth Stübigen« (prayer room). Whereas the vaults of the Green Vault with their isolated location were rather more structured like a storage facility, the prayer room was presumably a treasure cabinet belonging to the prince elector's private quarters. Comparable to Munich's *Kammergalerie* under Maximilian I, this space held the sovereign's personal selection of artifacts. Whereas until now, the exact location of the »beth Stübigen« has not been identified, it can be surmised that it was a small room immediately bordering the ruler's bedroom. The electoral living quarters were on the second floor of the south wing and in the southern reaches of the west wing. They occupied an area today partly identical with the Green Vault's exhibition galleries. The prayer room's existence is documented in the files begun in 1697 on the occasion of Prince Friedrich Augustus I's coronation voyage to Cracow. According to the documents, the prayer room accommodated numerous rock crystal works, diamond-studded gold beakers, as well as the prince elector's jewelry.[25]

Upon his coronation as Polish-Lithuanian king, the prince elector took the throne name Augustus II. One century later, he received the nickname August der Starke / Augustus the Strong. Born in 1670, he belonged to a generation whose princely education was coined by Baroque self-perception. As the son of a prince elector, Augustus the Strong grew up immersed in the antagonistic tension between imperial Hapsburg habits and customs and the temptingly fashionable ideas of the French Sun King at Versailles. He personally experienced both variants of rule and their artistic views of themselves, and in addition, he knew the courts of Spain, Portugal, Savoy, and Florence. Since the last quarter of the 17th century, the residences of the Holy Roman Empire's nobility had begun to open more towards other European entities. Part of this development entailed the fashion of creating cabinets of precious objects. These very intimate collections of Treasury Art served for the *recréation* and *divertissement* of the collecting prince. It appears that initially they were only small collections associated with the princes' private quarters, comparable to the prayer room, within the residences. However, this new type of collection soon evolved into a stage for princely competition. The composition of precious objects collections and their originality reflected the rank that many German princely houses aspired to within their own class.

Gallantries and Precious Things

Apart from jeweler's sculpture, courtly Treasury Art of the Late Baroque also entailed exquisitely mounted statuettes, state clocks, and complex cabinet pieces, most particularly items derived from the field of »gallantry.« At first, the term »gallantries« was applied to smaller-sized utilitarian luxury articles made of costly materials, among them decorative little bowls and boxes (p. 82/83), scent bottles, perfume phials,

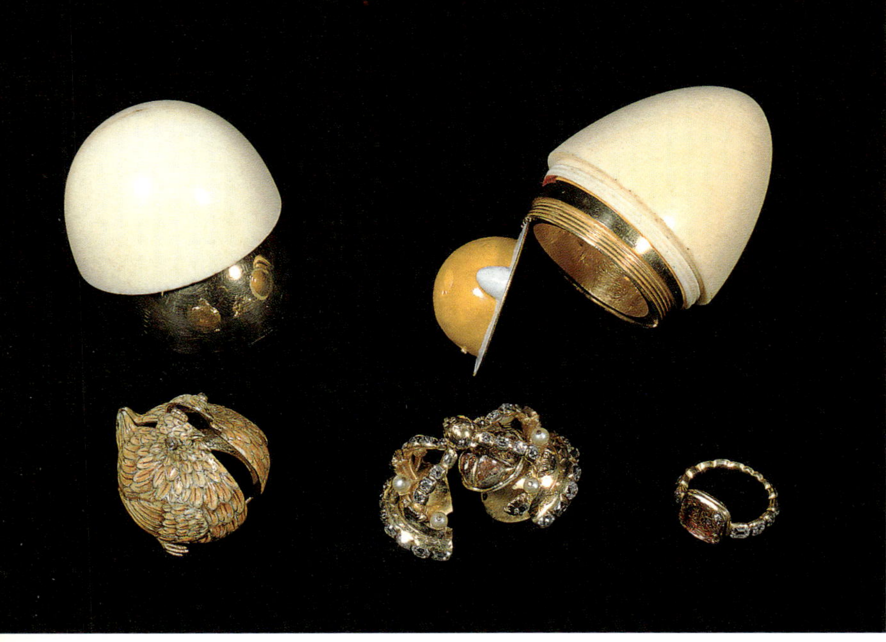

Ill. 5 Golden Egg
Ivory, gold, enamel, diamonds, pearls, carnelian
Germany, shortly after 1700
Egg: H. 6,1 cm, D. 4 cm
Amalienborg Palace, Copenhagen, Inv.-no. A2-728

as well as seal holders, receptacles, pommels, and small writing tablets. Especially minute and meticulously executed luxury works of this category became collector's items, and the expressions »gallantries« and »*Pretiosa*« became collective names for Treasury Art works in authoritative court documents. Hence, in the official German of the day, pearl figures or ivory statuettes were also associated with »gallantries.« Since the containers and the utensils were more or less concealed upon the wearer's person and were thus a surprise to beholders, they only quoted the original function of these items in a playful manner and emerged as writing tools, receptacles for sewing, articles for personal hygiene, or attachments for perfume bottles. Derived from utilitarian objects of princely extravagance, the reference to functionality and intentional imitation in these works of Treasury Art lends them an additional element of entertainment and amazement

A specific group within this precious art genre (p. 114/115) is constituted by a number of miniature minutely detailed and gemstone-studded ivory figures, some of which are mounted on elaborate pedestals. Figures derived from the *Commedia dell'Arte* or realistic depictions of merchants (Savoyards), peasants, and craftspeople were particularly popular. Pearl figures make up their own sub-category of Treasury Art (p. 116 – 119). Originating in Renaissance jewelry motifs, they became independent objects in the late 17th century. The point of departure for these playful designs with their free associations were large, irregularly formed pearls whose shapes began to be called »*barocco*« in Portugal beginning in the 16th century. Their bizarre shapes were turned into body parts for humans and animals, pieces of garments, and bags. Changes in fashion and variations in types may be pinpointed within the princely collections even for these individually fabricated objects.

The works of Baroque Treasury Art were intended for connoisseurs, and their intimate character did not readily lend itself to public display. They are mostly small-sized art objects inspiring the viewer to make playful discoveries and to study the items in-depth. Their material value and gracious design made them the most valuable of all collector's objects with the consequence that they were customarily stored in secure cabinets or trellised cabinets. When the princely proprietor removed them from storage, the fantastic objects would give him and his guests personal pleasure. As they were inspected from close-up or even »grasped« in one's own hand, they were the starting point for courteous conversations.

One example is the golden egg, a precious object characterized by the use of noble materials that qualifies it as a Late Baroque work of Treasury Art because of its surprise effect (ill. 5). On May 24, 1705, Augustus the Strong bought »Ein Ey, von Golde, worinnen eine Goldene Henne, und in der Henne eine kleine Crone mit Diamanten besezt ist;«[26] (a golden egg in which is placed a golden hen and in the hen a little, diamond-embellished crown) at the Leipzig Fair. Yet, this egg was not a unique piece: In 1725, the prince elector-king was offered another similar object for purchase that was included in the collection of precious objects from the duchess of Saxony-Coburg-Meiningen.[27] Two other gold royal surprise eggs are kept in Copenhagen's Amalienborg Palace and in the *Kunstkammer* of the Kunsthistorisches Museum in Vienna. Whereas the Danish example likely originates from George I, Prince Elector of Hanover and King of England, the Viennese egg's provenance is the imperial House of Hapsburg.[28] Finally, Sibylla Augusta von Lauenburg, wife of Margrave Ludwig Wilhelm von Baden – a politically important and militarily successful contemporary of Augustus the Strong – owned a fifth golden egg. This group illustrates that the high-ranking circle of imperial princes had a common view of Treasury Art. In all likelihood, the eggs – consistently worked with attention to particulars, despite differences in the details – originate from a goldsmith's studio located in southern Germany, where they were produced in the first decade of the 18th century and then sold to the fashion-conscious princes of the Holy Roman Empire. The latter actually moved to their winter quarters in Frankfurt / Main during the war with France, which explains in part the far-from-coincidental development of Frankfurt, city of fairs, into an important trading center for the jeweler's art.

As the case of the golden eggs points out, there was a demand for works of Treasury Art around 1700 of which we have only a vague grasp. The surviving objects are scattered and barely permit us to comprehend the former variety of types or the marketing routes. Thus, it is only infrequently that one can ascribe individual works to specific masters or date them with any exactitude.

In light of the fact that most Late Baroque collections of Treasury Art are lost, the Green Vault appears as the great exception. With its largely untouched holdings of precious objects, it occupies a singular rank today. While this status sometimes leads to the assumption that the residential city of Dresden – with its artistically significant jewelers and goldsmiths – was the leading center of German Late Baroque Treasury Art, a number of telling examples will underscore the point that Treasury Art was collected at almost all Late Baroque courts.

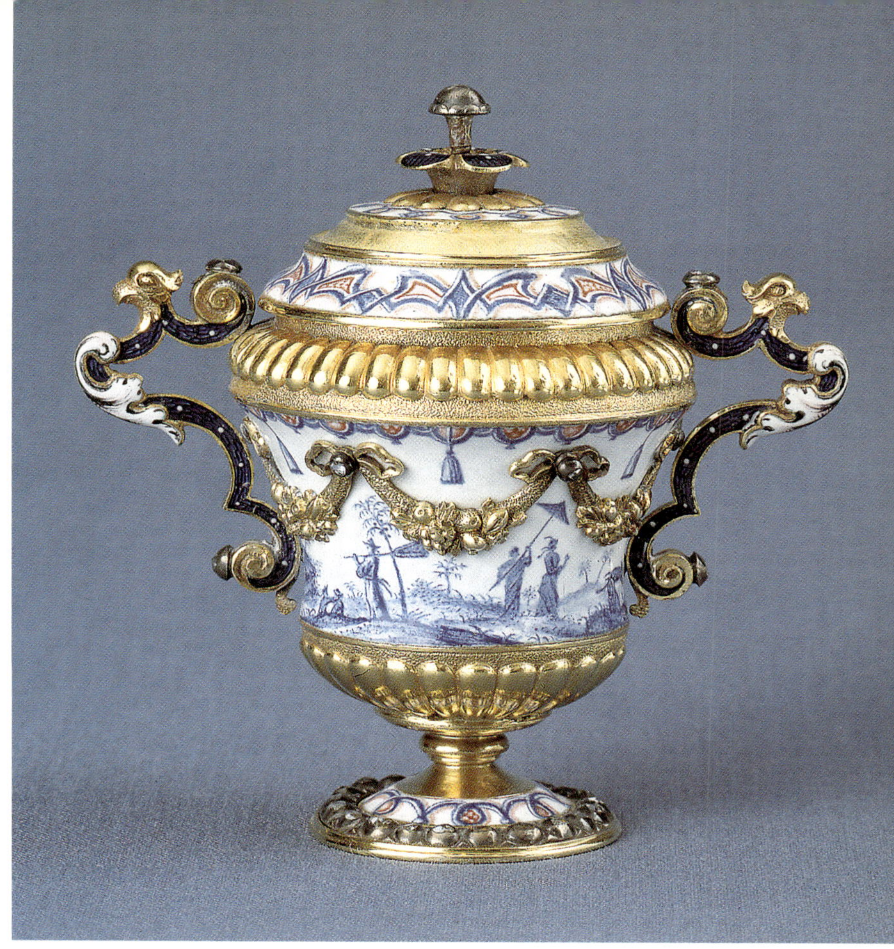

Ill. 6 Small Chinoiserie Covered Vase
Gold, silver, enamel, 30 diamond roses
Enamel painting: Georg Friedrich Dinglinger
Goldsmith work: Dinglinger workshop
Dresden, circa 1700
H. 5,4 cm, B. 5,4 cm
Rosenborg Palace, Copenhagen, Inv.-no. 5-214

A case in point is the rare surviving precious pearl objects and ivory figures from the collection of Prince Elector Johann Wilhelm of the Palatinate: Through the estate of his wife, Anna Maria Luisa de' Medici, they went to Florence.[29] Other portions of this once extensive collection of precious objects, procured between 1691 and 1719 for the Düsseldorf Court, were bequeathed to Munich's Treasury in the Residenz. Remnants of Baroque Treasury Art from the Danish royal house have likewise survived in Copenhagen's Rosenborg Palace. As is the case in the Green Vault, it contains important examples of this art genre, among them such items like the tiny gold enamel box that was brought directly from the workshop of Dinglinger to the court of Augustus the Strong's Danish cousin (ill. 6). Further traces of a Late Baroque courtly passion for collecting may be encountered in the traditional collection of the Ernestine dukes of Saxony-Gotha-Altenburg in Gotha's Schloss Friedenstein.

Reports concerning lost collections of Treasury Art have survived in archives, inventories, and other registers. Another remarkably comprehensive collection of which hundreds of ivories and objects made from different materials still survive today in the Herzog Anton Ulrich-Museum, was owned by the dukes of Brunswick-Lüneburg. The museum also owns five of the initial ten collection cabinets, expressly manufactured for Brunswick Palace; they once contained the ivories, among them some important Balthasar Permoser works and materially expensive objects of Treasury Art. The vitrine-cabinets measure about eight feet in height (240 cm) and were made in circa 1730 to house the collection of precious objects in the *Grauer Hof* (ill. 7).[30] From 1724 to 1726, Duke August Wilhelm had an illustrated inventory drawn up that incorporated the 250 most valuable objects in his *Pretiosensammlung*. The ducal Treasury Art collection consisted of more than 500 objects and was closely related to the one in Dresden, also with respect to its contents. Its focal point was – apart from the Mantuan onyx ewer from the collection of Isabella d'Este – the *Mons Parnassos* or *Mons Philosophorum*, a well over three-foot high (100 cm) cabinet piece that Johann Melchior Dinglinger, Augustus the Strong's court jeweler, executed using Permoser ivories.[31] Except for a very few pieces, August Wilhelm's collection of precious objects has disappeared. Meanwhile, the House of Brunswick-Lüneburg's ducal collection reveals the influence Dresden's collecting activities exerted on princely contemporaries.

Between Intimacy and the Public

In his own time, Augustus the Strong was certainly the most important collector of Treasury Art. During a reign that lasted from 1694 to 1733, he repeatedly obtained such artworks. His first documented purchase was »Eine Gallanterie büchse von goldt,« (a golden gallantry box) for which Johann Melchior Dinglinger wrote the invoice on October 4, 1692.[32] At that time, Augustus the Strong's brother was still the ruling prince elector and Dinglinger was a young goldsmith who had only recently moved to Dresden. Augustus' last purchase has also survived: »Ein großer oval halbrund geschnittener elffenbeinern Pocal mit Silber … haben Ihro Königl. Majt. in Leipziger NeuJahrsMesse 1733 erkauffet«[33] (His Royal Highness has bought at the Leipzig New Year's Fair 1733 … a large, oval ivory goblet with silver, cut in a semi-circular way.) The fact that the goblet has a Leipzig Fair provenance is absolutely in keeping with his acquisition habits. As an international market, Leipzig was an important source for the prince elector-king, where even court artists such as Permoser offered their works, and it was by this route that some of the material entered the royal collection. This is especially the case for the works by foreign goldsmiths and jewelers, such as Guillaume Verbecq, a jewelry merchant based in Frankfurt, or the goldsmith Christoph Ertel who worked in the Saxon town of Zittau. Today, his sumptuous group of the Four Seasons (ill. 8) is kept in Hamburg's Museum für Kunst und Gewerbe, proving that Saxon Treasury Art items did not exclusively come to the Dresden collections.

Whereas at first Augustus the Strong went to Leipzig alone, starting in 1701, the secret counsel Georg Baron von Rechenberg began to scrutinize the Leipzig Fair, acting as the art buyer for his sovereign, who often stayed in Poland. This explains how a comprehensive collection of Treasury Art was quickly assembled whose most opulent items are documented in a register dated January 1706. The latter is a pawn list,

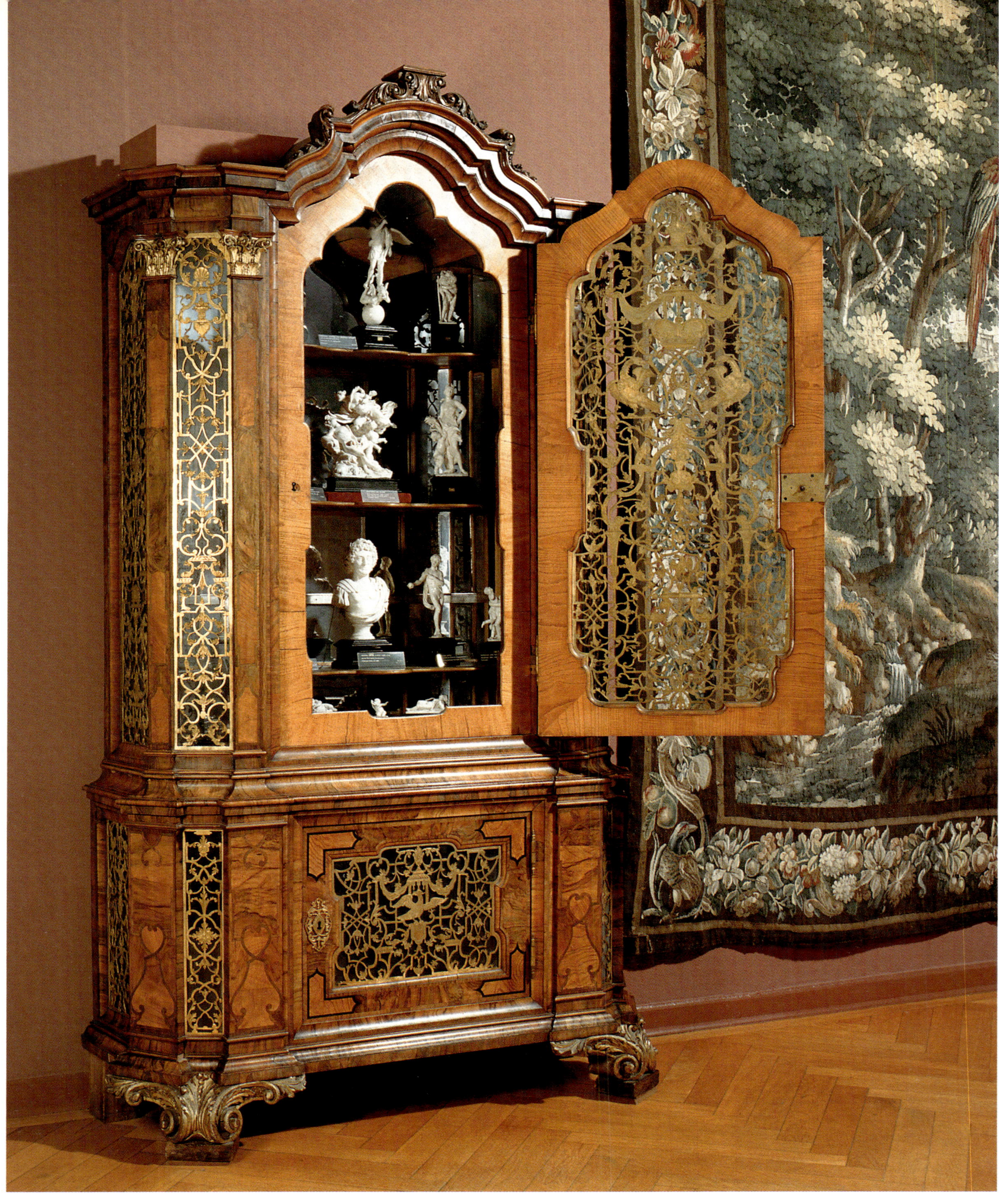

Left side:
Ill. 7 Vitrine-Cabinet
Walnut, ash, rosewood, fruitwood, burl wood, gilt brass
Brunswick, circa 1730
H. 240 cm
Herzog Anton Ulrich-Museum, Brunswick, Inv.-no. Moe 10

Ill. 8 Cabinet piece with Allegory of Fall from a Series of the Four Seasons
Ivory, polychromy, gilt silver, enamel, molten glass, scallop shells, agate
Christoph Ertel
Zittau, circa 1706
H. 19,2 cm, B. 9,6 cm
Museum für Kunst und Gewerbe, Hamburg, Inv.-no. 1926.54c

specifying 102 cabinet pieces, gems, and precious objects that were supposed to be brought to Hamburg during the Nordic War.

When the record was drawn up, the collection of Treasury Art had already gone through an eventful history. Thanks to the golden coffee service (p. 92/93) the prince elector-king had received from his court jeweler Dinglinger in December 1701, his collection had attained royal status. A handed-down document written by his secret chamberlain Starcke gives evidence that Augustus the Strong utilized his collection of precious objects for his own diversion. Pursuant to his return from Poland on November 30, 1704, the ruler commanded numerous precious objects and rock crystal works to be brought from his treasure depot in the Green Vault to the »*Praetiosen Cabinet*,« presumably situated directly above it, »Alwo Sr. Königl. Majt. Selbst in einen express dazu Verferttigten Schranck mit eigener Hoher Handt rangiret und Gesezt haben, wie auch ebenfalls das Christall de Roch Trinkgeschir,«[34] (where His Royal Highness with His own high hand arranged and placed, in a most rapidly and expressly fabricated cabinet, also the rock crystal drinking service.) With regards to the use of the Cabinet of Precious Objects, Starcke continues a little more specifically. »Die Schlüssel aber zu diesem praetiosen Cabinet haben S. Königl. Majt. von Dato an jederzeit bey sich behalten, undt zwar haben solche auff dero Schreibe Tisch in der Schlaff Gemach jedes Mahl versiegelt gelegen, da Sie denn bißweilen gantz alleine, auch zum öffteren mit Damens undt Cavalliers hinein gegangen, ihre Praetiosa besehen, unter weilen verändert auch einige anders faßen laßen;« (But from this date on, His Royal Majesty always kept the keys to this Cabinet of Precious Objects with himself. They were placed sealed on the desk in the bedchamber. Because he entered, at times alone, often times in the company of ladies or cavaliers to look at the precious things. Sometimes he also had some of them altered or mounted differently). On December 16, 1704 – barely two weeks after its inception – for the Cabinet of Precious Objects a notable acquisition was made: For the total sum of 20,600 thaler, Augustus the Strong bought »einige Curiöse Jubelen und pretiosa,« (a number of curious jewels and precious items) from Dinglinger. Apart from his portrait that was cut into a large ruby for 3,600 thaler, the additions encompassed one »große Schale aus Chalcedonick der Diana Bad vorstellend,« (a large chalcedony bowl representing Diana's bath) for 8,000 thaler (p. 98), four »Cabinets in 55 raren stücken bestehend« (cabinets filled with 55 rare pieces) for 6,000 thaler, and one further cabinet item »von Tiroler Türkisen für 3.000 Taler,«[35] (made of Tirolese turquoise for 3,000 thaler). With Diana's bath, Dinglinger's first display bowl, Augustus the Strong secured an artwork of exceptional class, whose significance furthered the Cabinet of Precious Objects' significance.

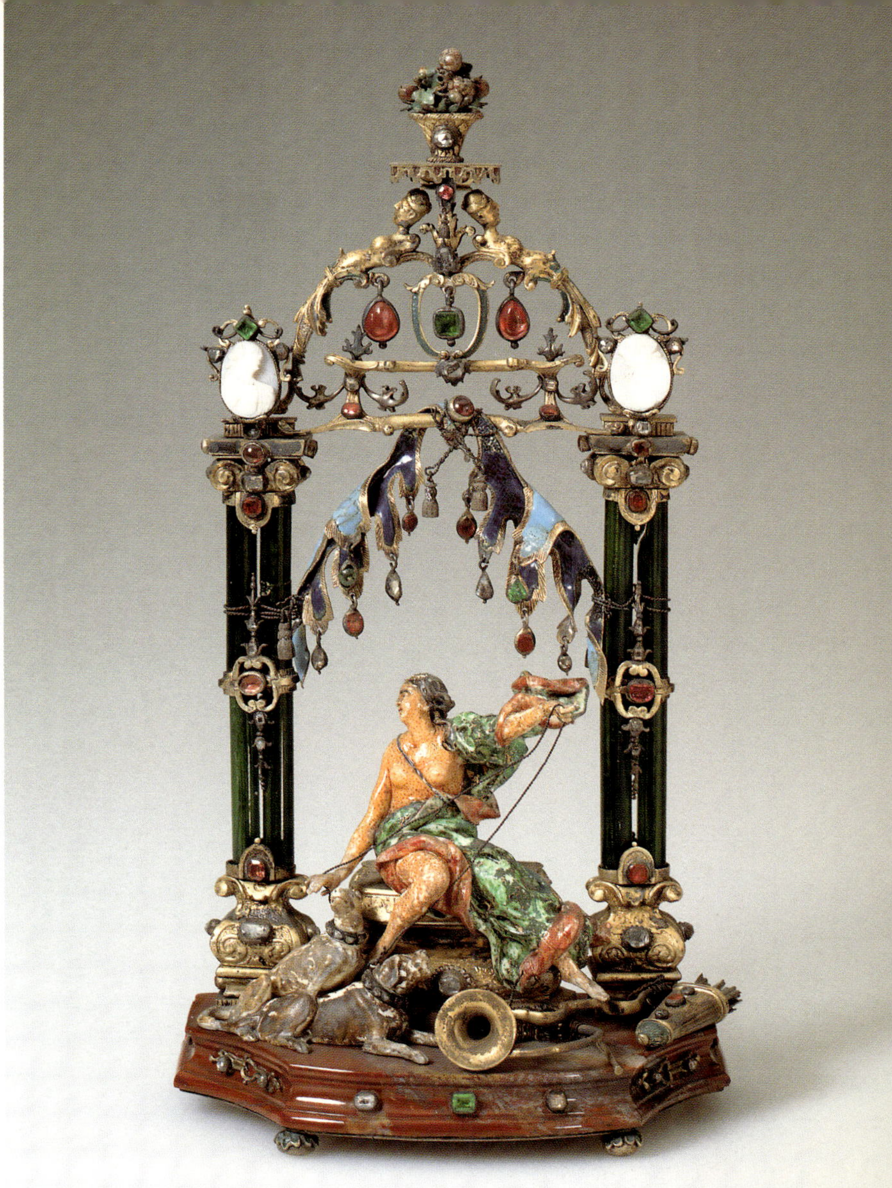

Neither war-related pawning of his precious objects collection's most sumptuous items nor the growing dearth of money could prevent Augustus the Strong from pursuing his collecting passions. On February 6, 1709, Dinglinger's »Throne of the Grand Mogul Aureng-Zeb« (p. 94 – 97) came into royal possession, soon followed by diverse eccentric display bowls by his court jeweler, whose fame continued to increase. Apparently, the large »Throne of the Grand Mogul Aureng-Zeb« could not be fitted into the little Cabinet of Precious Objects and was therefore installed directly in the Green Vault, at that point certainly not much of a place for stately display. Soon, more marvels followed, such as Dinglinger's Medea bowl in April 1709. In the ensuing years, the Cabinet of Precious Objects and the Secret Safe (*Geheimer Tresor*) continued to coexist and apparently were both shown to high-ranking visitors such as King Frederick V of Denmark.

When the pawned objects returned from Hamburg in October 1714, a satisfactory solution had be found for the royal Treasury. The abundant possessions had reached such numbers and a high standards of quality that the Augustan collection began to approach the level of those belonging to the Hapsburgs in Vienna or even the Medici in Florence. Hence, in 1715 Augustus the Strong determined to employ a suite of rooms on the second floor of the Dresden Residential Palace's west wing – formerly his mother's and later his wife Christiane Eberhardine's suite of private rooms – to present his »*Praetiosa*.« In November 1715, small Treasury Art works and rock crystals were brought to the marble chamber of the »Frau Mutter Zimmer« (Madame Mother's enfilade). They were the same spaces that since September 2004 house the New Green Vault as Museum of Renaissance and Baroque Treasury Art (*Neues Grünes Gewölbe*). On April 2, 1716, a few months after the inauguration of the Cabinet of Precious Objects, a serious incident occurred: Due to the architectural alterations, a portion of the window zone and the ceiling collapsed, damaging multiple Treasury Art objects. Despite the bruised precious objects, a Jewel Cabinet was instituted in October 1716 in a neighboring small room that directly bordered the hall »ou le Roy mange ordinairement,« (where the king ordinarily dines). The art agent and interior architect Leplat commissioned the mirrored interior decoration, extending over the walls and the ceiling, in Paris. Until the summer of 1719, the collection of impressively displayed jewelry was still significantly increased. This enabled Augustus the Strong to shine before the public and all princes present on the occasion of the Electoral Prince Friedrich Augustus' marriage to the emperor's daughter Maria Josepha and the related, week-long festivities. In this setting, the ruler not only distinguished himself as the owner of a unique group of jewel garnitures (p. 130 – 131), but also thanks to his well organized and richly-filled Cabinets of Jewels and Precious Objects. When the wedding ceremonies were over, in December 1719, the prince elector-king dedicated a number of weeks to evaluating his jewel garnitures and oversaw their subsequent presentation in a large jewel closet that he had manufactured for the Green Vault's main hall. Thereby the ultimate rise of the secret vaults to the royal museum of Treasury Art began.

The Green Vault as Treasury Museum

In the end, it was yet another huge purchase made by Augustus the Strong from his court jeweler Dinglinger in February 1722 that confirmed this development. At this point, he bought the *Obeliscus Augustalis*. This remarkable and immense cabinet piece in honor of the collector-king required a mirrored back wall to be appropriately installed. It is the first piece of Treasury Art that is inaccessible to individual close-up scrutiny because as an effective artwork, it fills the entire space and thus addresses the amazed beholder. The necessary spatial alterations in the Green Vault – based on a concept by Augustus the Strong – seem to have been undertaken by master builder (*Oberlandbaumeiter*) Matthäus Daniel Pöppelmann from June 1723 until August 1724. The result was a complete Late Baroque interior space. In it, the free-standing objects, exhibited on numerous consoles and tables, appear to have developed a singular coherence with the festive architecture. The installation of the new museum of Treasury Art equally required a new order for Treasure Art preserved in various areas of the Residential Palace. Beside the bronze statuettes, this applied to the majority of turned ivories from the *Kunstkammer* that were transferred to the Green Vault's Treasury Art museum. Nevertheless, soon Augustus the Strong found the freshly designed rooms of the Treasury Safe inadequate. Therefore, in February 1727, a considerable extension of the museum area began, ultimately filling the entire ground floor of the west wing. In September 1729, the Treasury museum was finally completed as a Baroque *Gesamtkunstwerk*. Surrounded by a festively escalating interior architecture, the House of Wettin's hereditary collection and Augustus the Strong's Collection of Precious Objects were hence united in eight rooms.

The circuit began in the Room of Small Bronzes, leading to the Ivory Room, a type of cabinet as well. The next two rooms, the White Silver and the Silver Gilt Room, served as the permanent silver buffet, intended to make visible the splendor and wealth of the monarch. A highlight was the Large Hall of Precious Objects: Measuring nearly 1,700 square feet (180 square meters), it was the former Treasury Vault's main space and facilitated the presentation of Treasury Art objects to a larger circle of visitors, while testifying to the fact that even intimate artworks could become public objects. Surrounded by the air of a princely cabinet of precious objects, the Corner Cabinet was only fourteen square meters in size (circa 130 square feet), filled with some 400 works of Treasury Art, and accessible via the Large Hall of Precious Objects. The visitor, guided by a court official, reached the Jewel Room by way of the Coat-of-arms Room that underscored the House of Wettin's political claims (ill. 9). The effect of the beauty and the material value of the jewel treasure, displayed in glass cases and on lavishly designed tables, must have been overwhelming for contemporaries of Augustus the Strong. Among the material exhibited were key works of the Late Baroque era. The royal treasury was not only accessible to the potentate's personal guests, but also to visitors with prior reservations. This alone made the Green Vault a unique museum in the early 18th century.

A description written by the experienced traveler Georg Keyssler and dated 1730 confirms the continuing success of this exhibition method when he states at the end: »Denn alle besonderen Kostbarkeiten anzudeuten, ist nicht möglich, wird auch von Jahren zu Jahren schwerer, weil sich die Sachen immer mehren. Die florentinische Tribuna mit demjenigen, was dazu gehöret, übertrifft vielleicht am Werthe diesen itztgemeldten Schatz; allein es ist nicht zu leugnen, daß the Fassungen und die wohl ausgesonnene Ordnung, welche man den hiesigen Sachen zu geben gewußt hat, ihnen ein Ansehen machet, welches viel mehr als der florentinische Schatz in the Augen fällt;«[36] (It is impossible to point out all the special sensations, and it gets increasingly more difficult by the year because the number of things keeps increasing. Maybe, the Florentine Tribuna surpasses, in its value and with all it entails, the treasure mentioned just before; however, it cannot be denied that the mounts and the well-conceived order one knew to give to domestic things, lends them a look that catches the eye much more than does the Florentine treasure.)

The existence of Treasury Art collections was much more threatened than *Kunstkammer*s were. The reason for this threat was the greed awakened by the use of the costly applied materials such as gold, silver,

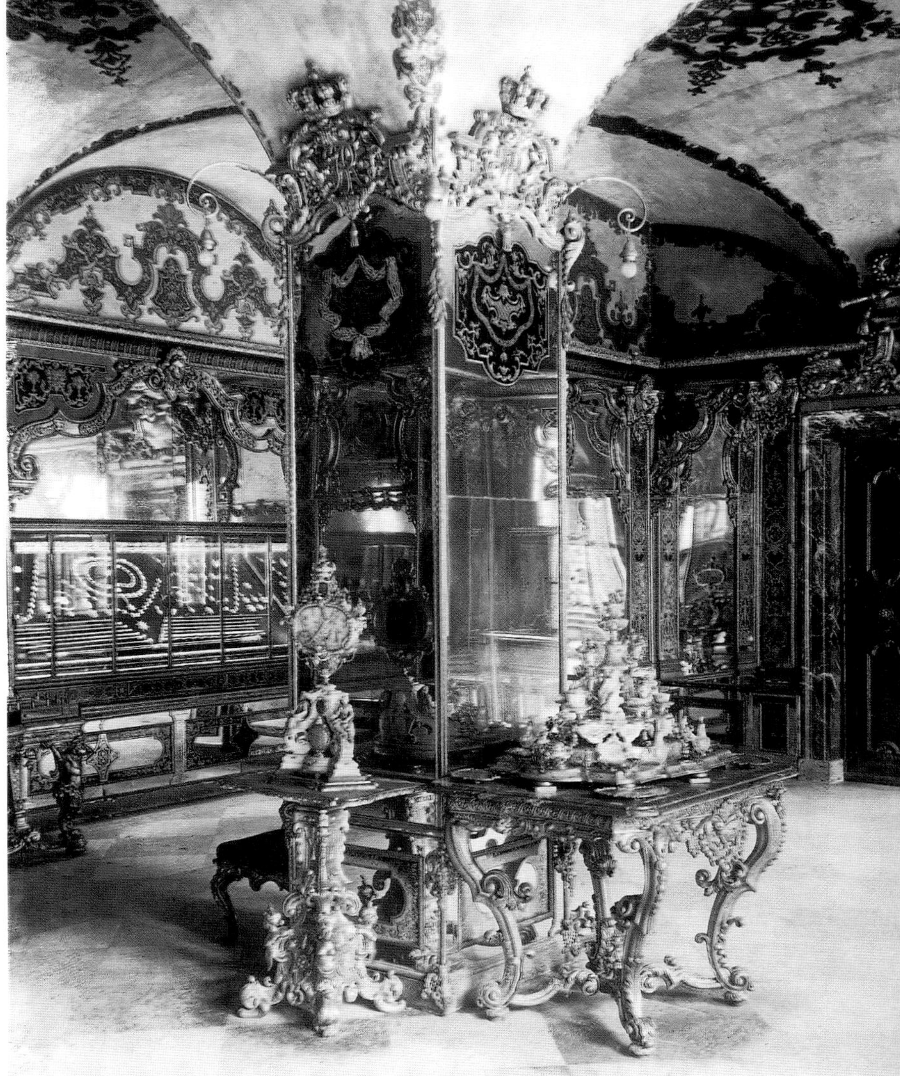

Ill. 9 Jewel Room, The Green Vault
North and west walls, center column
Appearance in 1933

diamonds, and other precious stones. Time and again, collections of Treasury Art were divided due to inheritance, or were acquired by strangers when a family of collectors died out. In the 17th and 18th centuries, they fell victim to war because the cash required to wage war had to be raised or Treasury Art collections were pillaged. Starting in the second half of the 18th century, enlightened but financially poor princely inheritors themselves increasingly became the individuals who overcame old customs and called themselves supporters of progressive thought. Perhaps it was all due to the changing fashions between the passing Rococo era and a strengthening Classicism that they began to attack what their ancestors had loved.

The survival of the Green Vault's abundant holdings to this day is in part owed to the fact that the collection has had a partially public status since 1730. Most importantly, however, was the awareness that Augustus the Strong had erected a monument that prevented his successors from touching the otherwise fugitive collection of Treasury Art in his Treasury Museum. Thus, the holdings of the Green Vault continue to document the nature, wealth, and beauty of Renaissance and Baroque Treasury Art until today.

1 SächsHStA Dresden Loc. 8694/10 Inventoryia über Schmuck und Silber Geschirr, Anno 1541. 1662., fol. 78r.
2 K. Renner, Mollusken-Schalen – faszinierender Glanz von Weichtieren des Meeres, in: D. Syndram (ed.), Naturschätze – Kunstschätze. Vom organischen und mineralischen Naturprodukt zum Kunstobjekt, Bielefeld 1991, p. 63.
3 *Kunstkammer* inventory 1595, fol. 306v.
4 J. Menzhausen, Kurfürst Augusts Kunstkammer. Eine Analyse des Inventars von 1587, in: Jahrbuch der Dresdener Kunstsammlungen, 17, 1985, p. 26.
5 Zur Rekonstruktion des Sammlungsbestandes unter Kurfürst August: D. Syndram, Von fürstlicher Lustbarkeit und höfischer Repräsentation. Die Kunstkammer und die Dresdner Sammlungen der Renaissance, in: Exh.-cat. Hamburg 2004, p. 58 – 60.
6 G. Kugler, Kunst und Geschichte im Leben Ferdinands I., in: Exh.-cat. Vienna 2003, p. 210.
7 L. Seelig, Die Münchner Kunstkammer. Geschichte, Anlage, Ausstattung, in: Jahrbuch der Bayerischen Denkmalpflege, 40, 1989, p. 119 – 124.
8 H. Brunner, Die Schatzkammer der Residenz. München, in: Erich Steingräber, Schatzkammern Europas, Munich 1968, p. 45.
9 E. Scheicher, Die Kunst- und Wunderkammern der Habsburger, Vienna 1979, p. 73.
10 B. T. Moran, German Prince-Practitioners: Aspects in the Development of Courtly Science, Technology, and Procedures in the Renaissance, in: Technology and Culture, 22, 1981, p. 260f.
11 See also: D. Syndram, Von fürstlicher Lustbarkeit und höfischer Repräsentation. Die Kunstkammer und die Dresdner Sammlungen der Renaissance, in: Exh-cat. Hamburg 2004, p. 54 – 69.
12 SächsHStA Dresden, Loc. 8696/12, fol. 374r – 378r.
13 SächsHStA Dresden, Loc. 894, Inventar über Schmuck und Silbergeschirr. Anno 1541 bis 1662, fol. 62 – 91. With the emerald step, the inventory cites an object also included in the 1587 *Kunstkammer* inventory.
14 J. L. Sponsel, Das Grüne Gewölbe. Vol. 3, Kleinodien der Goldschmiedekunst, Leipzig 1929, p. 105.
15 Seelig 1989, p. 104.
16 L. Seelig, The Munich Kunstkammer, 1565 – 1807, in: O. Impey and A. Mac Gregor, The Origins of Museums, Oxford 1985, p. 87.
17 For the beginnings of this area of collecting see: H. Lietzmann, Valentin Drausch, and Herzog Wilhelm V of Bavaria, Munich/Berlin 1998, p. 88, see also H. Brunner, Die Schatzkammer der Residenz. München, in: Erich Steingräber, Schatzkammern Europas, Munich 1968, p. 46.
18 Seelig 1989, p. 124.
19 Scheicher 1979, p. 84.
20 T. DaCosta Kaufmann, Remarks on the Collections of Rudolf II: the Kunstkammer as a Form of Representation, in: Art Journal, 38, 1978/1979, p. 22.
21 DaCosta Kaufmann 1978/1979, p. 22.
22 R. Distelberger, The Hapsburg Collections in Vienna during the Seventeenth Century, in: Impey/Mac Gregor 1985, p. 39f.
23 Distelberger 1985, p. 40.
24 T. Beutel, Cur-Fürstlicher Sächsischer stets grünender hoher Cedern-Wald…, Dresden 1671 and 1683, no page (p. 48).
25 D. Syndram, Die Schatzkammer Augusts des Starken. Von der Pretiosensammlung zum Grünen Gewölbe, Leipig 1999, p. 46.
26 SächsHStA Dresden Loc. 896 (Geheimes Kabinett), Sachen das Grüne Gewölbe, Deßen Revision, und die denen geheimen Cämmerieren Starcken und Marchen darüber aufgetragene Aufsicht betr. ao 1687 – 1704 seq., fol. 39r. The golden egg remained in the collection of the Green Vault until 1924, then it became part of the princely compensation and was given to the House of Wettin, in 1988 it reappeared at auction.

27 »Ein goldenes Ey worinnen eine henne in solcher ein Königl. Crone, diese mit Brillanten und Perlen guarnirt, in der Crone einen Ring mit einer grünen Hertz Roßen, mit Brillanten guarnirt… .« (a golden egg in which is contained a hen, in the hen a royal crown garnished with brilliant cut diamonds and pearls, in the crown a ring with green heart-shaped roses, adorned with brilliant cut diamonds). SächsHStA Dresden, Loc. 895, fol. 44r – 54v, quotes fol. 46r and fol. 45v. Apart from pearl figures, this list also contains ivory statuettes that are, as similar types, still part of the Green Vault's collection today.

28 M. Bencard, The Hen in the Egg, Amalienborg 1999, p. 24 – 30. He refers to additional works of this type.

29 One pearl figure in Florence originally belonged to the imperial collection in Vienna. See Y. Hackenbroch and M. Sframeli, I goielli dell' Elettrice Palatina al Museo degli Argenti, Florence 1988, cat.-no. 48, p. 124f.

30 A. Walz, Braunschweiger Stadtschloss, in: Exh.-cat. Brunswick 2004, p. 144.

31 A. Büttner, Die Sammlungen der Herzöge des Neuen Hauses Braunschweig bis zur Gründung des Herzoglichen Kunst- und Naturalienkabinetts, in: Exh.-cat. Brunswick 2004, p. 40.

32 E. von Watzdorf, Johann Melchior Dinglinger. Der Goldschmied des deutschen Barock, Berlin 1962, vol. 1, p. 22.

33 Nachtrag zum Pretieusen Cabinet Stücken=Inventoryio, 1725 – 1733, fol. 97v f., Green Vault inv.-no. II 19.

34 Syndram 1999, p. 76.

35 Loc. 898, Hoff-Casse-Sachen de Anno 1704. Vol. V, fol. 115.

36 Johann Georg Keyssler, Neueste Reisen durch Teutschland, Böhmen, Ungarn, der Schweitz, Italien und Lothringen, worinn der Zustand und das merckwürdigste dieser Länder beschrieben wird, written 1730, published Hannover 1741 and 1752, vol. II.

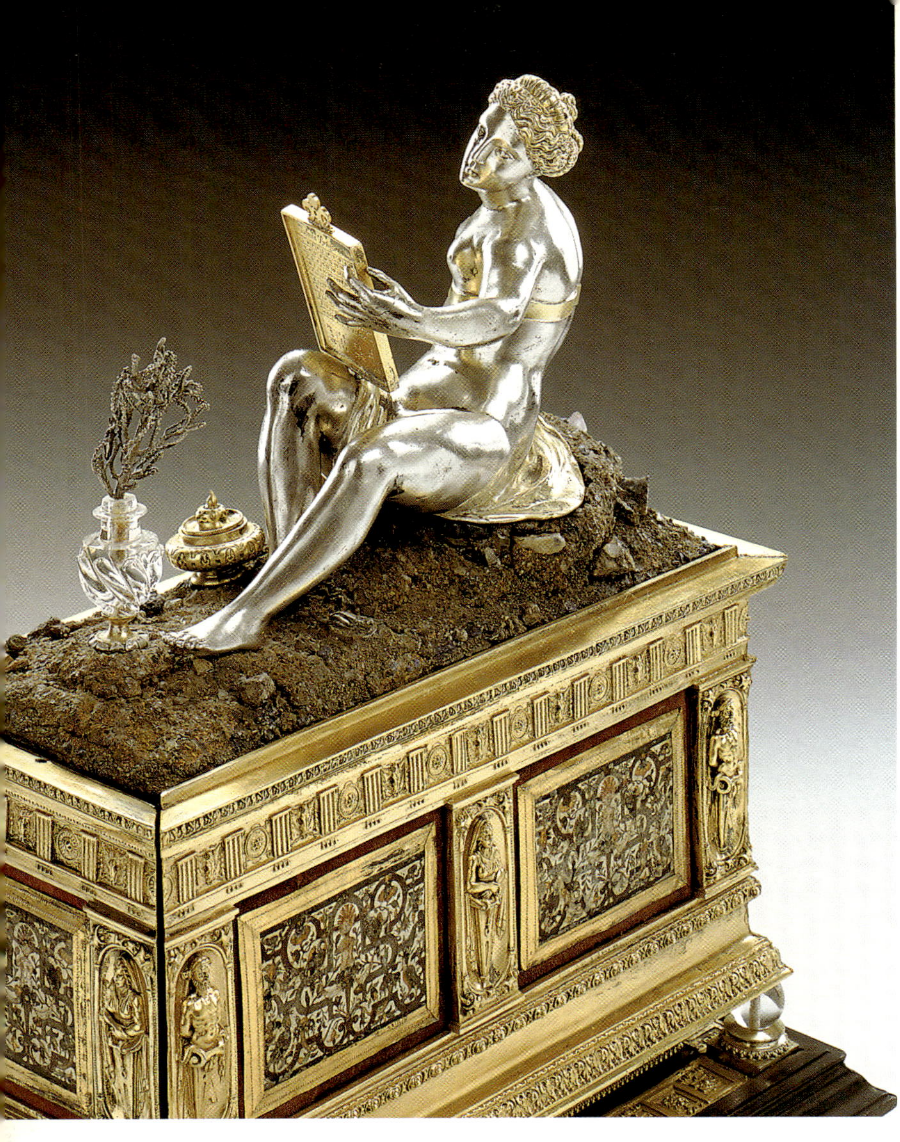

Display Casket with an Allegory of Philosophy

Silver, partly gilt, enamel, velvet, silk, rock crystal, ebony
Wenzel Jamnitzer
Nuremberg, dated 1562
H. 31 cm, W. 24 cm, D. 11 cm, Inv.-no. V 599

»Litere rebus memorē caducis / Suscitāt vitā monumenta fida /Artiū condūt revocāt ad auras /Lapsa sub umbras MDLXII«

»Scholarship lends perishable goods a life with memories; it erects art memorials and brings back to light what fell into the realm of shadows 1562.«

The firstly princely *Kunstkammers* were founded within the Holy Roman Empire of the German Nation around 1560. At the same time, Wenzel Jamnitzer (1507 – 1585), one of the most important German Renaissance artists, created a small precious casket in Nuremberg. Unlike nearly any other, this collector's item mirrors the world view characterized by a *Kunstkammer*. The Latin inscription on a gilt tablet held by the crowning figure, who is clothed in antique garments, notes: The human spirit, aided by the science and scholarship he created, surpasses the creations of nature, improves upon them by transforming them into artworks, and makes eternal the otherwise perishable actions of humankind. The back of the tablet reveals a Pythagorean number square on whose vertical and horizontal axis multiplication columns may be found. The written word and the invention of numbers determine human culture.

The female statuette, with her contrasting shiny silver surface, represents the personification of philosophy, i. e. the »love of wisdom.« With this *Casket*, Wenzel Jamnitzer created a monumental memorial to the human spirit, despite its diminutive size. In his oeuvre, the Nuremberg goldsmith also turned to the sensuous interplay between nature and art. The silver statuette of the young woman is artistically accomplished. She was influenced by the subtle French court style that was in turn influenced by Italian art, especially by the golden saltcellar, the *Saliera*, of Benvenuto Cellini. Philosophy rests on an artificial stone step. Two silver cast animals – a frog and a beetle – as well as a silver coral branch in a rock crystal vase and a small, lidded gilt vessel are added to the allegory.

The *Display Casket* itself is a work of art filled with surprises. The small box, whose sides are covered with antique Renaissance ornaments, serves as a pedestal for the personification. Its narrow sides may be opened near the young woman's feet with the help of a secret mechanism. Inside the *Casket*, there are four silk-covered drawers.

When Jamnitzer created his almost programmatic *Casket* shortly before 1560 he had reached the climax of his international fame. Among his patrons were kings and emperors, but also powerful German princes such as August of Saxony. The prince elector owned scientific instruments from Jamnitzer's workshop, as well as a number of his goldsmith's works. The *Display Casket* with an allegory of philosophy may have been mentioned in the 1587 inventory of the electoral Treasury which lists »1 Silbern vorgult kestlein oben vf dem deckel sizet ein nackent bildt, mit aus ziehe kestlein so mit Roth seiden attlas gefuttert;« i.e. »1 silver gilt casket with a nude on its top and drawers embellished with red silk atlas.« A later addition reads »sambt andern Instrumentich so zum nehen gehört;« i.e. »along with other sewing tools.« Apparently, the *Casket* came to the Dresden *Kunstkammer* in 1623 as the bequest of the elector's widow, Sophie, wife of Christian I.

Thanks to its unusual richness of decorative details including the profuse application of rare and precious materials, the virtuosity of its artisan techniques, its intellectual content, and its hidden surprise element, this *Writing Casket* is an excellent example of a *Kunstkammer* piece. These criteria are at the same time characteristic of treasury art objects that were of pivotal importance for high-ranking princely collectors from the Renaissance to the late Baroque eras.

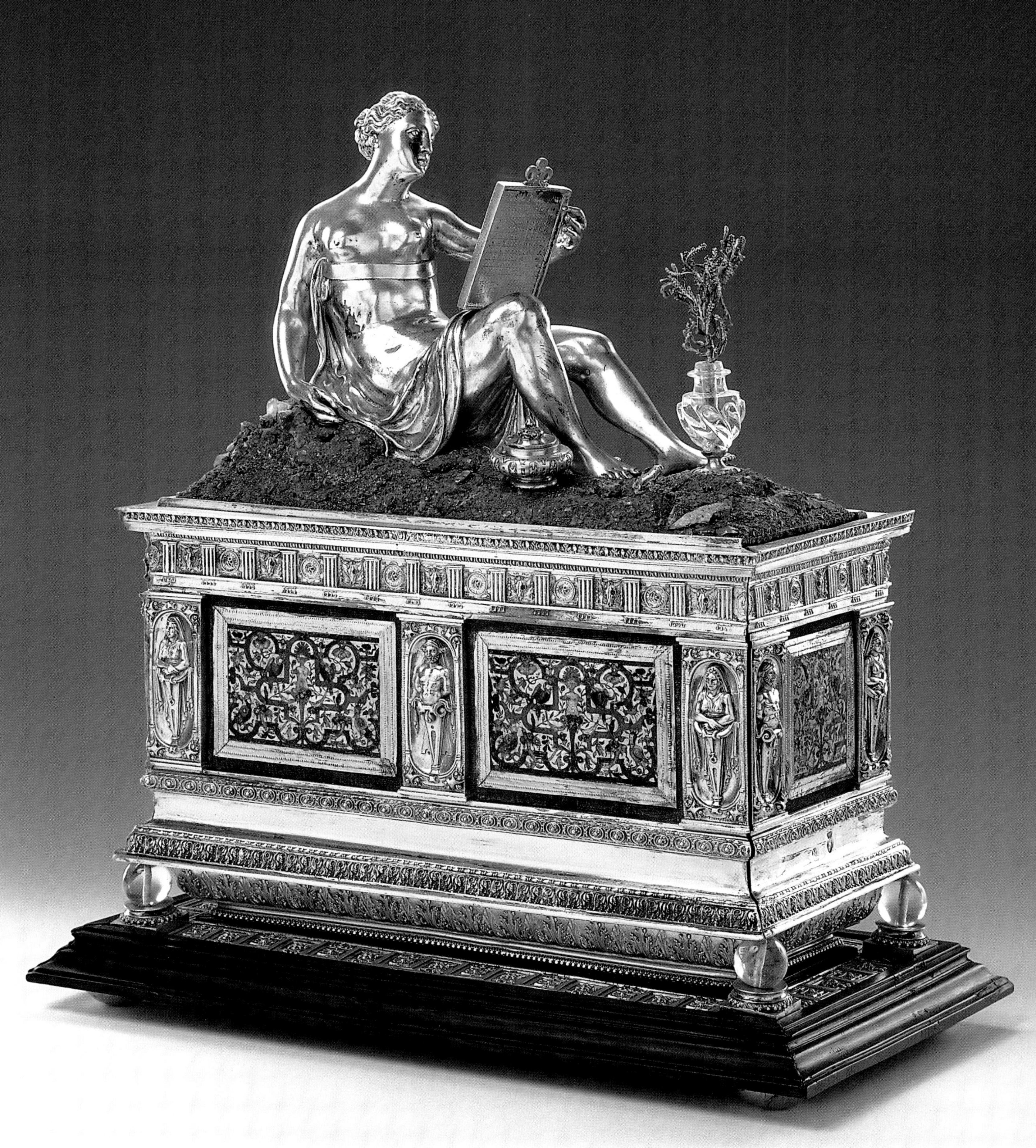

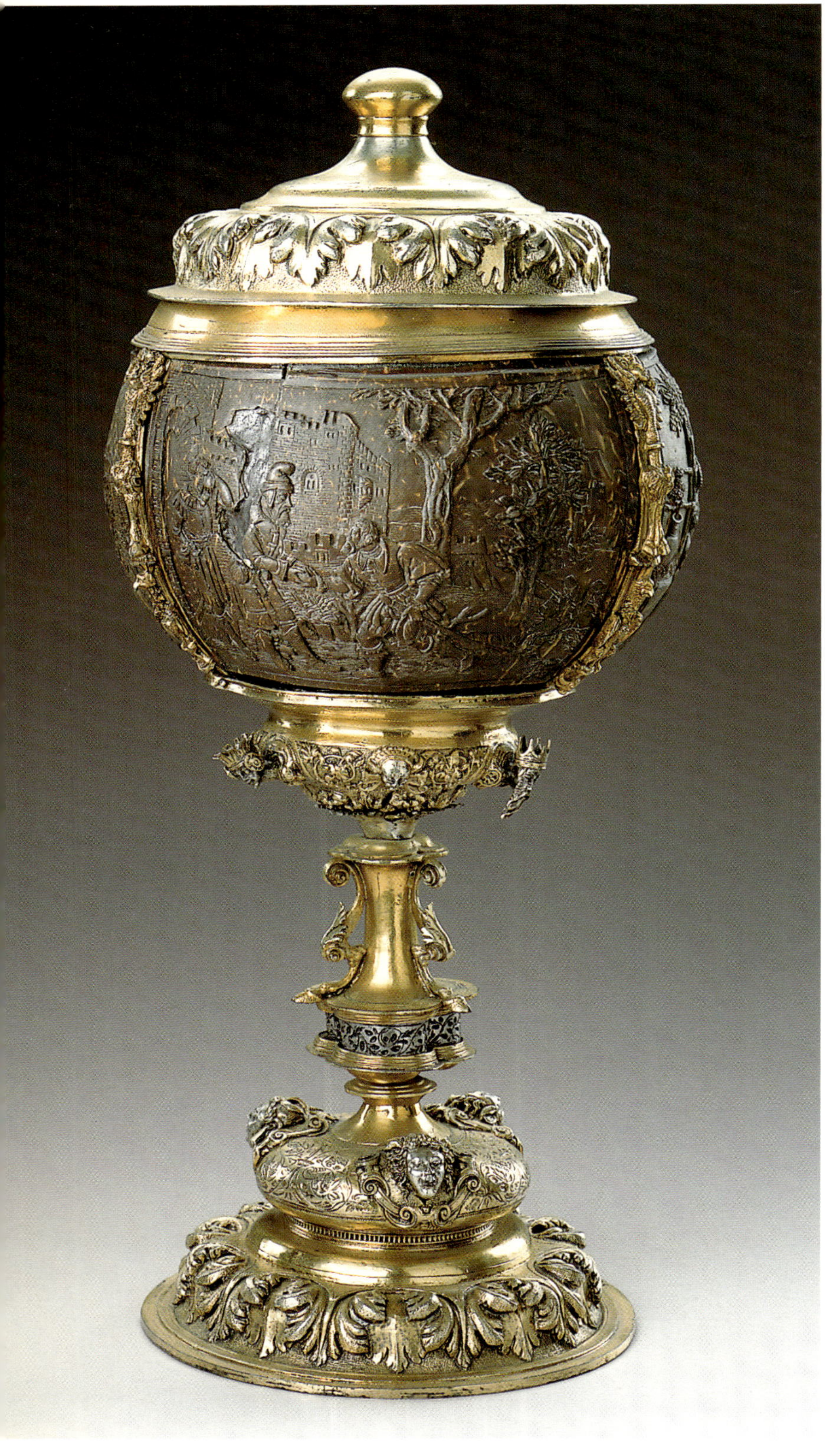

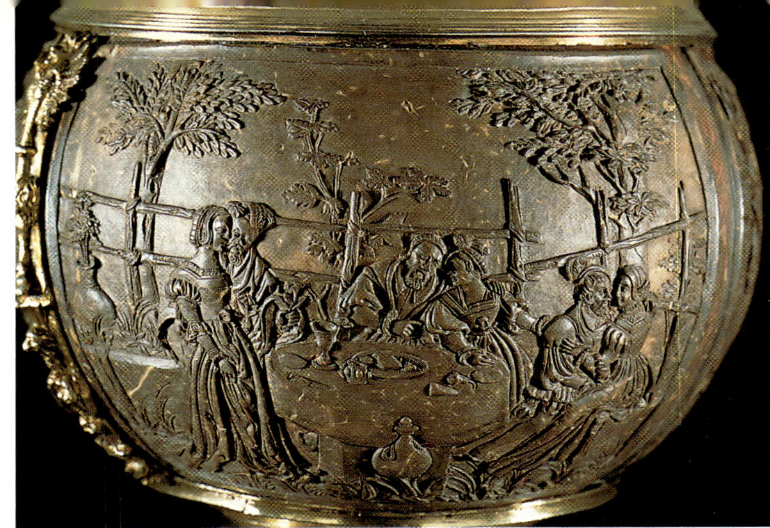

Carved Coconut Shell Goblet with Scenes from the Biblical Story of the Prodigal Son

Gilt silver, coconut shell
presumably Nuremberg, middle of the 16th century
H. 28 cm, Inv.-no. V 330

Silver Sculpture in the Shape of a Wheelbarrow Group

Gilt silver
Christoph Lindenberger
Nuremberg, between 1571 and 1575
H. 19 cm, Inv.-no. IV 337

Among the first products of nature that were turned into European luxury items were coconut shells. Even in ancient times they had reached the Occident. The oldest surviving silver gilt vessels made from the hard shell of this tropical nut originate from the 13th century. In Europe, the fruit of the palm tree was considered a »sea nut« until the 16th century. Thought to grow in »eternal night on the bottom of the sea,« it reached the European markets in larger numbers with the colonization of the West Indies, beginning in the second half of the 16th century. It became known as the »Indian« nut and was used by German and Dutch goldsmiths to create fantastic goblets and ewers. As collector's items of exotic rarity, mounted coconut shells were integrated into princely Treasuries and *Kunstkammers*. In the Protestant regions of Germany, goblets with carved biblical scenes were held in particularly high esteem. The preferred renderings dealt with wine and its abuse. Especially popular was the parable of the Prodigal Son (Luke 15:11-32), most notably his encounter with the prostitutes.

Reliefs with this subject matter may also be found on the walls of a mid-16th-century coconut goblet, presumably made in Nuremberg. Whereas the three carefully executed scenes from the parable may have been made by the goldsmith himself, they were more likely created by a specialized image carver who carved the high reliefs into the hard nut's shell. The source for the images is a series of copperplate engravings by Hans Sebald Behaim, which the artist skillfully transformed from two dimensions into relief. The »Indian« nut was thus ennobled and subsequently received a rather elaborate silver gilt mount. A gilt medal with the image of Christ and the inscription »ego sum Ihesus A et O« is placed on the ground of the cup. The inside of the nut is varnished, revealing that the *Goblet*, in contrast to many other similar objects, could indeed be used.

An impressive Nuremberg silver statuette shows images of the vices of alcoholism and gluttony, widespread in the 16th century. The goldsmith Christoph Lindenberger created this burlesque and subtle depiction of the mortal sins, condemned by the different Christian faiths and having repeatedly fatal consequences within the German high aristocracy during the course of the 16th century.

Equipped with the attributes of a servant of Satan, a little devil – he looks like a Satyr and is enveloped by a wine barrel – pushes a wheelbarrow. A barking little dog runs at the left side of the barrel devil. While the barrel is surrounded by pieces of meat and cooking utensils suspended from ropes, the sides of the wheelbarrow are adorned with bundles of fruit. An obese glutton »*Prasser*« stoically rests on the wheelbarrow. The bearded old man wears a bespectacled cuckold's cap with a pilgrim's shell. Below his right arm he holds a raven-like bird, and in his right hand a *Kuttrolf* (i.e. a wine bottle). His left hand is wrapped in a densely filled moneybag. In front of him, a lantern and a pilgrim's flask may be spotted. The apron of the barrel devil and the wheelbarrow's sides are inscribed with coarse drinking toasts. They offer insight into the »Epicurean's« way of life, one who all but ignores the Lord's word. Both the devil's head and the cuckold's cap can be detached. Worked in the guise of lids, they really turn this figural group into a true »drinking game« (*Trinkspiel*) that lends itself to the abuse of alcohol.

Lindenberger, the creator of this smart piece of goldsmith's sculpture, was active in Nuremberg from 1546 until 1586. His richly detailed work of art was presumably already included in the electoral Treasury inventory of 1587. In 1663, it came to the Dresden *Kunstkammer*. Such humorous glutton groups with their admonitory implications were popular until circa 1600. As suggested in a drawing by his hand, it can be assumed that the Hamburg goldsmith Jacob Mores the Elder (1542 – 1612) repeated this group for the royal Danish house.

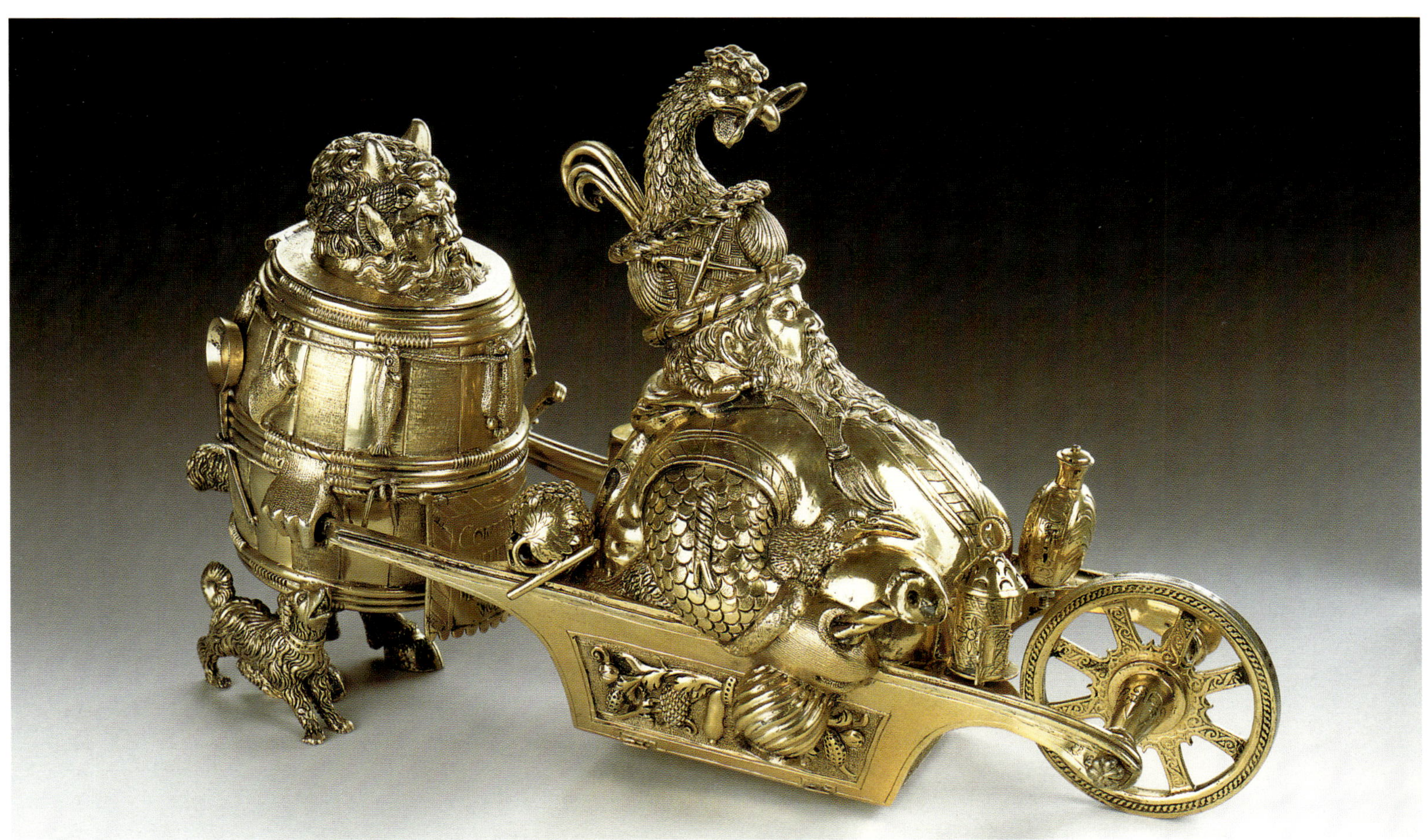

Ewer Made from a Seychelles Nut

Seychelles nut, gilt silver
Portugal, between 1570 and 1590
H. 32,5 cm, W. 41 cm, Inv.-no. IV 314

Leaping Unicorn

Brass
Unknown artist
Cast by Hans Reisinger
Augsburg, purchased 1589
H. 37,8 cm, Inv.-no. IX 51

The extraordinarily large fruits of the Seychelles palm were far more precious than coconuts. Today, no more than ten of the formerly famous and extremely valuable wonders of nature that were brought to Europe until the end of the 18th century are known. Starting in circa 1570, these »Cocos de malediva« were imported to Europe by Portuguese merchants. Seven Seychelles nuts were transformed by goldsmiths »pro vasis« and thus turned into vessels. In 1590, one of them came to the electoral Saxon *Kunstkammer*.

The surface of the Dresden Seychelles nut, largely left in its natural raw state, was merely varnished. The goldsmith – he presumably worked in Portugal – cut an ovoid opening into the center of the shell's upper side and added a shell-shaped lid worked in repoussé and equipped with a spherical handle. The spout on one of the narrow sides is designed in the form of a lion's mask. Four clips – sawn from a sheet of silver and embellished with ornamental perforations – connect the nut with the baluster-shaped shaft that is then mounted onto an engraved, circular foot.

It was not until 1769 that French sailors discovered the tree from which the fruit originated in the Seychelles. The nuts, weighing up to 35 pounds each, were repeatedly found floating through the ocean to such far-off beaches as those in the Maledives, located southwest of Ceylon, hence the name »Maledives' nut.« Since the Middle Ages they were con-

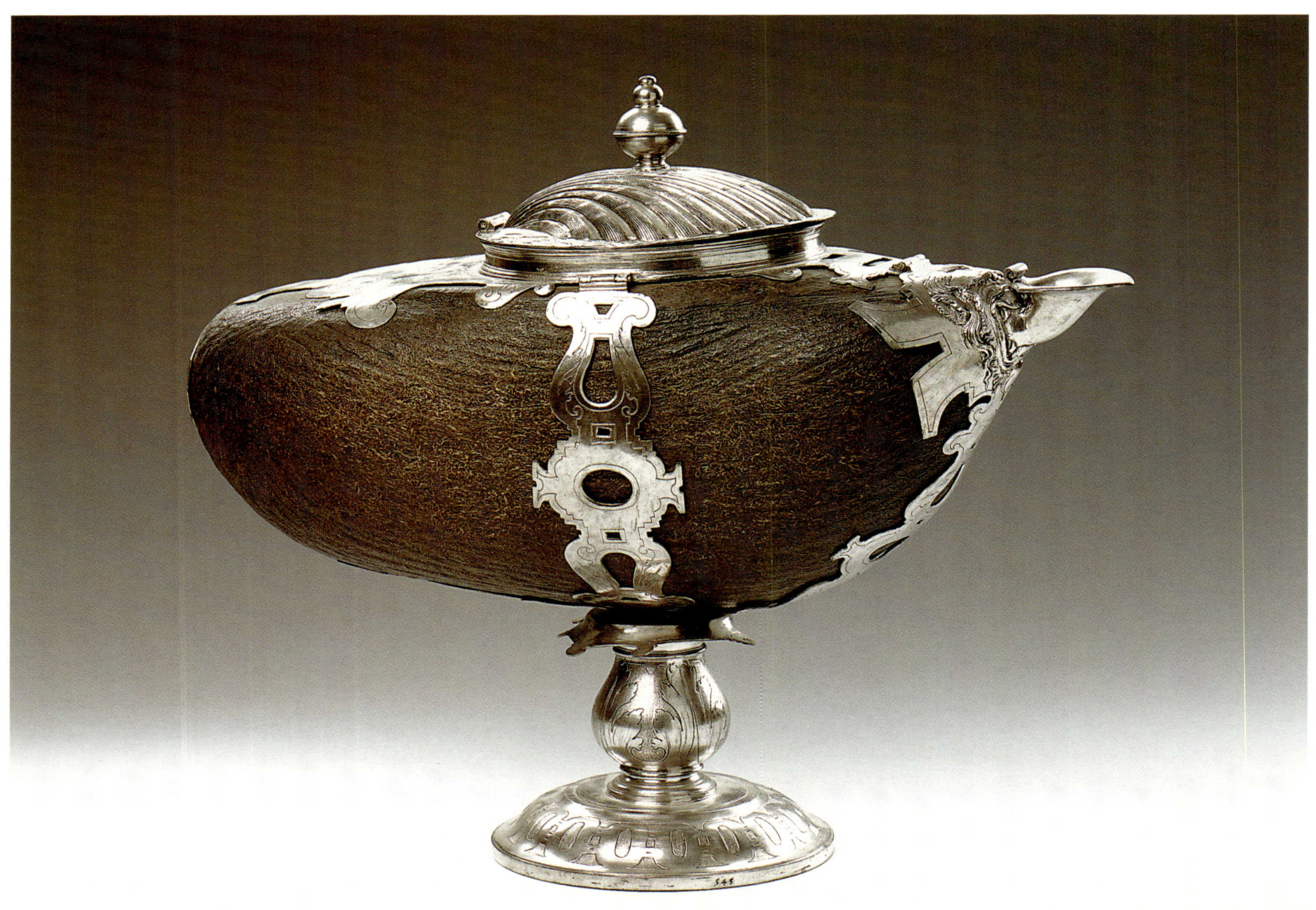

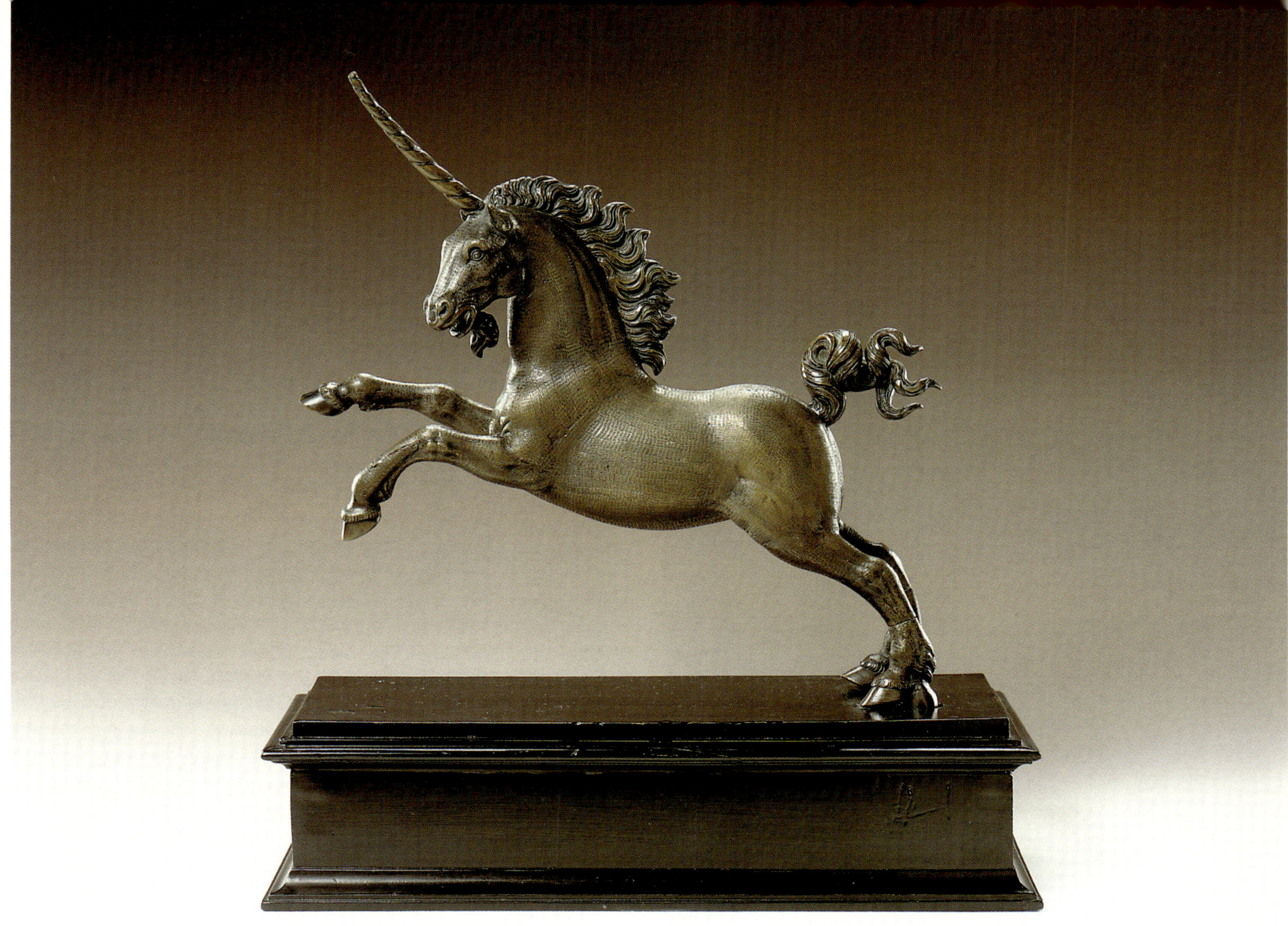

sidered to be magical fruits that grew in the sea, and they were traded as princely rarities in southeast Asia. Like the Asian princes, their European counterparts were also convinced that a »Cocla de Maladiua,« such as the one mentioned in the Dresden *Kunstkammer* inventory of 1595, would overcome the most powerful poison.

An integral part of human fantasy since Babylonian antiquity, the unicorn was surrounded by a mythical reality until the 17th century. Although the fabulous animal's looks were altered during the course of our cultural history, its main characteristics remained virtually unchanged. Adapted by the Greeks from Persia and reminiscent of a rhinoceros, the unicorn is characterized as a particularly wild, strong, and very versatile animal, whose horn possesses a mysterious healing power that renders poison ineffective. Like the ancient authors and the writer of the Physiologus, the Bible also mentions the »unicornis.« Later legends report that only a virgin can capture it or that it can only find rest in a virgin's lap.

The possession of a complete unicorn horn – with its miraculous healing powers – or at least objects made from such a horn, was a fundamental element in any princely Renaissance *Kunstkammer*. Therefore, in May 1587, Christian I commissioned a costly mount of enameled gold for the unicorn horn already in the electoral collection. The item in question was the then conventional, long and twisted tooth of a male arctic narwhal, subsequently suspended from its precious mount in the Dresden *Kunstkammer*. Two years later, Christian I acquired the statuettes of a crouching stag and a unicorn from the founder and fountain builder Hans Reisinger. He was an art founder who specialized in fountains with figures of moveable animals that were much sought after by German princely courts in the late 16th century. His *Unicorn* embodies the savage nature attributed to the fabled animal in the most lively manner. The equine look of the creature with its twisted horn that originates from the center of its forehead is the work of an unknown modeler who presumably also created models for Augsburg goldsmiths. In Dresden, both the *Unicorn* and the *Stag* served as the prototypes for wooden animals that crowned two artificial silver ore mountains erected under Christian I in the electoral chambers of the New Stable. However, the exquisite animal casts by Reisinger were immediately transferred to the Dresden *Kunstkammer*.

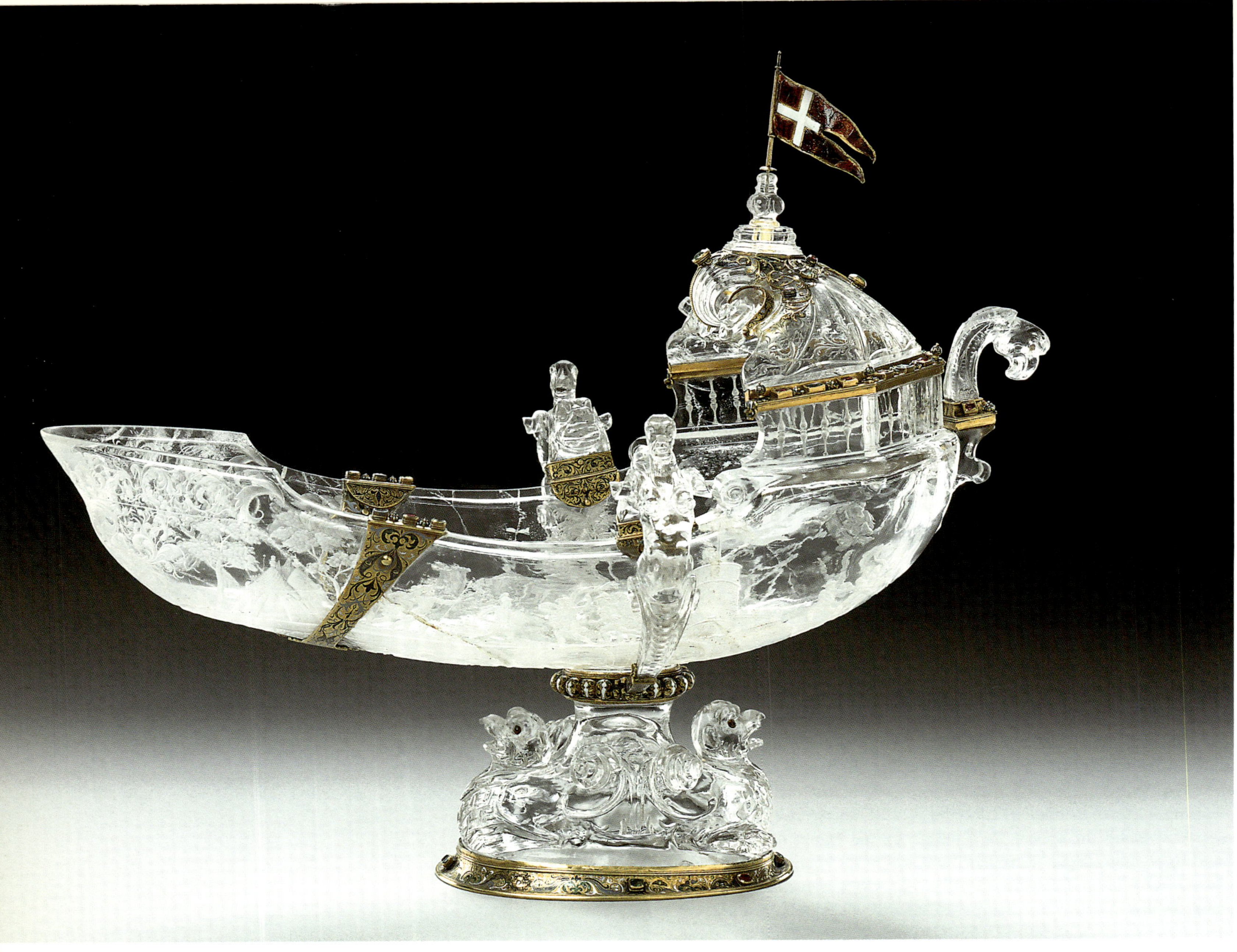

Galley with Depictions from Ancient Mythology

Rock crystal, gold, enamel, precious stones
Workshop of the Saracchi
Milan, end of the 16th century
Mount: Dresden, added between 1705 and 1709
H. 37 cm, L. 44 cm, Inv.-no. V 185

Flask with Scenes from the Story of Noah

Rock crystal, gold, enamel, rubies, emeralds
Design: Annibale Fontana, Milan after 1572
Carving: workshop of the Saracchi
Milan, circa 1580
H. 31,5 cm, Inv.-no. V 186

Large display vessels made of rock crystal are among the most precious artifacts of the Late Renaissance; ownership of these objects was considered a token of princely affluence. The price of these items was determined by a number of factors, among them their size, the purity of the crystal, the difficulty of creating them, but also the time-consuming process by which a skilled master rendered the rather coarse quartz into splendid containers. Precious mounts made of gilt silver or pure gold, as well as embellishments of precious stones or subtle enamel adornment underscored the material and the representational value of such vessels. Since the middle of the 16th century, Milan had been the center for artistic rock crystal cutting. Only a few families of artists – most notably the Miseroni, the Saracchi, and the Caroni – were responsible for the creation of these unique objects of art there.

During the last third of the 16th century, rock crystal carving experienced its artistic zenith. At the same time, a special competition occurred throughout Europe for the most comprehensive and highest quality princely collection of rock crystal vessels. The Hapsburg emperors, the kings of Spain, the Medici grand dukes, and the dukes of Bavaria contended for first place. As a court of political and cultural importance Saxony maintained a middle position. The Saxon prince electors procured most of their rock crystal vessels from dealers. However, goblets, handled ewers, bowls, and containers in the shapes of grotesque animals also came to the Dresden Treasury as diplomatic gifts from the dukes of Savoy, whose neighboring territory was Milan.

The most precious of the more than half a dozen rock crystal galleys once united in the holdings of the Green Vault was made in the workshop of the Saracchi brothers. It is presumed that its fabulous mount with gold applications also originated in Milan. The ship's hull rests on a foot composed of two reclining dolphins whose backs touch. From a formal point of view, the *Display Vessel* is closely related to the typical Mediterranean ships of the time. While the *Galley* has a broad stern and a pointed bow, its sides are deeply cut from the outside with decorative scenes derived from Greek mythology. On the broad hull with its slightly elevated bow and attached handles in the shape of female devil herms, numerous deeply cut scenes may be found. They are the Rape of Europa, the Rescue of Andromeda, the Abduction of Helen, and the Siege of Troy. The Danish flag can be seen above the roof of the so-called card house – behind which a dragon's head made of rock crystal is mounted as another handle. Both the banner and the crowning monogram of Augustus the Strong that is applied to a gold horizontal band inside the ship, stem from repairs executed after 1705.

The large *Flask* (bouteille) was also made in the workshop of the Saracchi brothers and belongs to the most technically ambitious rock crystal works of its time. Very few comparable flasks of this material have survived; the one in Dresden is the largest. The slightly flattened shape of the otherwise bulging *Display Vessel*, reminiscent of a pilgrim's flask, was predetermined by the rock crystal's natural shape. Carved into the body of the container are scenes from the biblical story of the drunken patriarch Noah, derived from a design of the Italian sculptor Annibale Fontana, another relative of the Saracchi family. Thanks to his differentiated cutting technique, the skilled carver managed to lend the appearance of movement to the figures' muscles and the texture of their garments, as well as to the ornaments and the vegetal structure of the trees. This all culminates in the utmost artistic elegance. Another feature of the utmost quality is the motif of the two matte gold double-tailed and winged sirens attached to the shoulder of the bottle. The 1588 Treasury inventory in which the *Flask* is mentioned for the first time relates that it was originally crowned by a ruby stopper.

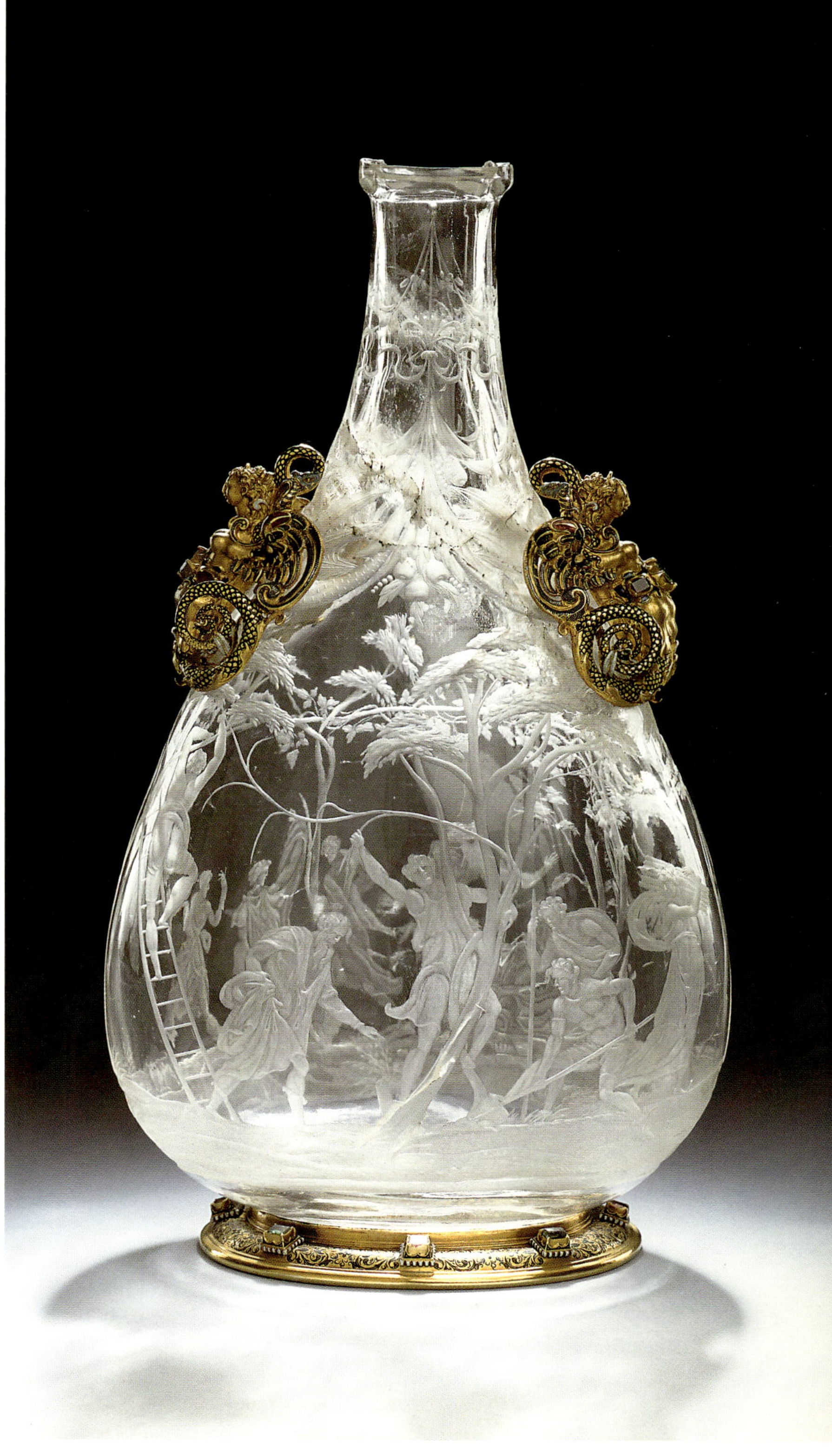

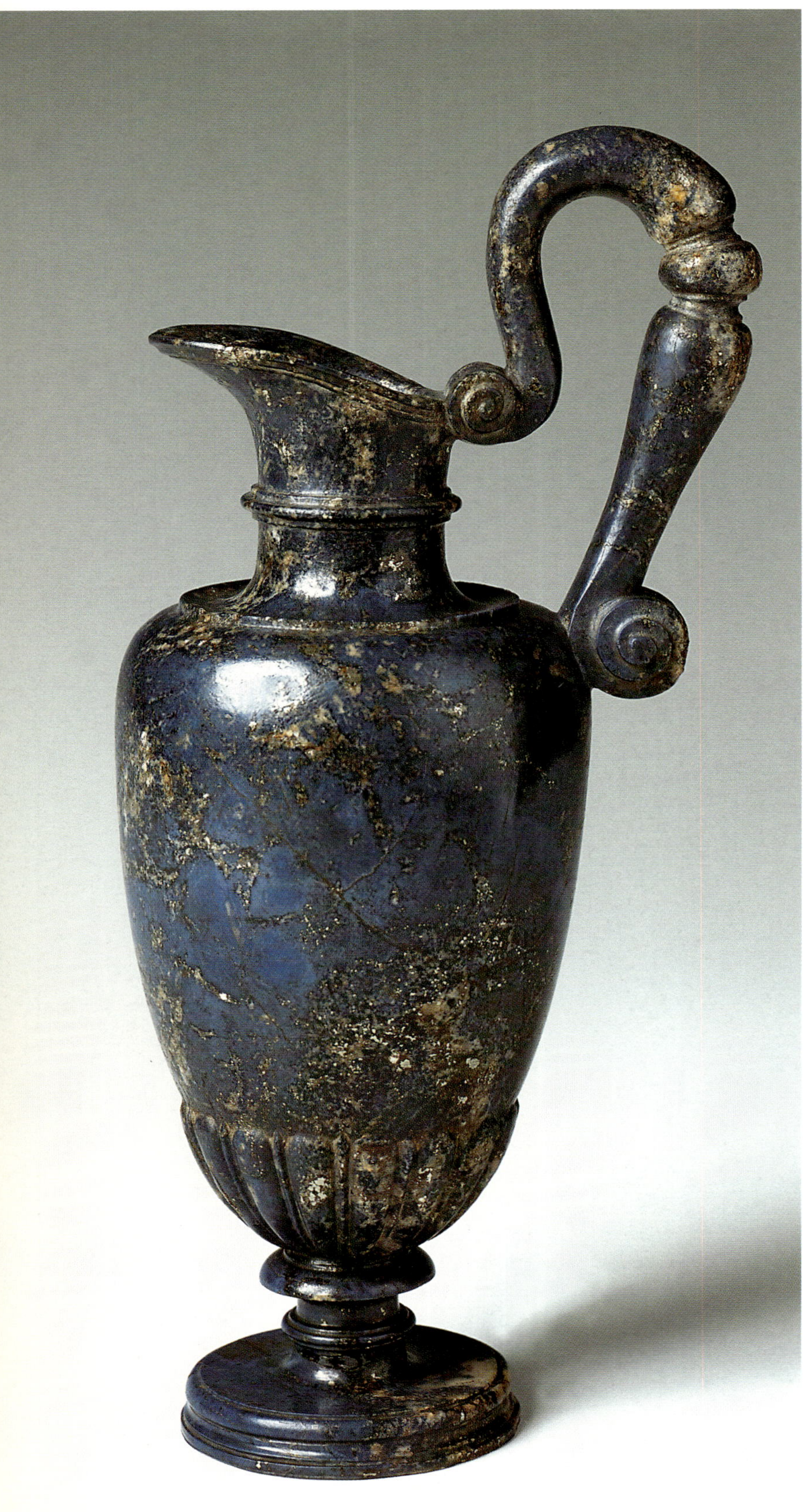

Ewer

Lapis lazuli
Design: presumably Bernardo Buontalenti
Execution: Opificio delle Pietra Dure
Florence, between 1575 and 1580
H. 27 cm, Inv.-no. V 56

Five Display Vessels

Serpentine from Zöblitz in Saxony, gilt silver
Design: presumably Giovanni Maria Nosseni
Mount: Urban Schneeweiß
Dresden, before 1585
(from left to right) H. 29,2 cm, 30,4 cm, 31,3 cm, 30,6 cm, 29,9 cm
Inv.-no. V 397, V 389, V 390, V 386, V 399

It is highly likely that these seemingly heterogeneous vessels made of precious stones are based on the designs of two court artists who worked almost simultaneously in Florence and in Dresden. Despite the geographical and cultural distance, the artistic and intellectual backgrounds of their creators, Bernardo Buontalenti (1536 – 1608) and Giovanni Maria Nosseni (1544 – 1620), were closely related. Both were active as consultants in their workplaces. During the second half of the 16th century, this particular type of court artist also began to emerge outside Italy. As employees of the court, they belonged to the court family that surrounded the ruler and his closest relatives. An artist like Nosseni was expected to be artistically successful; he was also an advisor to his patron on issues concerning building and collecting. Furthermore, he organized festivals and tournaments, and kept close ties to other courts – most notably in Italy – in order to remain on top of the most current developments and to be able to react promptly.

Nosseni was from northern Italy; he received his training as sculptor and architect in Florence. There, the slightly older Buontalenti was already working for the future Grand Duke Francesco I in the 1560s. In 1575, Nosseni was called from Florence to provide his services to electoral Saxony.

It was presumably between 1574 and 1576 that Buontalenti created a number of designs for precious stone containers for the grand duke, preserved today in the Uffizi. Some of them were rendered in Afghan lapis lazuli, especially venerated by the Medici. The *Handled Ewer* from Dresden – manufactured in the grand ducal workshop of San Marco – was cut from one single, particularly beautifully patterned and large piece of this mineral with its golden pyrite deposits. Its elegant silhouette appears to derive from a drawing by the architect and painter Buontalenti. The elegant handle that rises from the body of the *Ewer* and the provocatively turned spout at the top display the most discreet ornamental embellishment. It requires no goldsmith's mount

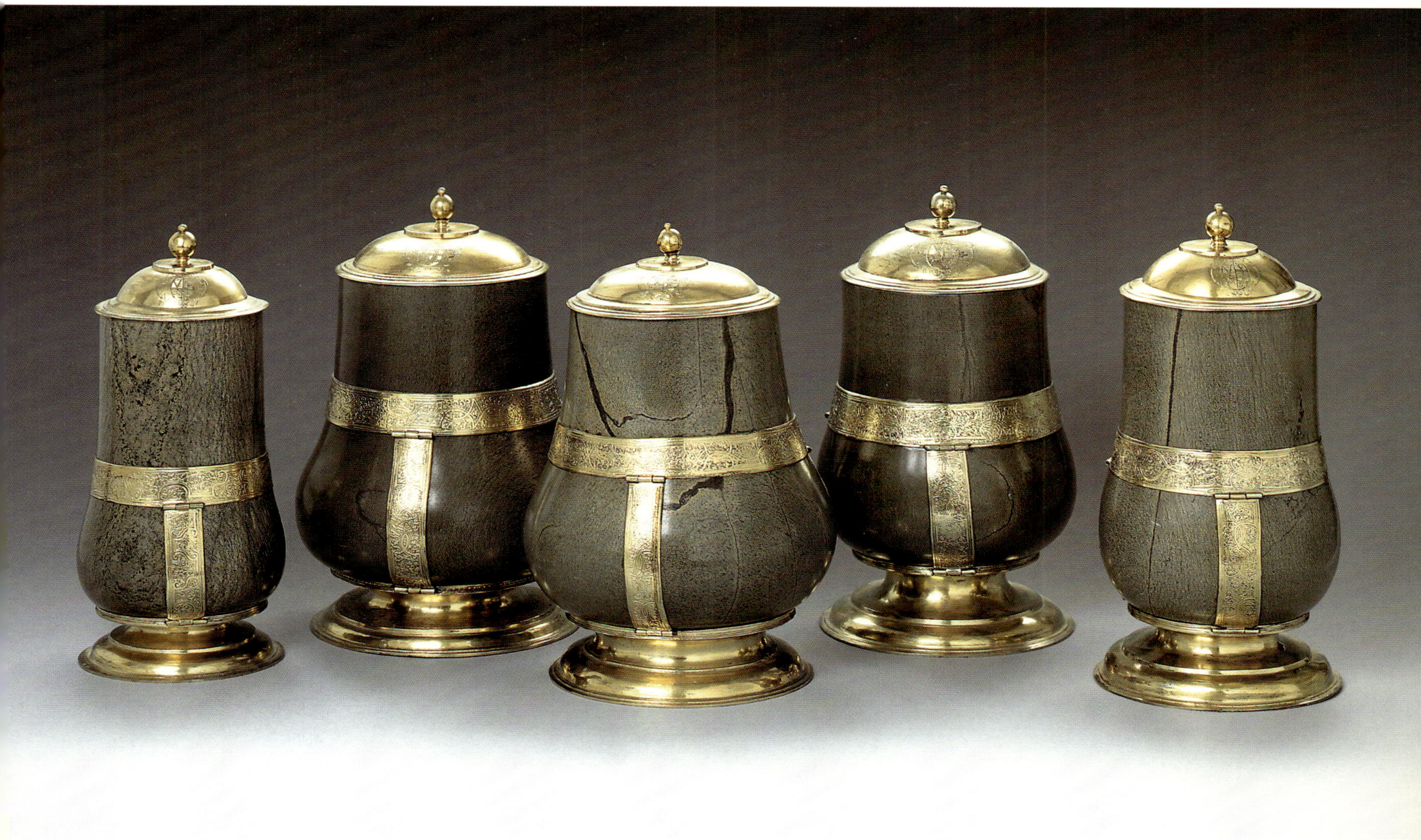

in order to clarify its material value. Until now, the path taken by this vessel with its classical appeal to Dresden and its provenance from the Florentine court workshop remain unknown.

During his first few years in office, Giovanni Maria Nosseni served Prince Elector August by exploring newly discovered marble and alabaster deposits. He investigated to what degree the stones might be put to artistic use. This process also entailed the already known serpentine. It was not until 1583 that Nosseni moved his primary residence from Torgau to Dresden.

It is almost inconceivable that a total of *Six Display Vessels* in convex shapes turned from gray-green serpentine were not based on Nosseni's design. As artistic exercises on a design theme, they are of almost identical height but have differing circumferences. Between 1575 and 1585, the cylindrical containers were decorated with silver gilt base rings and bands adorned with arabesques by the Dresden goldsmith Urban Schneeweiß. The lids are bedecked with the Saxon coat-of-arms of Prince Elector August and the coat-of-arms of his wife, the royal Danish princess Anna. The fact that they are already included in the 1587 electoral Treasury inventory testifies to the collecting sovereign's high esteem for the unusual artistic form of this otherwise not very precious material.

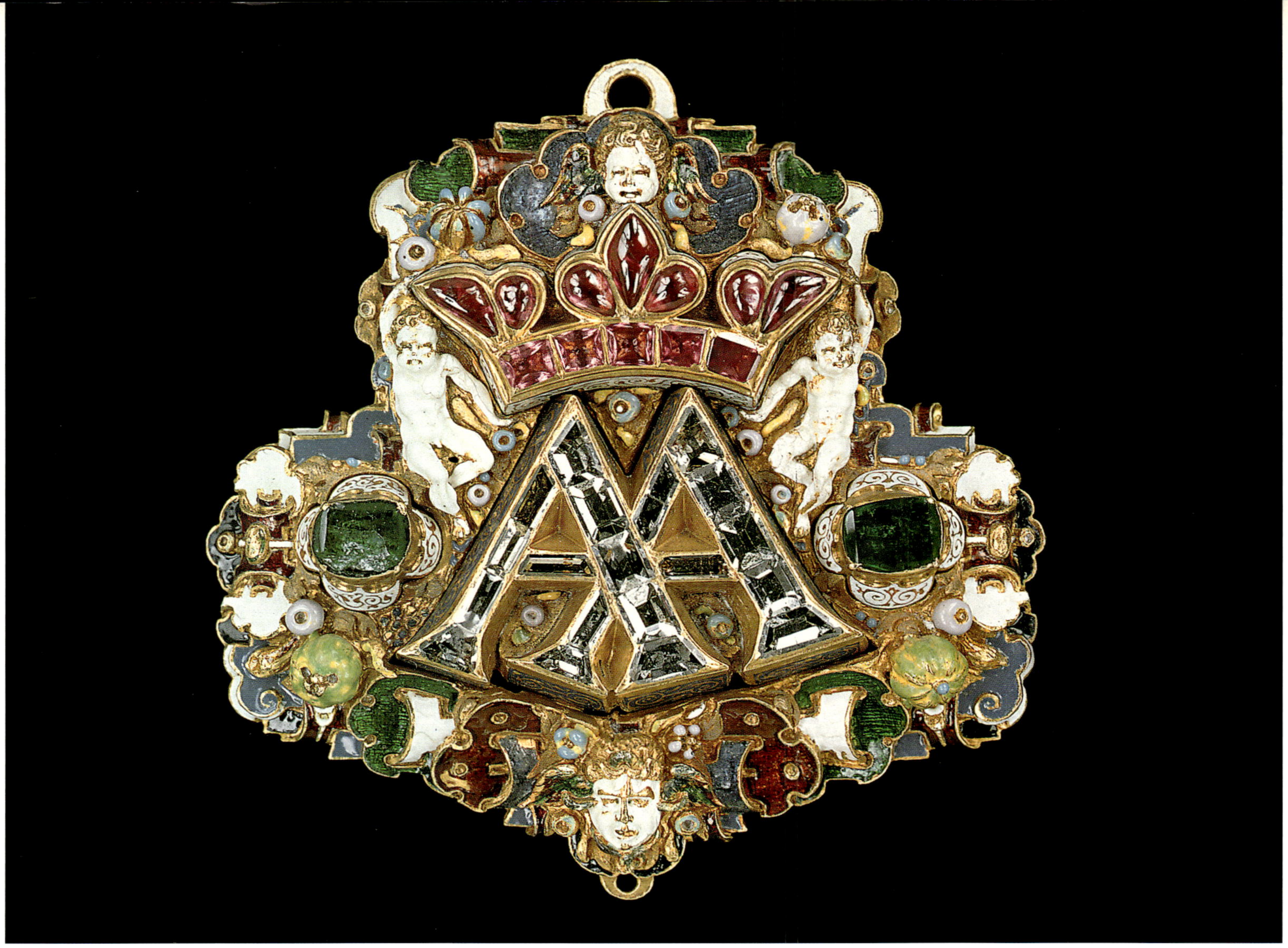

Pendant with the Monogram AA

Gold, enamel, twenty diamonds, ten rubies, two emeralds
Germany, second third of the 16th century
H. 6,5 cm, Inv.-no. VIII 286

Pendant with David and Goliath

Gold, enamel, diamonds, rubies
Germany, end of the 16th century
H. 9,9 cm, Inv.-no. VIII 294

Pendant with Saint George

Gold, enamel, ten diamonds, six rubies, one emerald, one ruby
Germany, end of the 16th century
H. 8,3 cm, Inv.-no. VIII 265

The Green Vault's collection of treasury objects includes well over two dozen necklaces and belt chains, nearly forty pendants and trimmings, and more than ten finger rings. This group, however, represents only a fragment of the abundant Renaissance and early Baroque holdings of jewels and other small precious objects made for the Dresden court during these epochs. Unlike most other items, the members of the electoral House of Wettin were prepared to spend sizable sums for their jewels. Gold and precious stone jewels served as independent beautification and as generous presents for other princes or aristocratic subordinates. Despite severe losses, mainly due to changing tastes, the Green Vault's collection of jewels dating from the early 16th to the late 17th century is still one of the most comprehensive of its kind. It is sometimes possible to trace the provenance of individual pieces of jewelry back to the individual who commissioned them. Yet, the places of origin and the names of the goldsmiths can only rarely be determined. During the Renaissance and the Baroque eras, jewelry style was international. Its design adhered to surprisingly quickly transmitted fashion trends and only rarely reveals local idiosyncrasies. The Dresden court attempted to remain informed about the most current fashion

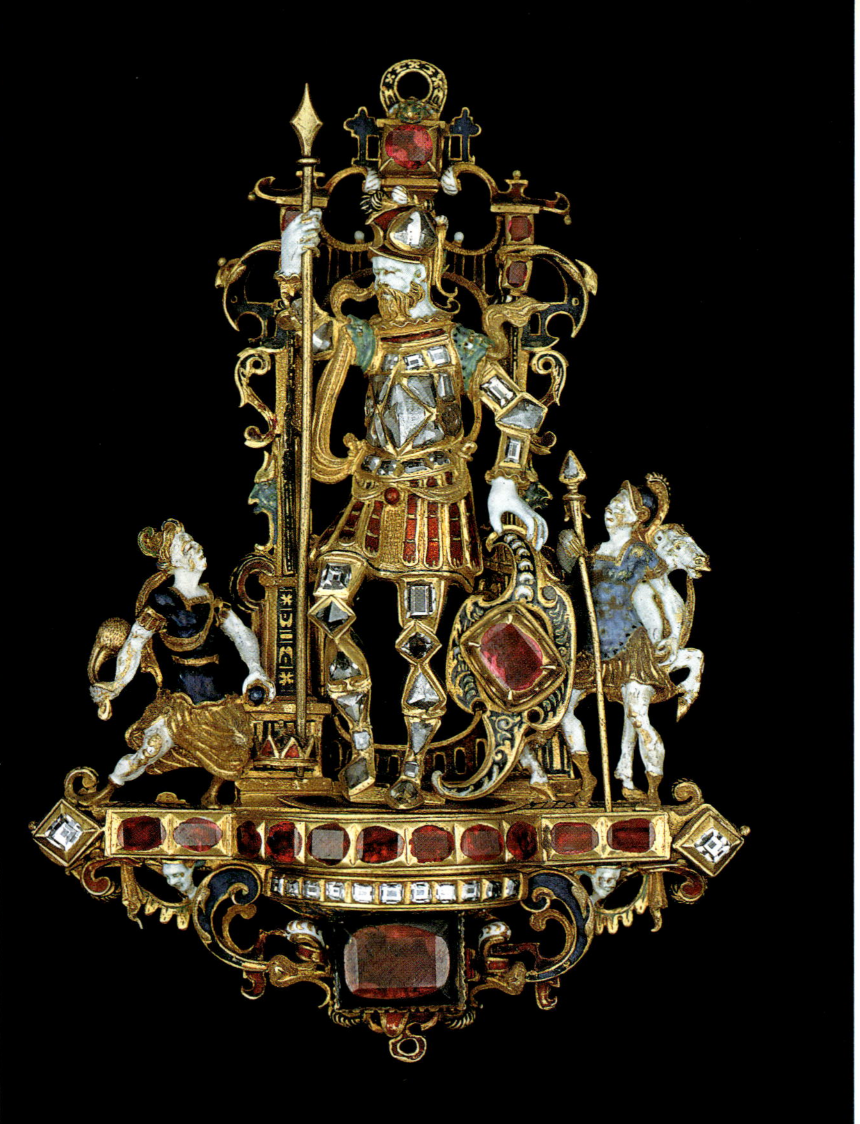

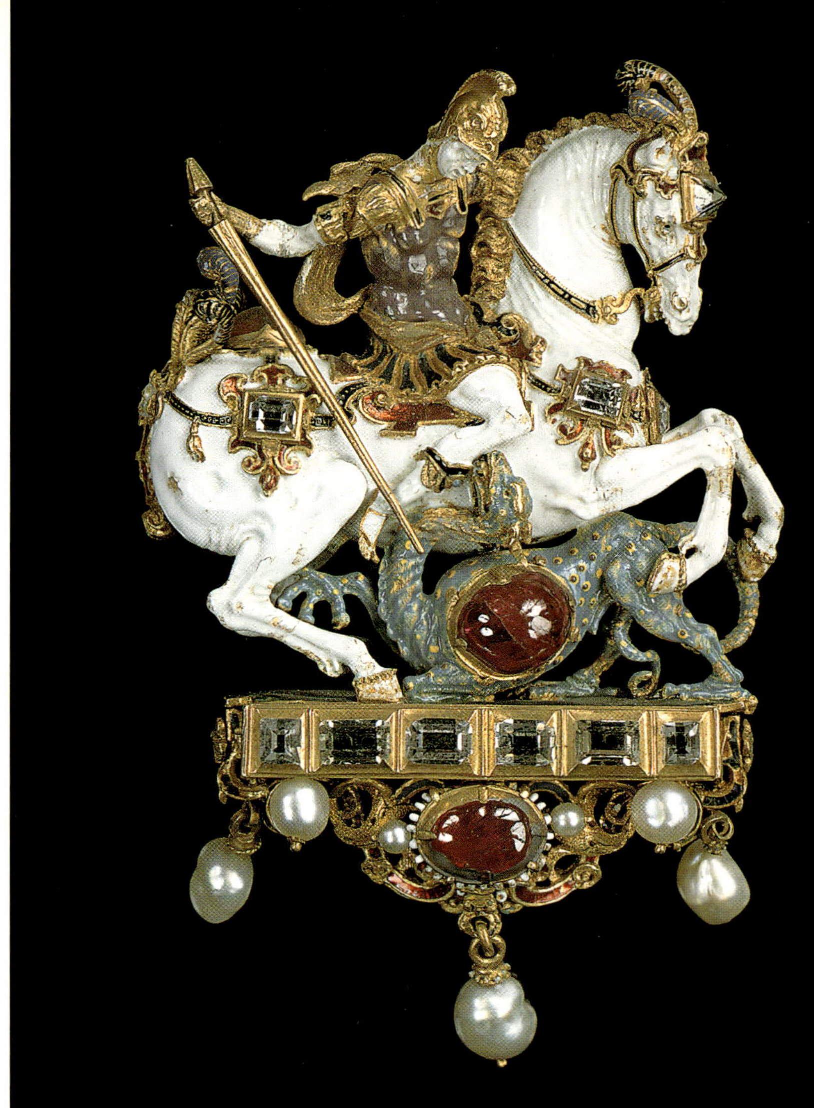

trends in France and Italy. This was assured by jewelers from the metropolitan centers for luxury items, Augsburg and Nuremberg, who reacted instantly and counted the electoral Saxon house among their customers.

The *Golden Pendant* with two overlapping letter »A's« refers directly to the electoral couple August (1526/1553 – 1586) and Anna (1532 – 1585). The letters are appropriately made of diamonds, which were increasingly popular at the time, whereas the ducal crown above consists of rubies. The double monogram is flanked by two emeralds. Originally, the piece of jewelry terminated in a suspended pearl. The decorative elements on the cast ground plate – fruit, putti heads, and two sculptural putti – mirror the fashion trends after 1560. Precious objects of this type were integral parts of the severe Spanish court fashion. It was customary for both sexes to wear numerous long necklaces, one over the other on the mostly dark, high-necked garments made of precious fabrics.

The *Pendant with the Equestrian Saint George* battling the Dragon must be counted among the most significant artistic pieces of Renaissance jewelry in the Green Vault. The modeling of this three-dimensional object is remarkably powerful and reveals a finely differentiated anatomy. Equally masterful is the subtle coloration of the pendant's opaque enamel: It is so thinly applied that the precious metal shines through in the raised sections. The *Pendant with David and Goliath* may presumably also be dated to the last decades of the 16th century. Like *Saint George*, it is also influenced by the progressively stronger sway of French fashion. The latter determined the shape of the ground plate with its perforated ornament as well as the appearance of the entire composition in the way the minuscule David is juxtaposed to the gargantuan Goliath. Similar pendants with Christian and other meaningful themes may be found repeatedly in the extensive jewelry listings of the prince elector's widow Sophia (1568 – 1622) from 1599 onward. One of her jewelry cabinets contained, in four drawers alone, 164 pendants. The inventory lists various instances of decorative-figural gems depicting the battle between David and Goliath.

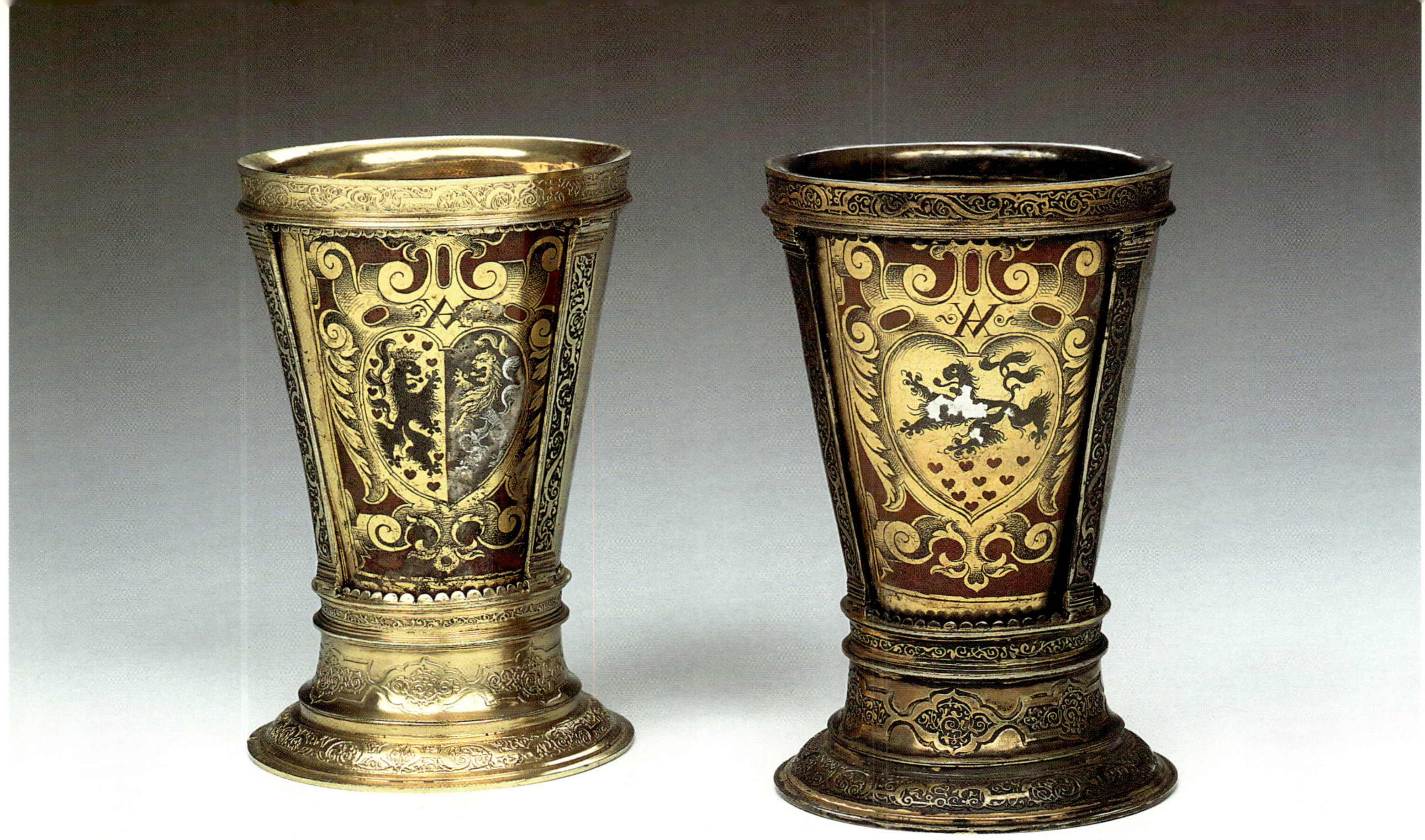

Two Double-Walled Goblets with the Coats-of-arms of August and Anna

Glass, gilt silver
Glass painting: Nicolaus Solis
Mount: Hans Selber
Augsburg, circa 1580
H. ca. 10 cm, edge of the lip D. 7 cm, Inv.-no. IV 208, IV 273

Armorial Panel

Glass painting, gold, enamel, miniature in oil on copper
Glass painting: Augsburg or Nuremberg
Goldsmith's work: Valentin Geitner
Dresden, dated 1586
D. 12,5 cm, Inv.-no. V 614

Only a few masters active in the last third of the 16th century were familiar with the art of »amelieren,« the art of glass painting. One of them was Nicolaus Solis (1542 – 1583/85). Born in Nuremberg, he settled in Augsburg in 1565, where he introduced a technique that had been perfected in his hometown: Painting in gouache on gold or silver foil under glass, until then a specialty of Nuremberg, was thereby introduced to the rising metropolis for the production of luxury items. Most glass painters who used this technique fabricated armorial panels that they then delivered to goldsmiths or ivory turners for embellishment. Larger vessels executed in this glass painting technique were only rarely produced. Because the painting behind the glass was sensitive to liquids the vessels could not be used. Display tankards therefore bore witness to the fugitive nature of this virtuoso art whose preservation required special care. They were pure collector's items whose place was in either a *Kunstkammer* or a Treasury.

The two Dresden *Goblets* are at the same time expressions of the dynastic self-definition of the Saxon electoral couple, August and Anna. The outer wall of the *Goblet* dedicated to Prince Elector August is articulated by three shields with the coats-of-arms of six provinces (the Palatinates of Thuringia and Saxony, Orlamünde and Pleißen, Landsberg and Altenburg). On the ground, the coat-of-arms of the burgraviate of Magdeburg may be seen, whereas one further coat-of-arms on the goblet's bottom side is destroyed. The interior of each *Goblet* is bedecked with green scrolls and colored flowers on a golden ground. The second *Goblet* refers to Prince Electress Anna and her royal Danish origin. Its outer wall is adorned with the coats-of-arms of Sweden, Jutland, and Wendenland, and the coats-of-arms of Schleswig-Holstein and Stormarn-Oldenburg can be seen on the ground of the goblet.

Like his father before him, Christian I valued the decorative function of engravings done in varnished gold and silver foil. This is why panels with Christian's coat-of-arms can oftentimes be found within silversmith's works. They were also inserted into the virtuoso ivories of his court turners. As owner's marks they ornated the interior lids, the

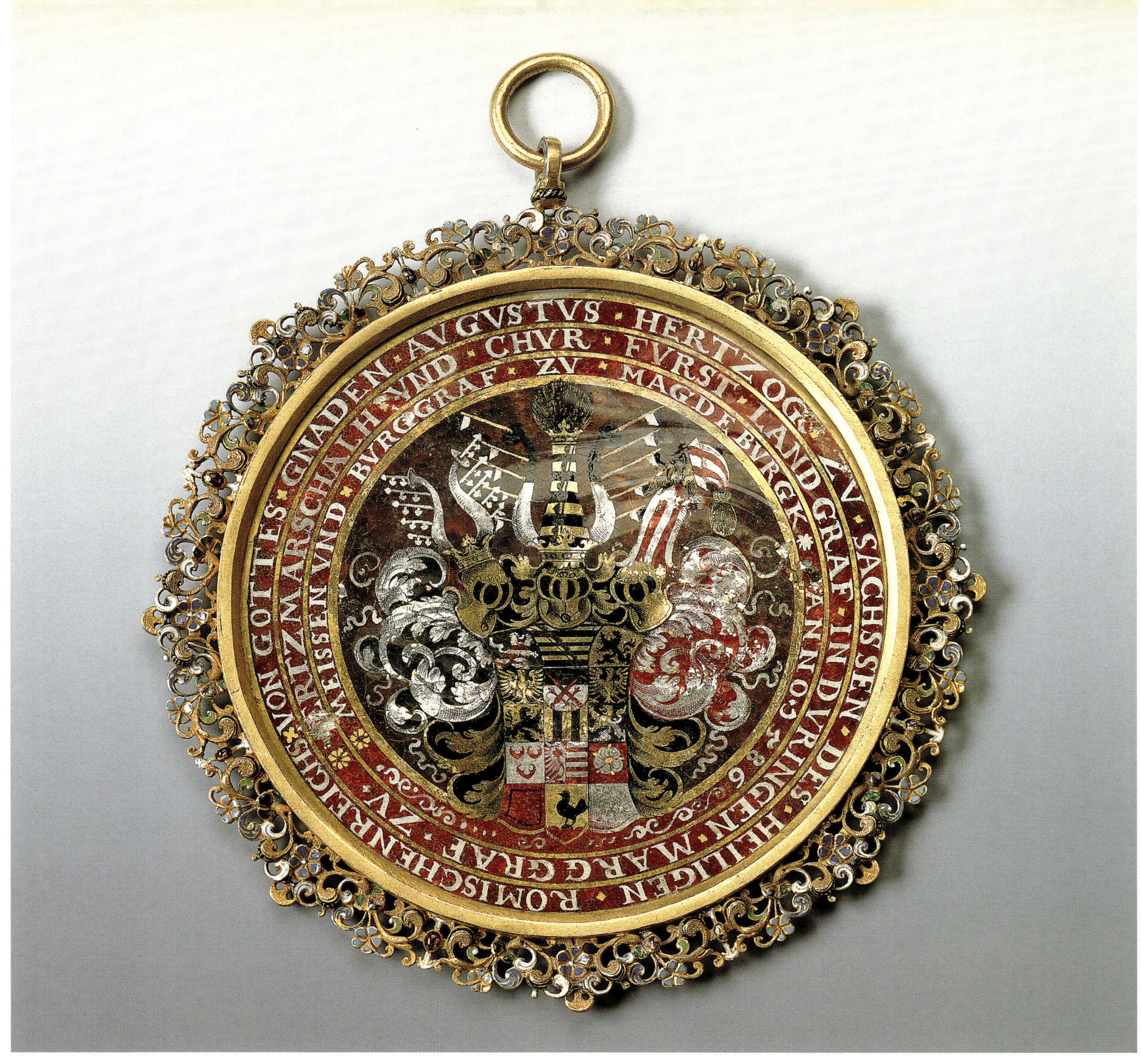

bases of objects, or they served as inlays on the lid's pommel. Thanks to a surviving invoice by Valentin Geitner, a busy Dresden goldsmith, the frequent use of smaller armorial glass panels can be ascertained. Geitner also created a »Cronengold« (i.e. crown gold) portrait of Prince Elector August that Christian I presented to his wife Sophia – presumably at Easter 1586 – in commemoration of her father-in-law, who had died barely two months before. In 1587 the image was already contained in the electoral Treasury. The back of this portrait – painted on copper, its present state of preservation is rather desolate – is a large and well-preserved armorial panel, presumably by a South German »Amelierer.« According to reports, the portrait showed August in half-length, dressed in a high hat and long cloak. The armorial panel shows the Saxon coat-of-arms of the Saxon prince elector with the electoral swords in a heart-shaped shield. The helmets are crowned with the coats-of-arms of the landgraviate of Thuringia, the Duchies of Saxony-Wittenberg, and the margraviate of Meissen. This is surrounded by three rings of inscriptions: »By God's grace, August, Duke of Saxony of the Holy Roman Empire / Imperial Arch-Marshal and Prince Elector in Duringen Margraviate of / Meissen and Feudal Lord of Magdeburg Anno 1586.«

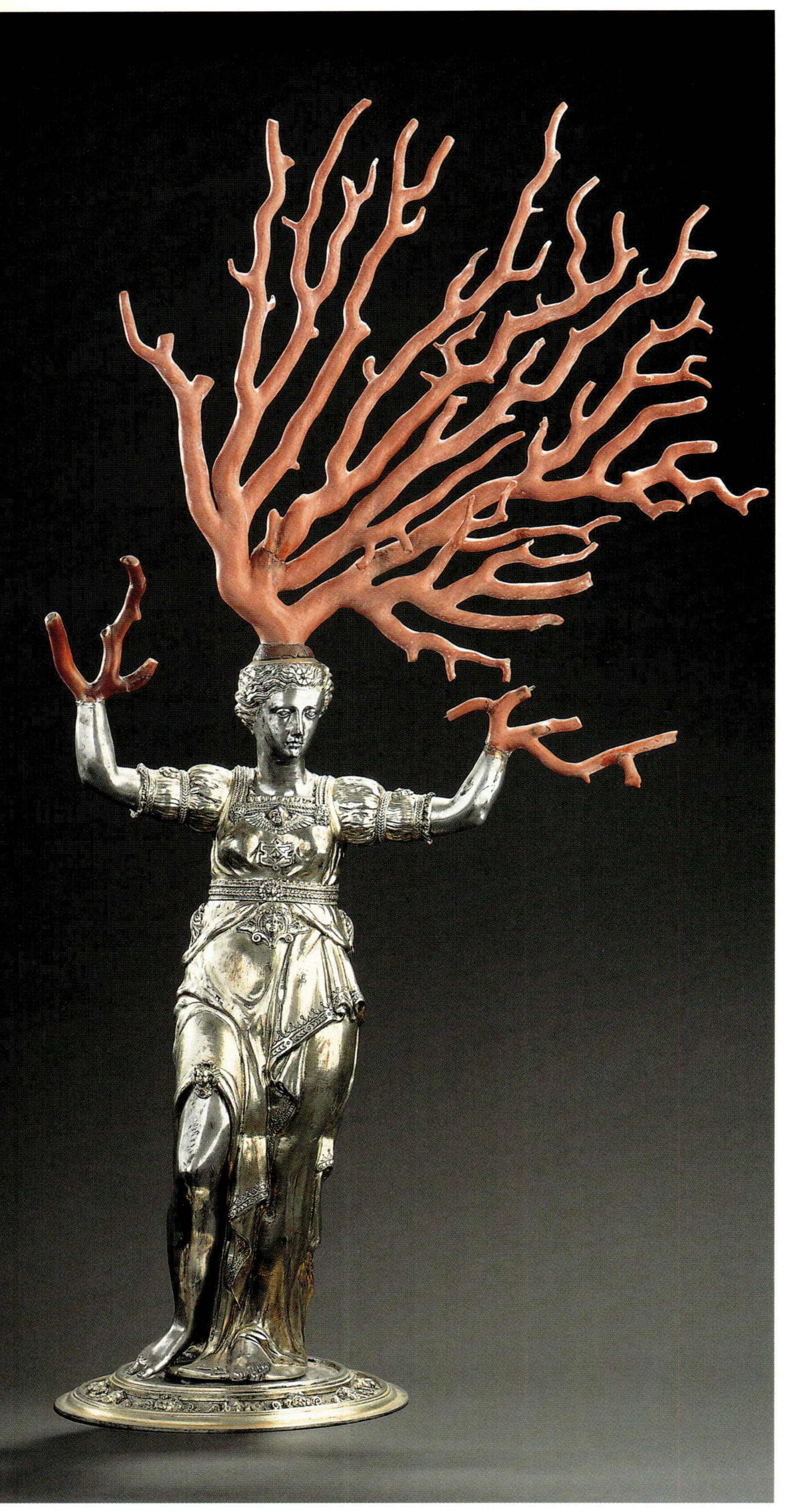

Statuette of Daphne

Silver, mostly gilt, coral
Design: Wenzel Jamnitzer
Execution: Abraham Jamnitzer
Nuremberg, between 1579 and 1586
H. 68 cm, Inv.-no. IV 260

Display Casket

Wooden core, silver, partly gilt, mother-of-pearl, velvet, silk, glass, precious stones
Design: Wenzel Jamnitzer
Execution: Nicolaus Schmidt
Nuremberg, circa 1585
H. 50 cm, W. 54 cm, D. 36 cm, Inv.-no. IV 115

Two works preserved in the Green Vault directly based on his designs testify to the fact that Wenzel Jamnitzer was an unusually creative goldsmith with scientific interests. He transgressed the tight boundaries of his guild with virtuoso works of art. Active in Nuremberg as a master between 1534 and 1585, his works attracted the attention of four consecutive emperors and two generations of princely collectors. He included the leading specialists of his hometown in putting his ideas into practice and they headed a workshop that spread his œuvre after his death.

One of the two works is already listed in the Treasury inventory of 1587 as »1 silbern brust bilt von einer Jungfrau, mit einem großen gewechß von Corallen Zincken ...« i.e. »1 silver half-portrait of a young woman with a large growth of coral spikes.« It is the shy nymph *Daphne*, who, in order to escape the impertinent pursuit of the god Apollo, is transformed into a laurel by her father. Reminiscent of an ancient draped statue, this sculptural masterpiece bears the goldsmith's mark of Abraham Jamnitzer (1555 – after 1591). Here, the son of Wenzel Jamnitzer, active as a master himself since 1579, repeated – in some instances down to tiny details – a statuette that is also crowned by a large piece of coral and was made by his father. According to the latest research of the maker's marks, this older work was made between 1571 and 1575. It is preserved in the Musée National de la Renaissance in the Château d'Ecouen and was produced for an unidentified patron. The model and the necessary casting moulds must have been preserved in the Jamnitzer workshop. When another particularly rare large coral spikes came to Nuremberg from Italy, Abraham was able to produce a second version of the sculpture for the Saxon prince elector.

The silver statuette of a *Nymph* can be taken apart at her belt. The upper body can be removed, while the lower portion may be used as a container. Closer scrutiny of the upper body reveals the technical challenges of its production. It was cast in two parts and sports a horizontal

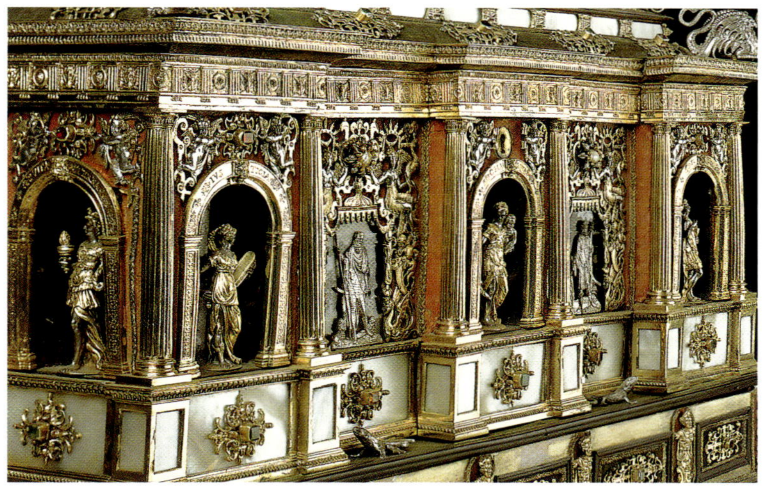

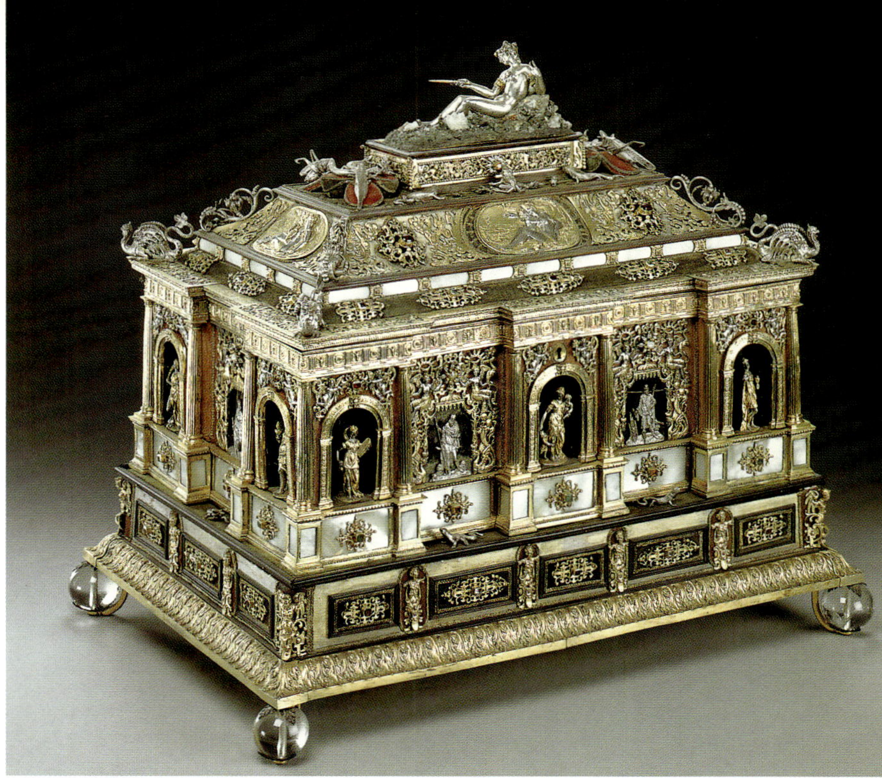

seam roughly in the center. The bare leg and the base plate were also individually cast.

The way Jamnitzer conceived the work was a stroke of a genius from both artistic and intellectual points of view. In the same way that Daphne – according to Ovid's *Metamorphosis* – was transformed from a human being into a tree, the drops of blood from the Medusa's head that was severed by Perseus turned into stone-like coral in the Mediterranean Sea. Coral was considered to be the quintessential *Kunstkammer* material, because, according to the understanding of the time, it united the three realms of nature: mineral, animal, and vegetable.

Nicolaus Schmidt, active as a master goldsmith in Nuremberg from 1582 until 1602, was another close associate of Wenzel Jamnitzer's. With his *Display Casket*, he quotes the latter's designs directly and also reveals workshop idiosyncrasies. Therefore, Anne Veltrup suggests that this *Casket* was a collaboration with the aged master that was completed by the younger one after Jamnitzer's death in 1585. This would make the Dresden *Casket* one of Wenzel Jamnitzer's last works.

Christian I presented this *Display Casket* to his wife Sophia on Christmas in 1588. By January 1, 1589 the »Kestlein oder Nöhe Ledtlein« i.e. »Little Casket or Sewing Drawer« had already received a distinguished place within the electoral *Kunstkammer*. The large *Display Casket* with its architectural layout is a precious piece of furniture used to store items. It is of royal rank. However, not all of its refined details have survived. The clock's striking mechanism, once hidden in the lid, is as good as lost. And so is the face that could be turned and on which the elegant statuette of a Mannerist female would point out the hours with her staff. Fully preserved, on the other hand, is a richly embellished internal system of drawers covered with silk of different colors. Additional intact details include silver filigree work, plaques referring to a princely owner, and gold cords.

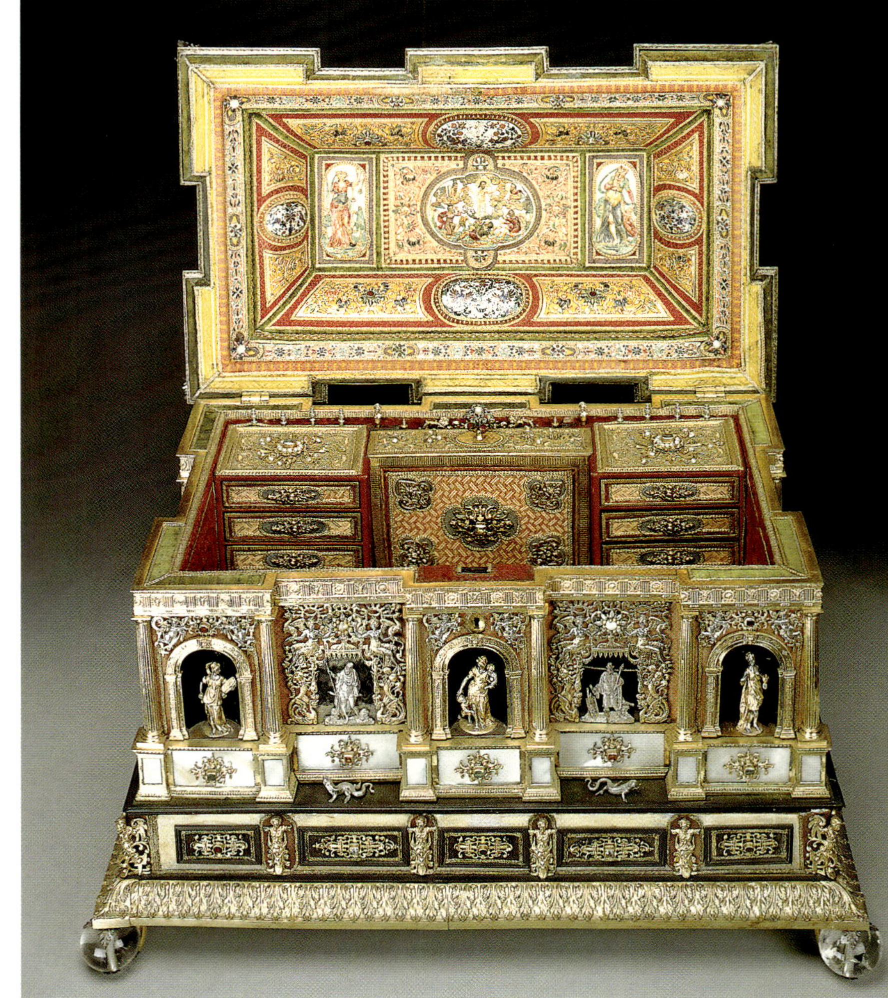

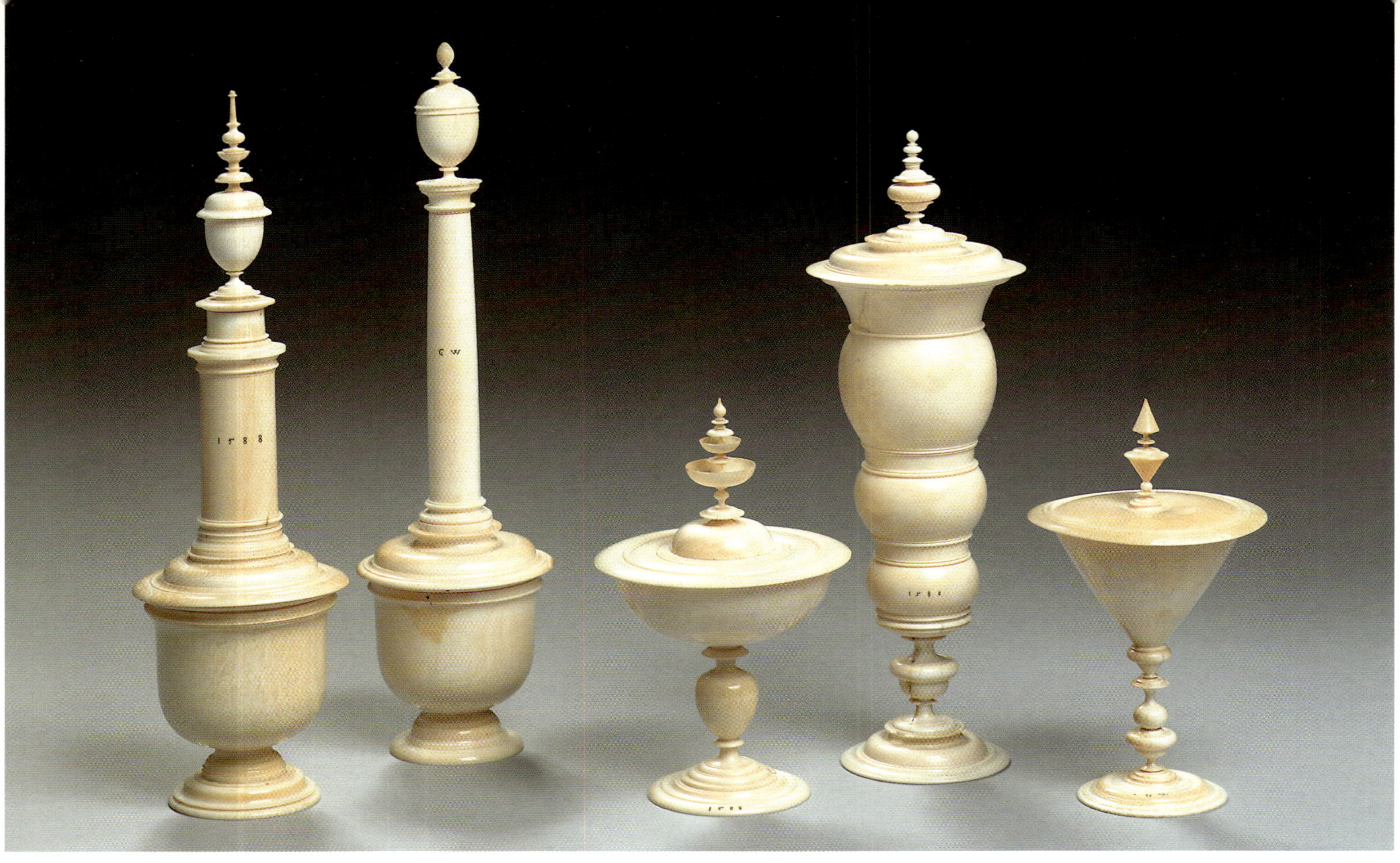

Pieces Turned on the Lathe: Two Writing Garnitures, and Three Lidded Goblets

Ivory
Signed Georg Wecker
Dresden, all dated 1588
H. 16,2 to 30,2 cm, Inv.-no. (from left to right) II 360, II 362, II 304, II 153, II 410

Ivory with Marcus Curtius

Ivory
Egidius Lobenigk
Dresden, presumably 1591 to 1595
H. 24 cm, Inv.-no. II 18

Court turners were highly paid artist-engineers. Not only did they create virtuoso works of art based on complicated calculations, but they also fabricated the necessary specialized tools. They were specialists of a mechanical art that was held in highest esteem during the decades around the year 1600; their art was the result of a perfect interplay of applied mathematics and advanced mechanical technology. Thus, in 1591 the workshop of the court turner Georg Wecker contained – besides tools to prepare the ivory – no less than five different lathes, two of which were used by Prince Elector August and his son Christian I. In addition, Wecker's workshop inventory lists 2,480 turning chisels, among them iron girders, concave drills, concave iron girders, and augers. The artist-engineer must therefore have manufactured numerous special tools for each of his works of art.

Court turners were, however, not only equipped with a mathematical and constructive spirit, they were also talented artists. Two turners worked simultaneously at the Dresden court: the Munich born Georg Wecker from 1576 until 1622 and Egidius Lobenigk from 1584 until 1595. Their salaries were paid by the otherwise frugal Prince Elector August. He was an admirer of applied mathematics, which enabled him to draw maps himself or to create works of art on the lathe. While his son Christian I was also trained in the active work of the lathe, he was more interested in collecting than in creating. During his reign – it lasted but five years – he was able to build on an already existing inventory to which he added a collection of artistically turned ivory objects that remains unsurpassed for its variety and multitude of forms. These holdings are preserved almost completely intact. Most of the turned objects in the collection were signed and dated by the collector's order.

Georg, son of the Bavarian court turner Hans Wecker, transferred the highly developed art technology from Munich to Dresden. He remained indebted to the monumental structures of the early phase of ivory turning. Wecker's works have the tendency to be stocky, although they are quite stable and often use goldsmith's works as their formal points of departure. With his fine sensitivity for shapes, he stressed horizontal lines and created solemn, clear structures. Still, Wecker commanded over the entire repertoire of shapes and forms that could be created on the lathe in a mechanical process. His works were technically brilliant. Because of the homogeneity of ivory with its silky shine, many of the turned works seem to be made in one part. However, they mostly consist of numerous independent elements that are joined thanks to individual connections – Wecker preferred bayonet joints, whereas Lobenigk opted for pegs.

Wecker's and Lobenigk's ivories toy with the possibilities of the contrast between concave and convex shapes, as well as smooth, striped, and perforated surfaces. The slightly younger Lobenigk preferred a somewhat abrupt change of form and turbulent, diminutive surfaces. In many turned works he pushed the limitations of the material to the edge of its stability. While Wecker tended to try numerous variations of a shape at the same time, Lobenigk searched for new solutions time and again. Lobenigk's work apparently left Christian I particularly impressed. The sovereign arranged for the payment of considerable allowances to him. In 1588, Lobenigk received an extra 1,000 thaler – five times his annual salary. This was the same year that both artists delivered large quantities of ivory objects to the *Kunstkammer*.

When Lobenigk died in 1595, it was determined that his entire estate should be purchased for the *Kunstkammer*. It is possible that among the items procured was the undated depiction of the legendary hero *Marcus Curtius*, a subject somewhat unusual within Lobenigk's œuvre. The object is first mentioned in 1595 in the *Kunstkammer* inventory. The mythological figure Marcus Curtius was considered to epitomize war-related bravery and patriotism during the Renaissance. The early Roman hero is said to have jumped courageously into a crevice on the Forum Romanum in order to prevent the predicted demise of Rome. For the genre of turning works on the lathe, the artist explored new avenues because he let the ivory sculpture dominate the turning.

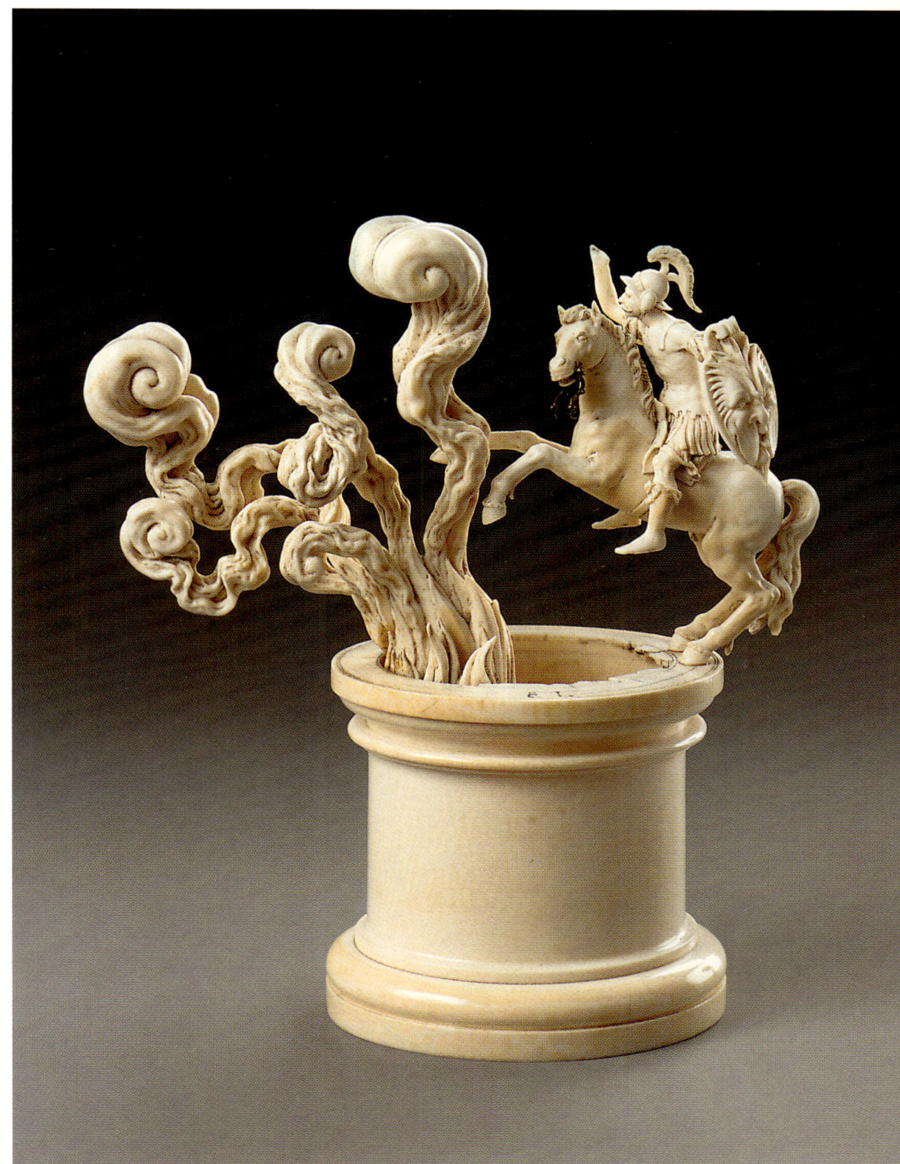

Bolted Column with Figure Clock and Music Automaton

Ivory, brass, partly gilt or painted, ebony, oak wood
Egidius Lobenigk and Hans Schlottheim
Dresden, dated 1589
H. 117 cm, Inv.-no. II 133

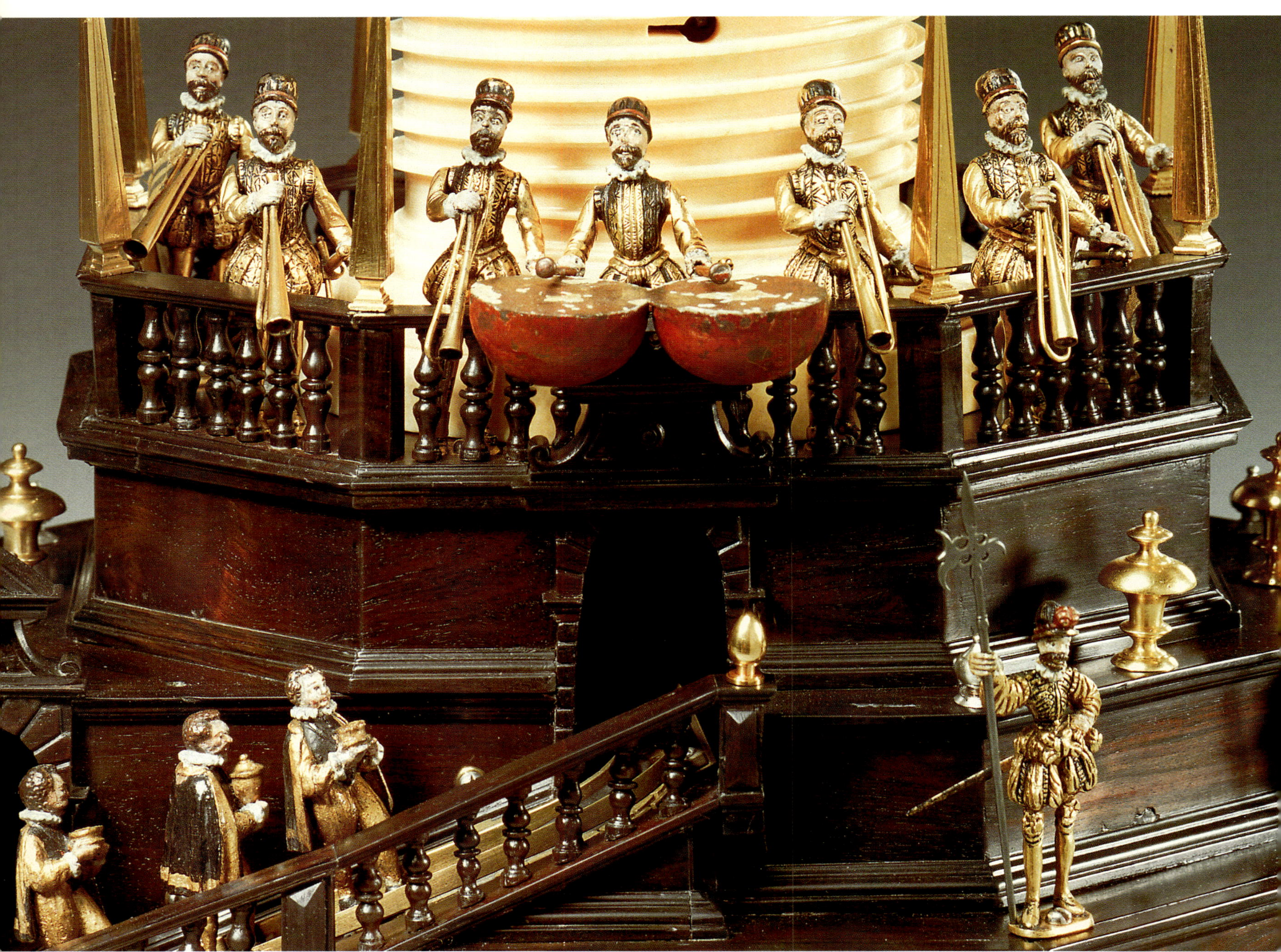

In one work of art, this large ivory column connects three masterful technical accomplishments of the German Late Renaissance. Thanks to automated machine art, a turned artwork of monumental effect was created. But it is at the same time a figural clock that toys with the illusion of liveliness and a music automaton that miraculously produced sound.

Called a pyramid in contemporary inventories, it was delivered to the Dresden *Kunstkammer* in 1589 by the court turner Lobenigk together with seven additional large pyramids. A compact organ work with a programmed cylinder and bellows is hidden in the stepped, ebony-veneered pedestal. The organ's music resonated through the lateral openings each hour. Connected to the work is a conveyer belt on which figures of three pages were pulled toward a door opening, as well as the mechanism that caused the six trumpet players located on the gallery to lift their arms. This mechanism also produced the sound of the drum in the foot's interior.

Two additional driving mechanisms and a clockwork are inserted into the lower end of the ivory column. With the aid of surprisingly long spindles, they caused movement within and above the perforated sphere on the top. When one looked into the sphere, one saw seven pages move around a table where a princely group of banquetters was gathered. Thanks to mechanical devices, three of the gentlemen and two of the ladies were able to lift their arms to their mouths. Driven by the second mechanism, the little polyhedron, as though driven by ghosts, circled the column top. The clockwork moved the reclining putto, who revolved around the upper side of the perforated sphere once an hour. The numerals of the hours are engraved in black into the surface of the sphere.

The hidden music implements, the mechanical drives, and the clockworks are cutting edge products of contemporary technology. The differentiated functions were effective due to the optimum use of space and the very complicated transmission of power. The technical fixtures represent the achievements of Hans Schlottheim, active in Augsburg, who is documented to have stayed in Dresden in 1589. It can be assumed that Schlottheim equipped the turned artwork (dated through the inscribed year) with prefabricated Augsburg products. These probably included the mechanisms, the prefabricated ebony base, and the gilt and painted brass figures, all of which he presumably assembled into a functioning, albeit quickly worn out, automaton.

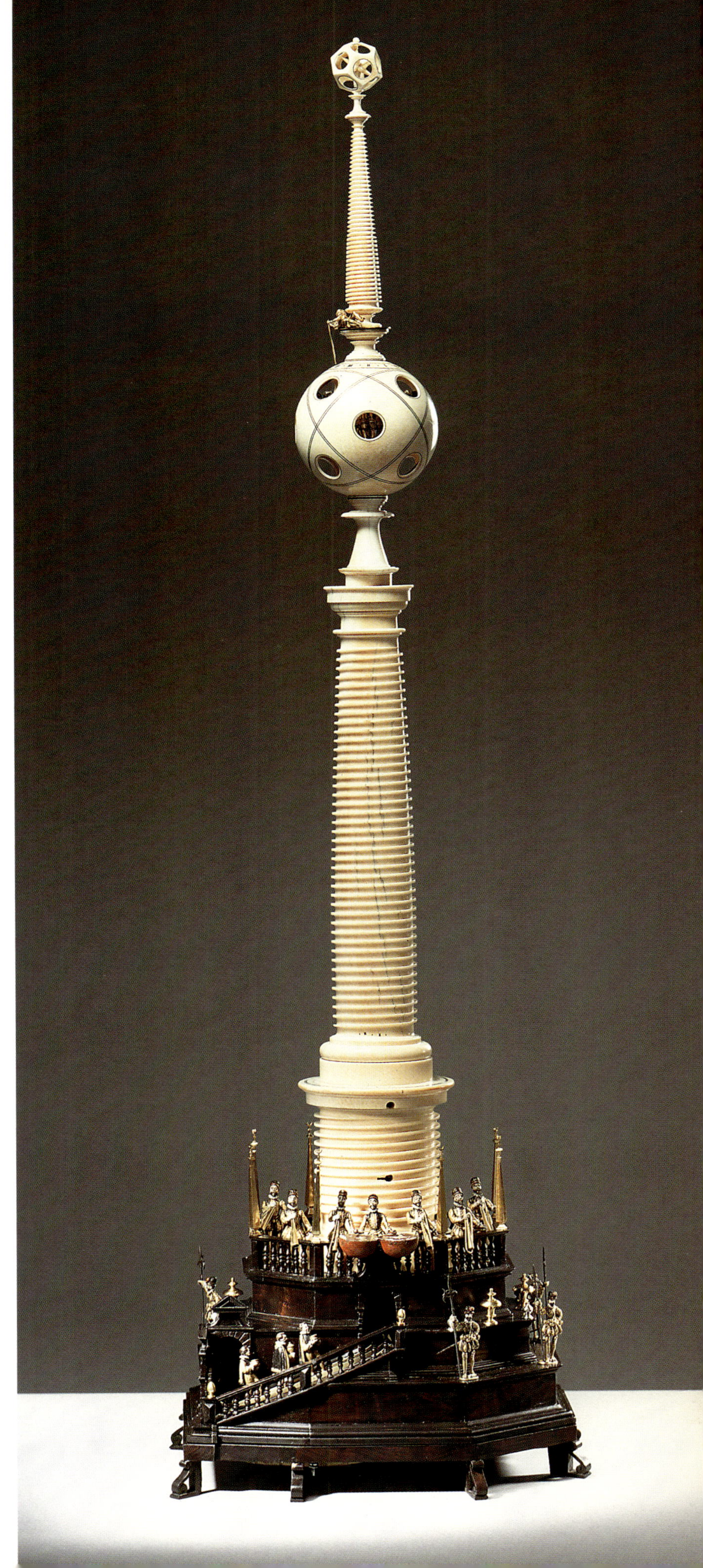

Kunstkammer Cabinet

Ebony, silver, partly gilt
Hans Kellerthaler
Dresden, between 1585 and 1611
H. 112 cm, Inv.-no. I 20

While the goldsmith Hans Kellerthaler (circa 1562 – 1611) was influenced by the fashionable trends of the Augsburg production of luxury items, he and his assistant, a Dresden cabinetmaker, also lent individual characteristics to the remarkable piece of display furniture they created from ebony and silver. It was only in 1612, one year after Kellerthaler's death, that his »schreibe schranck« (writing cabinet) was acquired by Prince Elector Johann Georg I for the hefty sum of 1,500 thaler. The year – coarsely embossed onto the flag of the crowning group – and the artist's initials lead to the assumption that the *Cabinet* was already finished by 1585. This would, however, lead to an unrealistic biography of the goldsmith, as Kellerthaler was then still working as a dependent journeyman who did not acquire his master status in Dresden until shortly after 1600. Ultimately, this is one of the earliest pieces of collector's furniture of its kind.

The piece is conceived as free standing; thus all four sides are equally worked. It consists of a broadly projecting base, a much narrower substructure and a richly decorated casket on top of the latter. In its unusual organization, the *Cabinet* remained unique. This is a *Kunstkammer* item, exclusively made to convey an extensive iconographic program via its silver statuettes and plaques. Originally, it was crowned by a silver cast figure group of high quality, lost during World War Two. The theme of this allegorical composition was the triumph of Christian truth over pagan vices and its imagery was the highlight of both content and aesthetics. Groups of silver statuettes are applied to the casket in a hierarchical manner from top to bottom. They are reliefs of the kings of the four Old World powers (Babylon, Persia, Greece, and Rome), as well as the eight virtues and the four continents. The backs of the casket's narrow sides include reliefs with the themes of war and peace. On the stepped pedestal, the Four Seasons may be found along with the four major metals (gold, silver, copper, and iron), and the world's four major rivers, among them the Elbe.

The creator of this piece of collector's furniture did not attribute much importance to its utilitarian aspects. Of the two dozen drawers, some of them minuscule, numerous ones can barely be opened due to construction details. The richly structured luxury object served as a tool for the depiction of the cosmic system according to an interpretation of King Nebucadnezar of Babylon's dream, often cited in the time around the year 1600. Its explication by the prophet Daniel delineates the vision of the demise of the four ancient world powers and the rise of an eternal Christian realm. It is conceivable that Kellerthaler created his *Cabinet* in close collaboration with Giovanni Maria Nosseni. It is known that the electoral art superintendent studied the dream of Nebucadnezar – from artistic and literary vantage points – around the year 1601.

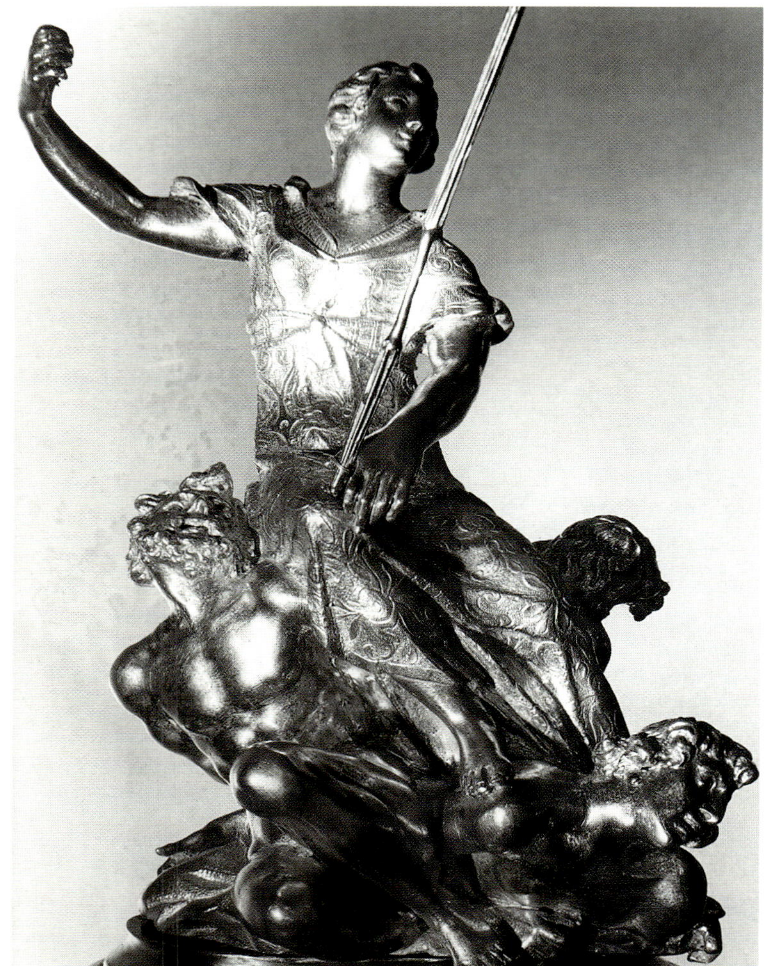

lost since 1945

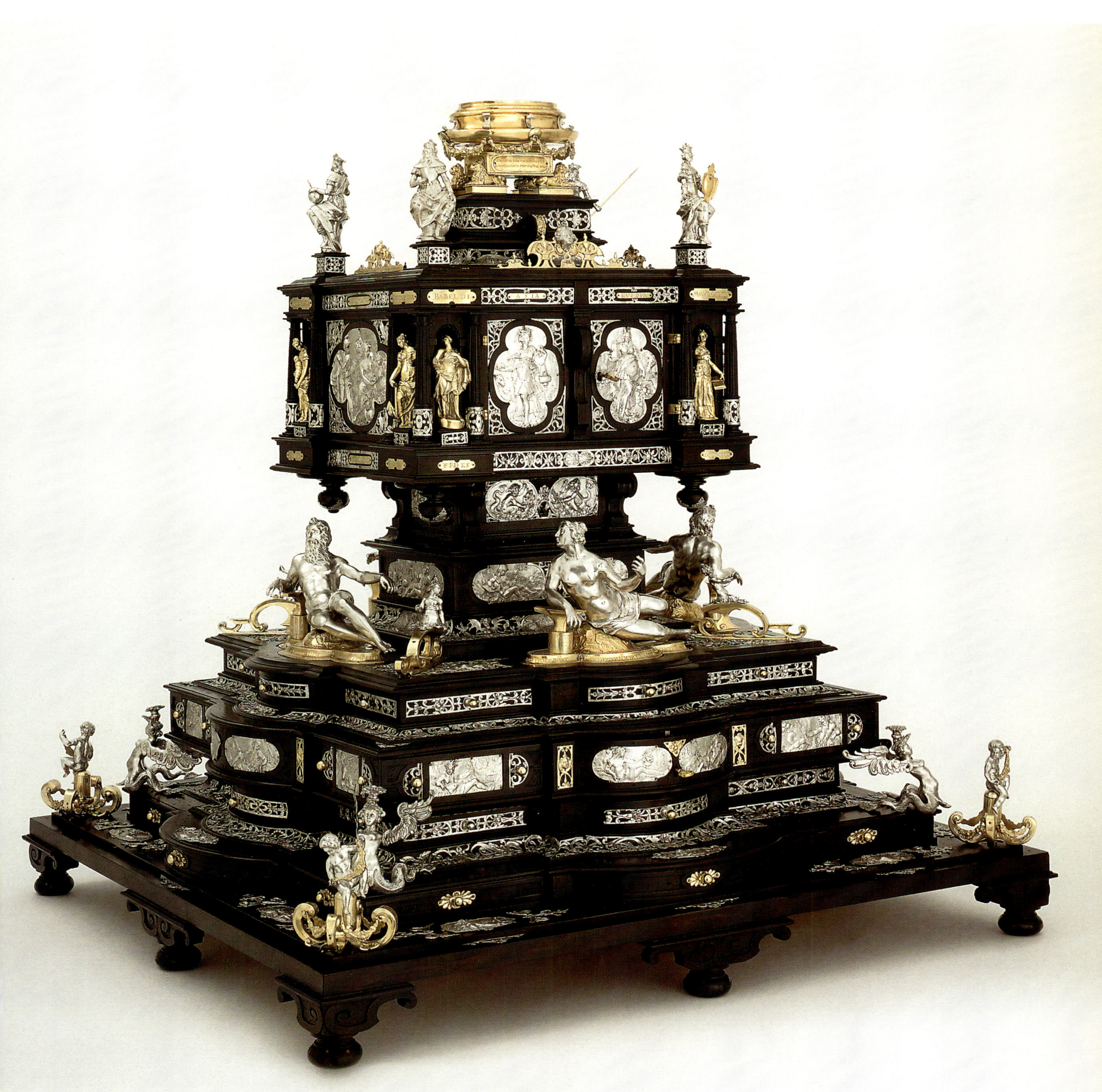

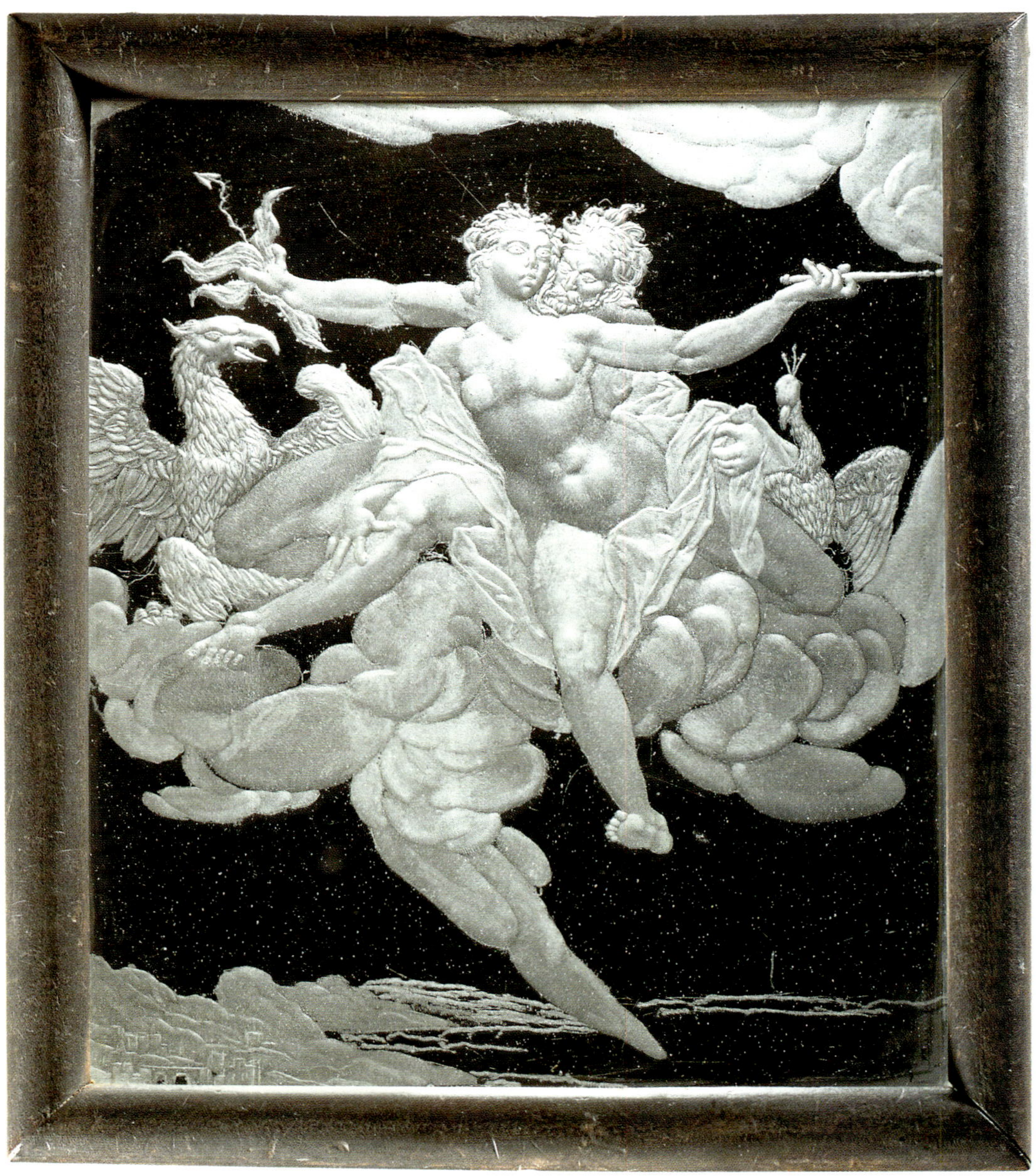

Glass Panel with Jupiter and Juno

Glass, wood
Caspar Lehmann
Prague, between 1588 and 1590
H. (with frame) 20,5 cm, W. 17,8 cm, Inv.-no. VI 70

Diana Goblet

Rock crystal, gilt silver
Stone cutter: Caspar Lehmann
Mount: presumably Daniel Kellerthaler
Dresden, 1606
H. 36,5 cm, Inv.-no. V 282

In 1590, Christian I procured an important example of Prague court art for his *Kunstkammer*. As remarked upon in the 1595 *Kunstkammer* inventory it was a »Christalen Glaß in birnbäumen Holtz eingefast, dorinnen einwarts geschnitten die Götter Juno mit dem Pfauen und Juppiter in Wolgken sitzend, [...]« i. e. »crystal glass framed in pear wood in which are cut the gods Juno with the peacock and Jupiter seated in the clouds.« The price of 30 thaler was half what the prince elector had to pay for a painting by the highly valued Bartholomäus Spranger. The imperial court painter was the author of a pen-and-ink drawing dated 1587, of almost identical size that served as the direct model for this first datable example of cut glass.

However, the master who cut the two gods into a rectangular glass panel was Caspar Lehmann. Originally from Munich, where he was trained a glass and rock crystal cutter for Duke Wilhelm V of Bavaria, he arrived in Prague in 1588 where he was appointed »court gentleman« to Emperor Rudolf II. Not until 1601 did the emperor promote him as his »chamber precious stone cutter« (*Cammeredelsteinschneider.*) Although Lehmann was not the first rock crystal cutter, he applied his technical abilities to the decoration of glass, a much cheaper material. He did this to much critical acclaim, that in 1609 Rudolf II bestowed upon him the privilege of glass cutter – comparable to a monopoly. A few years thereafter he was even elevated to the nobility.

The Dresden *Panel* with father of the gods, Jupiter, and his wife, Juno, is an incunabula of the art of glass cutting that stands at the beginning of the history of ennobling glass with this technique. The Green Vault preserves more artfully embellished glass panels besides this one, among them Lehmann's *Portrait of Duke Heinrich Julius of Brunswick-Lüneburg* of 1610, that belongs to the late phase of Rudolfian court art.

The chamber precious stone cutter Caspar Lehmann himself changed employers between January 1606 and late March 1608. Due to a court intrigue, he was forced to leave Prague. He moved to Dresden, where he began to work for the Saxon Prince Elector Christian II. The only art object to survive from this work-intense sojourn is the *Diana Goblet*, a lidded goblet with a gilt and silver mount. There is only one other rock crystal cut vessel, a pitcher with carved caryatids and flowers preserved in the Kunsthistorisches Museum in Vienna, that can be attributed to Lehmann beyond doubt.

In 1606, Christian II purchased the ovoid »Drinckgeschirr auß Behmischen Diamant mit Deckel und Fueß und Fighuren gesnitten« i.e. »goblet of Bohemian diamond with cut lid, feet, and figures,« depicting the tragic transformation of Actaeon based on Ovid's *Metamorphoses* for 200 thaler. Stupendously cut, the *Goblet's* cup shows the shy hunting goddess bathing with her nymphs. On the lid, Lehmann depicted the unlucky observer of this intimate scene being transformed into a stag. The foot presents a dynamic hunting scene, added to which are finely delineated shrubs, incised using the tip of a diamond.

Corresponding to the high quality of the cut crystal, unmatched by any other artist at the imperial court or in Dresden at the time, is the exquisite goldsmith mount. The ornamental clasps, the finely executed silver statuettes of the hunter with his dogs, and the reclining stag can all be attributed to Daniel Kellerthaler, who was then the most creative goldsmith working in Dresden.

The successors of Christian II also loved the *Diana Goblet* as a hunting goblet. Time and again, it was loaned from the electoral Saxon *Kunstkammer*, until it finally broke. But Augustus the Strong integrated it into his Treasury Museum – out of respect for the work of art – even in its damaged state.

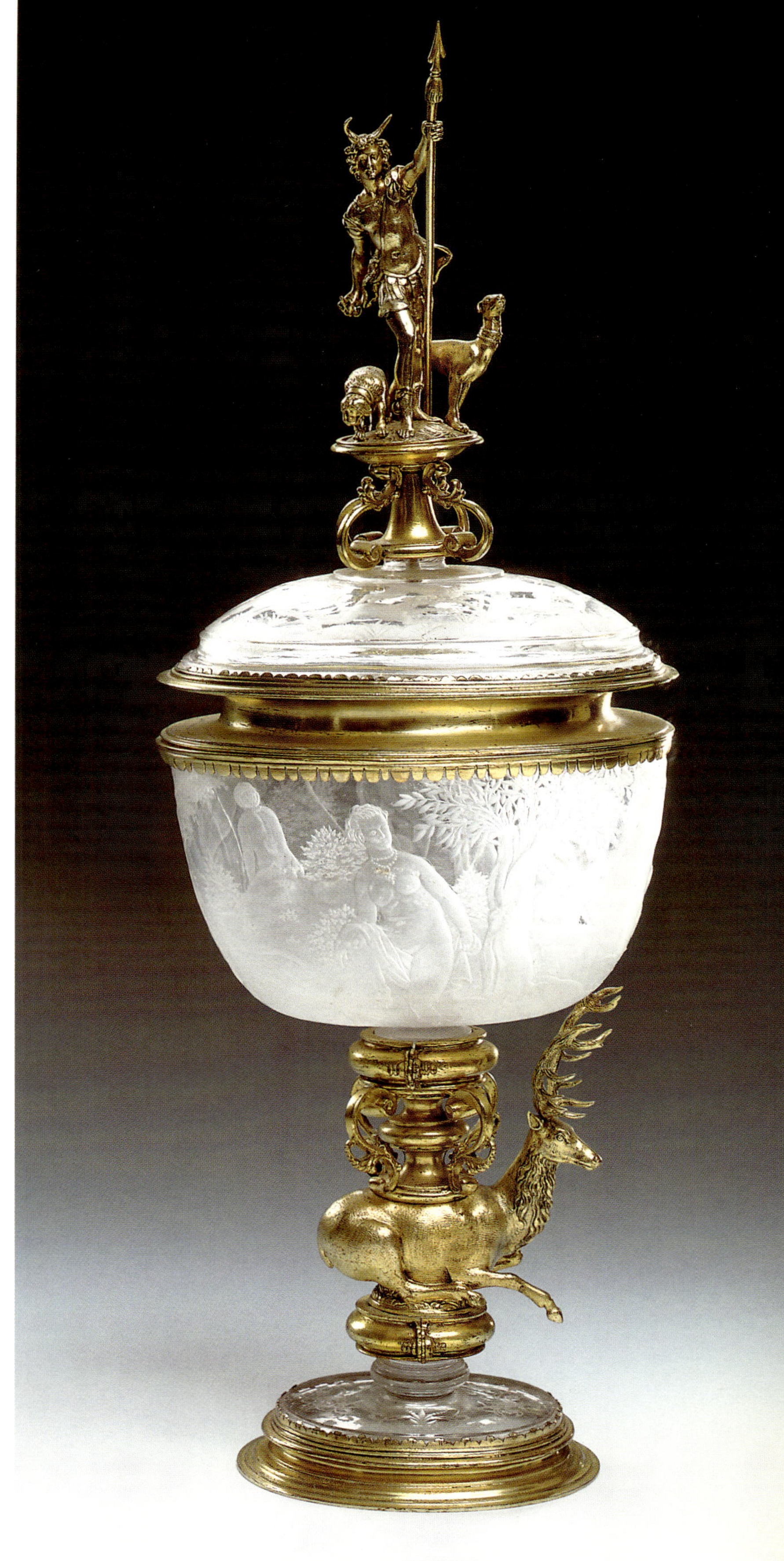

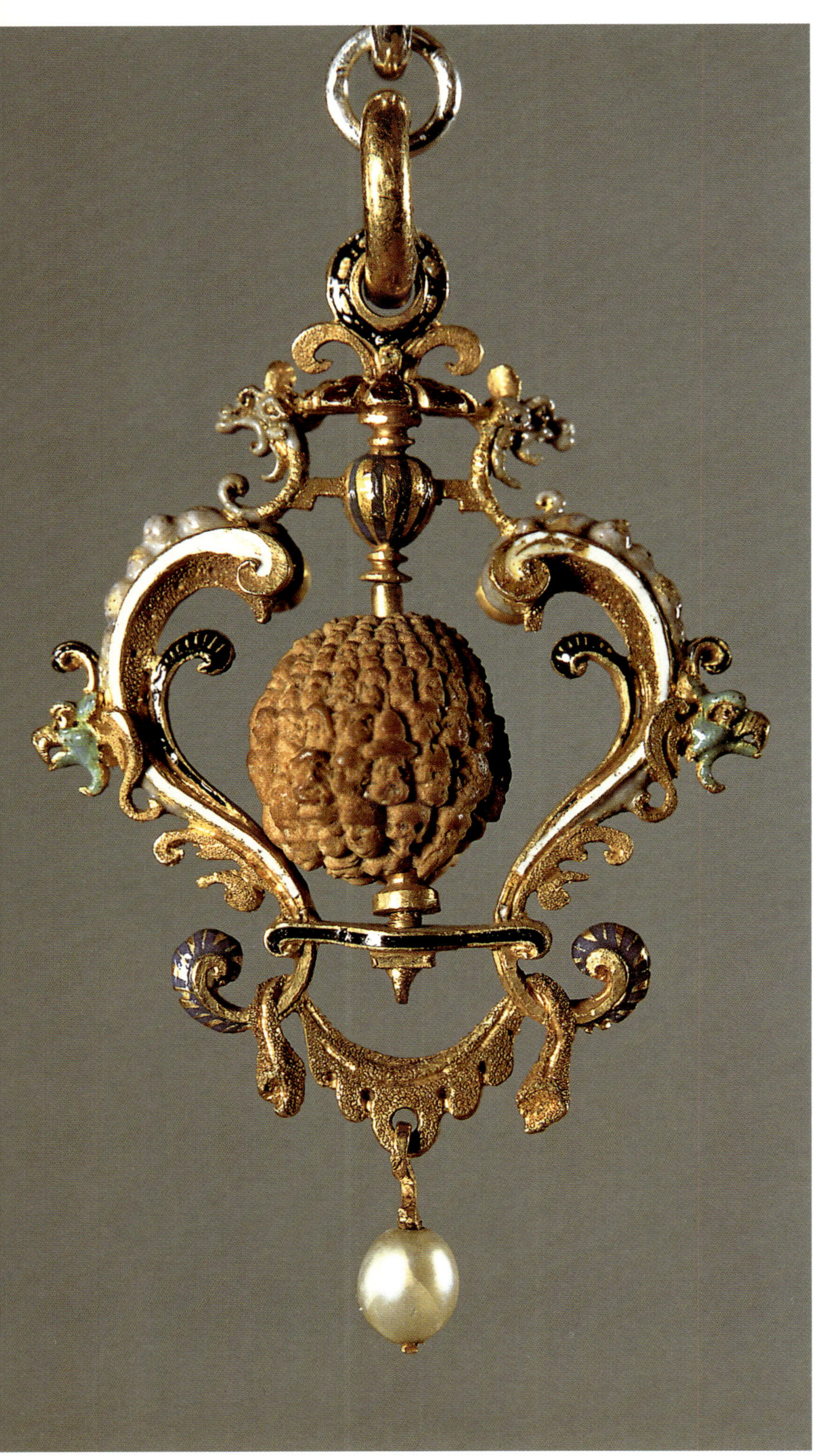

Cherry Pit with »185 Carved Heads«

Cherry pit, Gold, enamel, pearl
Germany, before 1589
H. 4,5 cm, Inv.-no. VII 32 ee

Little Mount of Calvary

Gold step, gold, enamel, ebony
End of the 16th century
H. 5 cm, Inv.-no. VI 8 dd

Spider Automaton

Brass, traces of paint, iron
Tobias Reichel
Dresden, before 1604
L. 2,6 cm, Inv.-no. VI 7 qq

Works of small size that could only be created by overcoming the greatest technical difficulties were always particularly fascinating to aristocratic collectors. As *mirabilia*, and thus as wonderworks of human creativity and artistic accomplishment, they occupied an important place in princely *Kunstkammer*s. From the Green Vault's vast holdings of micro-sculpture and small sculptures made of ivory, wood, and metals, only three are presented here, distinguished through the materials used.

Unlike almost any other object preserved in the Green Vault, the *Cherry Pit* decorated with uncounted human faces, has dumbfounded visitors for centuries. Upon his visit to Dresden 1629, the learned traveler Philipp Hainhofer, an outstanding connoisseur of the collections of his time, noted »Ain Kirschkern, darauf 185 todenkopf und gsichter wol kändtlich geschnitten, als ein kleinot zum ohrgeheng gefasset;« i. e. »one cherry pit into which are cut 185 identifiable skulls and heads; the gem has a mount and can be worn as an earring.« The 185 heads are first mentioned in the inventory of 1595 – according to a recent count, there are »only« 113. Using the finest tools, they were incised into the surface of the pit with the aid of a magnifying glass. Prince Elector Christian I received the *Kunstkammer* object par excellence in 1589 as a gift from Christoph von Loß zu Pillnitz (1545 – 1609). The Loß family also gave the sovereign three additional cherry pits still preserved today, two of them reveal portraits and coats-of-arms, and a third one has numerous biblical depictions (among them the Fall of Man, Noah's Ark, the erection of the Brazen Serpent, the Crucifixion) and four male portrait busts.

Whereas the carved cherry pits were made from a perfectly ordinary material, the minuscule *Crucifixion of Christ* over a »rock« rises from a solid piece of pure gold the size of a walnut. The white enameled

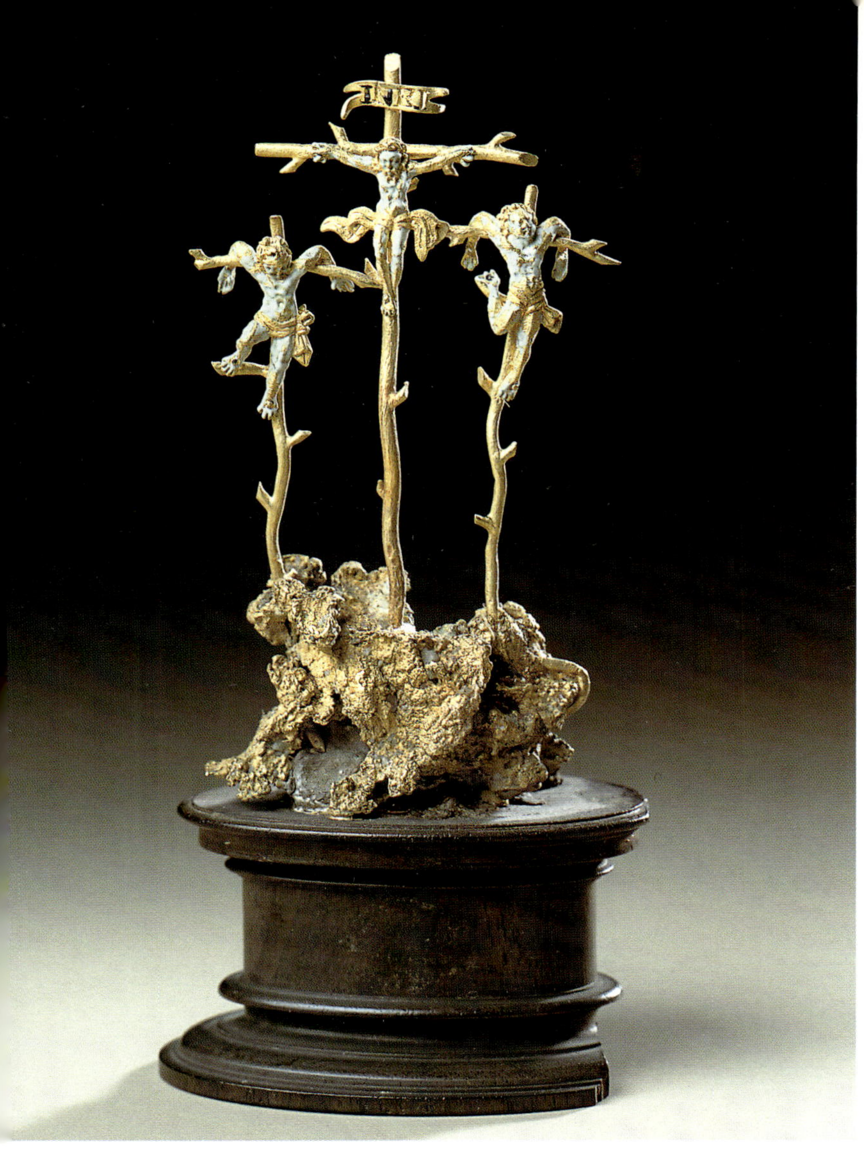

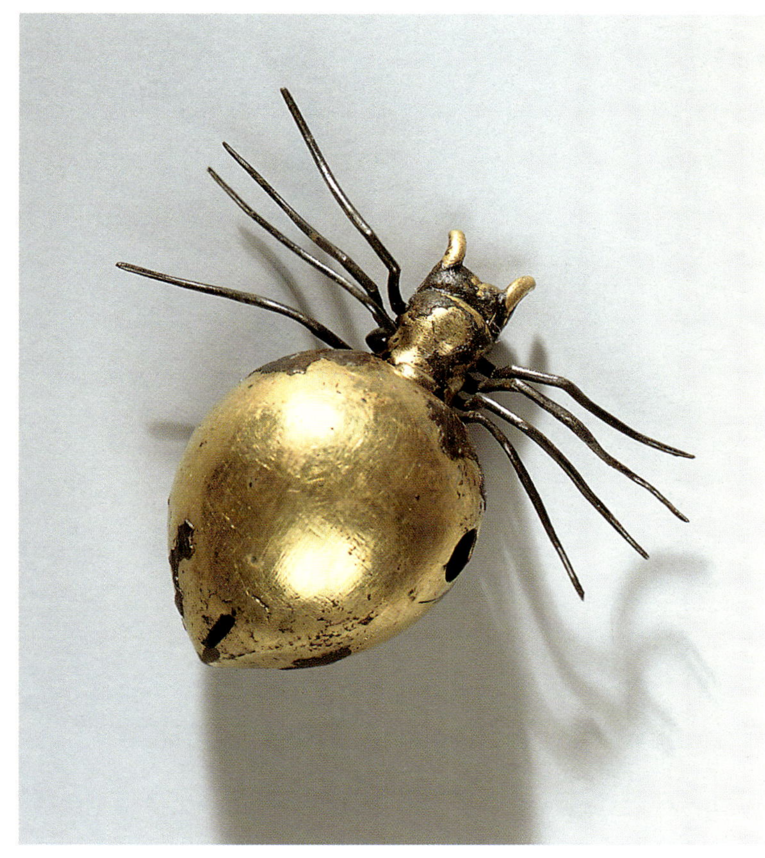

Crucifixion Group with the two thieves is worked from this same precious metal, considered invaluable in the 16th century.

Within the collection of the Green Vault, the precious *Crucifixion Group* belongs to the so-called *Handsteine* (literally hand stones). Around the year 1600, the terms *Erzstufe* (literally ore step) and *Handstein* were applied to bizarrely shaped stones consisting of more or less pure silver, copper, or even gold, some of them adorned with multiple figural beautification. The name *Handstein* refers to the Latin term *lapides manuales*, which translates as »filling one hand.« Artistically embellished ore steps were customarily erected in areas where mining played an important role. In addition to Bohemia, Hungary, and the Tyrol, Saxony was also a significant mining center. In the mining pits one would occasionally come across steps made of solid ore. Hand stones were much sought after collector's items that belonged to the basic holdings of a princely *Kunstkammer*. Starting in 1595, the Dresden *Kunstkammer* inventories list – besides a plethora of raw stone samples with high metal contents – dozens of artificially ennobled hand stones, of which the ones made of gold ore were especially rare. The priceless *Mount of Calvary* is first mentioned in the 1587 Treasury list as »1 small little golden ore step with the Crucifixion of Christ on a little wooden foot; gilt on the top and also with a pearl.« The base was presumably altered, and thus the pearl was lost. The golden hand stone came to the *Kunstkammer* during the first decades of the 17th century.

Automatons that could imitate movement and thereby life, were likewise integral to any princely collection around the year 1600. There is a vast quantity of these wonderworks of technical progress from the reigns of Christian I and Christian II preserved in the Dresden museums that illuminate the high esteem in which they were held at the time. The little *Spider Automaton* is driven straight ahead by a small mechanism. The energy affects two cog-wheels located just under the surface of the body. Powered in this way, the artificial animal – its once naturalistic coloration is only fragmentary today – was capable of moving over a smooth surface. In doing so, the eight wiry legs of the automaton spider – rendered almost faithfully to nature – moved up and down. This micro-automaton – whose finely worked movement was fabricated by Tobias Reichel, court clock maker of Christian II – came to the *Kunstkammer* in 1604 as the gift from Prince Electress Hedwig.

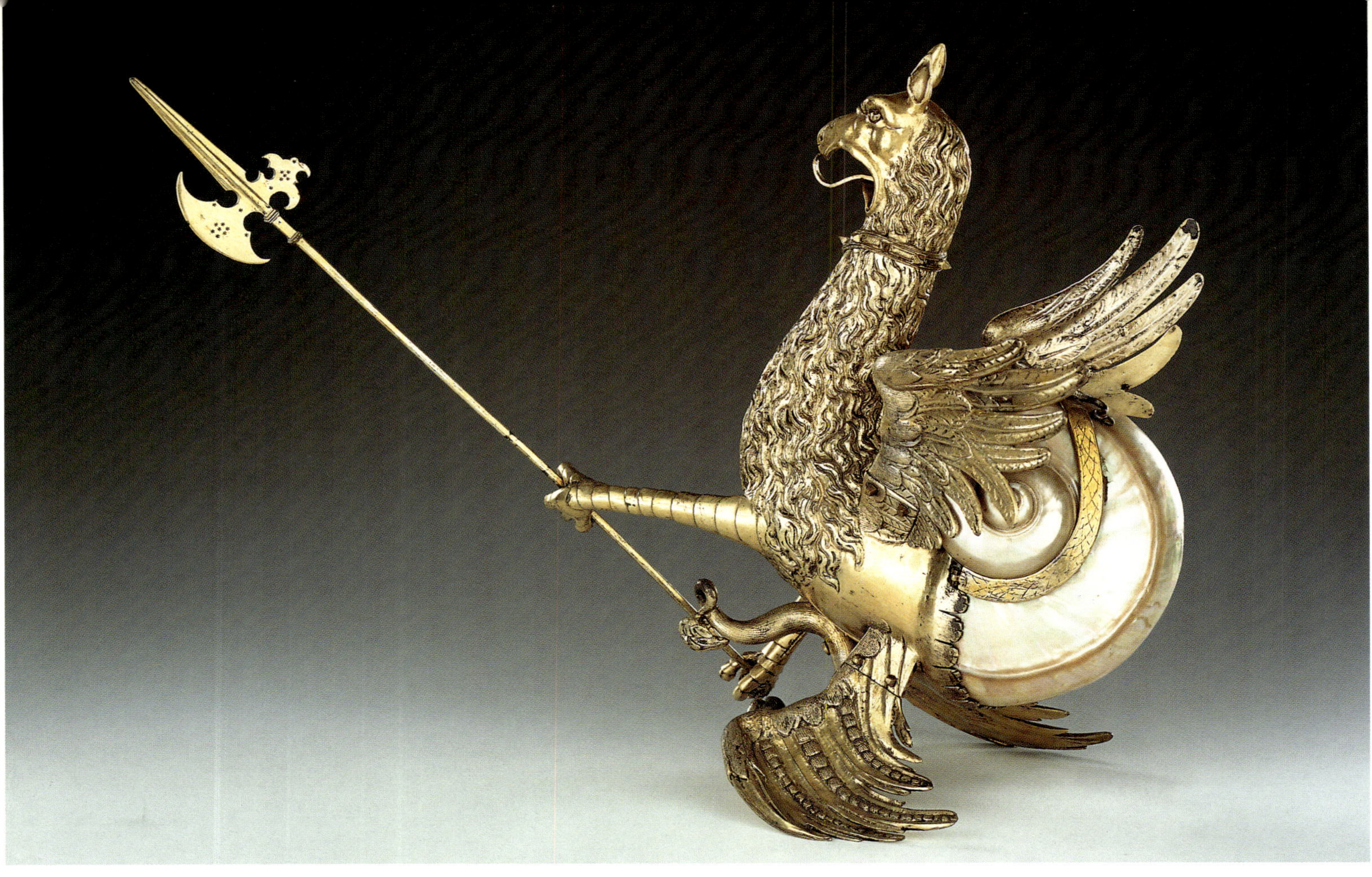

Griffin with Halberd

Silver, gilt, Sea-Snail Shell
Elias Geyer
Leipzig, 1608 until 1610
H. 38,4 cm, Inv.-no. IV 127

Centaur Automaton

Silver, partly gilt, enamel, rubies, emeralds, ebony
Johann Jacob Bachmann
Unknown clock maker
Augsburg, between 1600 and 1610
H. 51 cm, W. 33,3 cm, D. 21,3 cm, Inv.-no. IV 50

Elias Geyer was one of the most innovative masters of his time. He was, however, not active in any of the metropolis for luxury items, Nuremberg or Augsburg, but in the rather provincial commercial city of Leipzig. The roughly thirty works in the Green Vault's collection represent the largest quantity by far of Geyer's known œuvre. The *Kunstkammer* inventory of 1610 lists most of the works and even mentions an entire menagerie of fabled beasts that belonged to the prince electors. A »Meermänlein,« »Meerweibesbildt,« »Meerlewe,« »Basiliscus,« and »Meerpferdt« (little sea-man, sea maiden, sea lion, basilisk, and seahorse) are recorded there as well as one »Einhorn« and one »Greiff« (unicorn and griffin). The maker of these masterpieces was possibly unknown at the Saxon court. The person who negotiated the acquisitions was Veit Bötticher, a silver dealer who purchased numerous objects from Geyer for Christian II between 1601 and 1605. In 1609 Christian II gave Geyer's *Griffin* to his brother, Duke Johann Georg, as a Christmas or New Year's gift. In addition with a second similarly designed work by Geyer it formed a pair.

The winged griffin, a fabulous animal that originates in antiquity, was considered the guardian of treasures. It also served as the bearer of the shield for the German imperial coat-of-arms. The posterior part of the goldsmith's work – based on strict icongraphically correct terms, the body of a lion – consists of a very large and shiny sea-snail shell reminiscent of mother-of-pearl; here the fabled creature is turned into a maritime beast.

Functional the *Griffin with a Halberd* could be used as a drinking vessel, whereas its formal design is connected to the ornamental vocabulary and depictions of Renaissance era grotesques. From the art historical vantage point, this is an autonomous piece of silver sculpture. As part of a »curious« group, and as part of the competition between *naturalia* and *artificialia*, this item is a rare and priceless product of nature with the highest artistic merits.

Since antiquity, silver statues that appeared to move by themselves were considered as tokens of sublime human craftsmanship. In this respect, the table automaton by the Augsburg goldsmith Bachmann is not only a contribution to entertainment technology around the year 1600, but is of unusual artistic significance even within its own genre. The carefully worked sculptural group consists of a bearded centaur who is armed with bow and arrow and a young woman who rides upon his back and who may either be interpreted as Diana or one of her nymphs. The shape of the striding horse and the male torso that emerges from its chest testify to the maker's complete mastery of natural forms. The combination of animal and human body as well as the interplay of muscles and tendons beneath the skin seem organic. Bachmann created an exciting tension between the elegant composure of the youthful woman's body and the vitality of the animal-human creature. The goldsmith's meticulous technique reveals tangible sculptural details, for instance in the finely delineated fur of the horse's body or the hair of the centaur's head, derived from ancient prototypes.

Apart from the mechanism and the clockwork of a richly decorated clock, the high ebony base also hides numerous driving mechanisms. These devices enabled the heavy automaton to move in curves across a flat surface for a distance of about ten feet. At the same time, the large silver hunting dog on the right slowly turned its head to the left and right. The tiny gilt dog on the other side excitedly jumped up and down, and the centaur and nymph rolled with their eyes. The greatest amazement, however, was surely focused on the centaur, who shot an arrow from his bow. Calculations predicted that the springs' power could propel it as far as seven feet – not without potential danger to a surprised group of people gathered around a table. It appears that a slightly older *Centaur Automaton* by the same artist, kept in Rudolf II's *Kunstkammer*, stimulated Christian's purchase of this object in the imperial city of Prague. The *Automaton* with its repeatedly repaired drive mechanism remained in the electoral *Kunstkammer* until it was dissolved in 1832, when the object was transferred to the Green Vault.

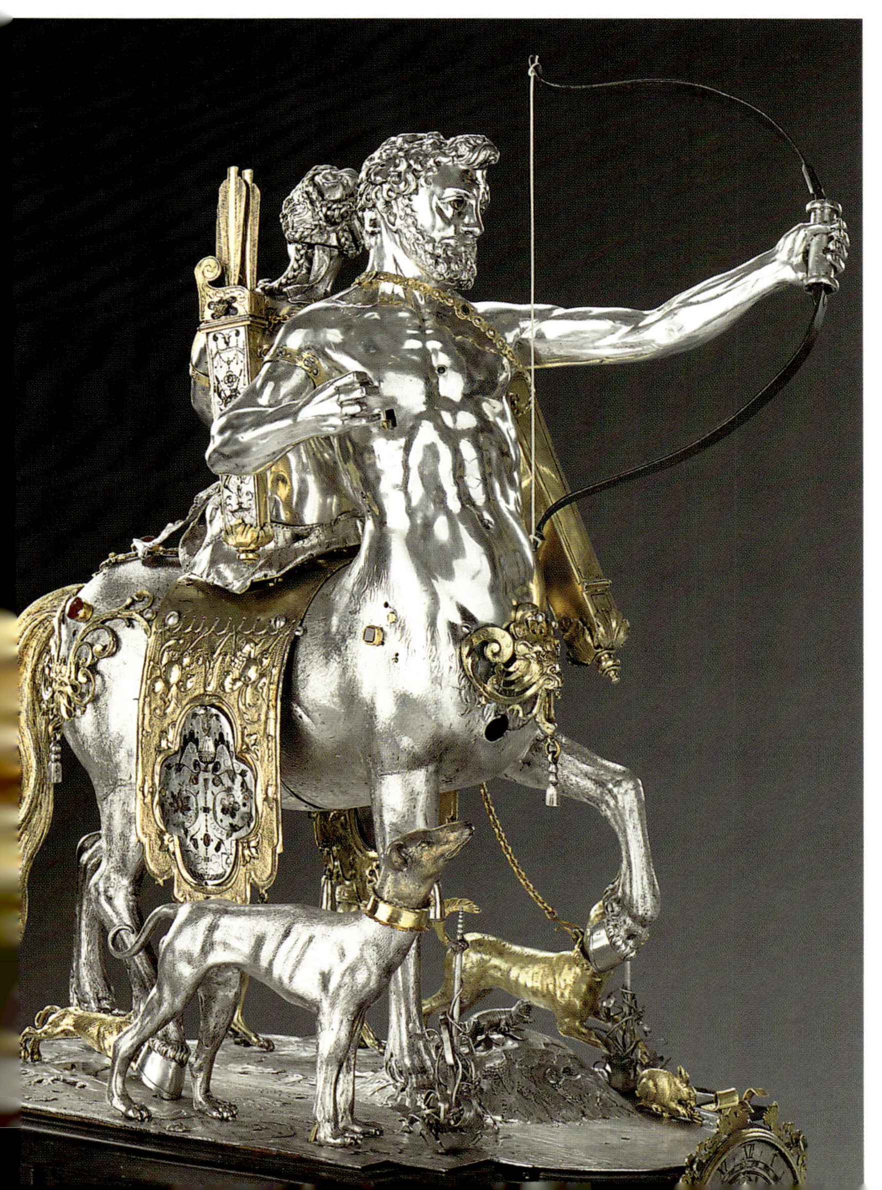

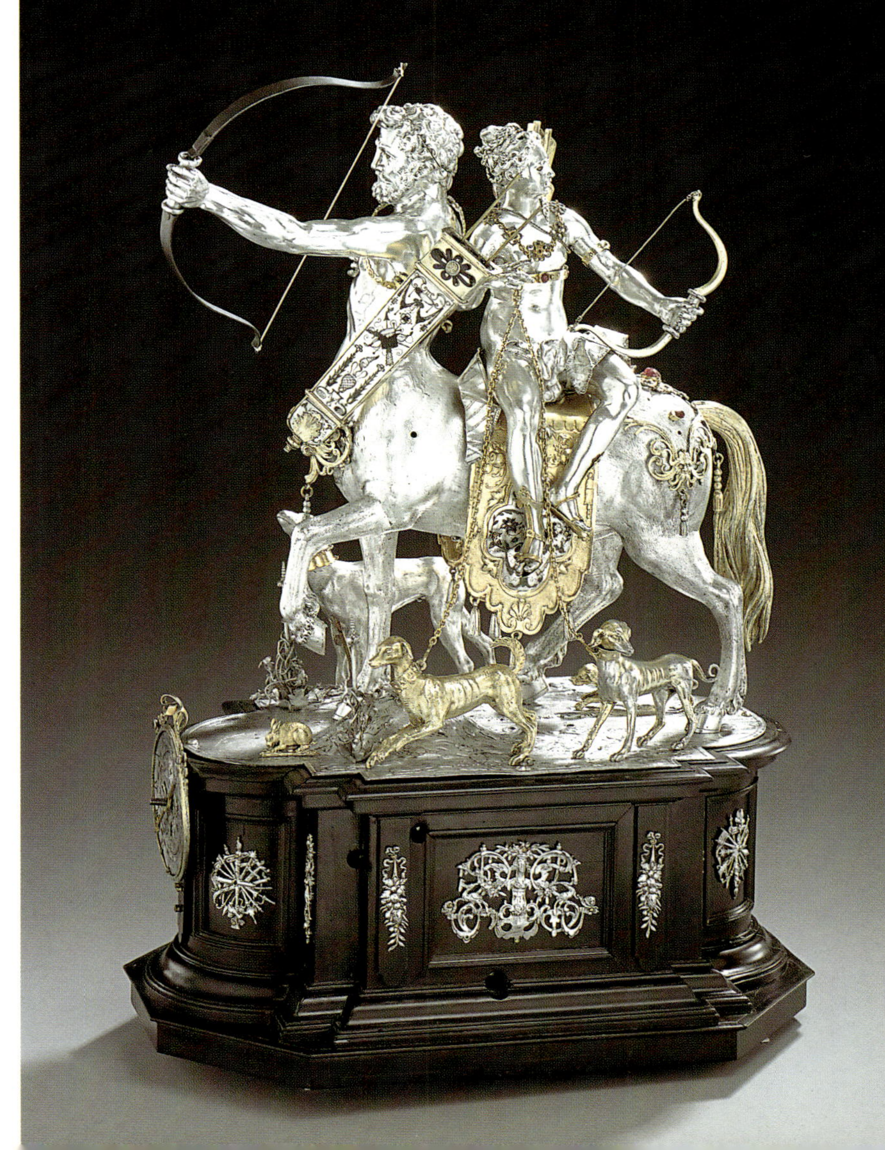

Travel Casket

Mother-of-pearl plates over wooden core, silver, gilt, putty paste, velvet
Mother-of-pearl work: Gujarat (India), end of the 16th century
Mount: Elias Geyer
Leipzig, circa 1600
H. 26,8 cm, W. 38,5 cm (without lions), D. 22,6 cm (without lions), Inv.-no. III 247

Pouring Garniture

Mother-of-pearl plates, sea-snail shell, silver, gilt
Mother-of-pearl work: India, end of the 16th century
Mount: Nicolaus Schmidt
Nuremberg, circa 1592
D. basin 56 cm, ewer H. 40 cm, Inv.-no. IV 248 and IV 157

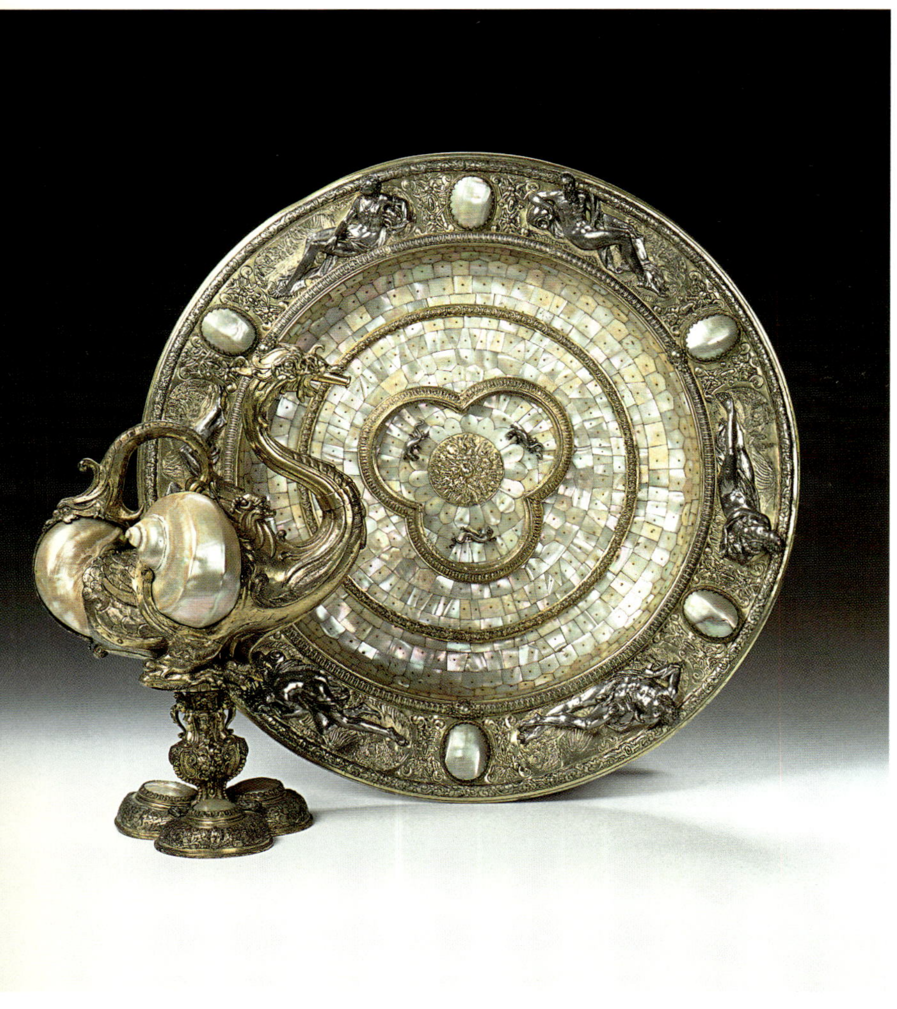

Since the creation of princely *Kunstkammers*, works made from mother-of-pearl were held in particularly high esteem. They belonged to the rare group of *exotica* as well as to the *naturalia* that originated from far-off lands. No other material matched the almost magical luster of polished shells and sea-snail shells. The combination of the velvety iridescent sparkle of Indian mother-of-pearl works combined with the reflections cast by the European goldsmith's mounts resulted in a particularly unique effect.

In the 16th century, Indian objects made of mother-of-pearl came into European markets by way of Portuguese merchants. The items mostly originated from the Gujarat area, where the production of similar luxury items had a centuries-long tradition. The goldsmiths procured their exotic caskets and pouring garnitures adorned with mounts corresponding to contemporary taste via international trading houses from Augsburg or Nuremberg, or through the fairs in Frankfurt and Leipzig.

Driven by his desire for precious and rare things, Christian II proceeded to make one of the most expensive acquisitions in the history of Dresden's *Kunstkammer* from the jeweler Veit Bötticher at the 1602 Leipzig Easter Fair. He paid 8,500 thaler for a group of objects made exclusively from mother-of-pearl. Apart from the richly embellished *Game Board* with Near Eastern mother-of-pearl and ebony (today Museum of Applied Arts, State Art Collections Dresden) the group included three mother-of-pearl caskets, two pouring garnitures, and five drinking services.

Elias Geyer created a carefully conceived mount for the largest of the three caskets. The Leipzig goldsmith added silver gilt corner and edge mounts to the *Casket*, as well as handles, a keyhole mount, and four feet in the shape of lions. With its stylized vegetal forms made of mother-of-pearl and surrounded by black bitumen varnish, the *Indian Casket* is one of the most precious and valuable of its kind.

Its function and its content are equally significant from the art historical viewpoint. The damascene and velvet covered insets accommodate the storage of large numbers of utilitarian luxury items in this *Casket*. The objects enabled a prince to pursue diverse activities, including dining and drinking, playing games, and writing, as well as grooming, in a fashion appropriate to his rank. In total, there are thirty-six individual pieces, among them two little goblets made of coconut shells and the shells of sea-snails, and a gilt silver bowl with a rock crystal sphere. None of the items reveal signs of use because the *Travel Casket* was immediately transferred to the *Kunstkammer*. The concentrated array of accessories of princely life that are gathered in the *Casket* thus became integral part of the *Kunstkammer*'s microcosm. On a small scale, Geyer's *Mother-of-pearl Casket* thus took over the same function as the slightly later Augsburg *Kunstkammer* cabinets that were made in far larger dimensions and in greater abundance.

Exhibited on the same table of the Dresden *Kunstkammer* as Geyer's *Mother-of-pearl Casket*, was the priceless *Pouring Garniture with a*

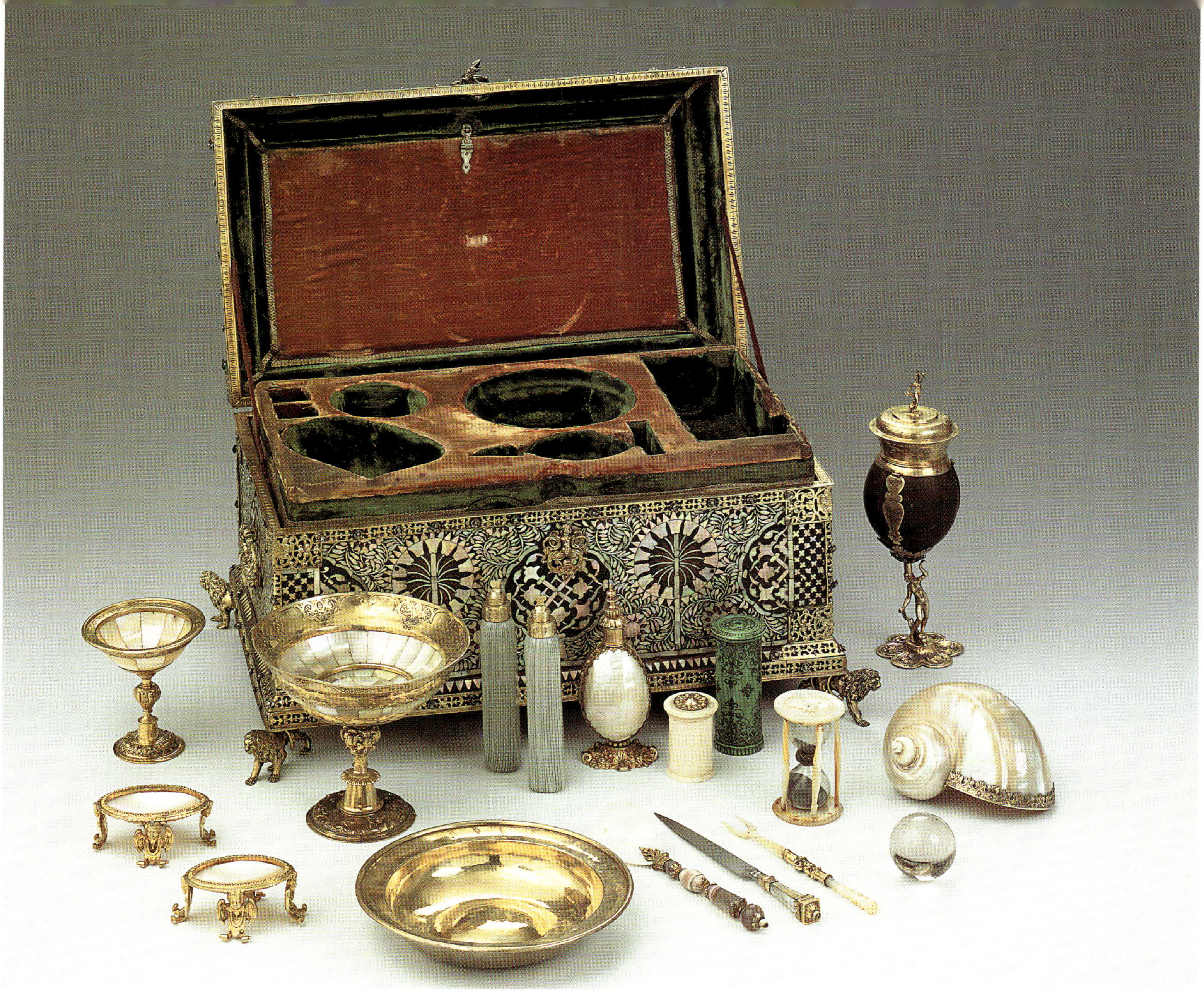

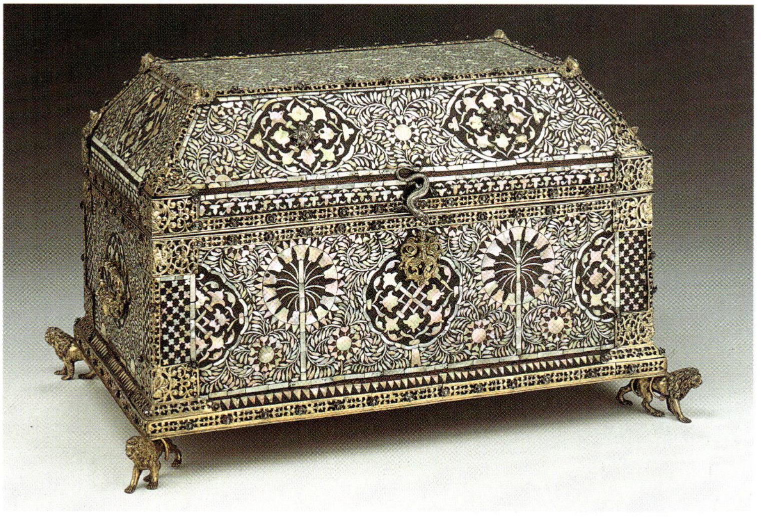

Basin created by Nicolaus Schmidt. It either came to the electoral collection together with the *Casket* in 1602, or was possibly already there in 1589. The fantastic, dragon-shaped *Ewer* of the Dresden *Garniture*, constructed of three turbo *mamoratus* snail shells, is a European work of art of high rank that reveals the influence of the naturalistic Mannerist style of Wenzel Jamnitzer. A notation in the *Kunstkammer* states that the basin was originally decorated with a colored mount; however, a post-script dated 1619 notes that the transparent colors came off during cleaning.

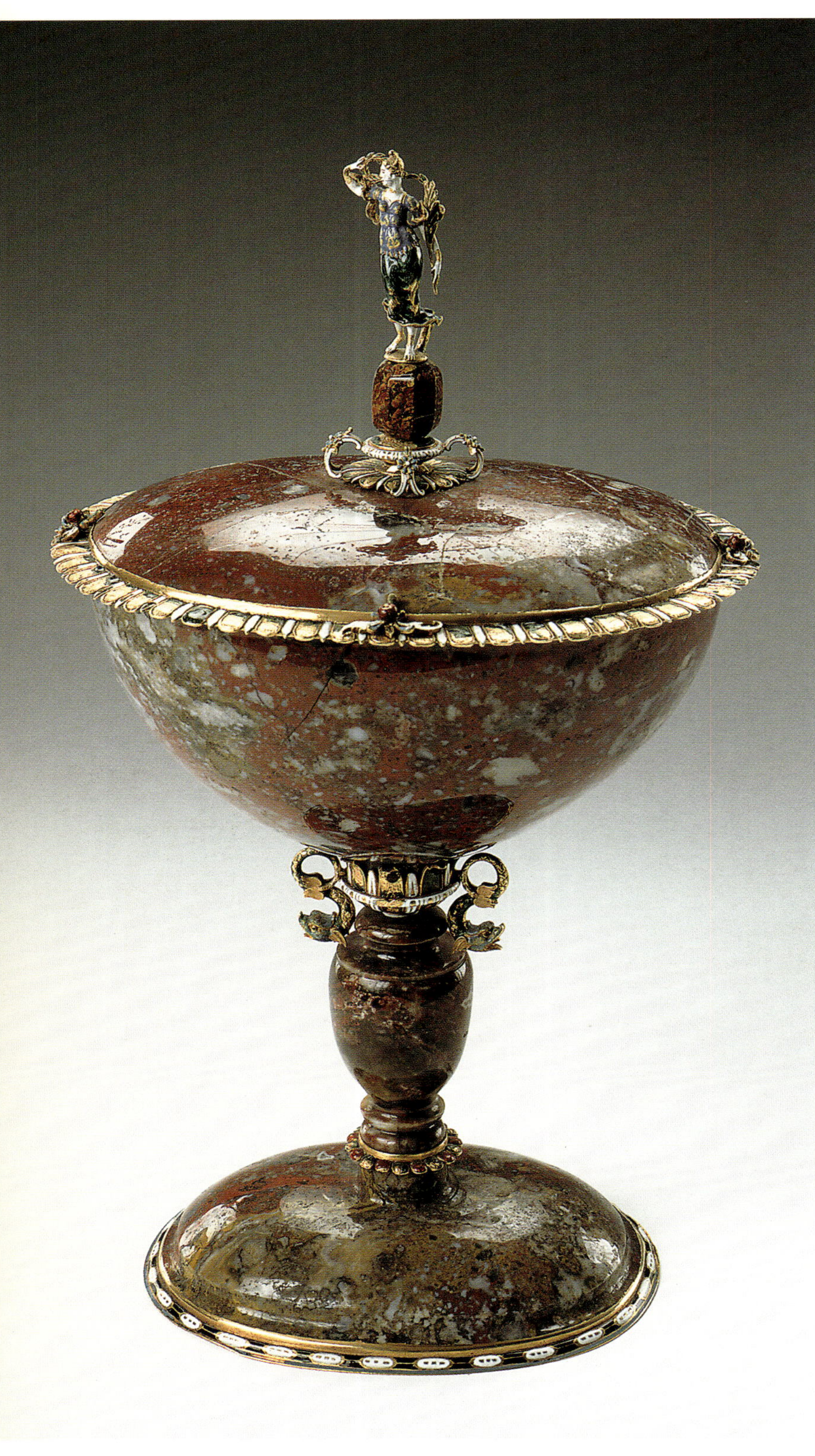

Bowl

Heliotrope, gold, enamel
Stonecutter: Ottavio Miseroni
Mount: Jan Vermeyen
Prague, between 1600 and 1605
H. 10,5 cm, Inv.-no. V 19

Lidded Bowl with Victory as Crowning Figure

Jasper agate, gold, enamel
Stonecutter: Hans Kobenhaupt
Mount: presumably François Guichard
Stuttgart, between 1610 and 1623
H. 23 cm, Inv.-no. V 6

During the 17th and 18th centuries, the Green Vault served as a »melting pot« into which other collections were at least partly absorbed. Although those collections thereby lost their independence, the various places of origin help to clarify the high quality and the diversity inherent in German Treasury collections at the time. Two remarkable works of the art of stone cutting originate from the Treasury of Duke Johann Adolf II of Saxony-Weißenfels. His death in 1746 brought about the extinction of his entire line; consequently, these objects were acquired by the electoral house of August III. Such precious stone objects united the beauty of the noble stone with the aesthetics of an elitist work of art.

One of the objects, an ovoid heliotrope *Bowl*, was made shortly after 1600 in the workshop of the stonecutter Ottavio Miseroni (1567 – 1624). Miseroni came from a famous Milanese family of stonecutters. In 1588, upon the order of Emperor Rudolf II, he established a stone-cutting workshop in Prague that was of paramount importance for Rudolfian court art.

Miseroni worked exclusively for the *Kunstkammer*, founded after 1576 by Rudolf II and continued until 1612. Only in exceptional cases did Miseroni work for individuals favored by the emperor. The opaque and colored precious stones found in Bohemia were ones for which the imperial collector harbored a particular partiality. For this reason, Miseroni began to specialize in the virtuoso cutting of vessels rather than – as was the custom in Milan – figural and ornamental cut rock crystal.

The ovoid and thin-walled *Bowl* with its distinguished decoration, sparingly cut in relief, is made of heliotrope, also known as blue jasper. This green chalcedony with red spots was believed to have special healing powers. The material and artistic values of this Indian stone are enhanced by the elegant gold enamel mounts on the stout shaft and the foot ring. The latter may be attributed to the emperor's chamber goldsmith Jan Vermeyen (before 1559 – 1606). The fascination with this type of carved vessel lay in the rarity and the natural beauty of the stone, as well as in the virtuosity of the artist-craftsman stonecutter. In an almost playful manner, Ottavio Miseroni overcame considerable technical obstacles in working the unyielding and tough material, forcing the uncommonly colored stone into unexpected shapes that contradict the mineral's hardness.

Hans Kobenhaupt was the maker of the second *Bowl* with a Weißenfels provenance (*Weißenfelser Verlassenschaft*). Until he founded a pulp-mill in 1601 in Zweibrücken / Rheinhessen-Palatinate, he worked in Prague. From 1609 until his death in 1623, Kobenhaupt worked for Duke Johann Friedrich of Württemberg. Kobenhaupt created numerous drinking services as well as saltcellars, cutlery, little boxes, and cut stone portraits mostly made of domestic jasper and agate for the duke and his family, who resided in Stuttgart. Well over twenty large precious stone drinking vessels have survived, three of them in the Green Vault.

The *Lidded Bowl* of red and yellow-brown marbleized jasper agate possesses the strong outline and profiled vase-like shaft that are typical Kobenhaupt features. Just as characteristic are the s-shaped dolphins at the joint between the shaft and cup. Most of the crowning figures in Kobenhaupt's oeuvre are very particular allegories, in this case the goddess of peace, Victory.

Most of the objects attributed to Kobenhaupt and preserved in Basel, Copenhagen, Munich, Paris, Stuttgart, and Vienna originate from princely collections. Those kept in Vienna and Munich go back to the looting of the Württemberg *Kunstkammer*s and Treasuries by imperial and Bavarian troops after the Battle of Nördlingen in 1634. In 1648, the remains of the Rudolfian *Kunstkammer* in Prague fell victim to the same fate when it was plundered by Swedish troops.

It is thus fair to state that each of the *Bowls* by Miseroni and Kobenhaupt were made long before the Duchy of Saxony-Weißenfels was founded in the year 1652.

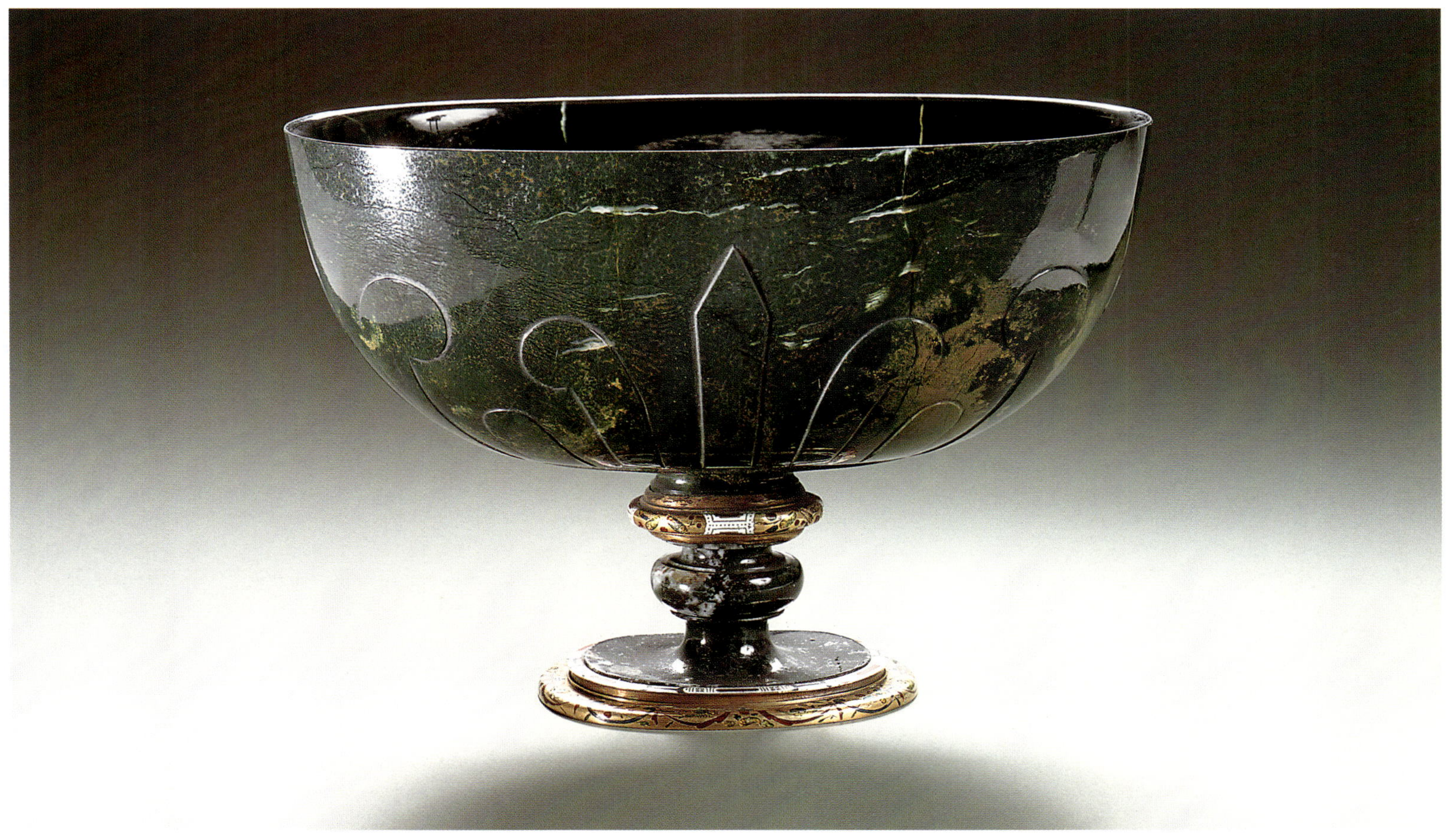

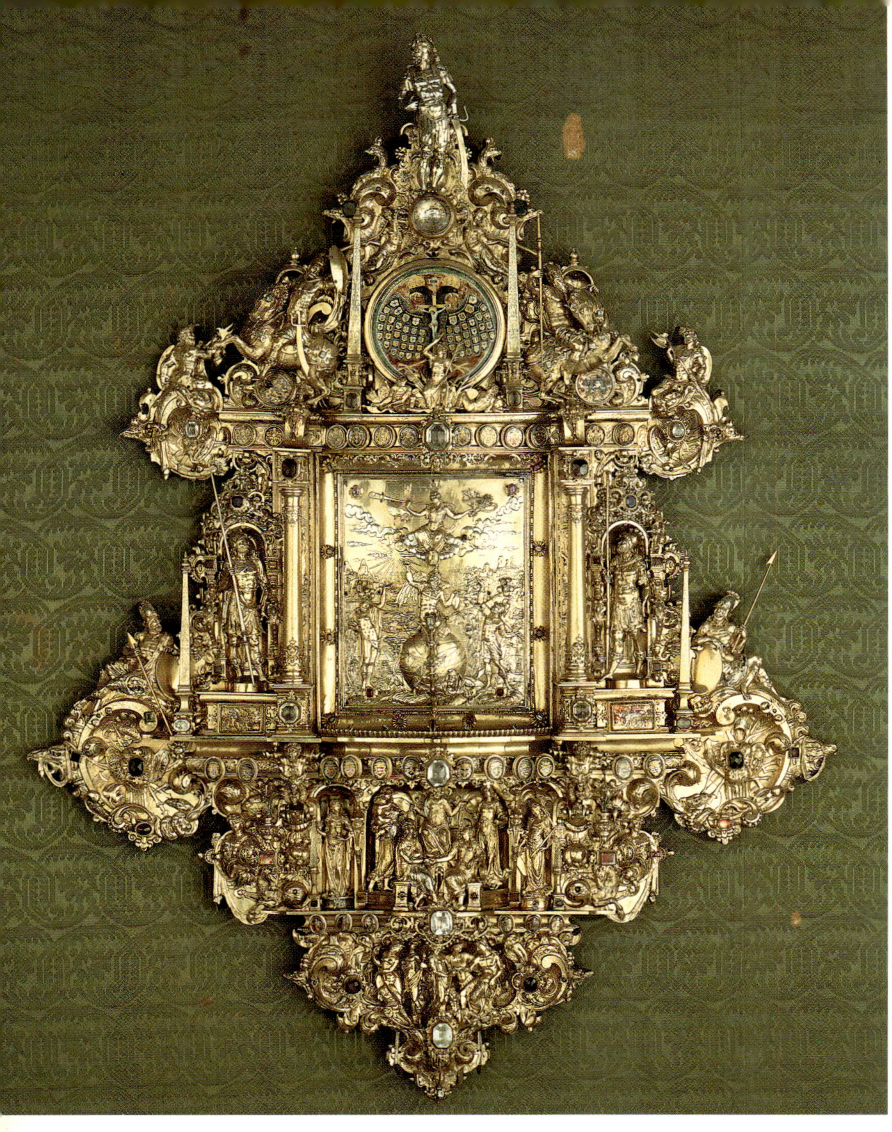

Mirror with Display Frame in the Shape of an Epitaph

Wooden core, silver, mostly gilt, mirror glass, glass painting, rock crystal, amethysts, garnets, cut glass stones
Luleff Meier and goldsmith Dirich Utermarke
Lüneburg, dated 1587 and 1592
H. 115 cm, W. 85 cm, Inv.-no. IV 110

The so-called »Lüneburg mirror« is an unusually large goldsmith's work of outstanding quality. The rectangular mirror is hidden behind a richly embellished cover on which the personification of time may be seen seated on a globe. Worked in high relief, the silver figure's mournful gaze is raised upwards. The cleverly concealed mirror is framed by an impressive abundance of cast and chased silver figures, voluptuous Baroque scrollwork enlivened with festoons, fruit bundles, trophies, animal heads, composite creatures, and masks, as well as more than thirty medallion-shaped glass paintings, and a plethora of precious stones. Despite the bountiful Mannerist ornaments, the mirror displays a rigid architectural structure due to the shape of the epitaph, a popular and customary type of church memorial around the year 1600. Monumental goldsmith epitaphs that functioned as display objects are particularly uncommon.

The complicated and multilayered iconographic program is an allegorical rendering of Nebuchadnezar's dream as related in the Old Testament book of Daniel (Dan. 2:27-45; 7 and 8). This work is crowned by a so-called »Statua Danielis,« an armored statuette, whose image appeared in the Babylonian king's dream. God's interpretation of the story by the prophet is attached to it. It predicts the demise of the four superpowers – Assyria, Persia, Greece, and Rome – and the emergence of a realm of truth and peace, the perpetual divine rule on earth. The mirror is framed by riding and standing armored knights symbolizing sovereigns of long-gone, ancient world powers. The divine empire is equated with the large coat-of-arms of the Holy Roman Empire of the German Nation, applied above the mirror. The symbolism of the latter, placed behind a round glass pane of about six inches in diameter, displays the imperial double eagle with the cross of Christ and the coat-of-arms of the empire's constituents. Mounted below the mirror are an allegory of good government and a parable of bad politics, visualized by the Judgment of Paris.

The Old Testament prophecy ties the »Lüneburg mirror« to the political situation just before 1600. At the time, the interpretation of the dreams included in the Book of Daniel was highly topical: It was considered to be a forewarning of imminent war between the different Christian faiths. This war did ultimately broke out in 1618. While within the boundaries of the Dresden court, the royal dream and its interpretation by the prophet especially found various artistic renderings, this goldsmith work was not a commissioned piece. The years 1587 and 1592, inscribed in the mirror's frame, denote the beginning and end of its fabrication. The marks of the Lüneburg goldsmith, jewel merchant, and mirror maker, Luleff Meier, as well as the name of his assistant, Dirich Utermarke – from 1599 active in Hamburg as master goldsmith – may also be found. The »Lüneburg mirror« did not become a Saxon possession until well over ten years after its completion.

For May 19, 1601, the Dresden *Rentkammer* lists that the sum of 1,450 guilders was to be paid to Johann Schlowern of Lüneburg »vor einen großen Spiegel, welcher mit 1000 lot vergültten silber beschlagen, Auch mit des gantzen Romischen reichs wappen, vnd viehlen darein versetzten Bemischen steihnen getziret« i.e. »for a large mirror embellished with 1,000 lots of gilt silver, also with the coat-of-arms of the Roman Empire and decorated with many mounted stones.« Although the prince elector's mother commissioned it, she also had the mirror moved »in dero geliebter Söhne kunst cammer« i.e. »into her beloved sons' *Kunstkammer*.« It was four months before her oldest son, Christian II, came of age that Sophie formulated her political testament through the purchase of this work of art: Only through close political ties between electoral Saxony and the emperor and by maintaining the imperial constitution would it be possible to retain peace for the empire.

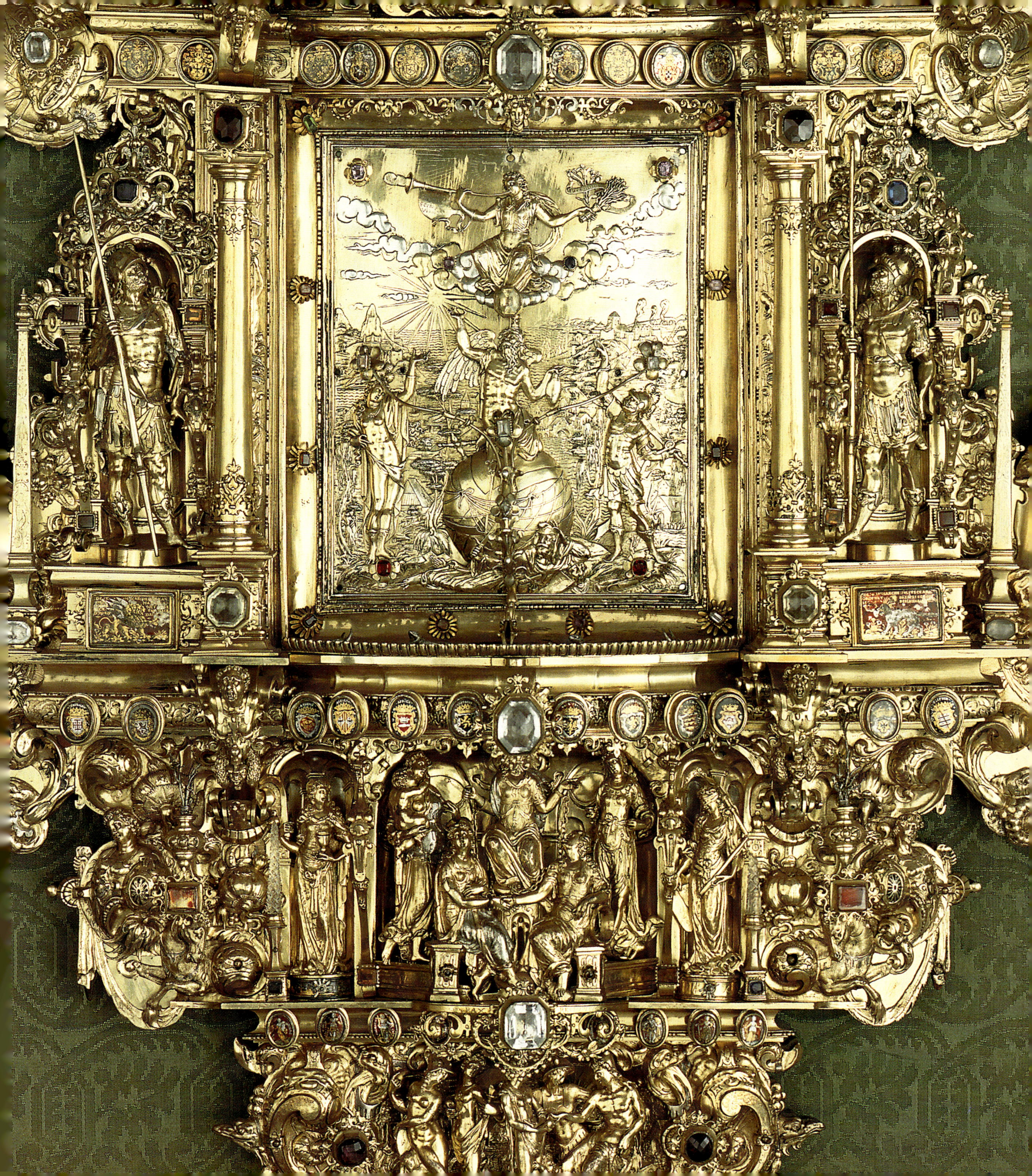

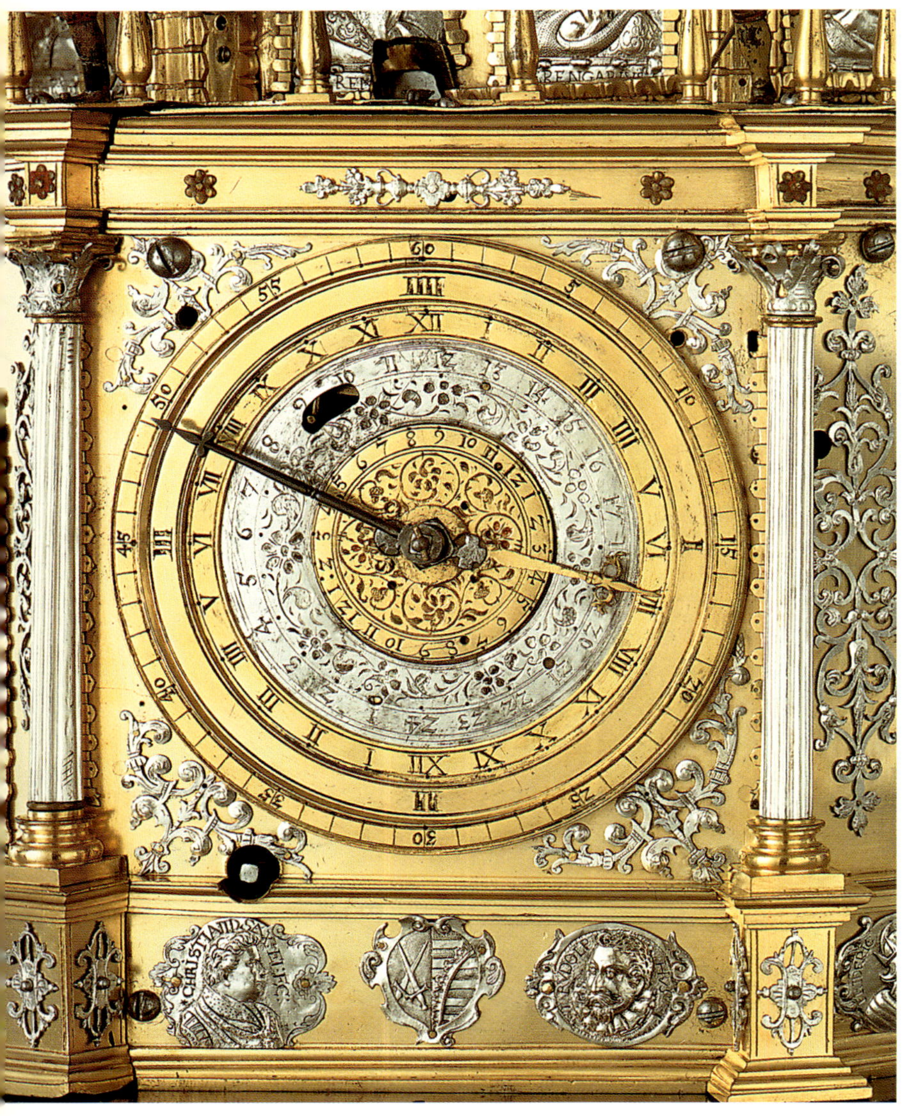

Rolling Ball Clock

Brass, gilt, silver, partly painted, ebony, iron
Hans Schlottheim
probably Augsburg, before 1602
H. 112 cm, Inv.-no. V 140

In July 1601, Hans Schlottheim received an advance of 300 guilder – instigated by the prince elector's widow Sophie – for the fabrication of a unique clock automaton. Even before 1585, the Saxon electoral house patronized this Augsburg-based creator of ingenious figure clocks and automatons. Born in the then electoral Saxon city of Naumburg an der Saale, the new commission was granted to the artist-engineer in the expectation that he would create an automaton that was to replace or even to surpass another one (presumably also made by him). The latter, removed from the Saxon *Kunstkammer*, had been presented to Emperor Rudolf II. In February 1603, Schlottheim delivered his new product: It was the huge *Rolling Ball Clock* for which he charged the sum of 2,400 guilder.

Built in the form of an octagonal tower, the *Rolling Ball Clock* is a mechanical wonderwork that combines the functions of music making with that of a figure automaton. At the same time, it was an attempt – based on the invention of Christoph Markgraf, court clock maker of Rudolf II – to create a more precise and dependable clock. To this end, a small rock crystal sphere rolled down a slope over sixteen turns in an exactly determined amount of time, while – simultaneous to this – an interior gear lifted another sphere. The god Saturn marked this event by hitting a bell with the hammer each time it occurred. The movement of the divine figures assigned to the planets was directly linked to the clock, as were the city pipers (*Stadtpfeifer*) located on the lower gallery. The eternal calendar, engraved into the lower gallery's floor, was likewise moveable and connected to the clock. Twice a day, an elaborate piece of music could be heard.

The pictorial program refers to the seven liberal arts: Grammar, rhetoric, dialectics, music, astronomy, geometry, and arithmetic. Their personifications are color varnished figures standing in niches along the base. Behind the slanted ramp for the sphere and arranged along the pedestal, there were additional fantastic silver portraits of emperors, possibly based on antique coins. The subject is a largely complete genealogy, beginning with Julius Caesar, continuing through the ancient and medieval emperors, and ending with the image of Rudolf II, mounted below the face. Opposite him is the portrait of the Saxon Prince Elector Christian II. The clock is crowned by an imperial double eagle which is located above a rock crystal globe in an aureole. The interior shield of the double eagle spots the ducal Saxon coat-of-arms. This testifies to the fact that our *Automaton* is a memorial to the friendship between the young Saxon prince elector and the emperor. At the same time, the object – based on Rudolf II's views – places the empire into a cosmological context. In this way, the *Rolling Ball Clock* complements in a rather subtle and hardly coincidental way the iconography of the epitaph-shaped »Lüneburg mirror,« also dedicated to the idea of the empire.

On December 31, 1603, Christian II presented this symbolic object in the shape of an automaton as a gift to his wife, Prince Electress Hedwig, who displayed it in her own *Kunstkammer*. In 1614, a few years after his brother Johann Georg I had assumed the reign, the *Clock* returned once again to the electoral *Kunstkammer*.

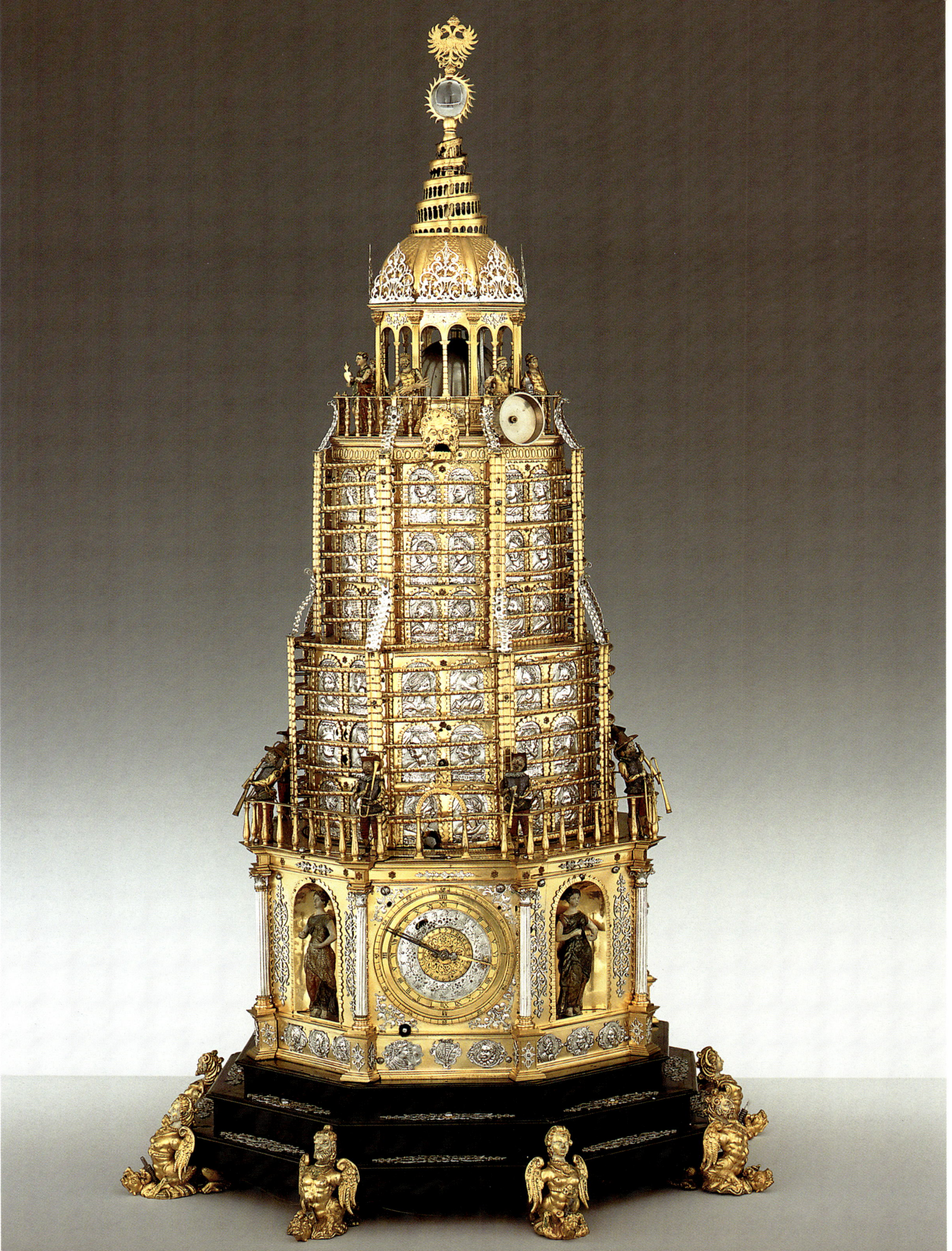

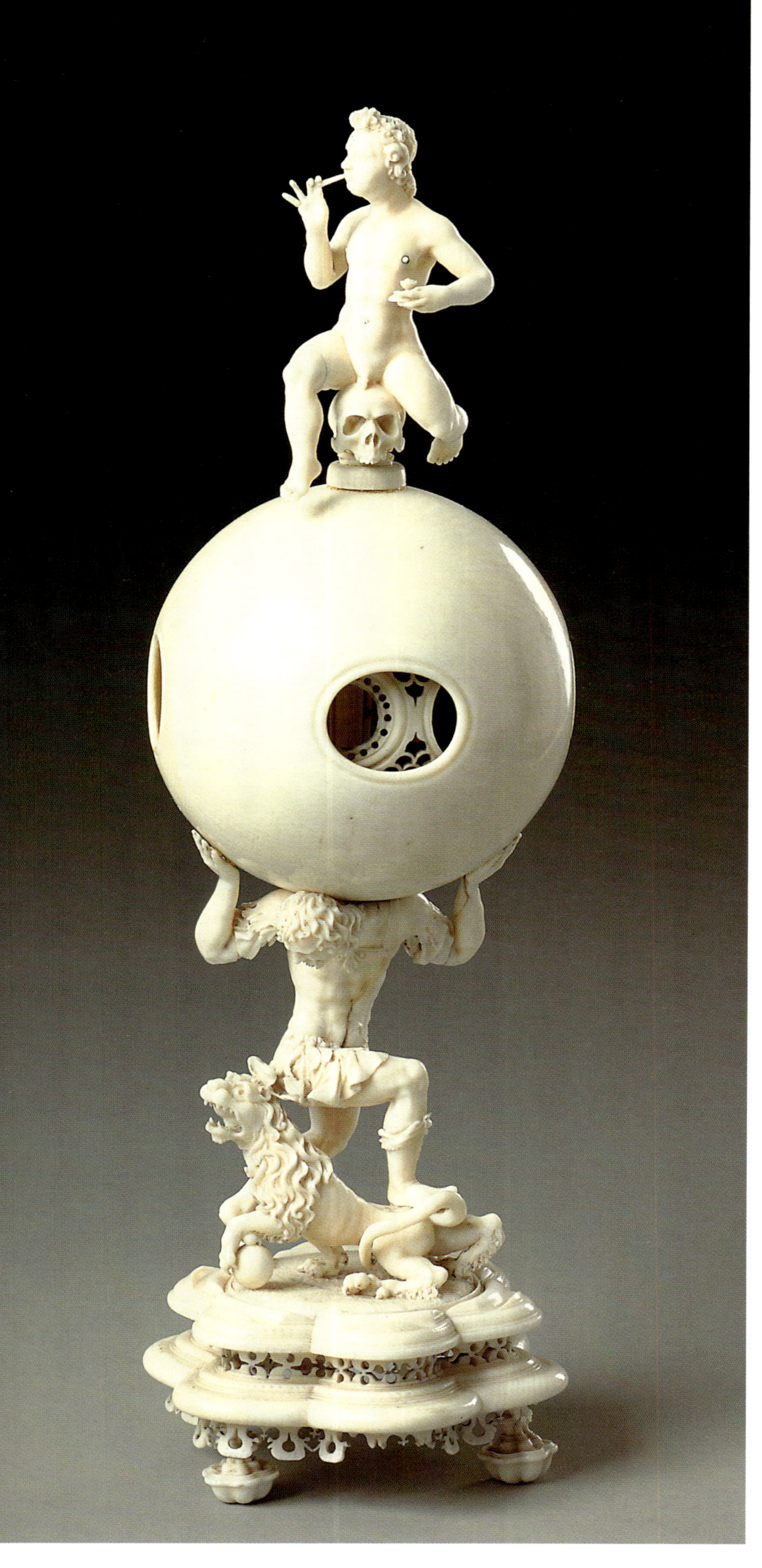

Contrefait Sphere with an Allegory of Transience

Ivory
Jacob Zeller
Dresden, dated 1611
H. 30,5 cm, Inv.-no. II 296

Frigate

Ivory, gold, iron
Signed Jacob Zeller
Dresden, dated 1620
H. 115 cm, W. 80 cm, Inv.-no. II 107

With the appointment of Jacob Zeller from Prague to Dresden in the summer of 1610, Christian II reverted to one of his ancestors' preferences. Thanks to the arrival of the new Saxon court turnes, the Dresden art of turning the lathe experienced its last climax. It was thanks to Zeller that the Saxon residence was the place of origin for a development that had remarkable consequences for German art. Among the most important works associated with this are two unusual ivories that should be understood as dynastic memorials.

The first, smaller work is a *Contrefait Sphere* with the portraits of Christian II and his wife, Hedwig of Denmark. The object was created immediately following the prince elector's death on June 26, 1611. *Contrefait Spheres* were exemplary virtuoso pieces in their own right; the turner hollowed out the sphere on a machine. From the material he removed from the inside, he carved one or more portrait medallions. They could be viewed through openings in the sphere. In Zeller's image sphere, the portraits are retained in two perforated and mutually adjustable, hollow spheres. The court artist did not restrict himself to working the lathe. By affixing carved ivory statuettes, he created a complex work of art whose subject is the fugitive nature of human existence. It is in this sense that the crowning figure of the nude boy who is seated on a skull and blows soap-bubbles must be understood. The prophet Daniel, located in the lions' den – comparable to Atlas in the way he painfully supports the portrait sphere – serves as the shaft for this object; he has been interpreted as a prefiguration of the risen Christ. This item was commissioned by Johann Georg I to commemorate his deceased brother, the prince elector who died at the age of 27. For New Year's 1613, Johann Georg once again appointed Jacob Zeller as court turner.

One of Zeller's last works was his famous *Ivory Frigate* that the court turner delivered to the prince electoral *Kunstkammer* in the summer of 1620 for the steep price of 3,000 guilder. With its full sails, the miniature state ship copies the early type of a frigate. The warship, on whose paper-thin ivory mainsails the coats-of-arms of the Saxon prince elector and his wife Magdalena Sibylla of Brandenburg are in-

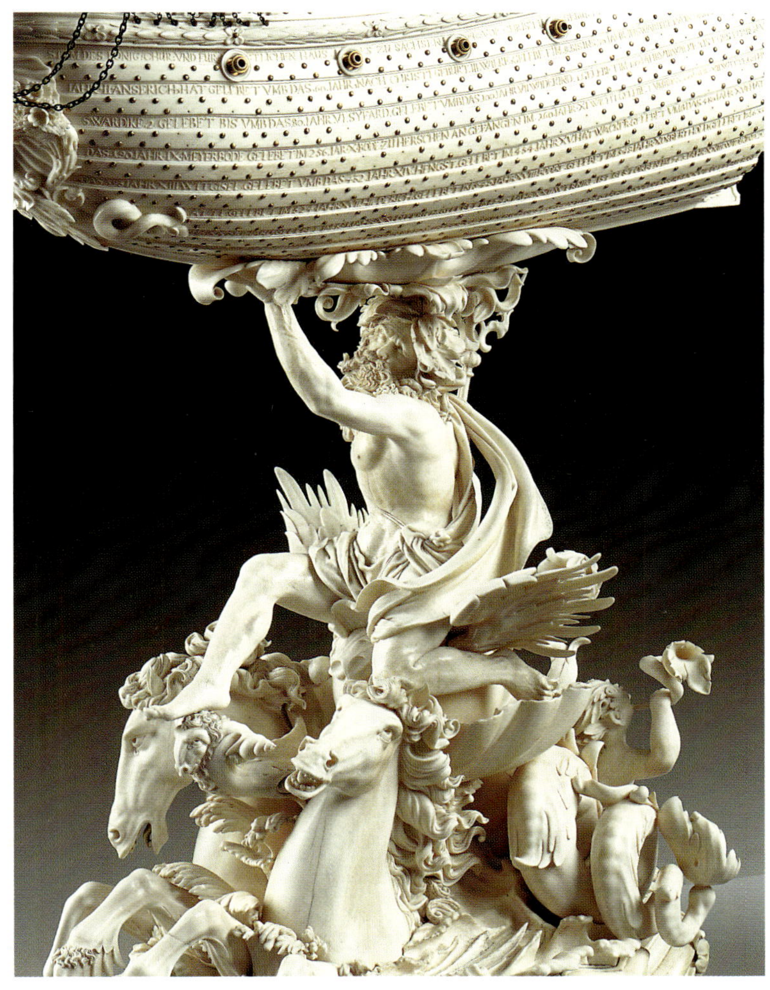

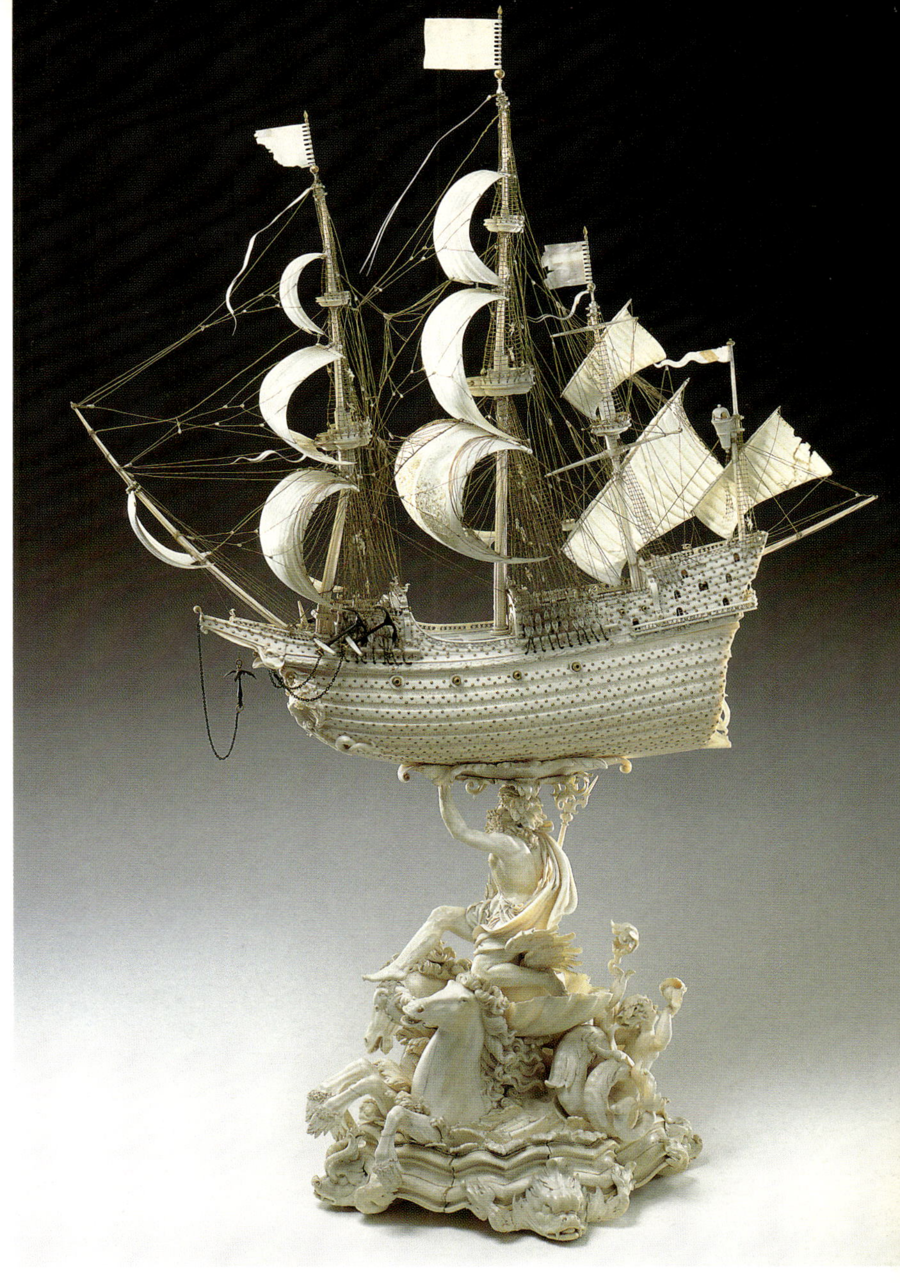

cised, has a whipping made of gold wire. Minute little ivory sailors can be seen, as well as also cannons, chains, and golden anchor. Eight inscribed banderoles – incised along the vessel's hull – turn the Saxon flagship into a dynastic monument. The scrolls contain the names of the Saxon sovereigns from Harderich, who apparently lived shortly after the birth of Christ, to the reigning Prince Elector Johann Georg I. This ancestral line was the result of historic speculation, as well as a proud reference to the venerable age of the House of Wettin.

The figured base on which the flagship rests has a particular artistic meaning. It appears to be safely carried by the lone figure of Neptune: the turned form of the powerful sea deity balances – like Fortune, goddess of changing luck – on a winged sphere that rests in a shell-shaped bowl. The moral forewarning about the uncertainty of a ruler's luck was realized in the case of Johann Georg I: During the course of the Thirty Years War, good fortune actually abandoned him at a crucial moment. The Neptune group gathered around the pedestal and located on shell-chariots pulled by sea horses and surrounded by tritons, goes back to a Prague model. The virtuoso Early Baroque ivory sculpture Zeller created is one of the major objects of its era. Before that, the *Ivory Frigate*, thanks to its size, subtle design, and recognizable artistic virtuosity, was an outstanding *Kunstkammer* piece. It lent a new quality to the collection of the Saxon prince electors, who were in competition with the emperors in Prague and Vienna. Jacob Zeller died on December 28, 1620, shortly after completing this work

Necklace with the Portrait Medallion of Johann Georg I

Ivory
Jacob Zeller
Dresden, before 1618
Medallion: H. 9,5 cm, W. 4 cm, max. L. of the necklace 55,5 cm, Inv.-no. II 145

Ivory Goblet with Saint George

Ivory
Signed Jacob Zeller
Dresden, dated 1613
H. 51 cm, Inv.-no. II 154

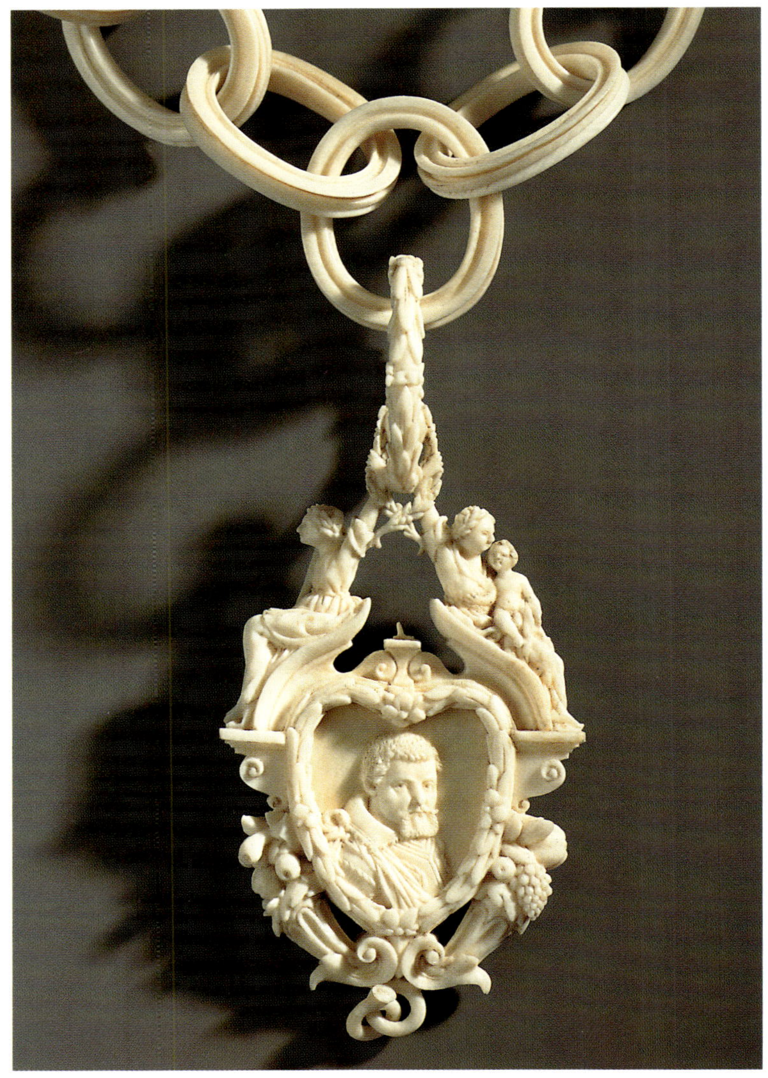

Part of princely representation could entail the gift of a golden necklace to an individual in gratitude for services rendered. Such gifts of patronage and honor were frequently embellished with precious princely portraits. The *Ivory Necklace* with the image of the youthful Prince Elector Johann Georg I by Jacob Zeller reflects this custom in a virtuoso turned piece of art reserved exclusively for the sovereign's use. The unworked pendant and the chain's segments were worked from one individual piece of elephant ivory on an eccentric turning lathe. After that, the artist continued his work on the portrait medallion as an ivory carver, while he separated the parts of the chain with the aid of a fret saw. Until the 17th century, the fabrication of a multi-segment chain with an image worked from one compact piece of ivory was considered a high valuable skill. Especially since the process was accompanied by technical obstacles that had to be mastered with bravura. The high quality of this ivory's craft and artistic treatment is characteristic of Zeller's work. The »gedröhete Helffenbeine Kette von einem stück inn einem ieden gliedt zweÿ vnterschiedene glieder, daran Churfürst Johann Georgen zu Sachssen p Bildnüß hangend« i.e. »turned ivory necklace from one piece, each segment containing two others, with the image of Prince Elector Johann Georg of Saxony suspended from it« is first listed in the 1619 *Kunstkammer* inventory. The prince elector bought it in May, 1618 along with twenty-two other turned works by Zeller for the total sum of 2,300 guilder. With this *Necklace,* he began a 17th-century family tradition; the succeeding Saxon rulers, Johann Georg II and Johann Georg III, also commissioned ivory necklaces with their portraits as lasting memorials for the prince electoral *Kunstkammer*.

By 1613 the court turner from Regensburg had created a large *Ivory Goblet.* The maker immortalized himself as the inventor and the creator of the vessel by virtue of an inscription cut in high relief beneath the foot. Zeller pushed the technical possibilities of machine-made art to its limits with the quatrefoil vessel's body and its diagonal ridges. The *Goblet* documents that the ivory artist was a sculptor who led the art of Baroque ivory carving in Germany to its zenith.

The *Goblet*'s octagonal foot rests on four grotesque busts. The shaft is formed by a fruit-laden tree trunk that is embraced by a bending Satyr, who represents the forest demon and at the same time symbolizes animal lust. The perforated lid is carried by four dolphins. On the top edge of the applied balustrade, a Latin inscription interprets the battle of Saint George with the dragon as Christ's combat against Satan. The dramatically staged struggle of the knightly saint crowns the symbolic *Kunstkammer* piece. George, dressed as a Roman hero and seated on horseback, attacks the rearing dragon with his sword.

This figure group goes beyond the sheer symbolic depiction of a duel between good and evil. During the Middle Ages, the legendary saint, who by virtue of his victory over the dragon saved a royal prin-

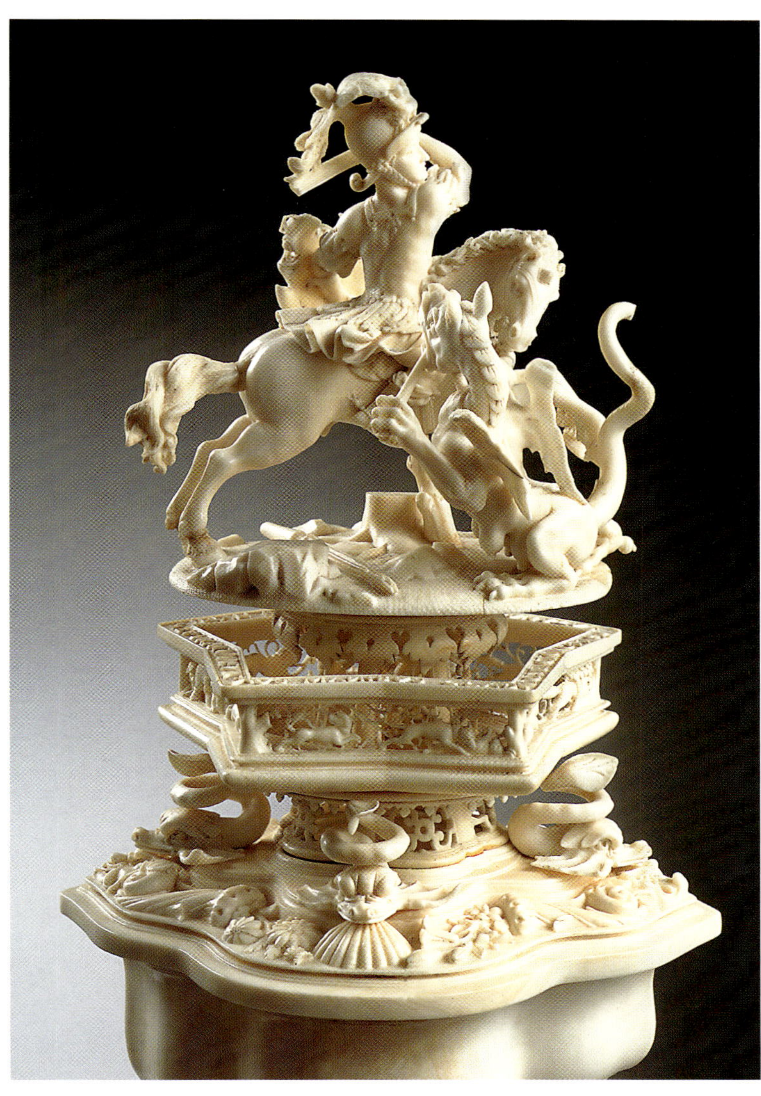

cess and converted an entire people to Christianity, was considered the ultimate virtuous knight. He was also the patron saint of Johann Georg I. In Zeller's Saint George's *Goblet* of 1613, Saxony's Protestant prince elector – in an act of princely self-documentation – is placed in direct succession of the venerable saint himself. Initially, a hollowed-out peppercorn was hidden inside of the goblet's lid. According to the 1619 inventory of the *Kunstkammer*, it contained »ezliche 100 helffenbeinerne becherlein von helffenbein gedrehet« i.e. »numerous 100 turned ivories beakers.« The object was thus elevated to the rank of *Kunstkammer* item.

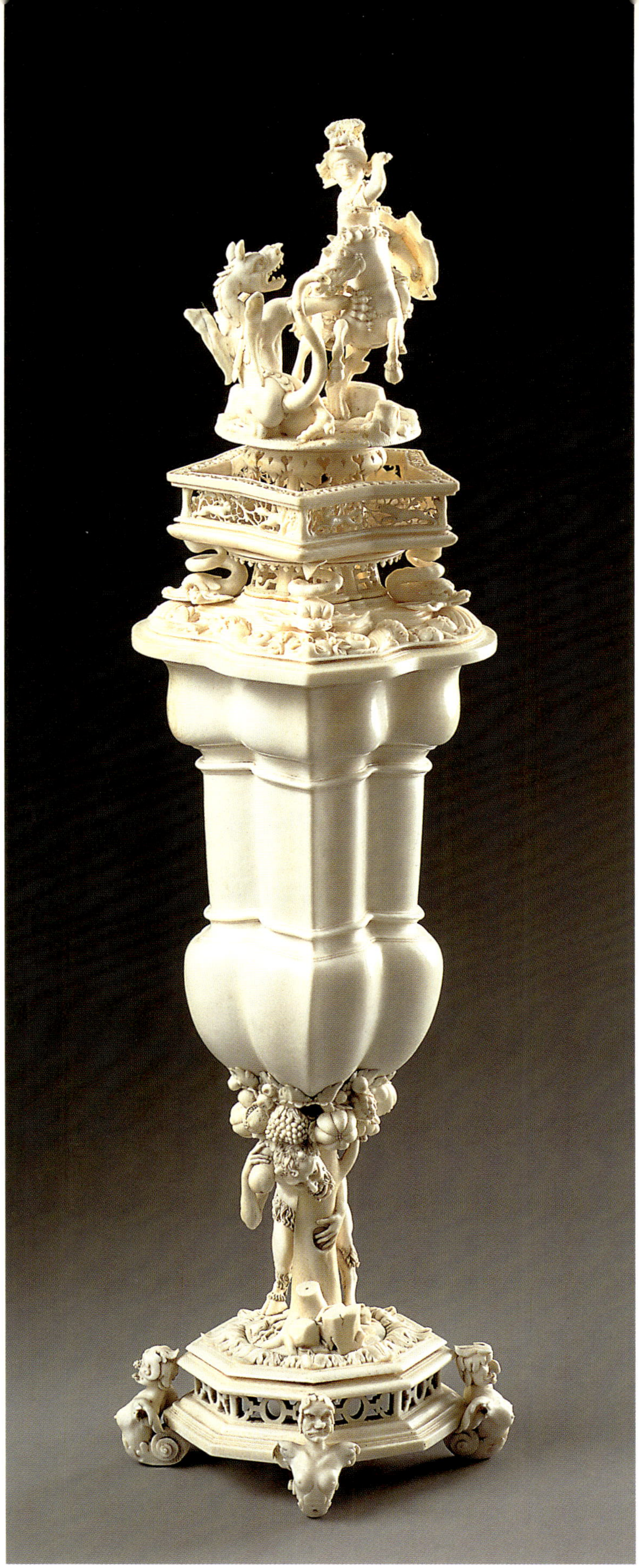

Ewer in the Shape of a Dragon

Silver, gilt
Christoph Jamnitzer
Nuremberg, circa 1610
H. 46,5 cm, Inv.-no. IV 293

Ewer with a Depiction of King Midas

Silver, gilt
Daniel Kellerthaler
Dresden, before 1629
H. 41 cm, Inv.-no. IV 9

Pouring garnitures consisting of a basin and ewer had a weighty function in courtly table ceremonies of the 17th century. On the one hand, they allowed one to wash one's hands with agreeably scented water, because until the end of the century, fingers remained the most important utensil with which to eat. On the other hand, the artistic and material splendor of silver lavabo garnitures – ornamentation and imagery of the individual items complemented each other – served to demonstrate, as they were arranged in ostentatious displays, their owners' power, affluence, and dynastic importance. Apart from garnitures with specific functions, there were some that had little practical purpose. They were even difficult to display on princely state buffets, intended to be seen from afar, because of their complex design and their rich abundance of material. Their creators took the needs of their princely collectors into account. This is why they were not exhibited in the silver chambers, but in the *Kunstkammer*s or the Treasuries. Two particularly fantastically designed *Ewers* of the Green Vault belong to this group of garnitures that were conceived as art objects.

Christoph Jamnitzer (1563 – 1618) created a ewer whose spout is reminiscent of a fabled animal. After Wenzel, Christoph was the second most significant master from the Nuremberg-based Jamnitzer goldsmiths dynasty. Like his grandfather before him, he worked repeatedly for the German high aristocracy. In 1612, Johann Georg I bought a number of goldsmith's works from him at the cost of 4,000 guilder. Presumably, this garniture with basin and ewer was among these.

The *Ewer* with the dragon-shaped spout and the tail-shaped handle is surrounded by dense ornamentation and bead molding. The vessel's form is determined by four heart-shaped bosses. They are located on the flat foot and the pear-shaped corpus. In tectonically prominent spots, rams' heads and snails, winged cherubs' heads and feline mascarons emerge from abundant relief ornaments. Time and again, the dragon motif is quoted, from which the title is derived. A statuette of the goddess Minerva crowns the lid with its vegetal clasps. The heart-shaped shields on the *Ewer*'s body indicate that this *Kunstkammer* piece was conceived for close-up inspection. The latter are embellished with finely embossed allegorical renderings of the four seasons. It appears that the matching *Basin* was melted down in 1772.

Daniel Kellerthaler's (circa 1575 – 1648) *King Midas Ewer* was made fifteen years after Christoph Jamnitzer's masterpiece. At the time, the court style of Prague – the epicenter of Northern European art production until Emperor Rudolf II's death in 1612 – witnessed a brief second blossoming in Dresden. Kellerthaler also originated from an important family of goldsmiths. He was the first outstanding artistic and intellectual personality in the history of Dresden goldsmith's art. This is most impressively confirmed – even when juxtaposed with Jamnitzer's masterpiece – by the *Ewer* with illustrations of an episode derived from Ovid's *Metamorphoses*. The sculptural scene with many figures, executed in high relief and worked in silver, can hardly be absorbed in a single gaze. The vessel is crowned by a statuette of King Midas. According to the god Apollo's viewpoint, the Phrygian ruler's disgraceful donkey's ears are the result of a severe misjudgment on the occasion of a musical competition between the god of light and Pan. This event is depicted on the inside of the corresponding *Basin*. Game, rendered in a brilliant chasing technique, emerges from the silver *Ewer*'s body and may be observed below the animated statuette. The form of the ovoid container with its voluminous impression corresponds to the Mannerist canon. It rests on a thin and short shaft on four delicate clip feet. Johann Georg I paid 2,700 guilder for the pouring garniture. This late Mannerist German masterpiece alone helps one grasp the notion expressed by Jacob Böhme in 1624, when the Holy Roman Empire began its demise due to war-related turmoil: »Dresden is a rejoicing city in the same way Prague was before.«

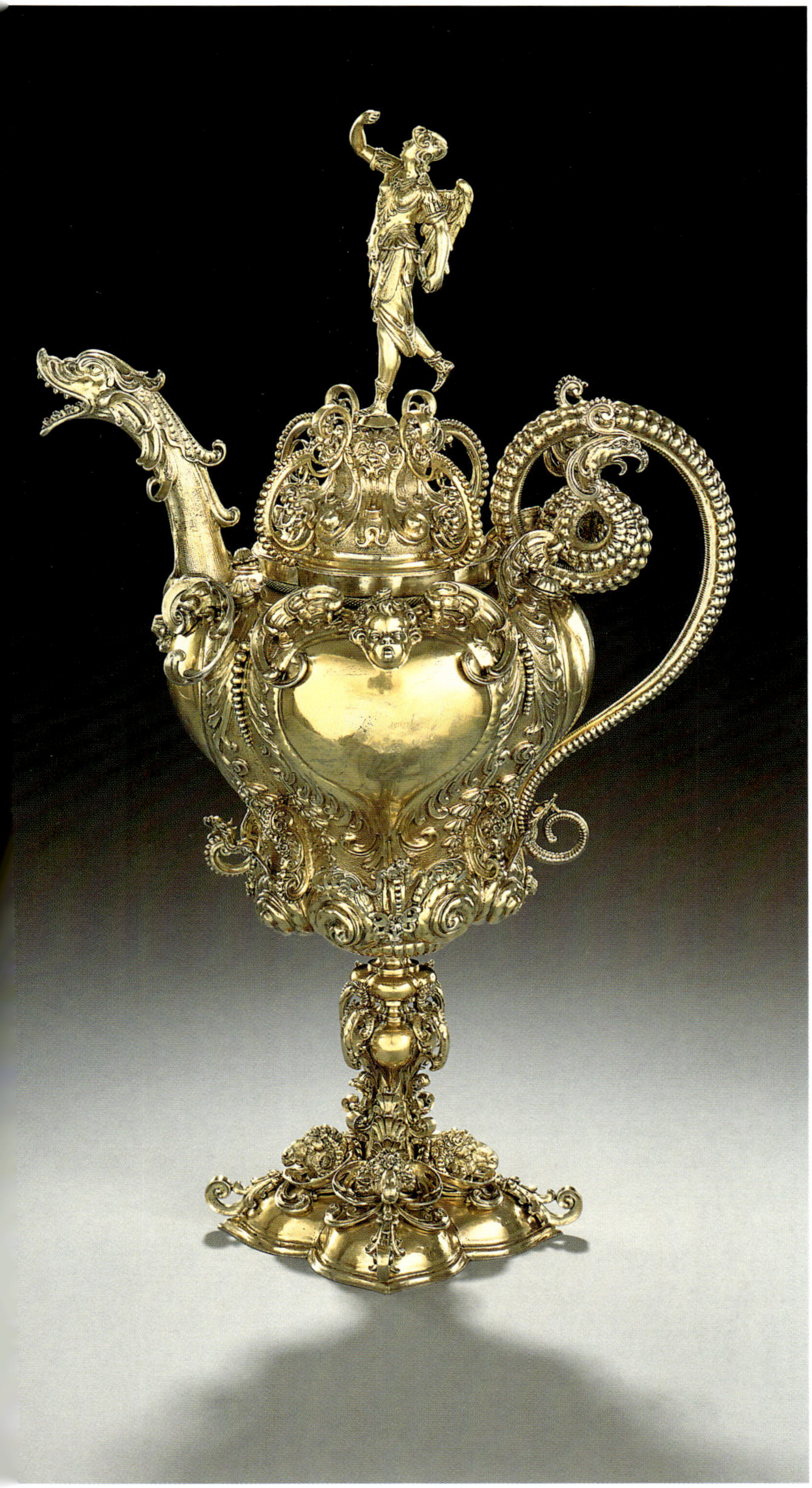

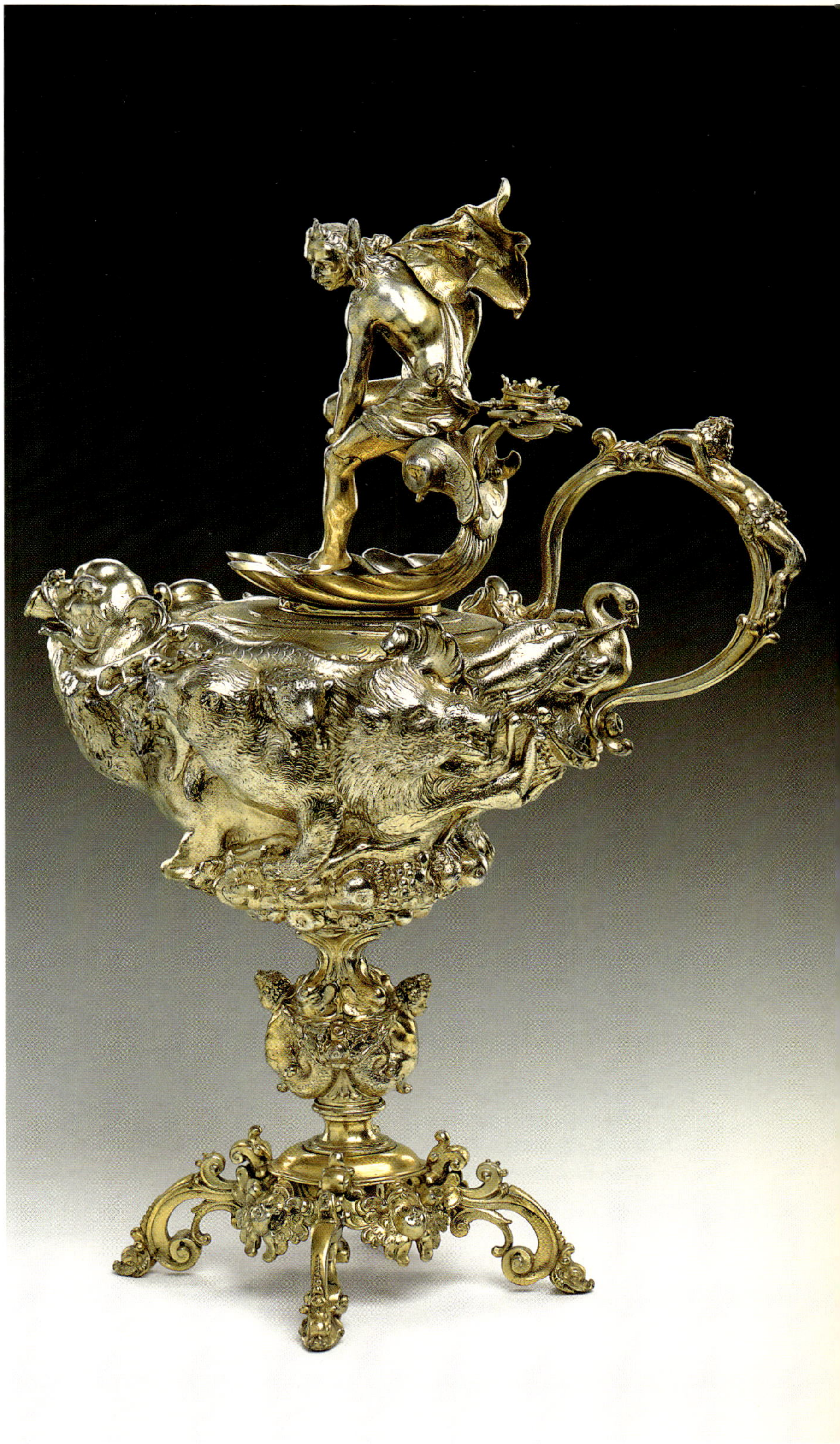

High Columbine Goblet

Silver, gilt
Georg Mond
Dresden, circa 1610
H. 70,4 cm, Inv.-no. IV 185

Lidded Goblet with Automaton Mechanism of Hercules with the Globe

Silver, gilt
Elias Lenker
Augsburg, between 1626 and 1629
H. 63,2 cm, Inv.-no. IV 294

In the 16th and 17th centuries, silver gilt goblets were immediate and visible expressions of princely power. While they served as luxurious tableware, they also functioned as state objects. On the ceremonial buffets, they bore witness to their owner's affluence and high standing. Lidded goblets were particularly popular. Their walls were embellished with chased rows of lobes whose reflections produced glorious light effects in candlelight. The *Columbine Goblet* was first made in Nuremberg. With the shape of its cup adapted from the flower of the ranunculae family, it represents a particularly exacting form of lobed goblet. The vegetal chase work is not restricted to the vessel's walls that consist of two rows of six overlapping mouchettes each; it also extends to the interior with a hexagonal tip reminiscent of the calyx. This made the columbine goblet one of the numerous items required as a master's piece by many goldsmith's guilds.

Whereas they were customarily about ten inches high, the *Columbine Goblet* created by Georg Mond in Dresden is over two feet high and thus extends far beyond all the others. Its monumentality significantly increased the challenge of executing – in consistently high quality – the chase work from one individual piece of silver. Ultimately, this work opened the way to the *Kunstkammer* for Mond.

Scrollwork and plant ornaments cover the spherical triangles of the cup's surface. Three embossed children's head and three warriors' heads in contemporary costumes were placed at the top and the bottom respectively. Instead of a shaft, a vase with three rings carries the high cup. Its lower portion is adorned with three female busts located between rams' heads. The vessel was originally decorated with an extra colorful mount and thus imitated the enamel embellishment of particularly exquisite goldsmith's works.

The Dresden *Columbine Goblet* represents a variant of a customary goldsmith's product worthy of a *Kunstkammer*, whereas the *Globe Bearer Goblet* of the Augsburg master Elias Lencker can instantly be recognized as an art object. The terrestrial globe, laboriously upheld by Hercules, can be opened near the equator and may thus be used as a drinking vessel. Together with its pendant, Saint Christopher carrying the firmament, it is the perfect *Kunstkammer* piece. The mature shapes of the muscular Hercules, influenced by large-scale sculpture from Augsburg, testify to the confident mastery of forms as well as an accomplished command of anatomy. Zeus' vigorous, silver cast and gilt eagle crowns the globe. This magnificent Early Baroque work of art combines artistic expression and artisan supremacy.

The earth's hemispheres were both cast from sheets of silver. Based on a model by Hondius, Johannes Schmidt engraved the most updated geographical knowledge of his time onto the surface. Hidden below the high pedestal, designed as a naturalistic forest floor with amphibious animals, are two cog-wheels that only barely protrude above the sheet. A third small, smooth wheel is fastened to serve as the pivoting steering wheel. The globe-shaped *Lidded Goblet* may thus be turned into an automaton that could move independently across the table if so desired. As a result, the *Goblet*, marked by Lenker, is a collaborative work of a technically versed goldsmith, an attentive silver engraver, an inventive automaton maker, and presumably one of the most important sculptors who invented the figure's models.

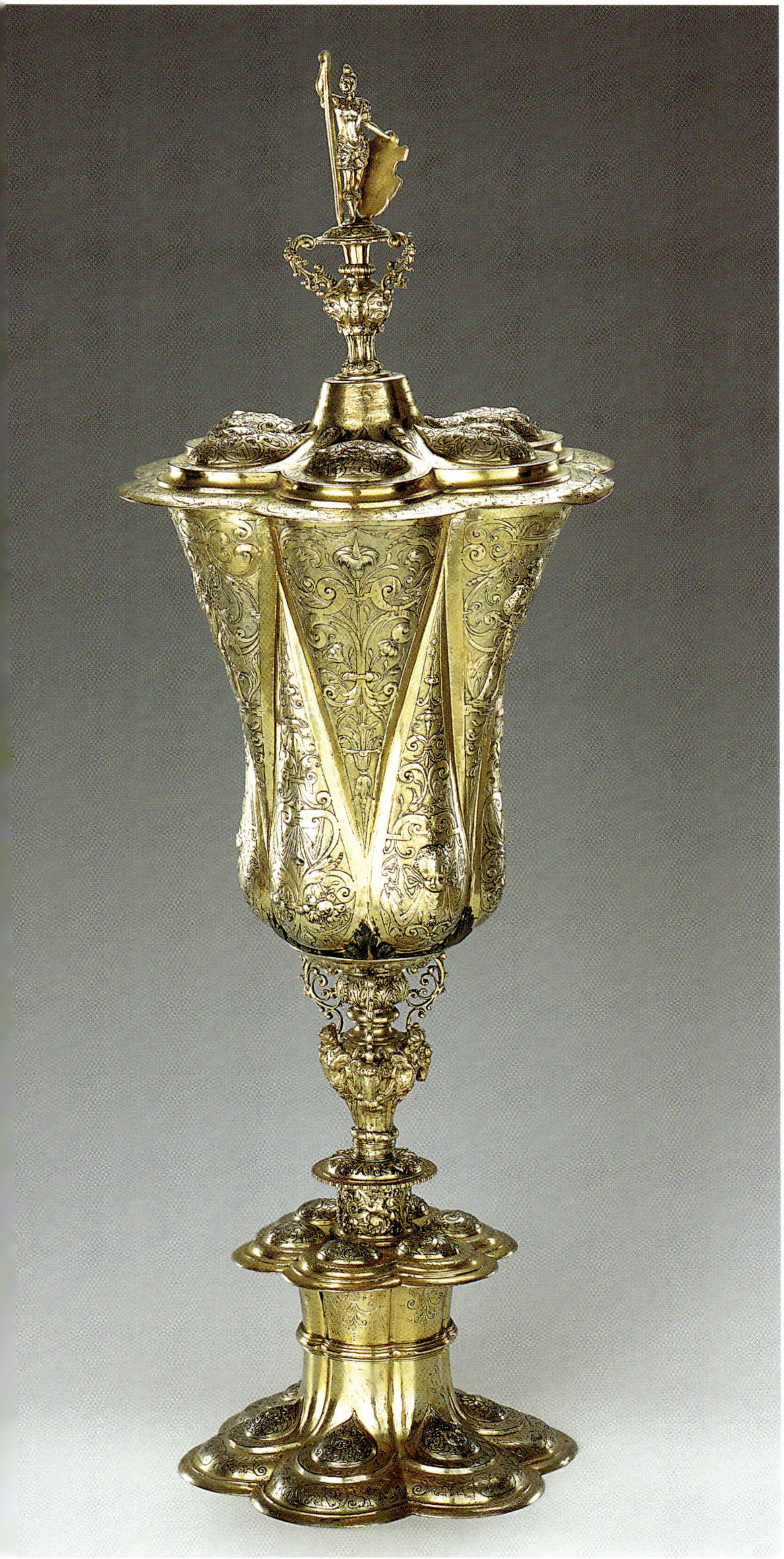

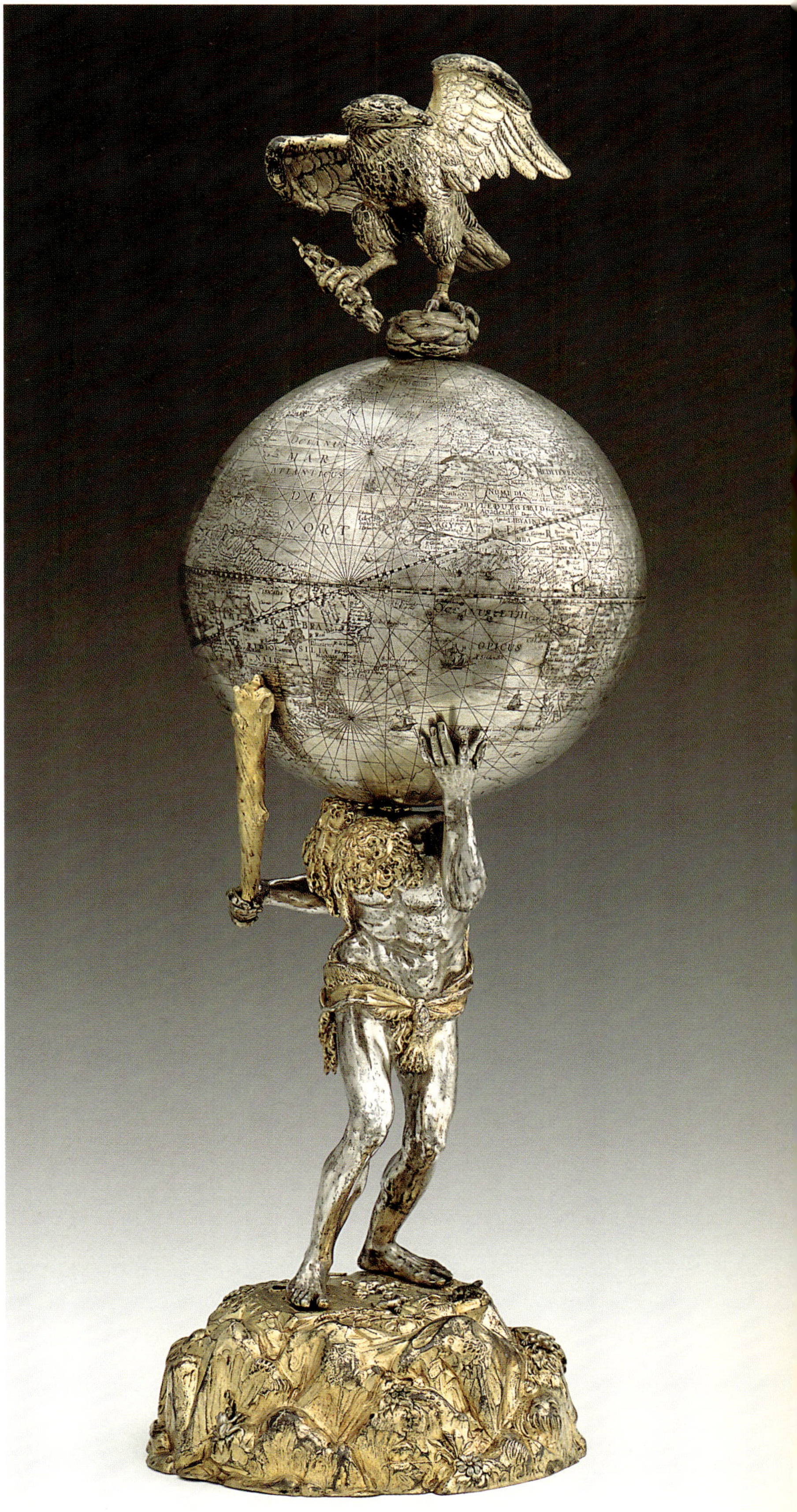

Ewer in the Shape of a Dragon's Head

Rock crystal, gilt silver, precious stones, cameos
Stonecutter: Dionysio Miseroni
Prague, between 1653 and 1656
H. 42 cm, Inv.-no. V 183

High Rock Crystal Goblet in the Shape of a Snail

Rock crystal, silver, enamel
Stonecutter: Johann Daniel Mayer or Lorenz Grießenbeck
Augsburg, circa 1660
H. 34 cm, Inv.-no. V 250

After the end of the Thirty Years War and the related economic crisis, art recovered rather slowly at the courts of the Holy Roman Empire. During the second half of the 17th century, the sensuous, finely shaped forms seen in earlier treasury art were admired less by the princely collectors of Northern Europe. Instead, their emphasis was on clearly recognizable preciousness and sumptuous materials; luscious gold mounts covered with colorful precious stones were particularly venerated.

The form of the approximately twenty-inch (42 cm) high *Display Ewer* is reminiscent of a dragon's head. Made during the mid 17th century by the imperial stonecutter Dionysio Miseroni in his Prague Castle studio, the structure of the hexagonal *Ewer* contains an unusually large and pure rock crystal. From this, the master created a vigorous vessel with a narrow opening and high spout. The chamfered edges are decorated with severe flutings, whereas the walls are filled with cartouches, feathered foliage, framed rows of pearls, and deeply cut palmettes. The separately worked rock crystal imitates one heavy, long, leaf-adorned volute. With its squat outline and the massive application of material, the *Display Ewer* represents, in an almost prototypical way, the shapes preferred by the last representative of the Miseroni dynasty of stonecutters.

This *Vessel* is closely related to a group formerly kept in Vienna's Treasury. Similar rock crystal works were commissioned by Emperor Ferdinand III. As opposed to the works by his famous father Ottavio, whose fantastic sculptural creations were expressions of the extremely refined culture dominant at the court of Emperor Rudolf II, the œuvre of Dionysio reflects the taste of a new era. Because the mount for the lid is shaped like a cockscomb and due to the innumerable precious stones that stud the foot and the springing point of the handle, the *Ewer* can be identified as an emperor's princely gift. Although archival sources identify a large rock crystal container in the guise of a *Barrel* as the emperor's gift to the Saxon prince elector, no references have yet been located specifying when and how this even richer and more lavishly mounted work came to Dresden from the imperial workshop.

Apart from the Prague-based Hapsburg workshop and the traditional rock crystal works from Freiburg im Breisgau, ambitious stonecutting studios were established in Augsburg in the mid-17th century. The latter specialized in princely patrons. The stonecutter Johann Daniel Mayer created numerous bowls from colored precious stones for the Duke of Württemberg. His works can likewise be documented for the historic collections in Vienna, Florence, Munich, and Dresden. The second stonecutting artist from Augsburg who can be named is Lorenz Grießenbeck. The large *Snail Goblet* originates from one of the two ateliers. The *Vessel*'s robust body – with a height of approximately eight inches (19 cm) and a diameter of approximately nine inches (23 to 21 cm) – is pointed at the bottom. Snail-like curls that do not imitate any natural forms are cut into either side. The cup's front is adorned with a stylized, relief-like leaf, whereas the broad back is occupied by the bearded head of a satyr, with pointed ears and a high forehead. In addition, fine, long-stemmed foliage with variously interspersed insects was deeply cut into the relief-like wall of the cup. The clear rock crystal shaft in the shape of an animated volute is remarkable. The stonecutter gave the foot the form of a sprawled out, stylized snail shell he also embellished with deeply cut plants. The foot's enamel mount and the two shaft rings are typical of south Germany. Naturalistic flowers – among them a tulip, daffodil, lily, carnation, and chrysanthemum – are painted onto the enameled ground. Strewn between them are smaller petals and ornamental scrollwork. A shell-shaped *Footed Bowl*, also attributed to Mayer and in the Green Vault's collection, has a nearly identical mount.

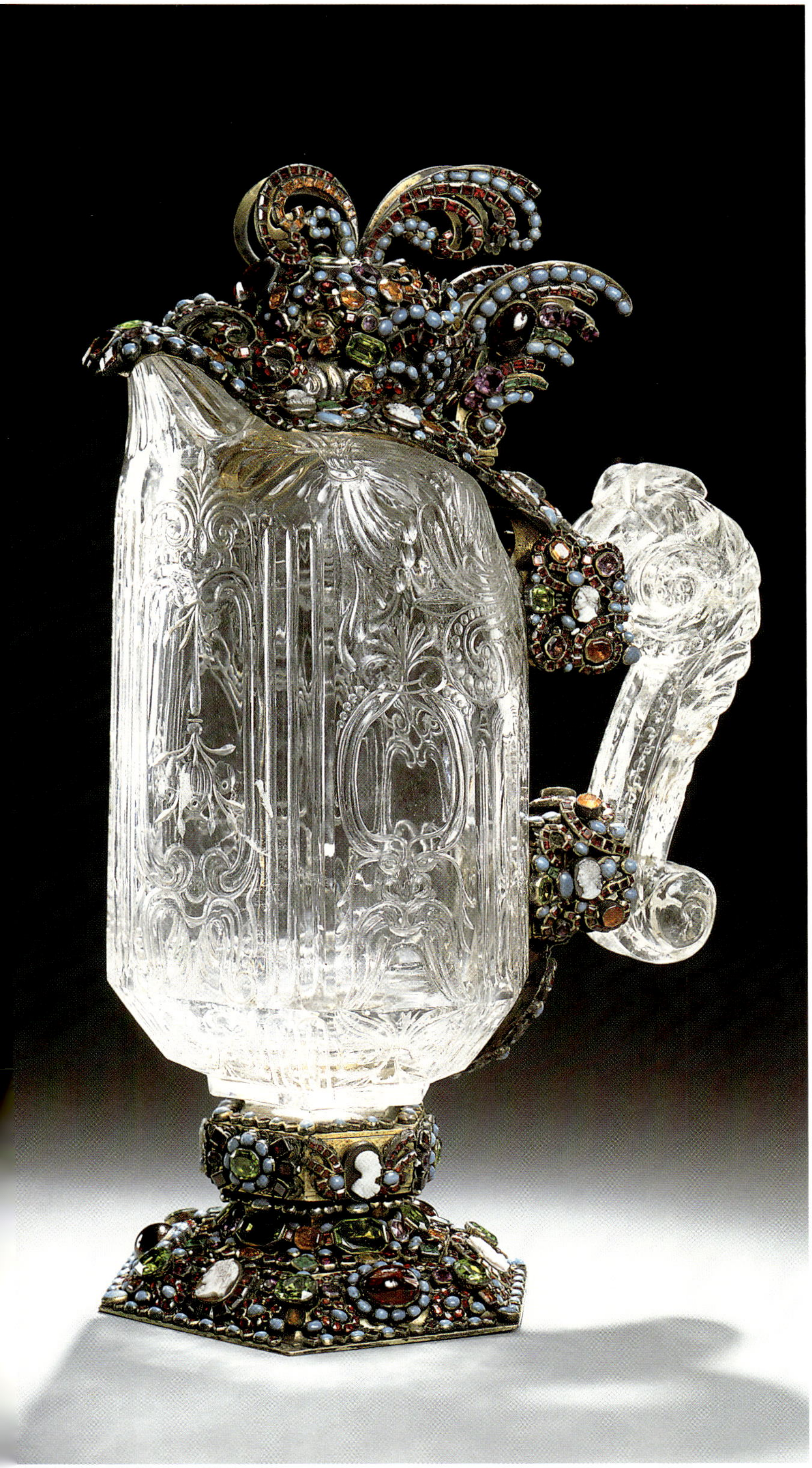

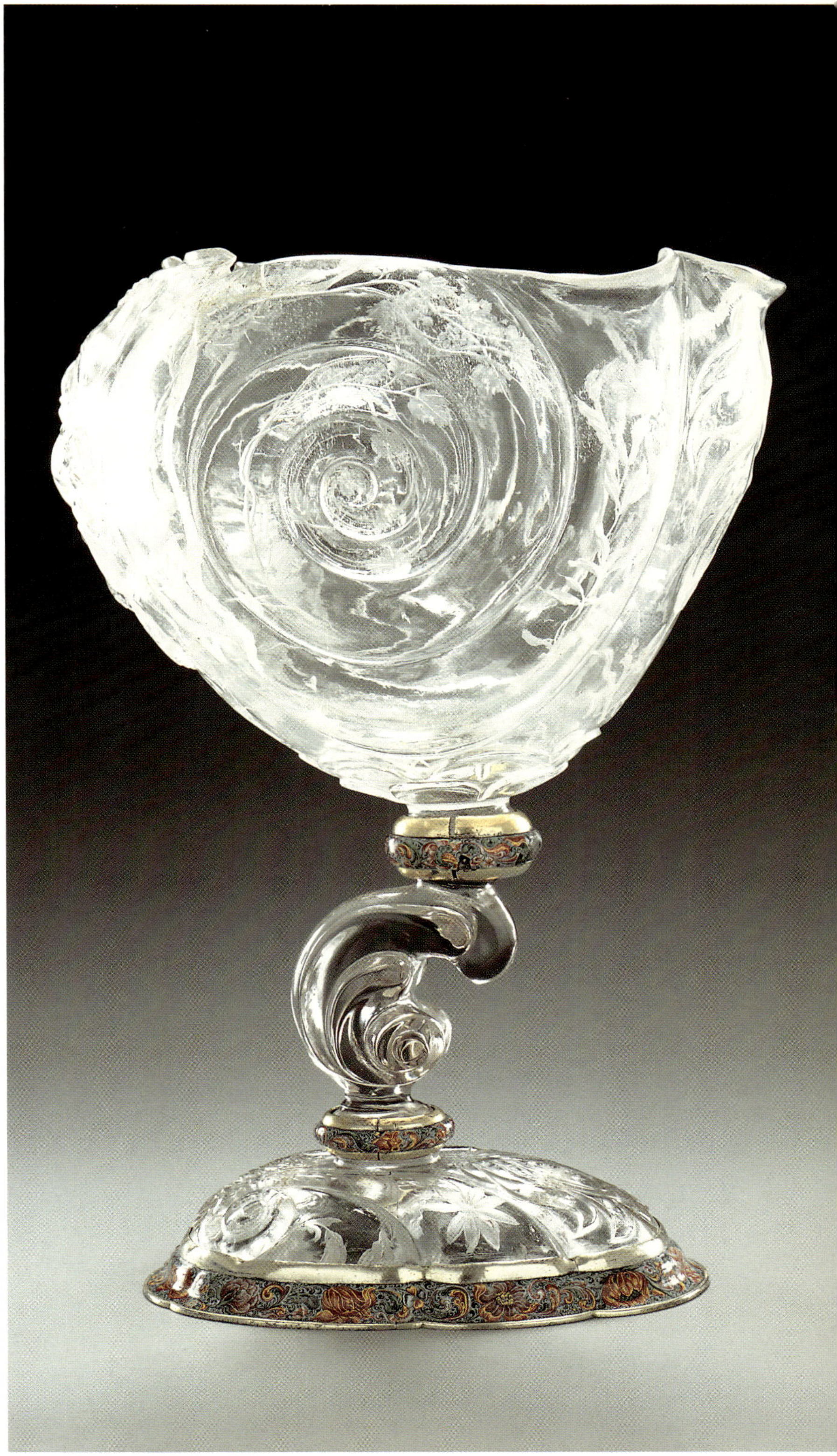

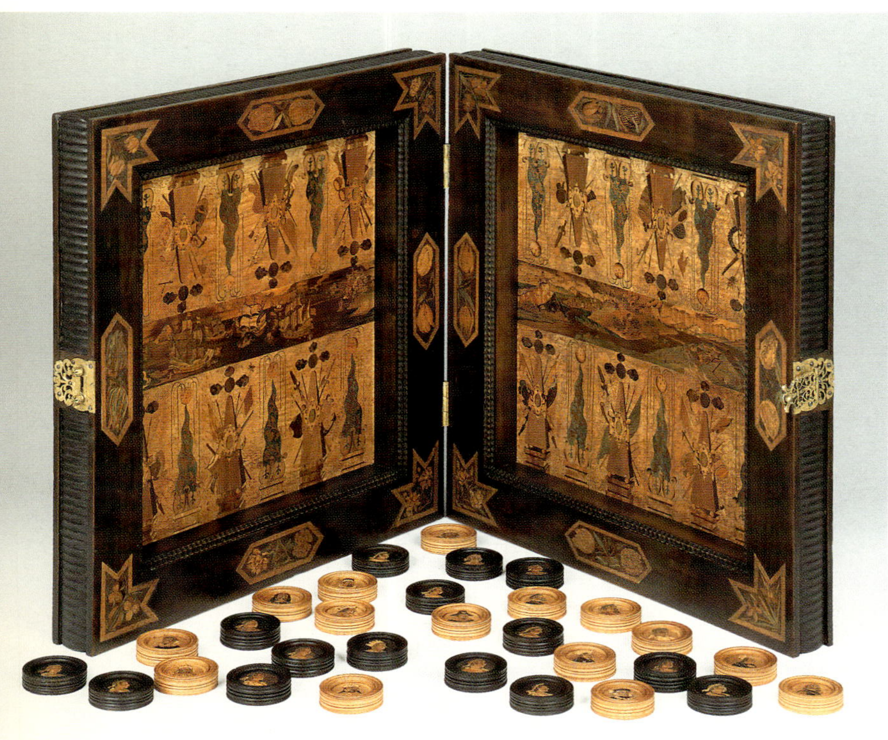

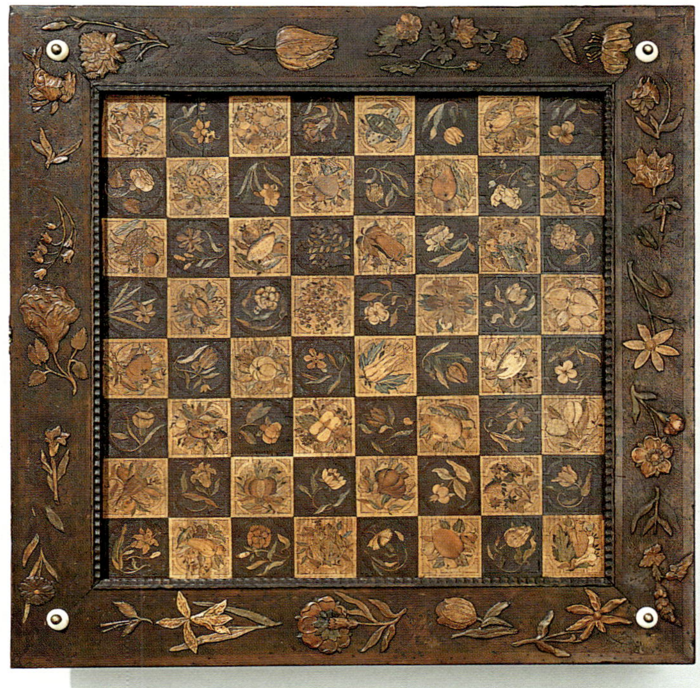

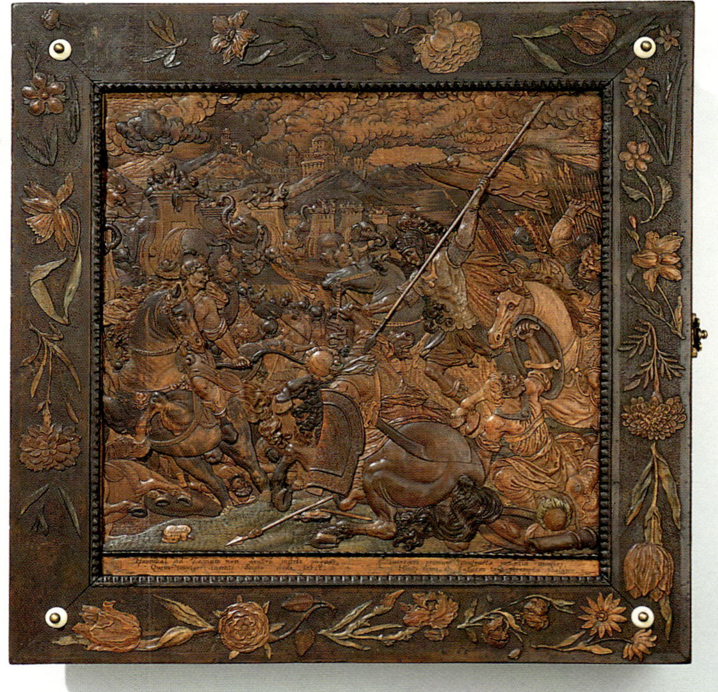

Board Game with the Battle near Zama

Various types of wood
Johann Georg Fischer
presumably Saxony, dated 1655
H. 13 cm, W. 54,5 cm, D. 54,5 cm, Inv.-no. VII 250

Golden Hunting and Drinking Horn

Gold, enamel, diamonds, rubies, emeralds
Presumably Henrik Langemack
Copenhagen, dated 1650
L. 49,5 cm, Inv.-no. IV 45

For his seventieth – and hence second to last – birthday, on March 5, 1655, Prince Elector Johann Georg I received one of the most beautiful 17th-century *Board Game*s as a gift from his son, Electoral Prince Johann Georg (II). The artist was Johann Georg Fischer, originally from the city of Eger in western Bohemia, which he was forced to flee due to the Thirty Years War in 1628; this object is signed and dated in the same year. The game's box counts among the most refined artistic accomplishments of relief intarsia, a technique developed in Eger. The latter are idiosyncratic and unmistakable inlay works fabricated from colored hard woods of differing thickness. With the aid of carving tools, the wood was composed in dynamic, colored high relief narratives that are reminiscent of a goldsmith's formal vocabulary. Fischer's work in Dresden is among the most artistically and technically prolific using this

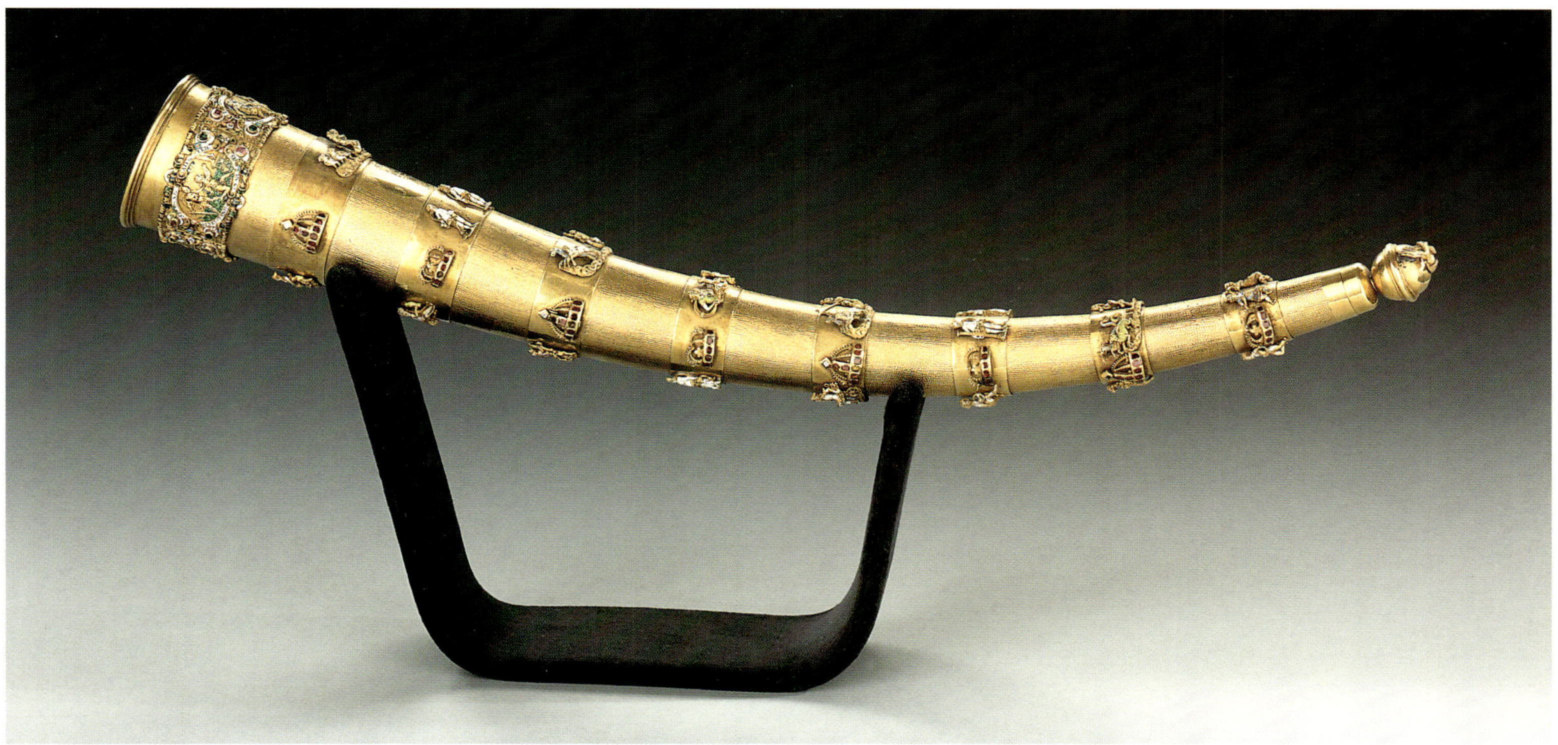

method, a technique that also produced cabinets, jewelry and board game boxes, and picture panels.

The depiction of the battle on the display side is a remarkable interpretation of the two games united inside the receptacle – they are the strategic trictrac on the inside and the chess game on the outside. The decisive combat near Zama in the Second Punic War is depicted, in which Scipio Africanus defeated his enemy Hannibal, the »master of strategies.« The superb rendition of the armed turmoil originates from a copperplate engraving Fischer flawlessly transformed from its rectangular format into the box's square shape. Whereas the trictrac board picks up the combat theme, the diversity of plants visible on the chessboard is reminiscent of a vegetable, fruit, or flower garden with abundant flora. The game box is still furnished with two complete sets of fifteen black and white stones ornamented with images of ancient and modern emperors. The board games reveal no signs of use.

Thanks to his perfect relief technique and microscopic inlay work, Fischer created a grandiose *Kunstkammer* piece whose rich details are revealed only upon close scrutiny or with the help of a magnifying glass. The universe of images thus offered the spectator a nearly endless source of historic and military discourse, but also contemplation of nature and botany.

The *Golden Horn* from Copenhagen was made for a member of the Saxon electoral family as well and was also intended to stimulate reflection on the part of the recipient. It bears the date 1650 and the »MS« monogram of Magdalena Sybilla, a daughter of Prince Elector Johann Georg I. In 1634, she married the Danish Crown Prince Christian, the oldest son of King Christian IV of Denmark. Five years later, a *Germanic Golden Horn*, excavated near Tondern, caused a sensation among scholars. The Danish king presented this rare precious object to his son. When the crown prince died in 1647, the *Golden Horn of Tondern* remained in the possession of his spouse – albeit under the condition that she remain in Denmark and not remarry. When Magdalena Sybilla returned to Saxony in 1650, she was given – as a substitute for the priceless original – the *Golden Horn* weighing about three pounds (1,368 grams), now preserved in the Green Vault. The object is a free copy of the original that dates to circa 500 AD. The decorative trimmings applied to the *Dresden Horn* are dated before 1650 and might have been part of the Saxon princess' rich bridal dowry. In 1652, the crown prince's widow married Duke Friedrich Wilhelm II of Saxony-Altenburg. Later her *Golden Horn* returned to Dresden as an inheritance. The *Golden Horn of Tondern*, found in 1638, has been missing since 1802. Hence, the Green Vault's exquisite Baroque copy is the only witness to one of the most spectacular 17th-century archaeological finds.

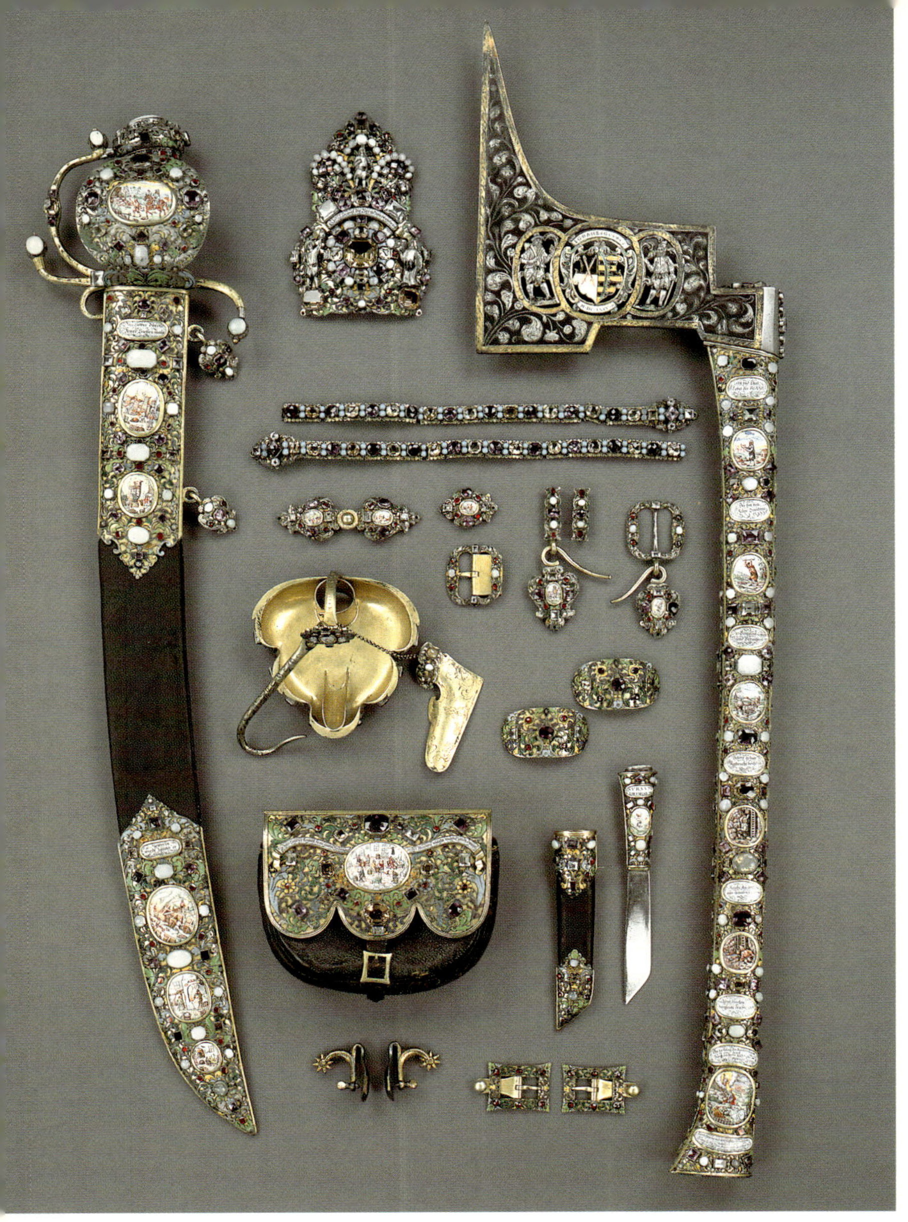

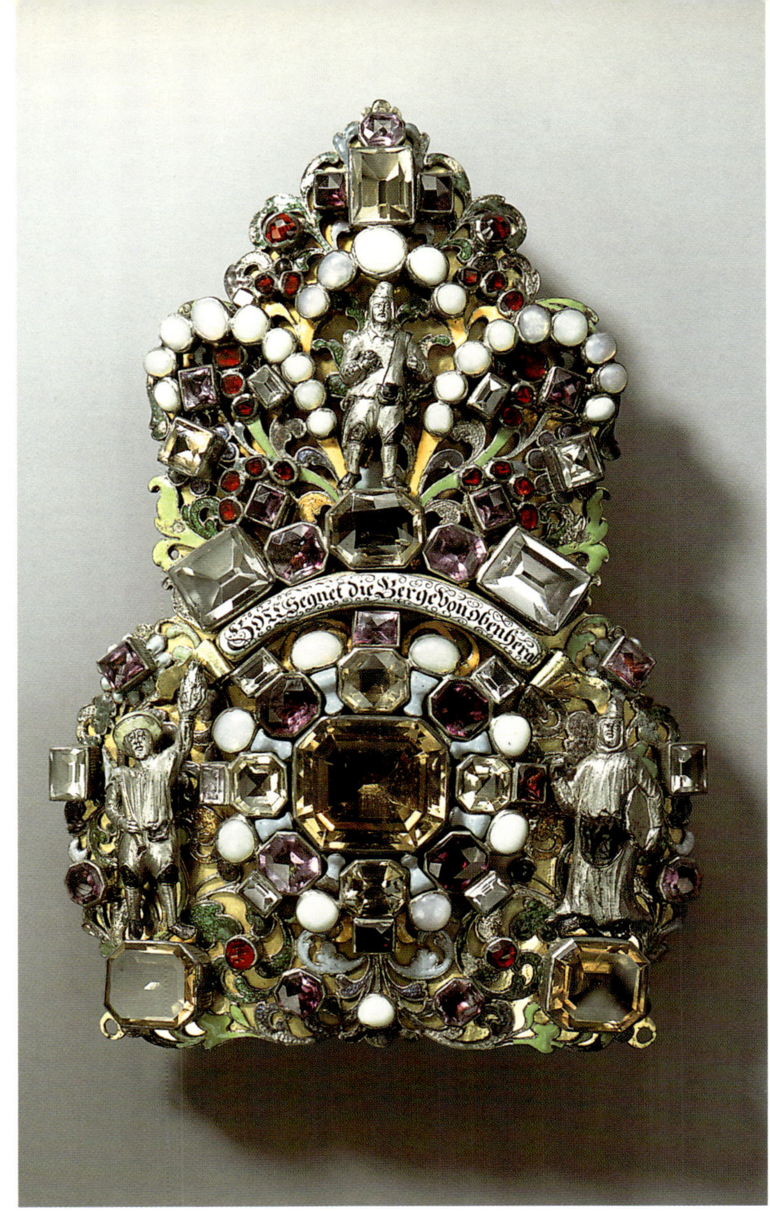

Hat Ornament, Knife Bag, and Shovel from the Miner's Garniture

Silver, partly gilt, enamel, garnets, rock crystal, amethysts, opals
Various types of quartz
Samuel Klemm
Freiberg, 1675 until 1677
Hat ornament: H. 16 cm, W. 11 cm, Inv.-no. VIII 317
Knife Bag: H. 17 cm, Inv.-no. VIII 324

Based on historic development, the *Miner's State Garniture* of Prince Elector Johann Georg II stands between the early 17th century stone-embellished *Hunting Garnitures* and Augustus the Strong's late Baroque *Jewel Garnitures*. From the historical vantage point, the *Miner's Garniture* is an important document of Saxony's economic and cultural growth following the Thirty Years War. It is one of the major works of 17th century Saxon precious stone processing, and from a mineralogical stance, the *Miner's Garniture* offers an overview of Saxon precious stone deposits known at the time of its fabrication – and this was indeed intentional.

The mountains were the possession of the prince electors and were thus part of the sovereigns' prerogative, and the rulers were consequently authorized to dispose of their territory's mineral resources. According to the theories of a controlled economy, this formed the basis of a state's wealth. Even in Saxony, certain financiers or economic conglomerates took over the development and the exploitation of mineral resources. The prince electors only participated sporadically in the operation of the mines, quarries, and foundries. Nosseni was the first to undertake a systematic investigation of Saxony's exploitable stone deposits in 1575. Due to the disorder caused by the long war, some finds fell into oblivion. Thus, the prince elector commissioned Saxony's chief building master (*Oberlandbaumeister*) and *Kunstkammer* supervisor Caspar von Klengel in 1659 to undertake a renewed »Revision derer Edelgestein- und Marmor-Brüche« (revision of the precious stone and marble quarries.) The *Miner's Garniture* reflects his success.

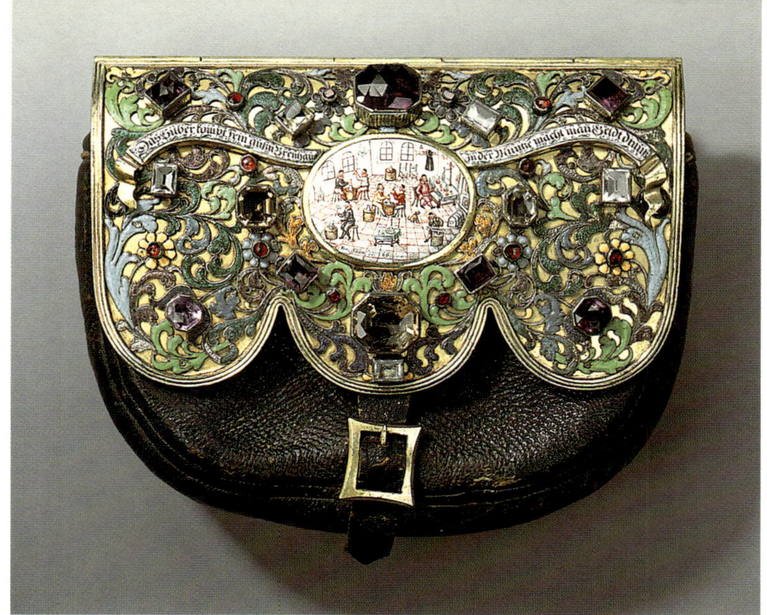

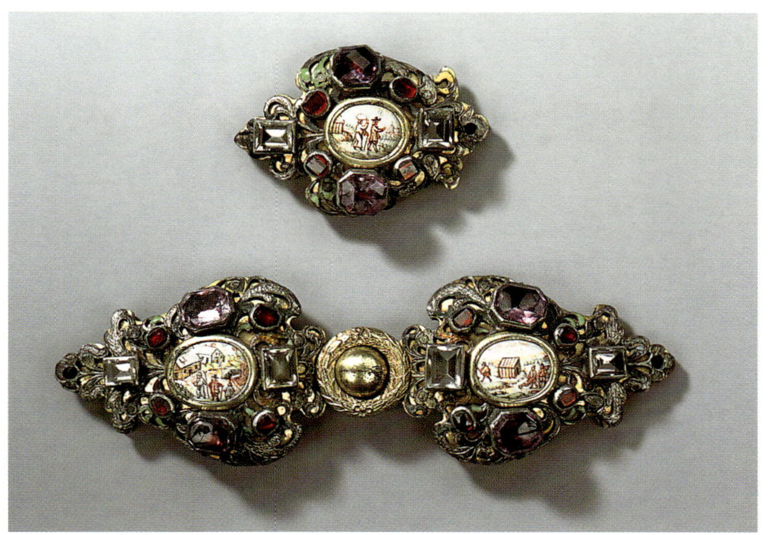

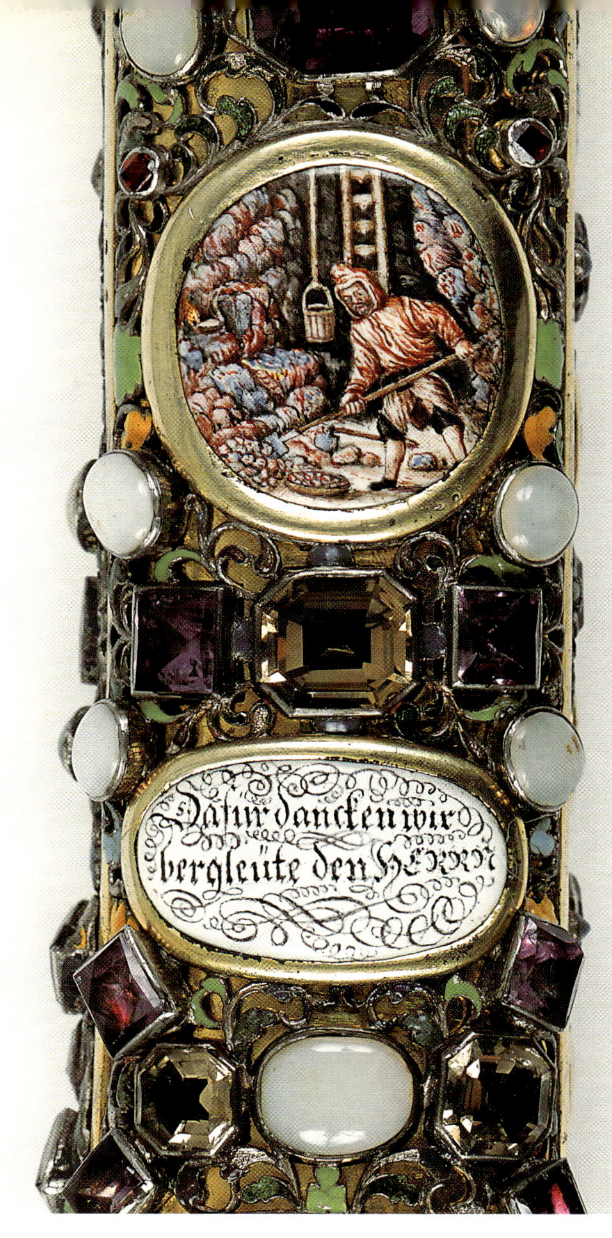

However, the immediate reason for the creation of the *Miner's Garniture* was the »Durchlauchtigste Zusammenkunft« (the illustrious meeting) of Prince Elector Georg II's three brothers in Dresden on February 13, 1678. The preparations for this festive family gathering began in 1674. For this reason, the inner and the outer façades of the Dresden Residential Palace were renovated, and even the crest of the palace tower (*Hausmannsturm*) was raised. For the prince elector, the meeting was of major importance because it served as a demonstration of his rank and his claim to power vis-à-vis his brothers and the public. This intention determined the iconography of the *Miner's Garniture*, made between 1675 and 1677 by the Freiberg goldsmith Samuel Klemm.

The decorative elements of a high-ranking mining official's festival attire were rendered from the perspective of ceremonial court culture. The ensemble consists of a hatchet (broad axe) and broad sword, a short knife (*Tscherper*) to work the tallow, the knife bag to hold the lighting agent, the pit lamp with wick scraper, a hat clasp with matching cord, as well as a clasp, buckles and pendants. Only minerals quarried in Saxony were used for the *Miner's Garniture*: silver and gold, rock crystal from various sites, amethysts, garnets, smoke and milk opals. With the aid of blue-green enamel, Klemm imitated turquoise, highly prized at the time but not found in Saxony. Klemm's specialty was the art of enameling. In his typical style and rich color palette, he produced numerous ovoid enamel medallions with which certain parts of the *Garniture* are studded. They offer detailed descriptions of how the silver ore is mined from the mountains' depths and enters the electoral Treasury: from the dowser as treasure finder, through the various steps of quarrying and smelting, to the minting of the precious metal. The electoral territories' coats-of-arms are placed on the shaft of the axe, the miner's most important tool.

The ensemble was only worn once by Johann Georg II on the occasion of the family festival: According to what the annals impart, his electoral highness was riding in the »Bergk-Habit« (the miner's outfit) during the great procession of the god Mercury, who protected mining.

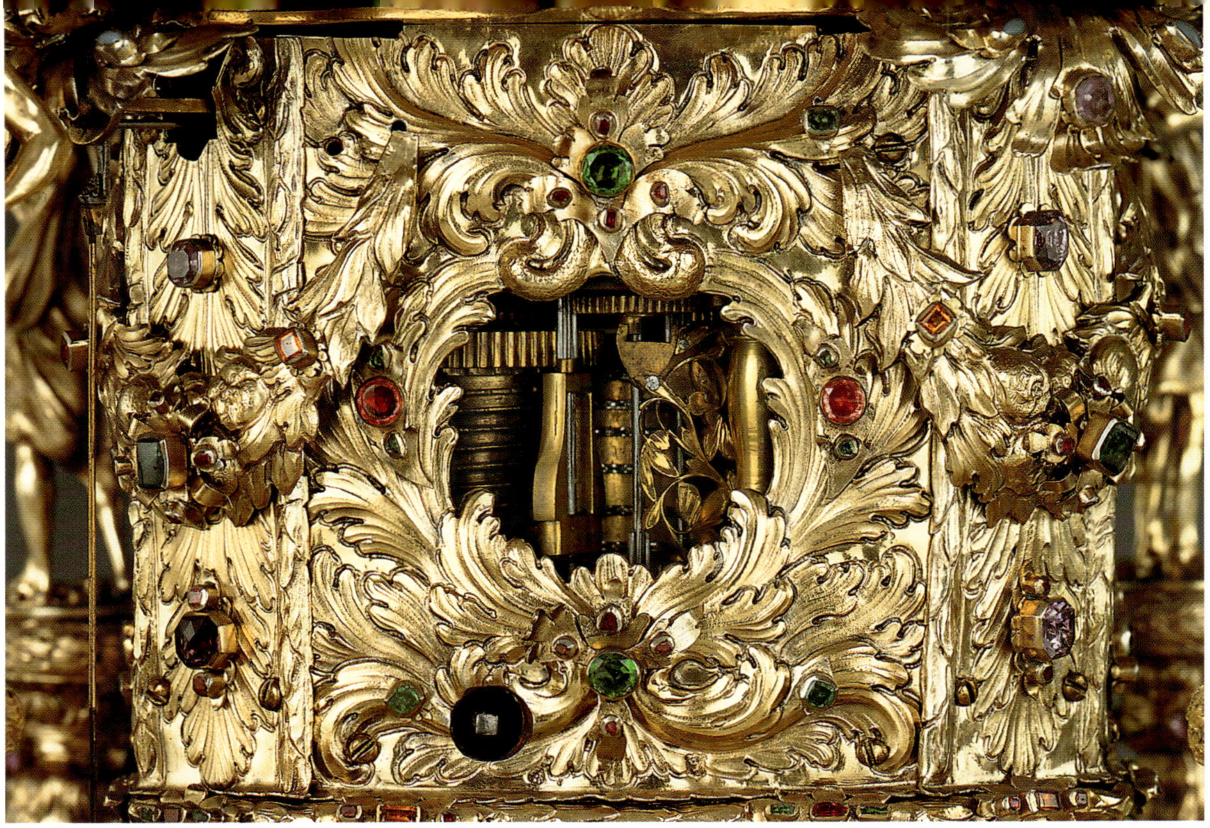

Table Clock of Christiane Eberhardine

Gilt silver, diamonds, emeralds, rubies, amethysts, garnets
Abraham II Drentwett
Augsburg, between 1680 and 1685
H. 46 cm, W. 37 cm, D. 36 cm, Inv.-no. IV 56

The Baroque *State Clock* was owned by Electress Christiane Eberhardine and is a particularly sumptuous example of a horizontal *Table Clock* adorned with exquisite precious stones. It belongs to a type created around 1600 that became particularly popular during the course of the 17th century. The square, almost box-like case with its elaborately decorated sides is characteristic of such clocks. While their dials are placed horizontally, these clocks frequently include a crowning statuette with a staff-shaped hand to indicated the time.

From an optical point of view, the Augsburg goldsmith Abraham II Drentwett lent the Dresden *State Clock* an air of lightness by equipping its case with four flat ball feet placed far apart from one another. The goldsmith turned out to be a master of contemporary fashion trends, especially regarding the acanthus style that came into vogue around 1680. The *Clock*'s decoration consists of thinly chased, zigzag acanthus vines with lightly rolled leaves. Garlands with fruit and baskets are suspended from the pedestal and the base plate. Equally trendy at the time, they are placed between the scrolls. The elements that bestow royal dignity to the luxuriously equipped *Clock* are most particularly the high-quality, valuable precious stones, dominated by emeralds, some of considerable size. The use of rubies and diamonds, as well as amethysts and garnets makes for a colorful frame. The extraordinary luxury of the *State Clock* is accentuated by its dial, whose Roman hour numerals are made entirely of green emeralds.

The iconographic message of the *State Clock* is delivered by four three-dimensional, silver cast allegorical figures placed over little balusters at the case's slightly beveled corners. The first mention of the *State Clock* in a 1733 Green Vault inventory notes that the figures – no longer be attributable beyond doubt – are representations of the five senses. The fifth statuette, rising in the middle of the face over a sphere, can also be identified as the goddess Athena.

The crowning figure is a reflection of the fundamental idea underlying Late Renaissance automatons: It is equipped with a mechanism on the inside and hence directly connected with the clockwork. This enables the statuette to move its head and its right arm. The sphere on which the goddess stands was also operable and served to indicate the phases of the moon. The *State Clock* stressed the quick passing of time in a sensual manner: Every minute one rock crystal sphere rotated around the dial that was furnished with only an hour hand, while at the same time, inside the clock's case, another sphere was lifted up to its point of origin. This is not a rolling ball clock in the sense of those dating circa 1600. Its rolling ball mechanism did not serve to measure time: Instead, it made time visible. The precise clockwork was regulated with the help of a visibly attached pendulum. A striking mechanism with three bells sounded every quarter hour and was also stocked with an alarm device. In addition, the *State Clock* had a date indicator.

When Electress Christiane Eberhardine, who had married Augustus the Strong in 1693, died in 1727 her husband transferred the *Parade Clock* to the Green Vault.

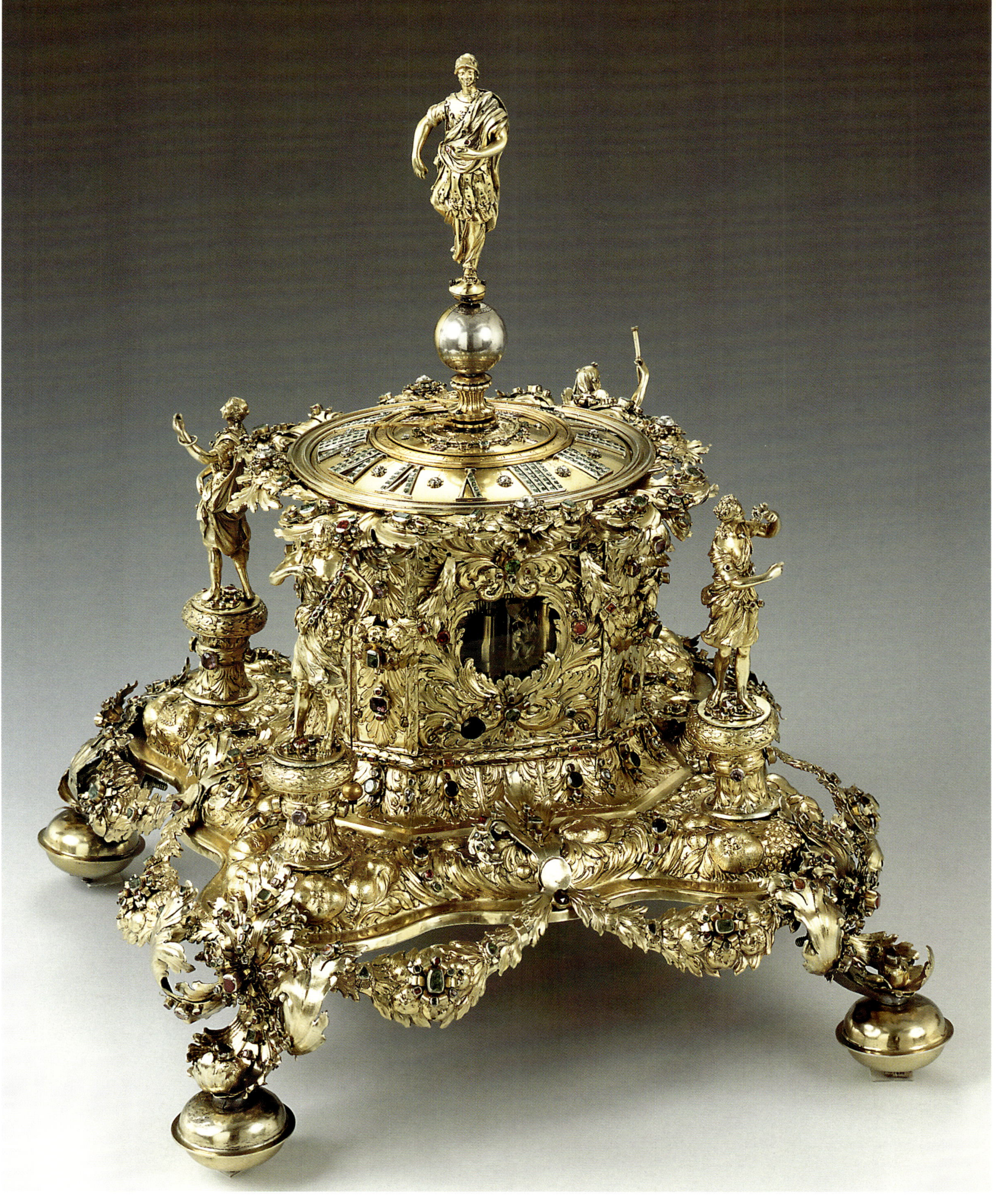

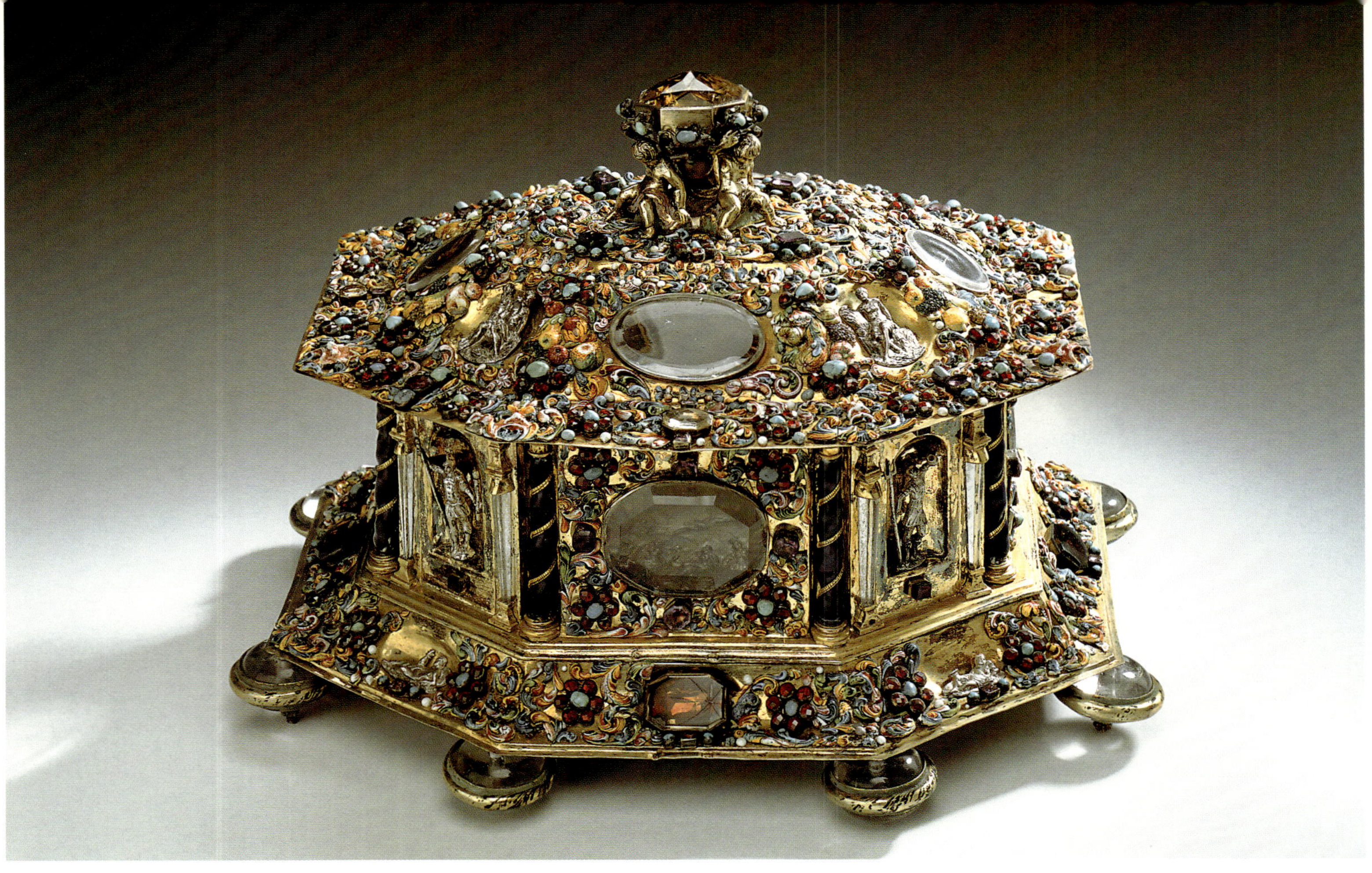

Display Casket

Silver, partly gilt, mirror, rock crystal, enamel, cameos, precious stones
Hans Jacob Mair
Augsburg, circa 1680
H. 15,5 cm, W. 27,3 cm, Inv.-no. V 600

Table Clock with Camel and Moor

Gilt silver, rock crystal, amethysts, turquoise, precious stones, enamel
Goldsmith's work: Hans Jacob Mair
Clockwork: Elias Weckherlin
Augsburg, circa 1674
H. 24,5 cm, W. 18 cm, Inv.-no. V 594 f

During the second half of the 17th century, colorful *Display Caskets*, lavishly studded with precious stones and embellished with ornamental enamels, were particularly popular with princely collectors. Characteristically, rock crystal discs enabled one to look inside. Such caskets only served in exceptional cases as containers for writing utensils or jewelry. One such *Display Casket* originates from the studio of the Augsburg goldsmith Hans Jacob Mair. It is an octagonal, oblong *Casket* covered with precious stone-studded petals, enamel pearls, and color enameled acanthus vines. The lid, supported by twisted columns, takes the shape of a curved roof and is particularly profusely adorned. Apart from scrollwork, seemingly arbitrarily intertwined fruit garlands and grotesque masks made of enamel may be found. The silver gilt putti support a huge topaz that crowns the lid. Little silver reliefs and figures on the lid and case walls are conventional references to the four seasons, the four elements, and the four cardinal points. The oval-shaped rock crystal discs placed into the lid and walls turn this tiny *Display Casket* into a purely decorative object for the princely collector, allowing him to view the silver relief mounted on the interior floor of the *Casket*. The theme of the relief is Phaeton and the sun chariot. The son of Helios was struck by Zeus' flash of lightning because his careless driving threatened to set the earth on fire. Witnessed by Zeus, towering on the clouds above the assembly of gods, the relief illustrates the moment when Helios was thrown off his sun chariot.

The creator of the *Display Casket* also made the *Table Clock with Camel and an Oriental Herdsman* preserved in the Green Vault. Mair alluded to the same clock type as Abraham II Drentwett did (p. 76). Just like the *Display Casket*, the *Table Clock*, too, is richly bedecked with multi-colored precious stones. Upon closer inspection, an orderly system can be discerned: Amethysts and garnets, almost completely covering the surface, determine the basic red-violet color of the precious stone adornment; The color is complemented by peridots, turquoise, and emeralds. The precious stone trimmings are surrounded by filigree tendrils made of white enamel and completed with sumptuous

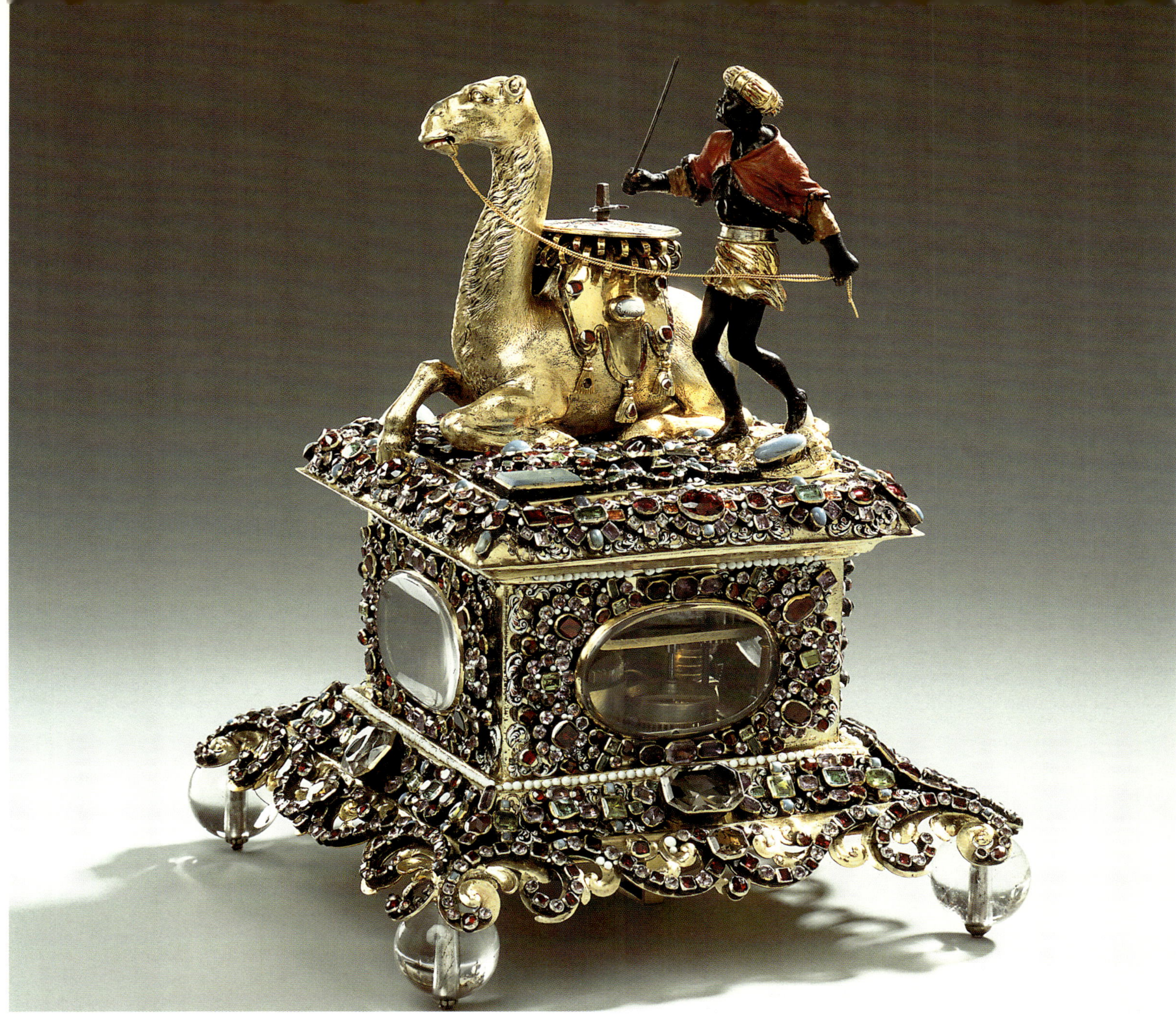

cold paint. Judging from technical considerations of the goldsmith's work, the case of this *Clock* is even more luxurious than the *Display Casket*. As observed in the latter, as well as in the case of the *Clock*, oblique oval-shaped rock crystal discs mounted in the sides allow one to view the fine clockwork inside. A seemingly exotic group crowns the *Table Clock*: It consists of a herdsman with a reposing camel on whose saddle the horizontal clock's face is placed.

This *Clock* is thus an example of the fashion for all things Turkish, cultivated at European courts since the end of the 15th century. In the last third of the 17th century, the admiration for the foreign neighbors' cultural and artistic achievements had once more been replaced by the fear of approaching military conflicts. Time and again threatening new battles flared up. It was not until after the victory over the Ottoman army near Vienna (1683), that a shift in the power structure between sultan and emperor was achieved.

Hans Jacob Mair was an important and versatile goldsmith, whom the Augsburg guild held in high regard. His documented œuvre is extensive, showing that Mair was perhaps best able to meet the late-17th-century preference for colorful and at the same time preciously garnished goldsmith's works. His masterworks must have been particularly popular with the European princely houses, since they may be encountered in important historic collections: among them Vienna, Moscow, Munich, and also Dresden.

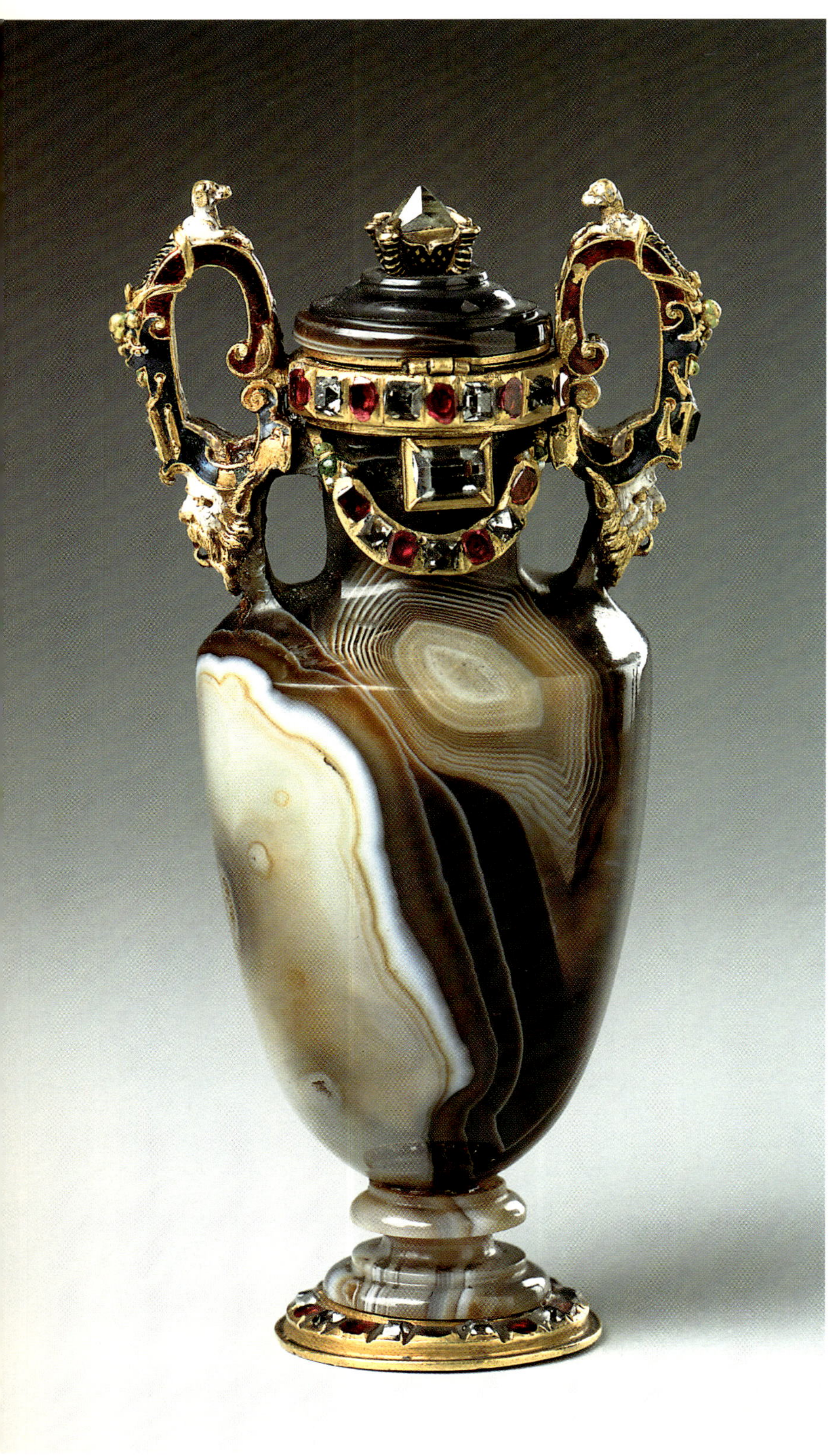

Phial

Onyx, gold, diamonds, rubies
Paris, circa 1600
H. 8 cm, Inv.-no. VI 8 o

Small Shell-shaped Bowl with Moor's Head

Gold, enamel, diamonds, pearls
Presumably France, last third of the 17th century
H. 5,5 cm, Inv.-no. VI 7 u

Mirror with Flower Painting on its Reverse

Gold, enamel, mirror glass
Presumably Copenhagen mid-17th century
H. 19 cm, W. 14,5 cm, Inv.-no. III 51

Fancy goods were decorative items whose form and function were adapted to perpetually changing fashions. The term »gallantry« came into being in the late Baroque period and described utilitarian luxury items. Together with refined garments and valuable jewels (*Bijouterien*), they mirrored the courtly society's lifestyle. Apart from little bowls and boxes, smelling bottles and perfume phials, these trinkets also included seal and signet holders, receptacles, pommels, mirrors, and small writing utensils. Thanks to their particularly extravagant design and material opulence, fancy goods reached an exaggerated level, earmarking them as a subject for treasury art. The utilitarian value of these collector's objects became secondary, whereas their gracious shapes gained prominence.

The oldest work of this type came into electoral Saxon ownership in 1709 as an »antique Urne von Onix in goldt gefasst« (antique onyx urn mounted in gold). It is a small, double-handled *Onyx Vase* whose golden mounts on the foot, neck, and opening are particularly delicately garnished with rubies and diamonds. A pointed diamond cut in a typical 16th-century fashion crowns the lid. The two golden handles reveal golden strapwork; in addition, they are bedecked with an enameled faun's mask and a minuscule bust of a dog. The latter detail leads to the supposition that the decorative vessel was manufactured in Paris around 1600. Augustus the Strong paid 200 thaler for this French Renaissance marvel at Leipzig's Easter Fair.

The first notes to diamond studded phials and toothpick cases appear in the Saxon chief chamberlain's lists in about 1680 – an unmistakable sign that the French fashion for these kinds of luxury commodities had gained ground in Dresden.

This was also approximately the time when the small *Golden Bowl* with rich enamel decoration was created. The bowl's body takes the shape of a scallop shell and is supported on a shaft shaped as an en-

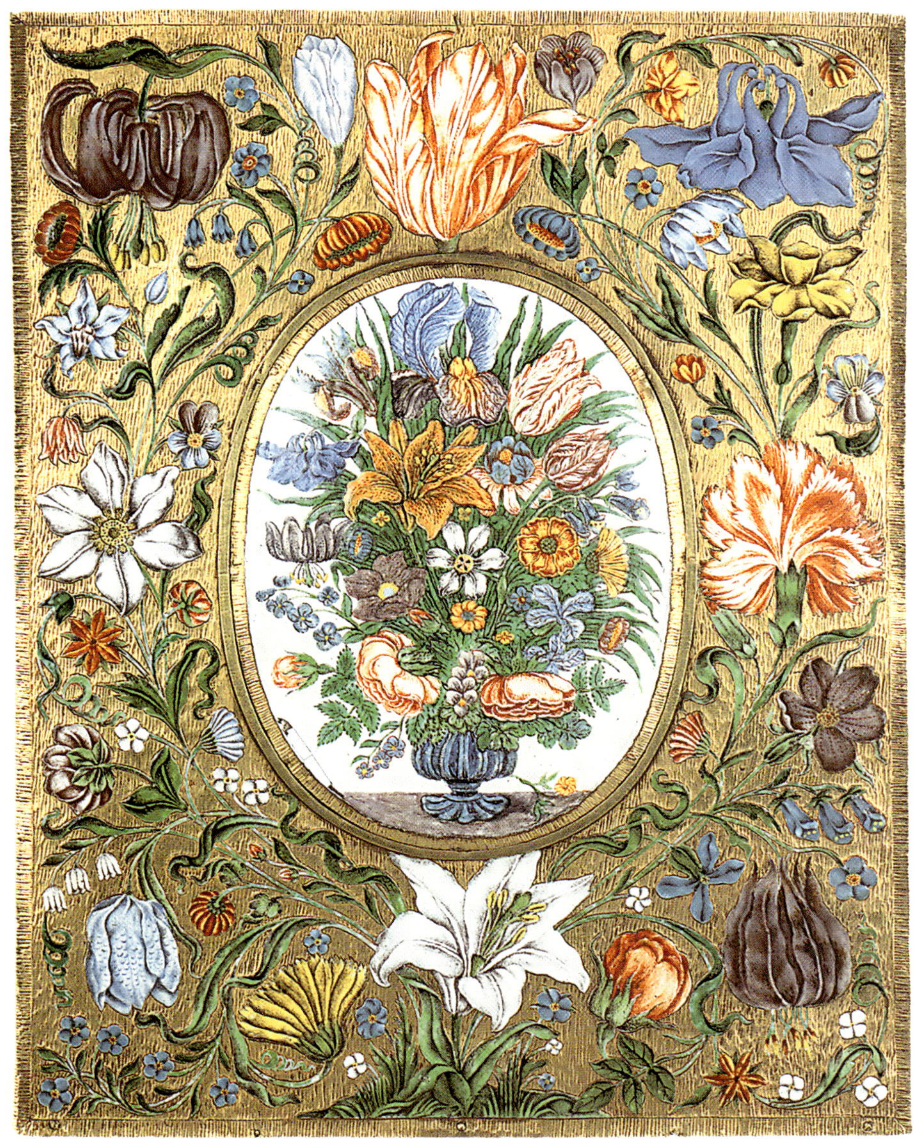

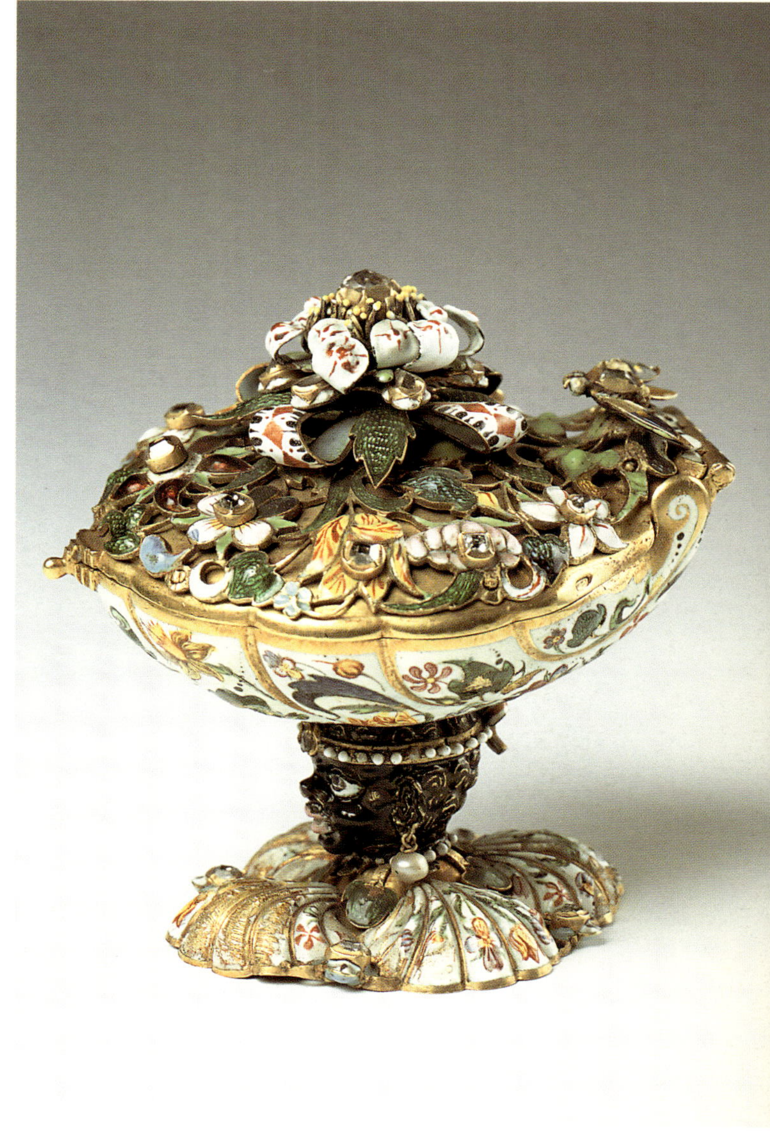

ameled Moor's head. The latter, in turn, is positioned on a foot made from four enamel-covered scallop shells. Following contemporary French fashion, the ground of the bowl's walls is white enamel with the addition of colorfully painted flowers. One additional three-dimensional flower arrangement rises over the lid.

A golden decorative *Mirror*, presumably made in Copenhagen, is likewise influenced by the Baroque flower fashion. Between the mid-16th and the late 17th centuries, such mirrors were favorite accessories for women of a certain rank. The mirror side was attributed less significance than the reverse, intended for the courtly public. In this case, its surface flowers with dense tendrils of various kinds, whereas the oval-shaped central field depicts a vase with an imposing bouquet. The goldsmith who created this work subtly contrasted the white enamel of the ground in the middle area with the frame's seemingly sculptural enamel, executed in *basse-taille* technique.

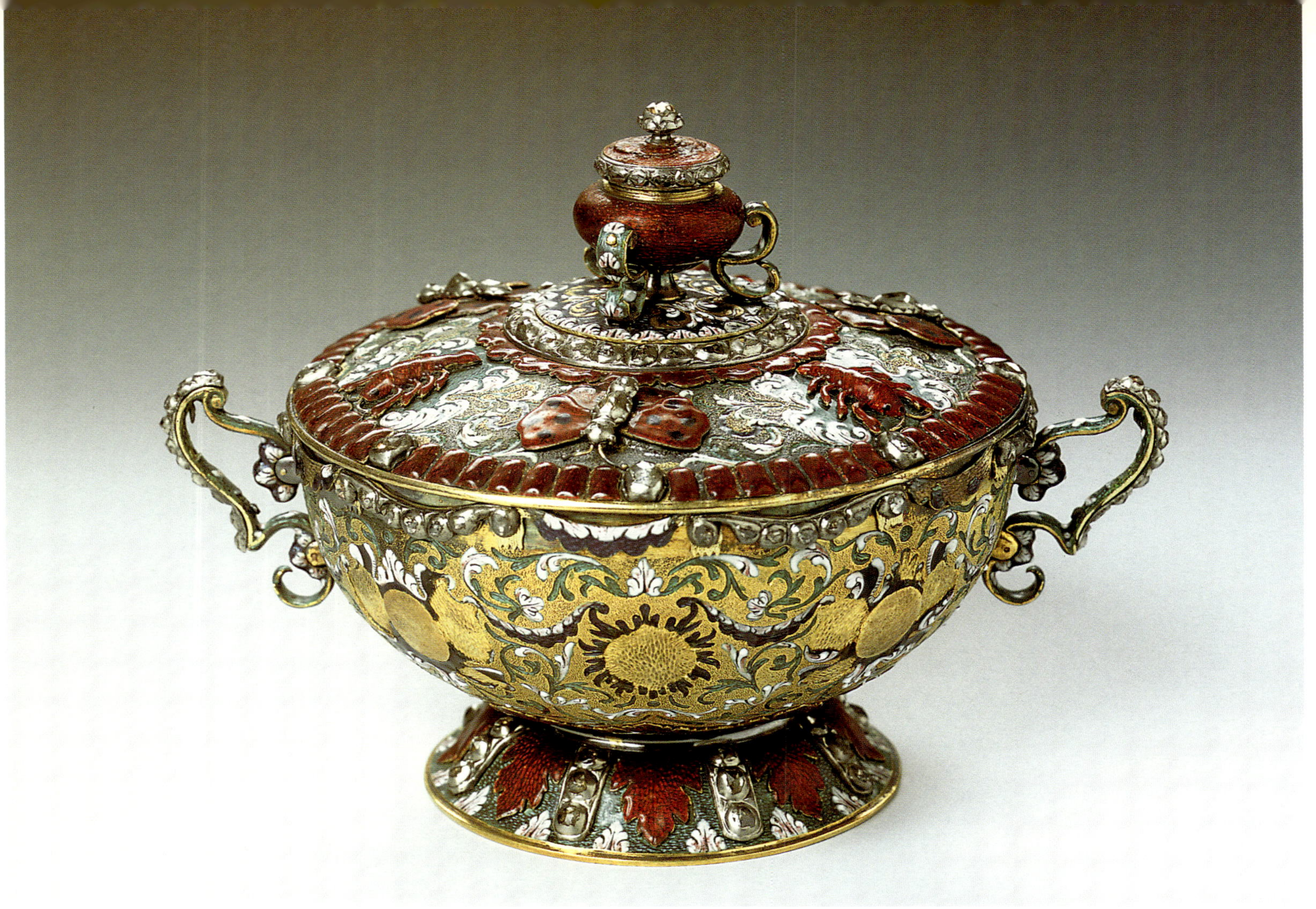

Handled Box with Butterflies and Crabs on its Lid

Gold, enamel, diamonds
Johann Melchior Dinglinger
Dresden, between 1692 and 1695
H. 7 cm, Inv.-no. VI 11

Golden Powder Box

Gold, enamel, diamonds
Johann Melchior Dinglinger
Dresden, between 1701 and 1708
H. 5,7 cm, Inv.-no. VI 8 t

Saint George Fighting the Dragon, Treasure from the English Order of the Garter

Gold, enamel, diamonds, emeralds, rubies
Johann Melchior Dinglinger
Dresden, between 1692 and 1694
H. 9,5 cm, Inv.-no. VIII 266

The arrival of Johann Melchior Dinglinger (1664 – 1731) in Dresden established the Saxon residence's leading position for the art of the goldsmiths within Europe. Within a few years, the goldsmith-artist – originally from the Swabian town of Biberach – created jewelry that counts among the most accomplished works created during the High Baroque era. The first written account documenting the presence of Johann Melchior is remarkable. In October 1692, he delivered, to the not yet ruling Duke Friedrich August, a diamond-studded »Gallanterie büchse« (*Gallantry Box*) as well as two golden rings.

Based on the feathery acanthus ornament, the red enameled *Handled Box*, whose lid is decorated with crabs and butterflies may be dated only slightly later. A similarly miniature *Lidded Bowl* of Dinglinger's with the same date is preserved in the Royal Danish collection in Rosenborg Palace. The tiny, cylindrical *Gold Box*, on the other hand, points to the early years of the 18th century. According to the inventory entry its purpose was to strew, with the aid of a miniature spoon, gold dust onto a letter whose ink was still wet.

Although Johann Melchior Dinglinger is primarily known today as the creator of exemplary cabinet pieces, his early oeuvre encompasses predominantly objects typical of a Late Baroque goldsmith and jeweler. Apart from jewelry, these entail fancy goods, little boxes, smel-

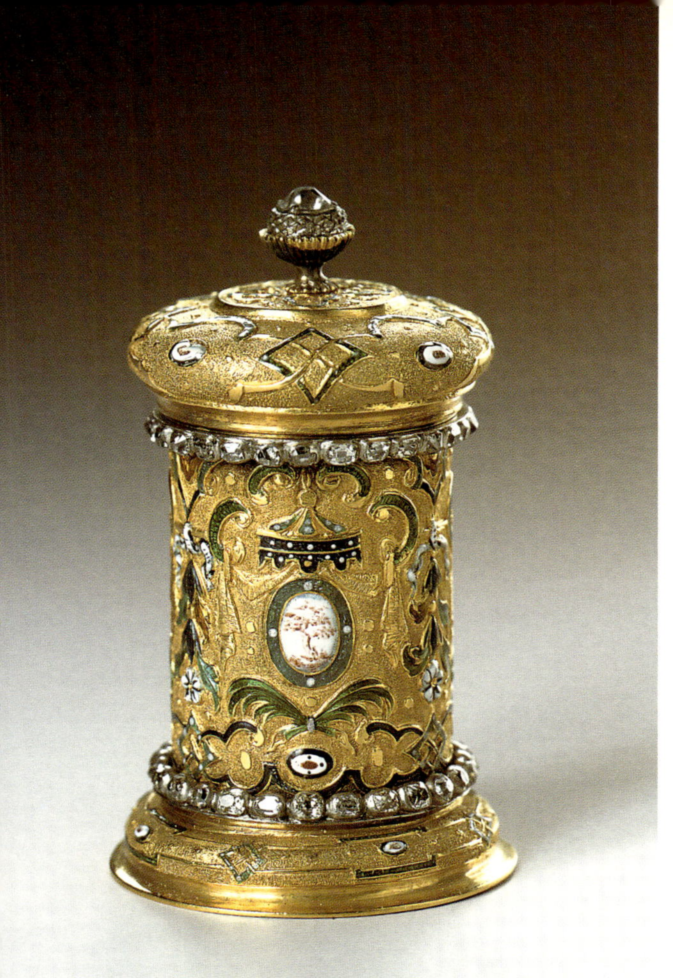

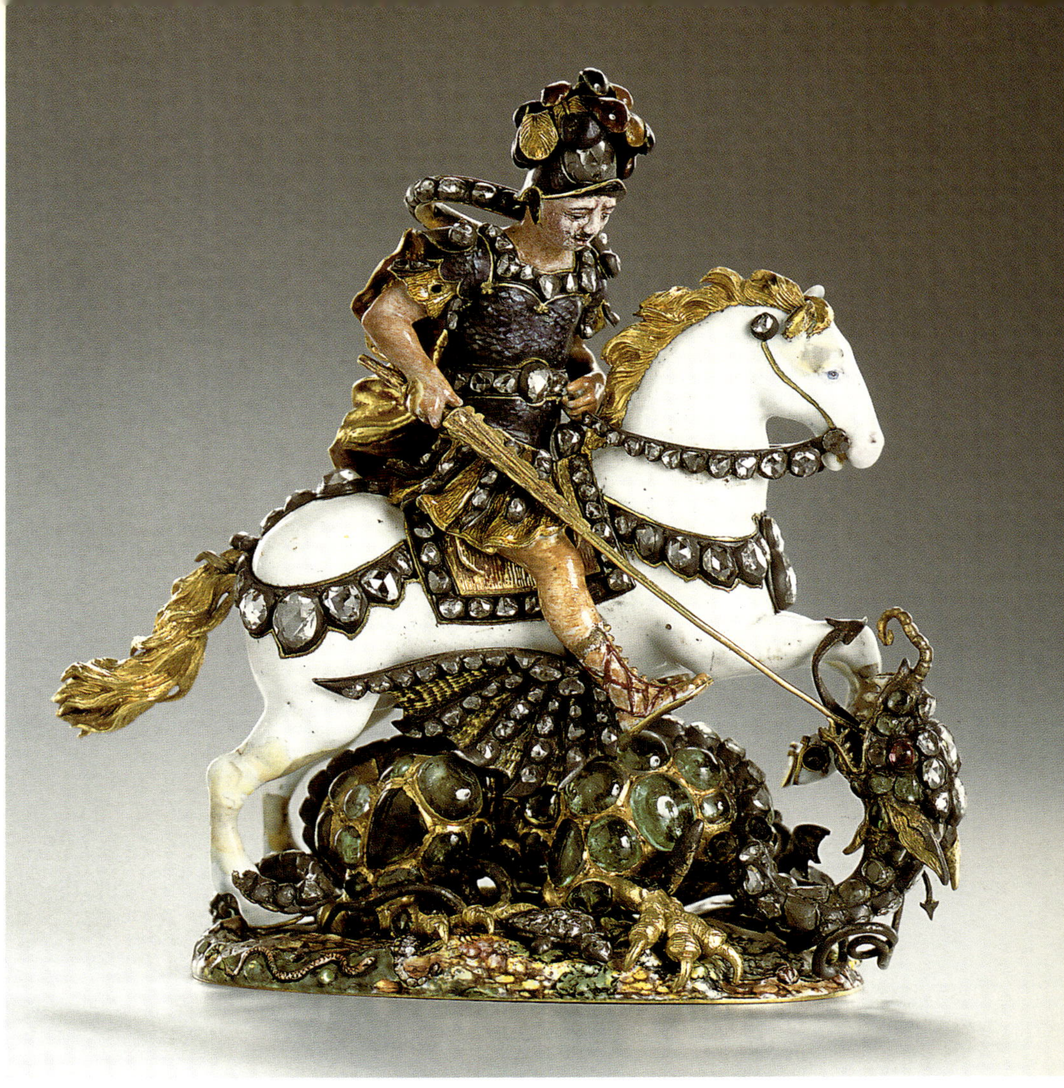

ling bottles, seal and signet holders, and walking stick knobs made of valuable materials. Thanks to their subtle goldsmith's mounts, excellent artisan enameling, elegant outline, and sumptuous diamond trimmings, his works are far superior to those of his contemporaries. Dinglinger's luxury articles were in fact not intended for actual use. Rather, they were collector's items for a princely patron who could appreciate their intelligent designs.

Dinglinger created his first accurately datable piece of jewelry for Johann Georg IV, the older brother of Augustus the Strong. While the small gold enameled statuette of the equestrian *Saint George Battling the Dragon* appears to be an independent work of art, it really is a jewel of the highest English knightly order, a so-called »Greater George.« On January 26, 1693, the prince elector – upon distinguishing himself as a worthy ally of England's in the war against France – was inducted as a knight in the »Order of the Blue Garter Belt« during a festive celebration in Dresden's Residential Palace. Within this context, Dinglinger was commissioned to produce the jewelry. In keeping with the prevailing rules, he portrayed the order's patron in profile on horseback as he energetically attacks the dragon with his lance. In comparison with later works by Dinglinger, the figures appear somewhat heavy-handed. However, the special qualities of his future oeuvre are already apparent when inspecting the individual shapes, such as the vibrating golden cloak, the fancifully armored dragon, or the forest soil enlivened with crawling creatures. The loop with which the artwork could be fastened to the order's blue band, is skillfully hidden behind the helmet's crest. Furthermore, it is characteristic of Dinglinger's jewelry that he understood how to give independent artistic meaning to traditional symbols. The unusual profusion of small diamonds bedecking the decorative emblem, sprinkles the pendant with radiant light effects.

Mercury and Putto

Ivory
Signed Adam Lenckhardt
Vienna, middle of the 17th century
H. 27,5 cm, Inv.-no. II 118

Figure Group of an Abduction of Women

Ivory
Melchior Barthel
Venice, before 1670 or Dresden, between 1670 and 1672
H. 43,7 cm, Inv.-no. II 341

The first half of the 17th century marked the beginning of an ivory sculpture's peak within the Holy Roman Empire. It was carried by a number of particularly mobile artists who adopted and further developed the most novel design ideas originating from Flanders and Italy. Apart from devotional objects intended for religious practice, increasing numbers of small sized collector's items, exhibited solely in the private sphere of art cabinets, began to be produced. By creating these figures, the carvers adapted the image tradition founded during the Renaissance for bronze statuettes that they translated into the formal Baroque language.

Mercury, messenger of the gods, was already a widespread motif during the 16th century. Adam Lenckhardt (1610 – 1661) shows him at the moment when the winged putto puts on his winged shoes. The cunning courier already sports his travel hat (*petasos*) and holds the hero's staff (*caduceus*) in his left hand. With his right index finger, the gorgeous youth points into the direction of heaven, a route he will soon take. In this ivory statuette, Lenckhardt varies a bronze sculpture from a fountain Adriaen de Vries created between 1596 and 1599 for a square, today called Moritzplatz, in the free imperial city of Augsburg. While the large sculpture with its long stride and the body's dynamic turn was indebted to the Mannerist ideal of movement, the small-scale work of Lenckhardt's is based upon the Baroque idea of only having one viewpoint. The body's soft modeling and the velvety shine of its surface are conducive to a collector's pleasurable contemplation.

The artist, born in Würzburg in 1610, began to work for princely patrons upon completing his travels through Italy, and settled down in Vienna in 1637. There, he enjoyed the privilege of a position as tenured court artist from 1642 until 1660, while working as chamber sculptor for Prince Karl Eusebius of Liechtenstein. Although it is still not clear when the *Mercury Statuette* came into Saxon possession, it ought to be noted that during the Baroque period *Mercury* was considered the patron of mining in the electorate of Saxony. In this function, the ancient god could be frequently encountered in 17th century festive processions.

The predilection for ivory statuettes reached back to circa 1600 and was kept up by the 17th century Saxon prince electors. The Green Vault's holdings of ivory testifie to this. In 1670, Prince Elector Johann Georg II even managed to commit the important ivory artist Melchior Barthel to Dresden's court. Prior to his hire, Barthel, born in Dresden in 1625, was active in Venice for many years, where he created his large-scale key works. Yet he already began to produce smaller ivory figures while still in Italy. Melchior Barthel's (1625 – 1672) statuettes in the electoral collection are indebted to the formal canon of antique and Italian Renaissance sculpture. Based on this, Barthel developed a personal style. His dynamic portrayal of an *Abduction of Women* goes back to a large marble group by Giambologna in Florence's *Loggia dei Lanzi*. But the adaptation of the motif is more than a mere literal repetition of an exemplary artwork. Thanks to slight alterations to the postures and mild changes in the theatrical gestures of his three-person group, Barthel managed to produce a discriminating tension. The result was an independent and psychologically developed version that would appear commendable to a princely collector. This ivory group was possibly begun in Venice but completed in Dresden. Only two years after being hired as court sculptor Barthel died in his hometown.

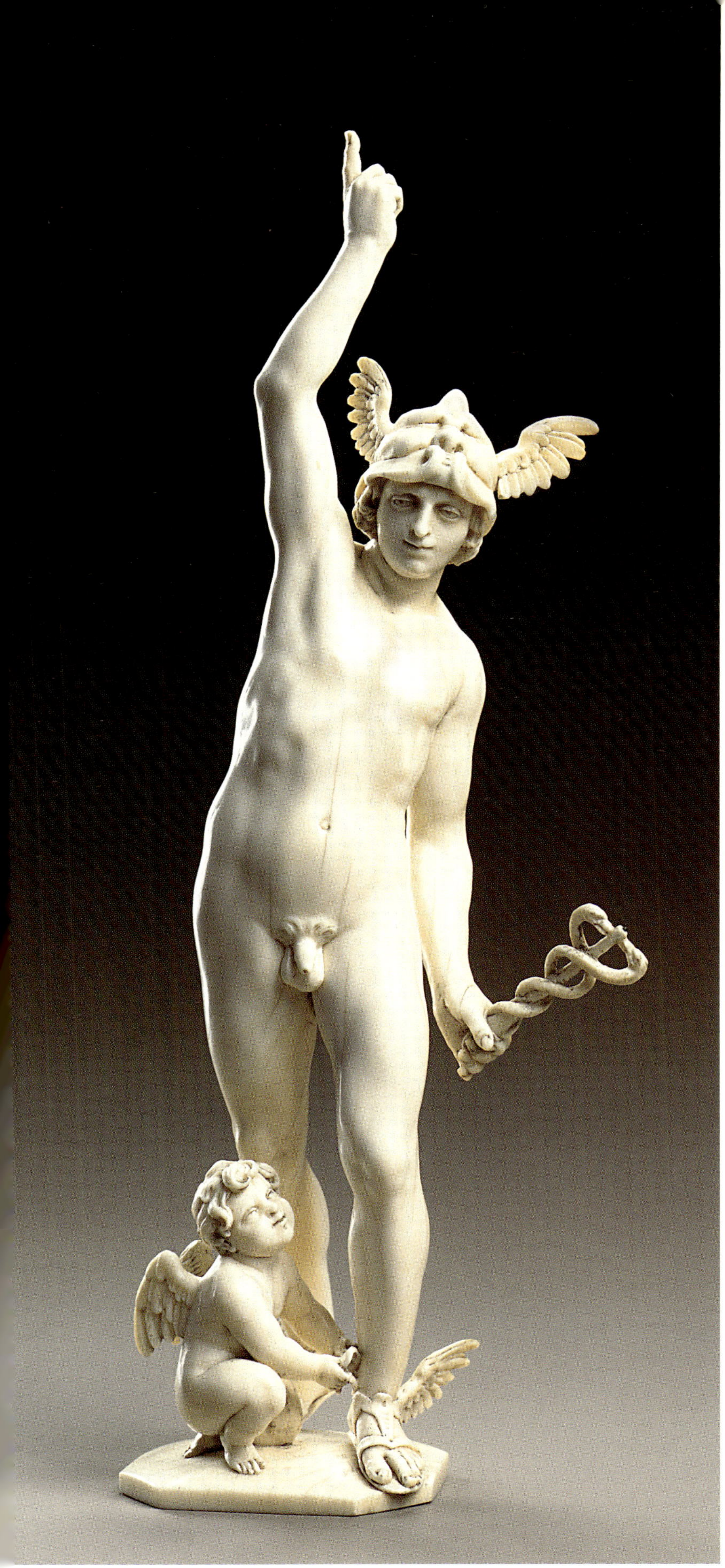

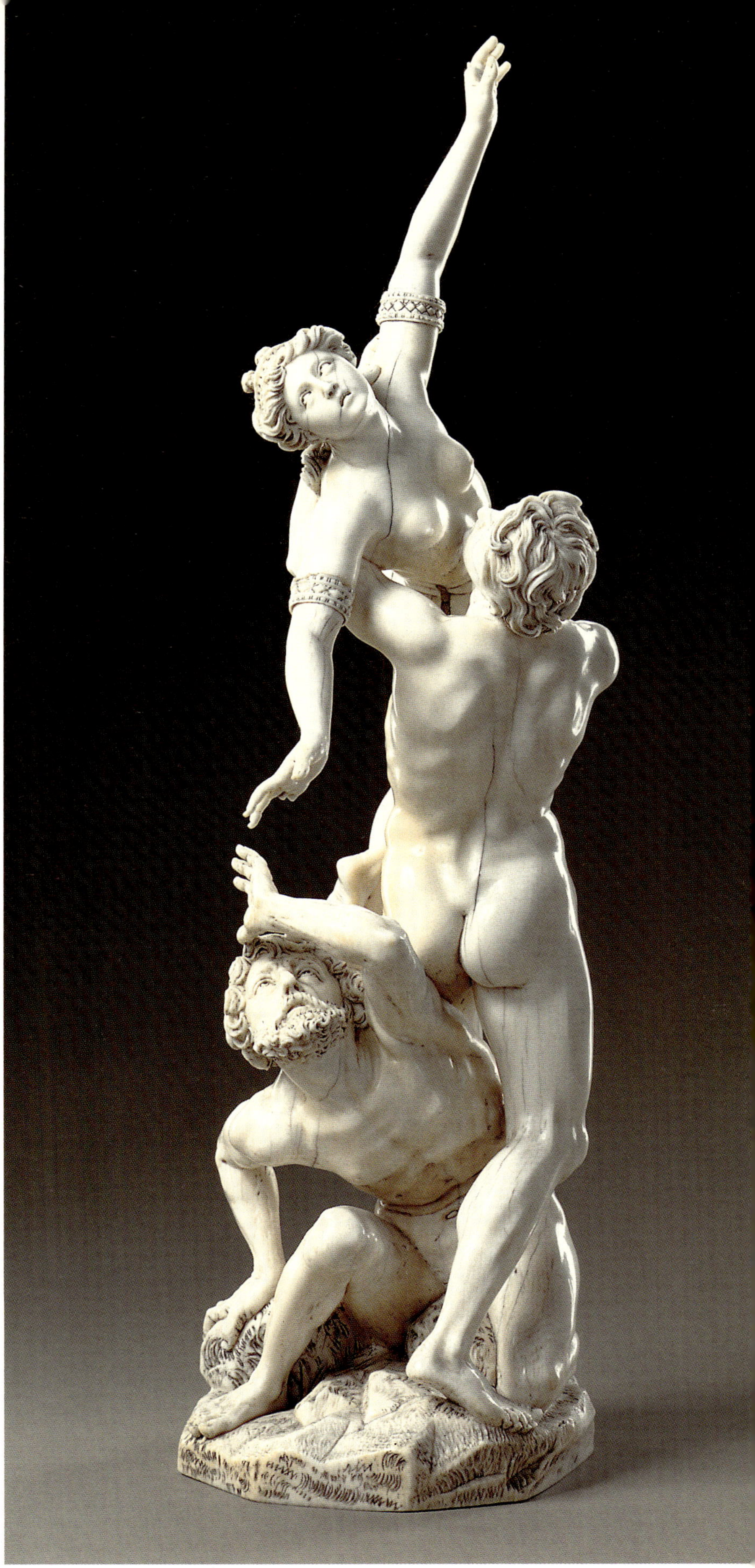

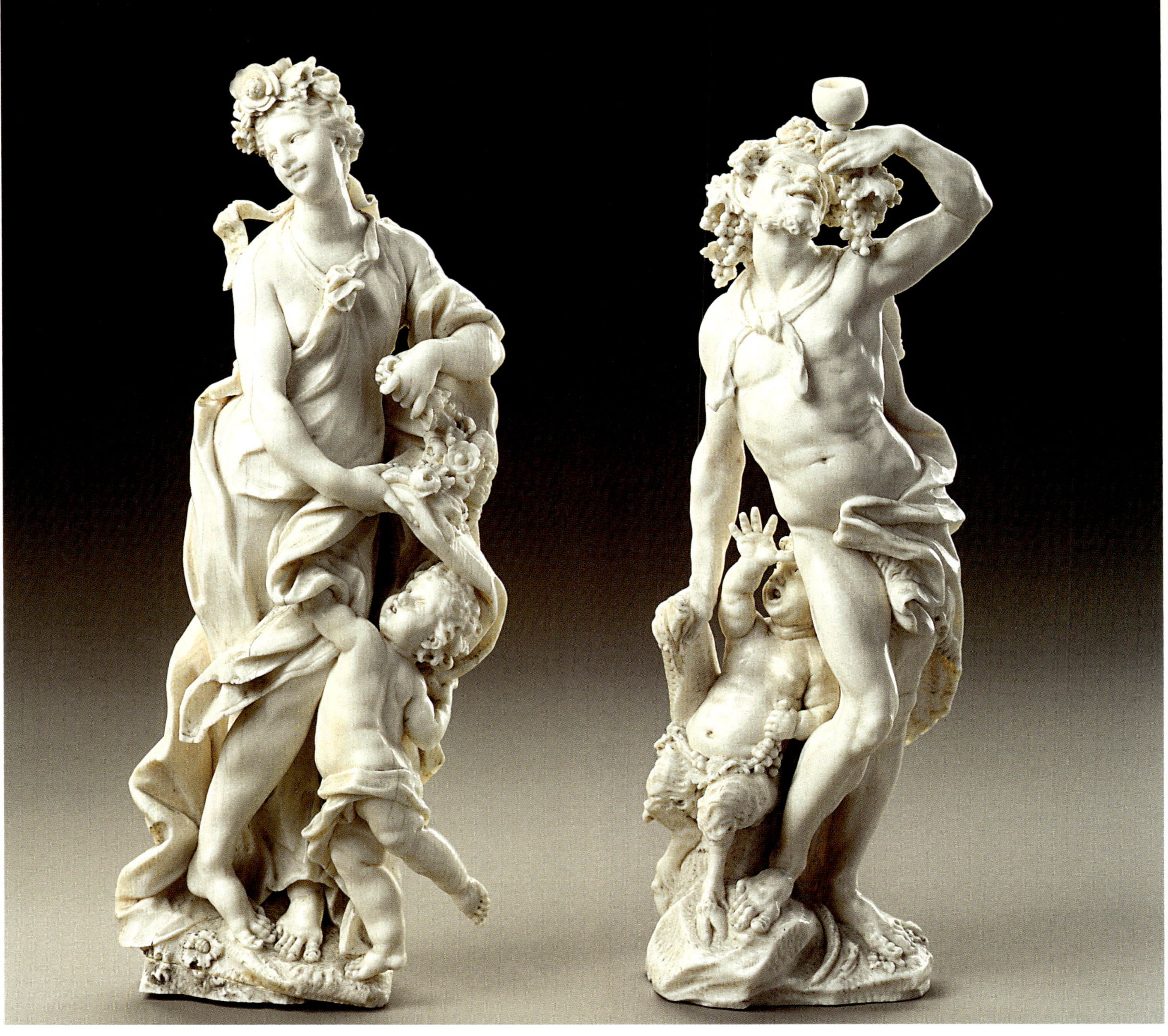

Spring and Fall from the Group of the Four Seasons

Ivory
Balthasar Permoser
Florence or Dresden, between 1685 and 1690
H. each 22,5 cm, Inv.-no. II 45, II 48

Hercules and Omphale

Ivory
Balthasar Permoser
Dresden, shortly after 1700
H. 26 cm, Inv.-no. II 42

Balthasar Permoser (1651 – 1732) was already thirty-nine years old and a successful sculptor in Florence when he began to work for the Saxon Prince Elector Johann Georg III in 1690. It was possibly Duke Friedrich August's brief visit to the Medici residence in the spring of 1689 that contributed to this decision – one that was not to remain without consequences for the further course of art history. When the second-born duke became Augustus the Strong, a forty-year-long, artistically extremely prolific relationship developed between the prince elector-king and the idiosyncratic Bavarian sculptor. During these decades, Permoser created famous sculptures, especially for the Zwinger and Dresden's Large Garden. He had already produced marble sculptures while in Florence, where he also created ivories for the Medici that belong to the genre of treasure art. Among the latter are four cutlery handles with depictions of the *Four Seasons*, today preserved in the Museo degli Argenti in Florence.

The Green Vault's allegorical ivory statuettes of the *Four Seasons* combine Balthasar Permoser's creative early Florentine compositions with his future Dresden creations. The portrayal of *Fall* as a drunken, slightly staggering faun is a direct adaptation of Michelangelo's famous Florentine marble sculpture of *Bacchus*. *Spring* received its shape from the dancing flower goddess Flora, whereas Ceres, goddess of agriculture, represents *Summer*. With the statuette of *Winter*, delineated as a strong old man in ragged clothes, ends the roundelay of blossoming, growth, harvest, and demise.

Each of the four ivories was carved from an approximately ten-inch (23 cm) long portion of tusk. Only *Fall*'s beaker was made from a separate piece. The artist made expert use of the tusk's nature-dictated dimensions, including its slight curvature, for the composition of his figures, lending them harmony and elegance. The statuettes are independent works of art intended for a collector's cabinet. It appears that they were mounted on ebony-veneered pedestals as early as the 18th century, lending them a presence similar to monumental sculptures.

Only a few years later, Balthasar Permoser composed a six-part ivory group signed on the front: »BALTHASAR / PERM: IN. V. F.« The artist thereby marked it as the final version of originally at least five variants of the same motif, of which one further example is likewise preserved in the Green Vault. It was procured from the alchemist Böttger in 1715 for 200 thaler.

Each of the pieces shows the moment when *Hercules* realizes that he is at the mercy of the voluptuous *Omphale*. Due to a divine sentence, the Greek hero was condemned to atone for a murder he committed in rage when he was the Lydian princess' slave. The lithe young woman made the he-man – deprived of his weapons – spin flax and even degraded him to the point of doing women's work. The sighing athlete looks up at *Omphale* with an imploring gaze, while she, appearing superior and amused, is on the verge of pulling the Nemean lion's hide over her nude body. A winged putto plays – like Amor, the god of love – with the hero's gigantic club. Permoser's thrilling composition of the delicate scene has the appearance of a relief with one main presentation side. Thanks to the fully three-dimensional figures, the artist exploits all the possibilities of rendering depth.

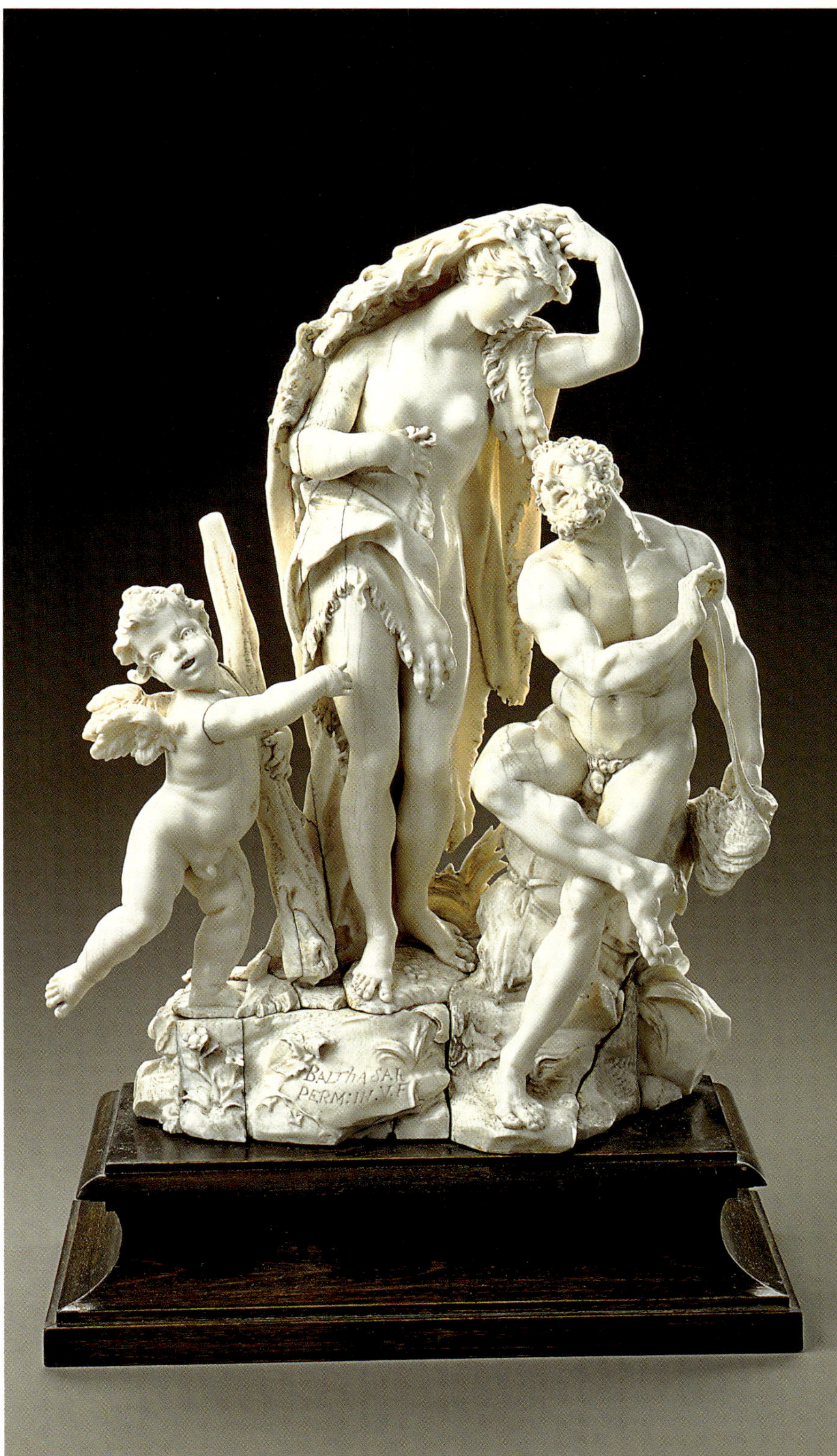

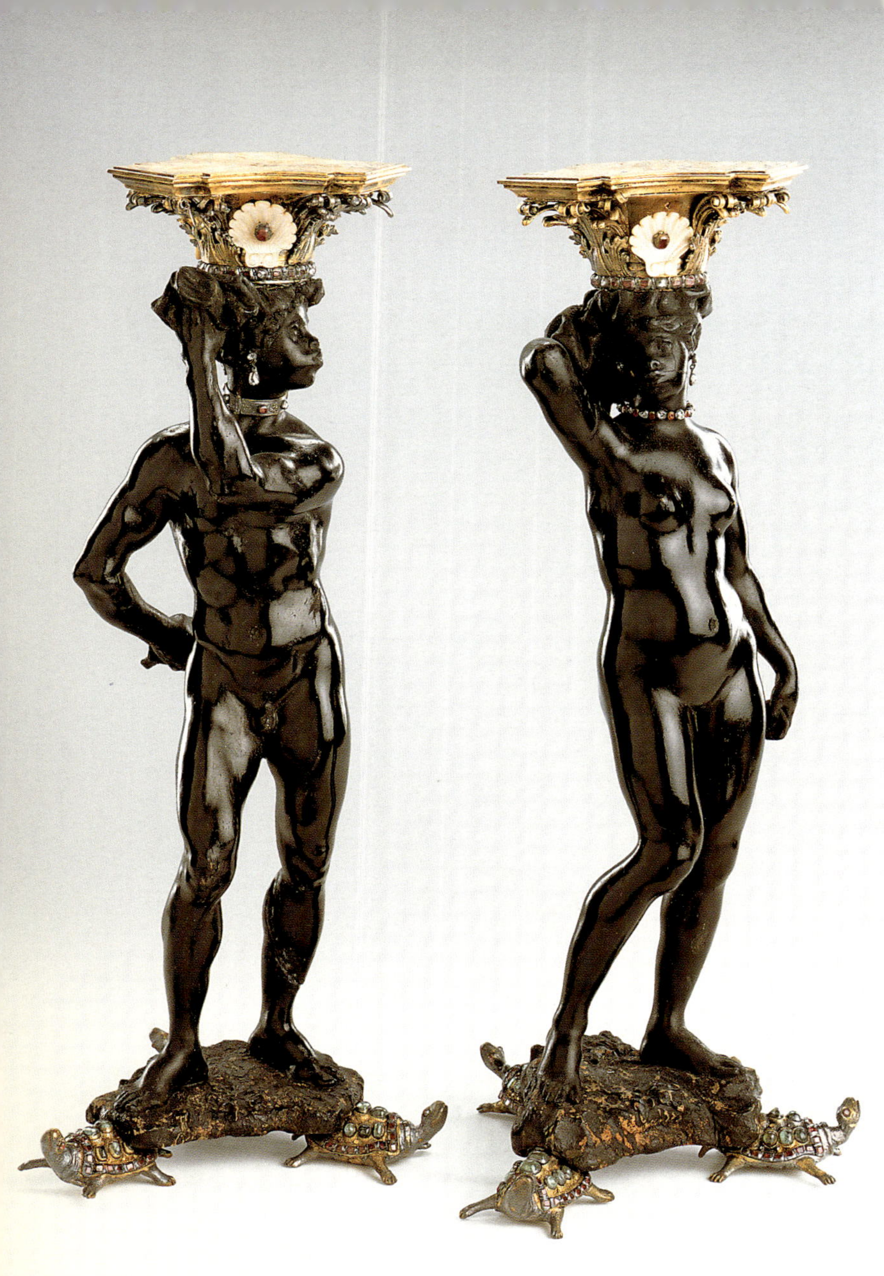

African Couple as Capital Supporters

Pearwood, varnished, silver, partly gilt, mother-of-pearl, emeralds
Balthasar Permoser
Dresden, between 1720 and 1725
H. 33 cm, Inv.-no. IV 153 and IV 165

Two Moors with Bowls made from Monstrous Pearls

Wood, varnished, gold, gilt silver, enamel, rubies, emeralds, diamonds, cameos, pearls, mother-of-pearl
Sculpture: Balthasar Permoser
Mount: Johann Melchior Dinglinger
Dresden, circa 1720
H. 19,4 cm and 20 cm, Inv.-no. VI 90 and VI 95

Permoser began portraying dark-skinned people when he was still working in Florence. The discourse of the exotic unfamiliarity and the sensuous beauty of Africa's inhabitants may be encountered throughout his œuvre. People of color were indeed known at the Saxon court and were integrated into court life. During the 1709 carnival, Augustus the Strong even decided to appear on horseback as king of the Moors and was accompanied by Moors.

From the beginning on, Balthasar Permoser had Dinglinger mount his skillfully delineated »Moors« as collector's items. It appears that the *Two Figures of an Athletic Man and a Well-Rounded Woman* – their entire aesthetic focus is the beautiful body – were made between 1720 and 1725. The figures each stand on a soil step that is supported by tortoises, while they lift the composite capital with ease and engage in a subtle dialogue through the movement of their bodies. Whereas the *Man*, arm loosely pressed into his hips, steps forward in a self-assured stride, the *Woman* turns toward him, as if dancing, with her right arm lifted upward. The sculptor's admiration for natural beauty and easily flowing movement are particularly apparent in this couple who bear resemblance to depictions of Adam and Eve.

In the early part of the 18th century, larger support figures with so-called Moor pillars served as side tables (*gueridons*) on which candlesticks were placed. In this instance, Permoser scaled the pair down to the point where they could no longer be utilized and thus elevated them to the rank of independent works of art.

His most famous rendition of a dark-skinned individual is his *Moor with an Emerald Step* of circa 1723, to which Augustus the Strong allotted a particular place in his Treasury Museum. Together with the *Moor with the Landsteinstufe*, it was displayed in the Jewel Room as a symbol of the world's foreign and domestic riches. The slender contours of two Native American (»Indian«) *Princes* who present knobby pieces of mother-of-pearl are related to the two *Large Moors* both thematically and formally. As both figures are on the verge of a spontaneous, fluid movement, they turn toward each other diagonally. While appearing to stride in a certain amount of haste, they simultaneously turn backwards. After their completion in about 1720, Dinglinger made minuscule, fine body jewelry for them from gold, silver, and precious stones. The body adornments are similar to those displayed by the slightly later and larger statuettes; their common prototype was a late-16th-century copperplate engraving depicting Native Americans from the Florida area. As objects found along the North American Gulf Coast, the monstrous pearl bowls make an appropriate iconographic match with their bearers – more so than in the case of their larger cousins from the ore steps. The *Carriers of Pearls*, intended for Augustus the Strong's collection of precious objects, were mounted on prudently prepared pedestals, comparable to similar ones furnished by Dinglinger and Köhler for other objects from the collection.

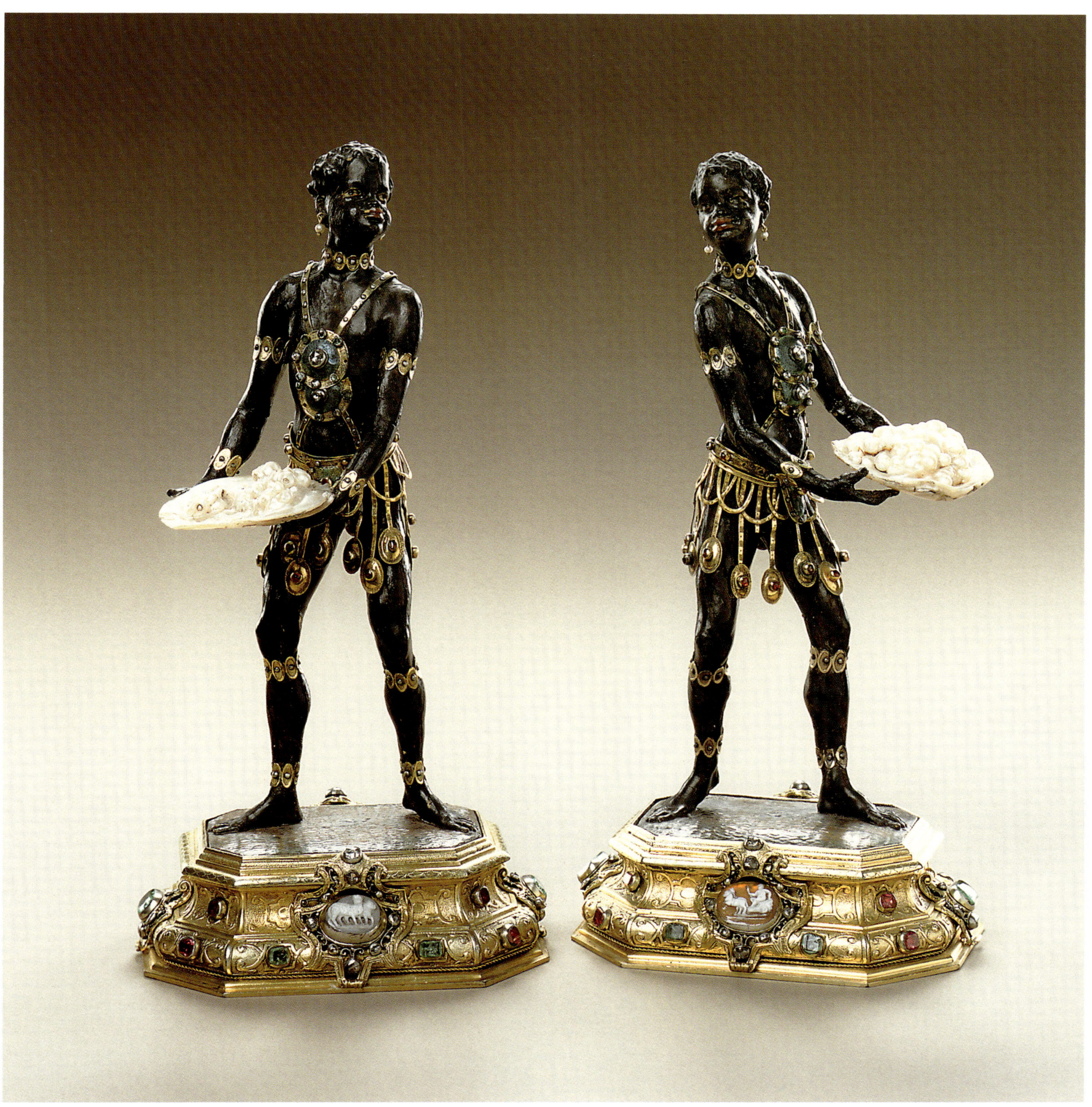

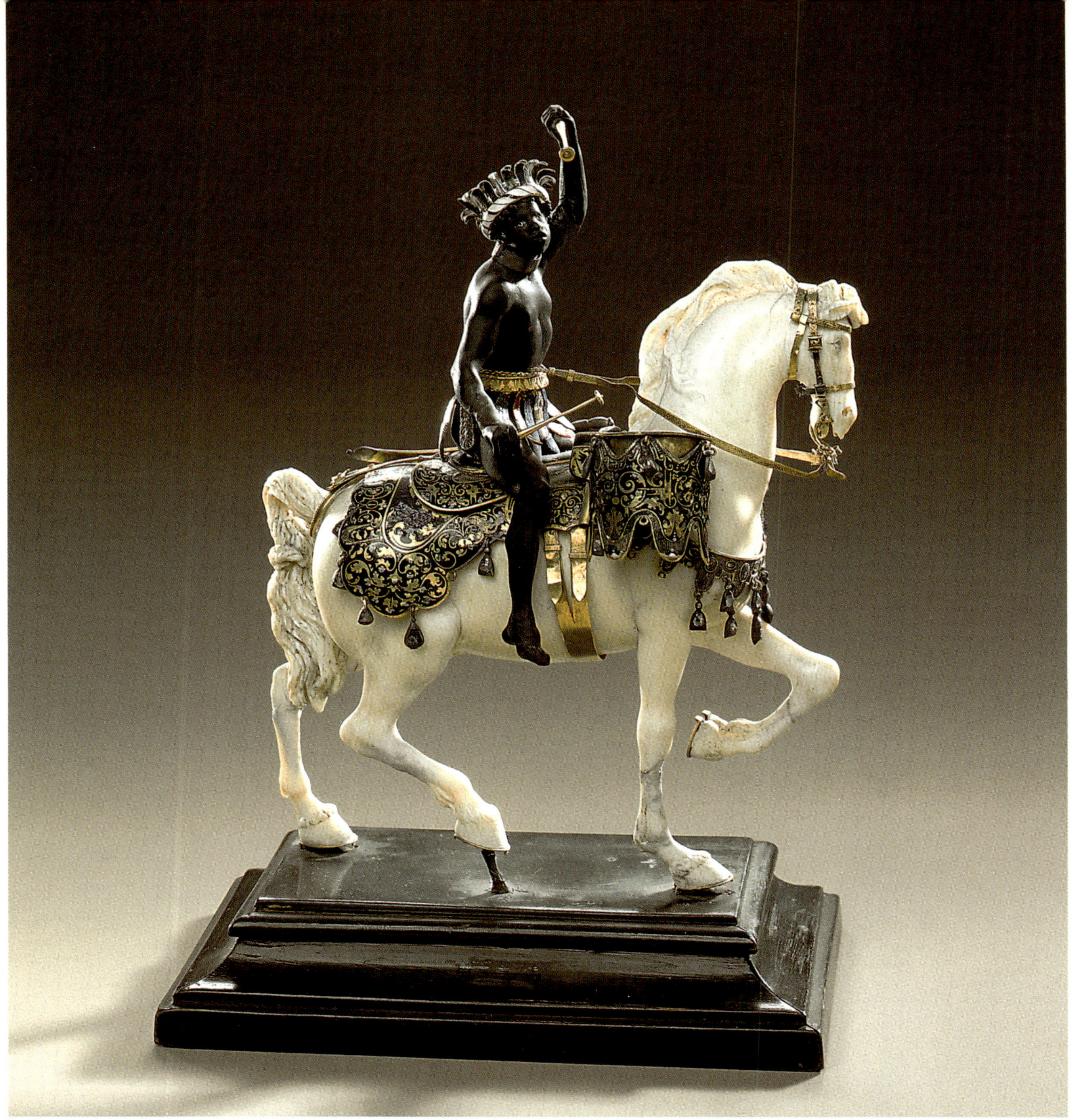

African Rider as Drummer

Wood, varnished, ivory, gold, enamel, precious stones
Sculpture: Balthasar Permoser
Mount: Johann Melchior Dinglinger
Dresden, between 1695 and 1700
H. 17,2 cm, Inv.-no. VI 193

Cabinet Piece in the Form of a Display Wall with Tea Service

Gilt silver, enamel, diamonds, glass paste
Presumably Dresden, between 1694 and 1697
H. 14,8 cm, W. 10,7 cm, Inv.-no. VI 133

It is assumed that the productive collaboration between the court sculptor Permoser and the jeweler Dinglinger began shortly before 1700 with *Two Small Black Ebony Warriors*. They are the earliest figures of this type that Permoser created in Dresden. The pair consists of barely four-inch (10 cm) high black Africans, one of whom has just shot an arrow whose course he observes, while the other one enthusiastically waves his bow. Permoser cites the same theme of ephemeral movement in a *Pair of African Musicians on Gray Ivory Horses*. Whereas the ethnographic depiction of the *Warriors with Bows* goes back to a 1692 engraving by Bodeneck, the two *Black Men on Horseback* cites a contemporary topic from the realm of the Saxon court. In general, the kettle-drummer and trumpeter belong to any Baroque prince's class-appropriate procession. The number who would appear on festive occasions was specifically defined and was dependent upon the sovereign's rank. In the courtly order, these highly paid musicians occupied the first position. The *Black Drummer*, who rhythmically beats his kettle-drum, was carefully equipped by Dinglinger with a highly precise and minutely shaped instrument, weapons, and riding gear. The jeweler produced the little sculpture to be viewed from close-up. Its multi-layered execution only becomes apparent when the pieces are picked up. Augustus the Strong was very fond of intimate encounters with miniature works of art that take on the character of jewels. This principle also determined the design of the *Golden Coffee Service* and the *Grand Mogul's Throne*. Consequently, both groups – with their diminutive, finely worked and outfitted Moor statuettes and dated to about 1700 – could conceivably have inspired the detailed and multi-figure *Grand Mogul* ensemble.

A little *Cabinet Piece* formerly owned by Augustus the Strong proves that the type of interior architecture created in the Green Vault between 1723 and 1729 had been generally known in Dresden for decades. The object is a *Display Wall* on whose protruding consoles an enameled *Tea Service* was exhibited. Augustus the Strong first encountered this accentuated type of presenting works of art in 1687/88 while sojourning in Versailles as a young duke. Bronze statuettes and precious stone vessels were displayed on consoles before mirrored walls in the *petite galerie*, finished two years earlier, and in the *cabinet du conseil*. Both spaces, still extant today, belonged to Louis XIV's chambers, to which only a select group of visitors was permitted access.

The artwork, reflecting an exhibition manner preferred by the French king, was presumably created in Dresden for Augustus the Strong and is crowned by an electoral hat. This means that it could only be dated between 1694 and 1697, because once he was crowned king of Poland-Lithuania, Augustus the Strong always used the crown to indicate his territories. The *Cabinet Piece* with its future references already belonged to the sovereign prior to 1705: It is included in a list of the prince elector-king's first collection of precious objects. Although the goldsmith who made the sumptuously displayed *State Service* remains unidentified, it was only a few years later that it was perfected to the level of royal splendor by Dinglinger's *Golden Coffee Service*.

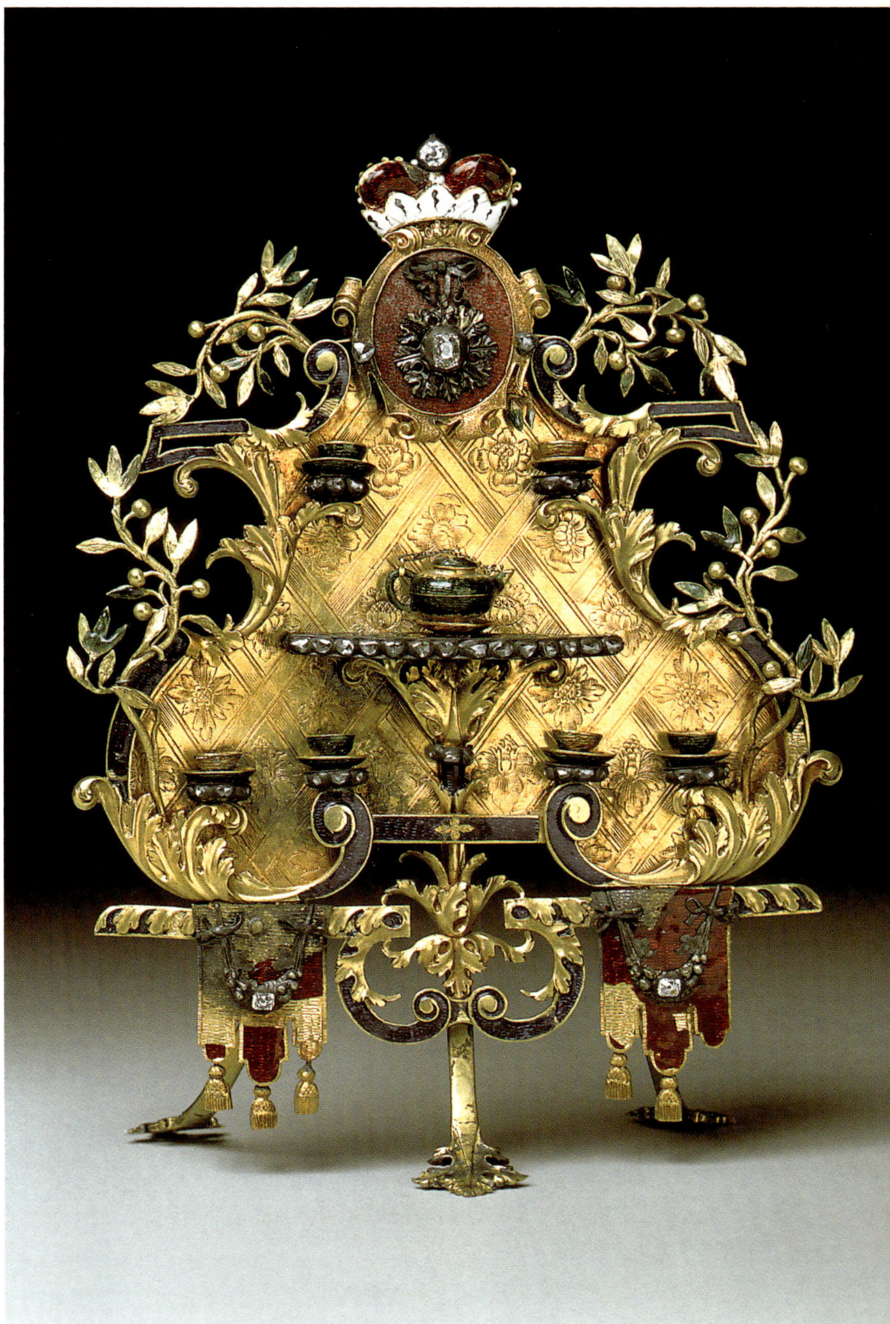

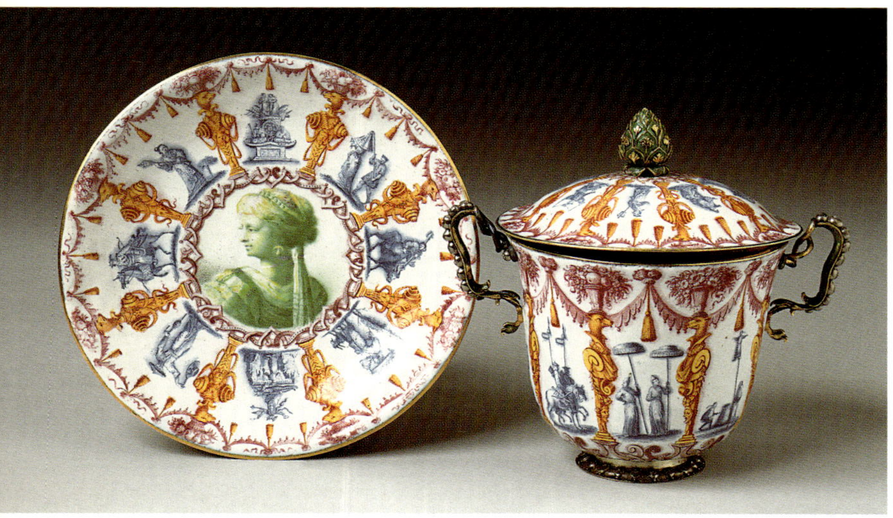

Golden Coffee Service

Wood core, gold, silver gilt, precious stones, enamel, ivory, iron
Design and goldsmith's work: Johann Melchior Dinglinger
Enamel painting: Georg Friedrich Dinglinger
Ivory sculptures: presumably Paul Heermann
Dresden, 1697 until 1701
H. 96 cm, W. 76 cm, Inv.-no. VIII 203

In June 1698, Augustus the Strong promoted Johann Melchior Dinglinger to the position of court jeweler »um seiner bis daher geleisteten untertänigsten treuen Aufwartung, auch gelieferten fleihsigen Arbeit willen« i.e. »because of his heretofore diligently and faithfully performed service and also for the sake of the industrious work he delivered.« At this time, the jeweler-artist had just begun to work on the *Golden Coffee Service*. In December 1701, his monarch ordered him »bey verlust Dero hohen Gnade« (at the risk of losing his high grace) to travel to Warsaw with the barely finished ensemble of treasury art in order to present it to him. Without a direct commission, Dinglinger had commenced work on this costly project after the prince elector's coronation as Polish-Lithuanian king, in September 1697. Now, Augustus the Strong accepted the asking price of 50,000 thaler for the »Coffe-Zeug von gold mit mehr denn 5600 Diamanten, nebst vielen Colerten steinen« i.e. »Golden Coffee Service« embellished »with more than 5,600 diamonds and many colored stones.« The passionate collector thus purchased a singular and at the same time prestigious work that established a royal standard for his cabinet of precious objects.

The *Service* consists of forty-five vessels arranged in five planes on a pyramidal centerpiece, whose central level is surrounded by four ivory figures, presumably made by court sculptor Paul Heermann. Representing the ancient deities Neptune and Ceres as well as Mercury and Minerva, they also symbolize the four elements and determine the *Service*'s iconography: The gods assigned to the respective cups, saucers, slop bowls, trays, and glass phials show symbols and mythological scenes referring to the elements fire, water, earth, and air, rendered in painted enamel, glass cutting techniques, and as ivory figures. The strong-colored small cups consist of golden bodies carefully enrobed on all sides by Georg Friedrich Dinglinger's masterful hand. On the narrow sides of the *Coffee Service*, two lidded cups with handles and white ground can be seen, their walls decorated with Far Eastern motifs. These are among the earliest examples of the European China fashion. A little over a decade before Böttger's invention of European hard-paste porcelain in Dresden, these gold enamel vessels reveal Augustus the Strong's desire for the capability of producing his own porcelain.

The other preciously executed containers, such as the crowning ewer with its dragon handle and the two display vessels with lids, or the sugar boxes decorated with swans, are also made of pure gold. They are likewise covered with diamonds, lending the items – most particularly under flickering candlelight – radiant light reflections.

Dinglinger's *Coffezeugk* was an innovative artwork on numerous counts. It marks the beginning of state services that began to be produced during the 18th century for European rulers. In addition, it reflects the preference for coffee, tea, and chocolate that emerged just before 1700. However, the vessels' artistry, as well as the application of gold and the gracious ewer would have led to unpleasant experiences had one tried to pour hot drinks. The sumptuous *Coffee Service* is thus a Baroque *Gesamtkunstwerk* par excellence and a ravishing initiation into the Augustan Baroque. As the first mature work of this epoch, it already incorporates characteristics of a style that was in the process of being developed in the realms of applied arts and architecture.

The history of displaying the *Golden Coffee Service* is symptomatic of the relationship its owner maintained with the collection of treasury objects. Due to his first defeats by the Swedes in the Nordic War, Augustus the Strong found himself in a tight spot in 1701. He thus put the magnificence of the *Golden Coffee Service* to practical use and proceeded to impress the Polish nobility with it. Treasury objects always served the prince elector-king as a figurative demonstration of his own claims to power and his rank within society. Although the *Golden Coffee Service* was brought to the electoral Saxon *Kunstkammer* in Dresden's Residential Palace in 1704, it was pawned to Hamburg in 1705 and then released in 1715. By 1725, when the *Golden Coffee Service* had received Dinglinger's finishing touches and taken its present form, it was transferred to the Green Vault and was finally moved, in 1730, to the newly-created Jewel Chamber, where it found a worthy place beside the Saxon-Polish crown treasure.

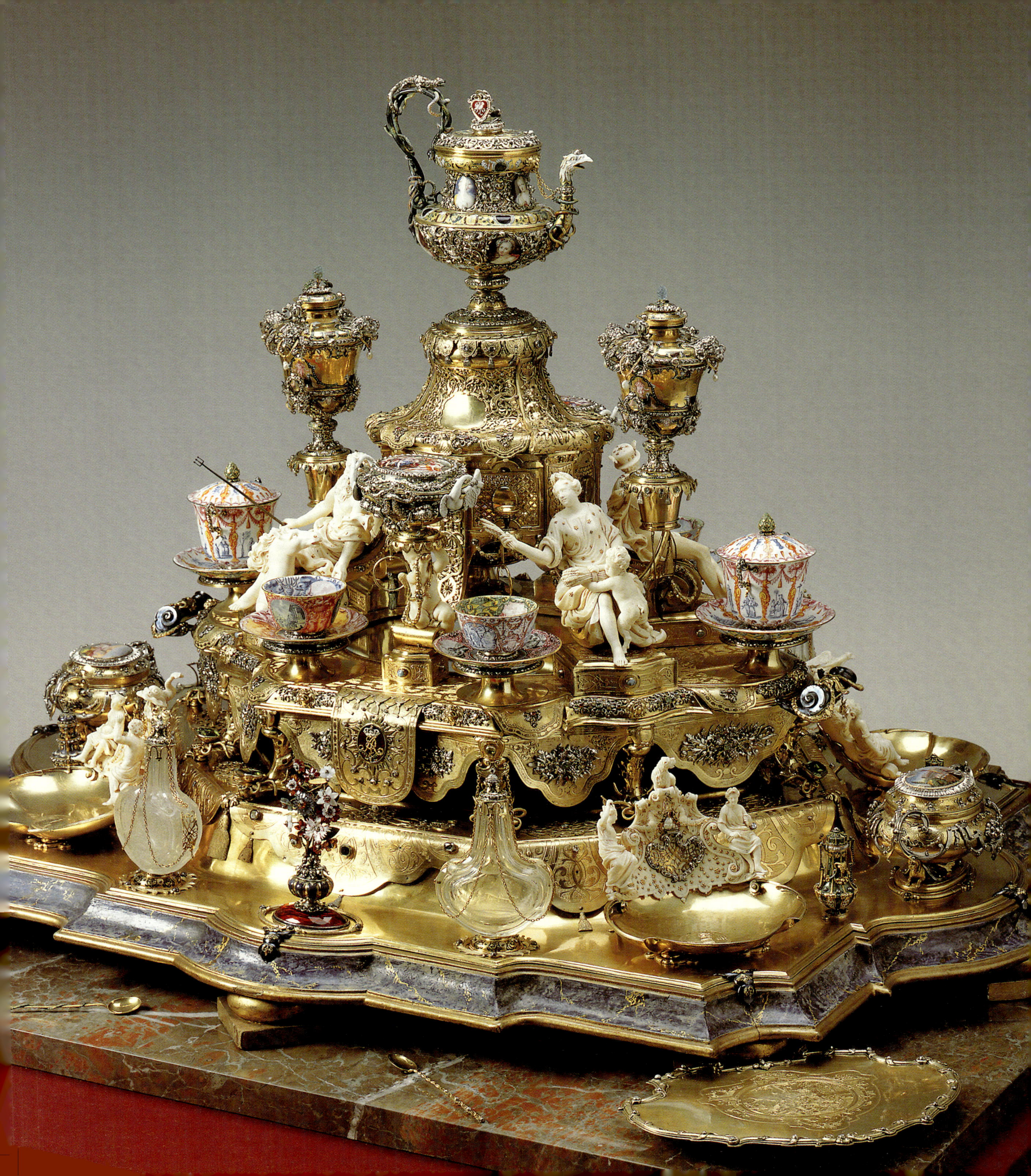

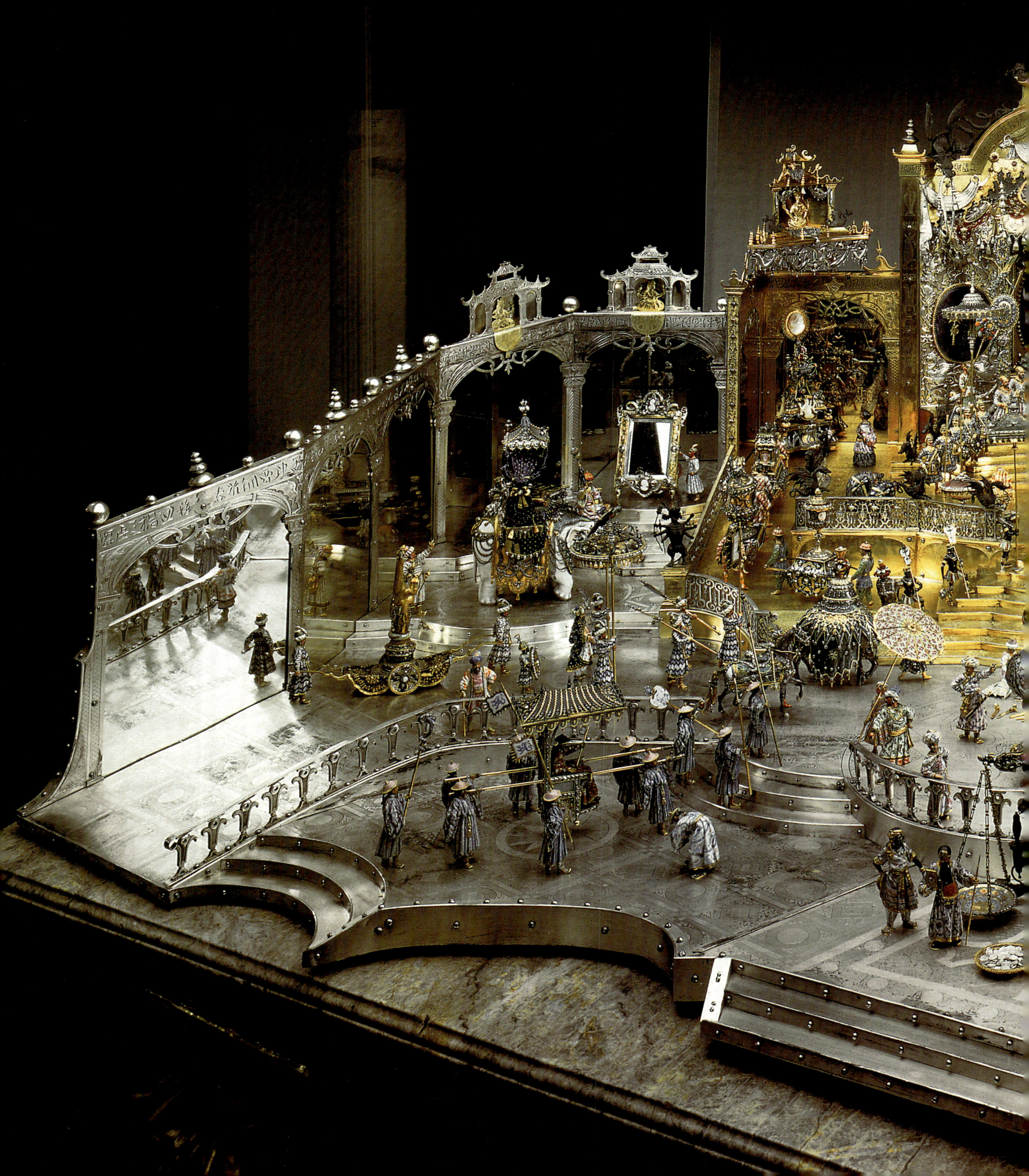

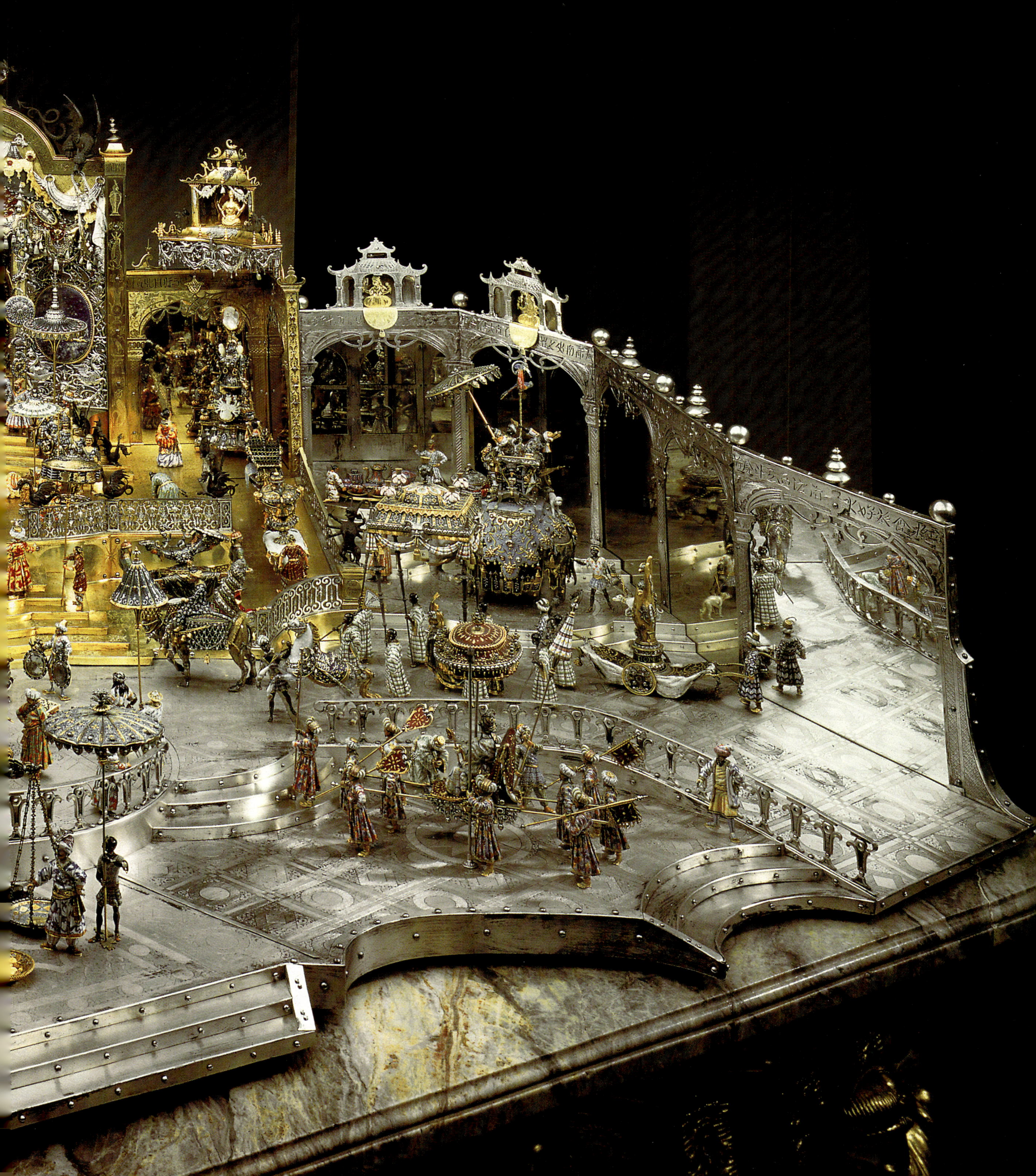

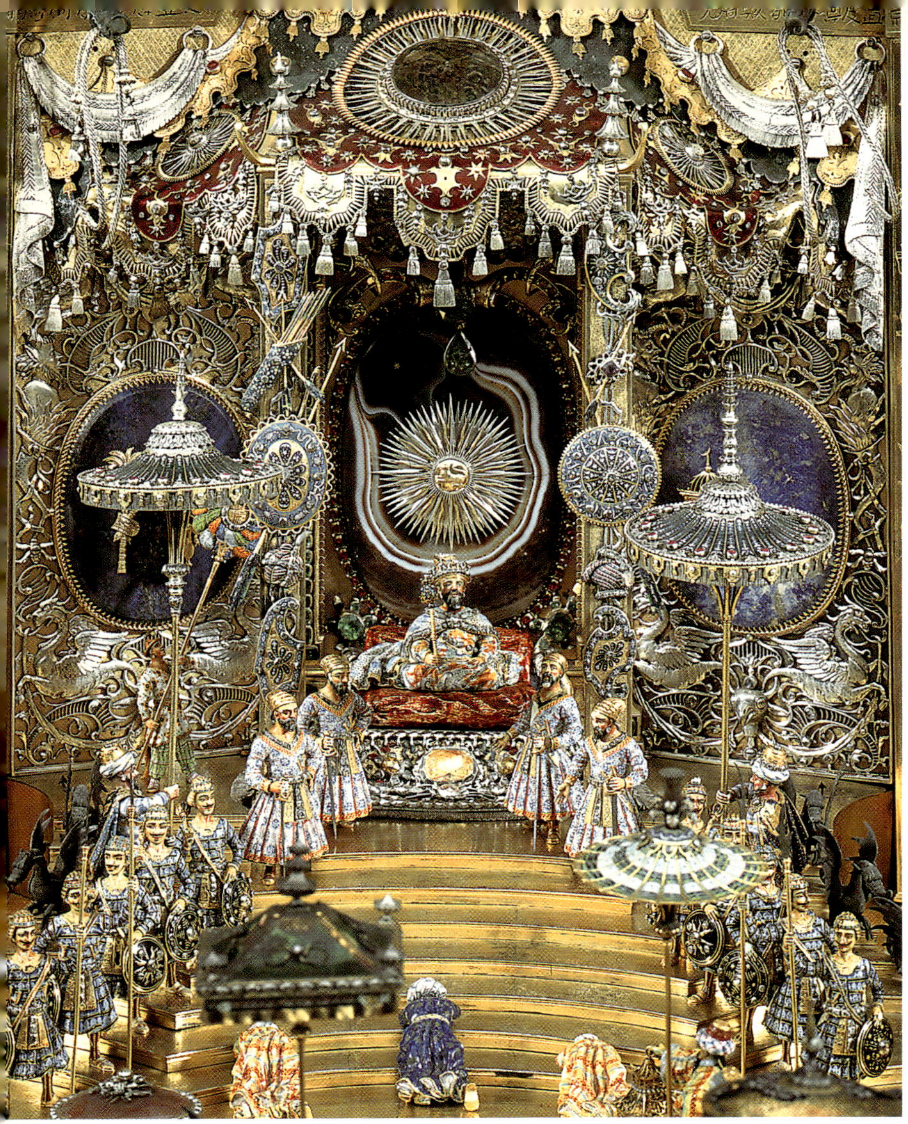

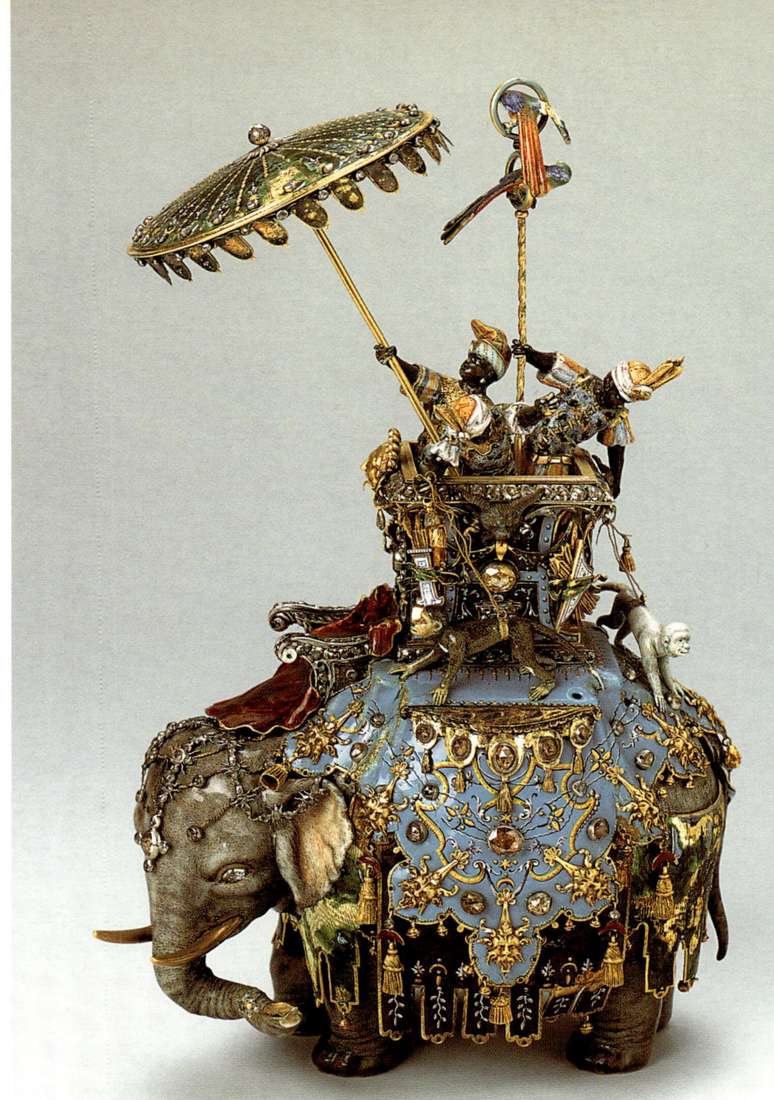

»The Throne of the Grand Mogul Aureng-Zeb«

Wood core, gold, silver, partly gilt, steel, enamel, precious stones, rock crystal, pearls, lacquer
Design: Johann Melchior Dinglinger
Goldsmith's work: Johann Melchior Dinglinger and workshop
Enamel painting: Georg Friedrich Dinglinger
Dresden, 1701 to 1708
H. 58 cm, W. 142 cm, D. 114 cm, Inv.-no. VIII 204

Augustus the Strong's urge to own treasury art objects that were both precious and unique led to his March 1709 acquisition of the *Grand Mogul's Throne* by Johann Melchior Dinglinger. In October 1707, the court jeweler had already invited his most important patron to view the work of which he was convinced that »dergleichen Arbeit noch niehmaln von einen Künstler ist vorgestellt worden, auch nach der Zeit nicht geschehen wird« i. e. »such work had never before been created by an artist and will maybe never be made again.« Dinglinger's assumption was completely justified. The *Grand Mogul's Throne*, as contemporary sources called it, is a chef d'oeuvre of European Baroque goldsmith art. Its overall design is the first extensive document of *Chinoiserie* in Germany. His combination of fashionable interlacing with Far Eastern elements that can easily be applied to organize the surface of objects, Dinglinger helped forge the style of the Dresden Baroque.

Today, the ensemble still consists of 132 figures and thirty-two gift items made of enameled gold. They are arranged on a silver, silver gilt, and gold stage that is conceived as an architectural feature. To this day, the group is placed on the same table that the court sculptor Thomae created for its display in the Green Vault. Between 1701 and 1708, Johann Melchior Dinglinger constructed the palace along with his brothers, the enamel artist Georg Friedrich (1666 – 1720) and the gold worker Georg Christoph (1668 – 1746). Once again, Dinglinger completed the work without a commission, in addition to his daily duties as court jeweler. The king encouraged him in his activity. Today, the opus is still bedecked with 4,909 diamonds, 160 rubies, 164 emeralds, one sapphire, sixteen pearls, and two cameos (391 precious stones and pearls have been lost over the course of its nearly three-hundred-year existence). Ultimately, Dinglinger wrote the prince elector-king an invoice in the amount of 58,485 thaler.

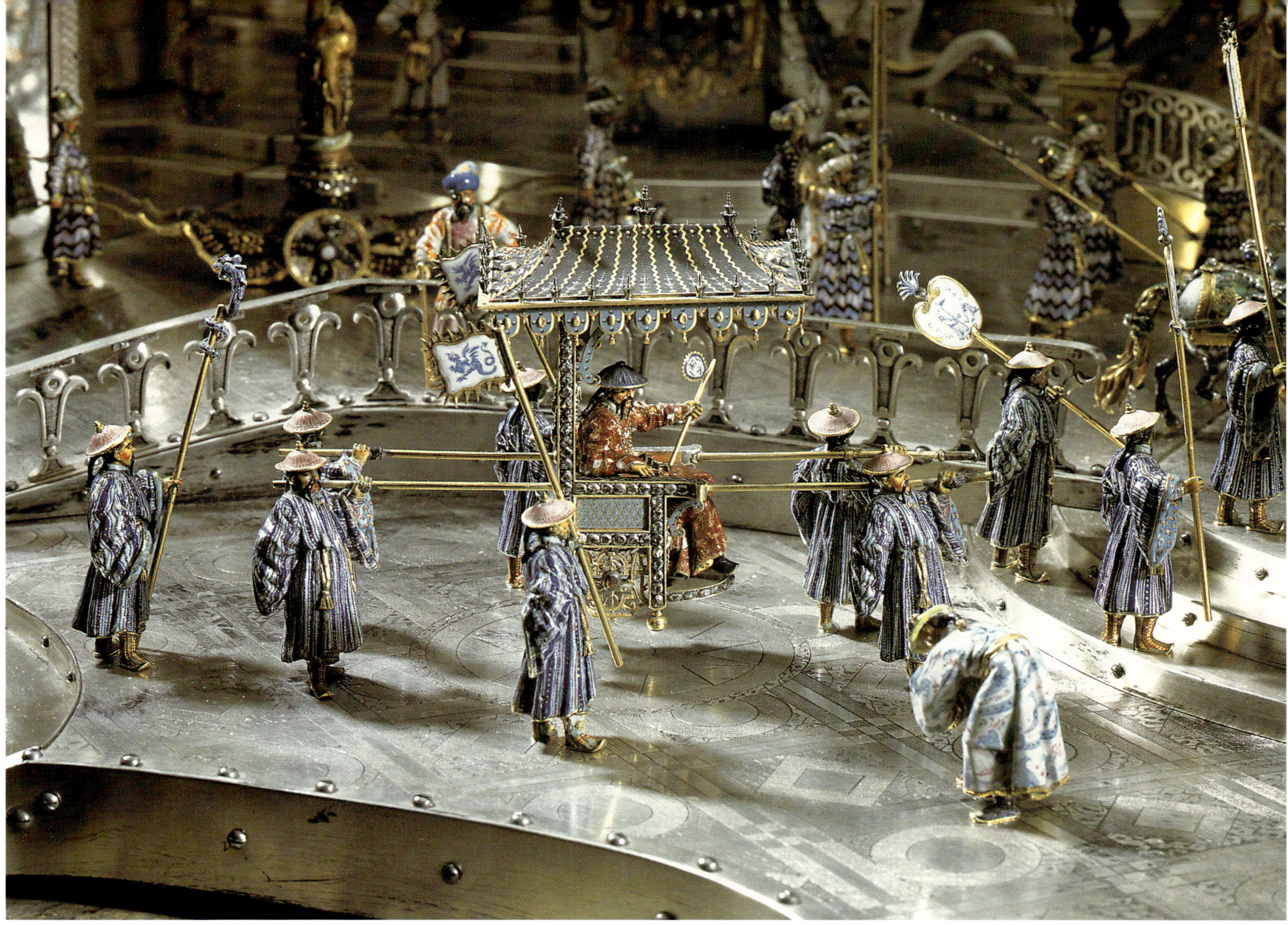

The Grand Mogul Aureng-Zeb, who is depicted, was a famous contemporary of Augustus the Strong who ruled over the Indian subcontinent from 1658 until his death in 1707 at the age of 88. Aureng-Zeb had the world monopoly on diamonds and also commanded over gold mines. His vast, centrally-ruled empire with uncounted riches in spices, ebony, silk, tea, and ivory made him the epitome of an Oriental sovereign in Europe. For Augustus the Strong and his time, Aureng-Zeb represented the zenith of absolutist power and unlimited wealth.

For his portrayal of the regent's exotic splendor – known from descriptions – Dinglinger chose the grand mogul's five-day long birthday celebration which occurred in his capital, Delhi. In order to find the appropriate form, the artist referred primarily to illustrations derived from travel accounts, as well as ethnographic and cultural-historic reports. He thus recreated the festivities with the utmost ethnological precision.

The structure of the stage, that measures more than ten square feet (one square meter), and its three courts corresponds to the palace court as described by travelers. This is also true for the clothing and the figures' postures. Anyone of any importance within the Indian Mogul Empire sought to retain the mogul's kindness through the presentation of gifts. Otherwise, the lingering threats included loss of favor, life, and fortune. Additional gifts were brought by delegations from China, Ethiopia, and Persia. In his choice of presents, Dinglinger combined Far Eastern items and symbols with ancient Egyptian, Chinese, Greek, and even Germanic commodities according to the antiquarian scholarship of his time. Very few of the figures are fastened to the stage and could thus be individually combined. Augustus the Strong, who loved to organize large festivities, certainly valued the liberties granted to him by his goldsmith. Ornaments engraved into the silver sheet do in fact indicate the ideal arrangement for the complex ensemble. Each portion was worked to artistic perfection and is of high aesthetic excellence. The *Cabinet Piece* remained unique and thereby corresponded – in its details and in its broader concept – to the desires Augustus the Strong harbored for his collections. On February 6, 1709 the *Grand Mogul's Throne*, which was too large at the time for the »praetiosen Cabinet« (Cabinet of Precious Objects) located immediately beside the royal chambers, was moved to the state safe in the Green Vault. This instigated a development that culminated in 1729 with the completion of the Augustan Treasury Museum.

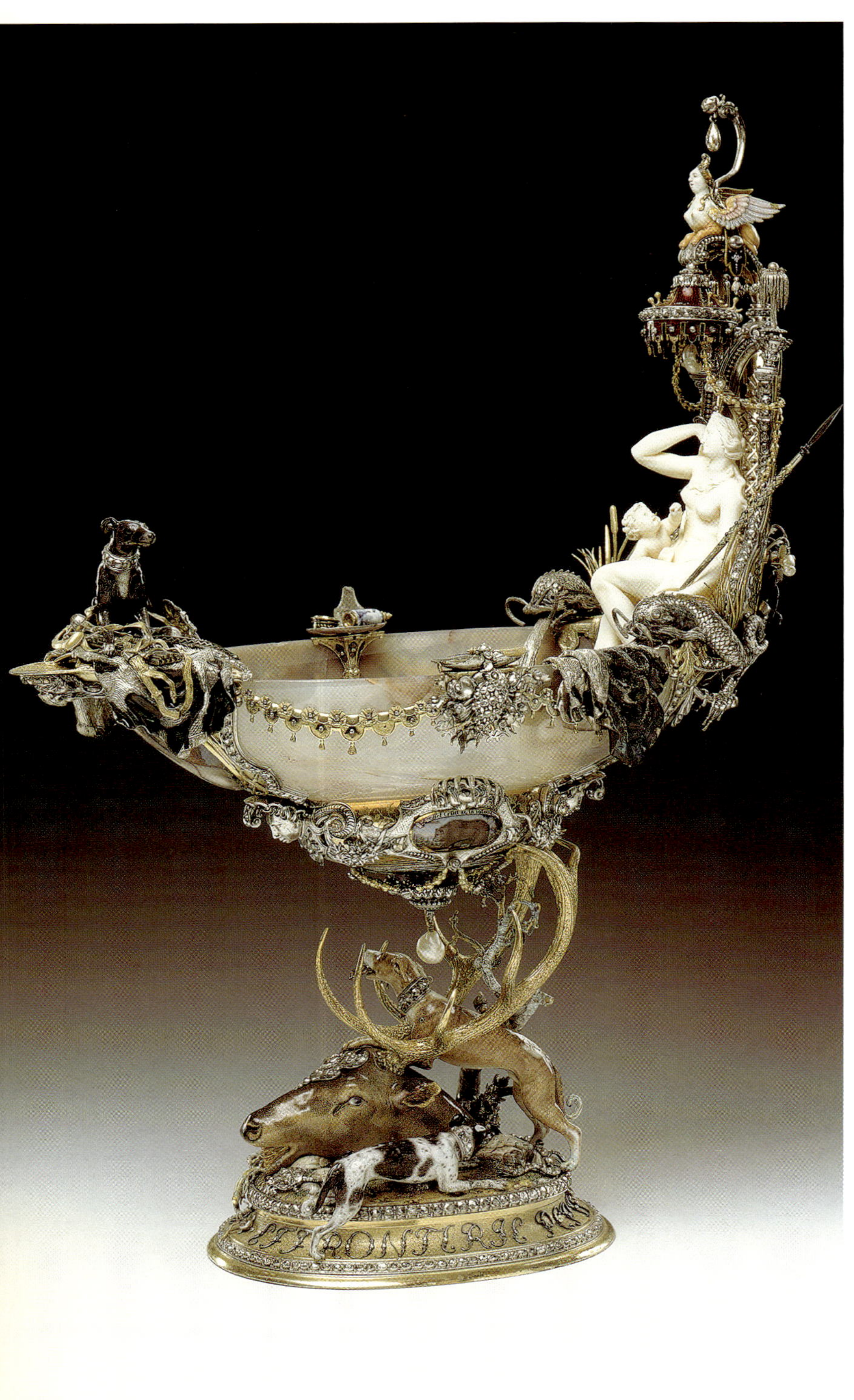

Display Bowl with Diana's Bath

Chalcedony, gold, silver, steel, ivory, diamonds, pearls, enamel
Design and goldsmith's work: Johann Melchior Dinglinger
Enamel painting: Georg Friedrich Dinglinger
Ivory sculpture: Balthasar Permoser
Dresden, before 1704
H. 38 cm, Inv.-no. VIII 305

Goblet with a Female Moor

Rhinoceros horn, gold, silver, enamel, diamonds
Design and goldsmith's work: Johann Melchior Dinglinger
Horn carving: Benjamin Thomae
Enamel painting: Georg Friedrich Dinglinger
Dresden, circa 1709
H. 37 cm, Inv.-no. VI 119

Within the course of a little over a decade, numerous display vessels were produced in the workshop of Johann Melchior Dinglinger that are as extraordinary within the confines of Late Baroque art as the jeweler-artist's large pieces are. The oldest of them, the decorative *Bowl with Diana's Bath*, is so outstanding, that, as a token of his proficiency, Dinglinger had himself portrayed with it.

Balthasar Permoser carved the naturally beautiful and graceful *Diana* from ivory. Together with a putto, she is seated beneath the canopy of a stately throne. Equipped with her hunting spear, the chaste goddess of the hunt prepares for her bath, while silvery water pours from the dolphins' mouths into the light-brown chalcedony bowl. Everything an early-18th-century lady required for her toilette is placed on two tables near the edge. Meanwhile, a wiry black hunting dog keeps a watchful eye on the discarded garments and the weapons of the virgin, whose nudity a shawl only barely covers. *Diana* can feel entirely undisturbed by the onlooker's indiscreet glare, because the head of the hunter Actaeon – who unintentionally saw her bathing – rests on the mossy forest soil at the foot of the bath. Once discovered by the outraged immortal, Actaeon was transformed into a stag that his own hunting dogs then tore to pieces. The legend along the edge of the *Display Vessel*'s foot relates the moral essence of the precious and elegant *Bowl*. There, one reads: DISCRETION SERT EFFRONTERIE PERD (Tact and manners adorn, whereas lack of tact is scorned). In this *Display Bowl*, Johann Melchior Dinglinger set to work with the utmost precision, artistic inspiration, and untamed narrative joy in relating the popular episode derived form Ovid's Metamorphoses. The *Diana Bowl* is also an artistic marvel because it successfully attempts to overcome gravity in a playful manner and achieves this goal: To the spectator, the precious stone *Bowl* with its abundant silver and precious stone ornamentation and its skillfully painted enamel medallions appears to be floating, because it rests on the mighty antlers at only three spots. Augustus the Strong bought this cabinet piece for 8,000 thaler in December 1704.

In February 1714, the Bowl with a *Female Moor-Herme* came into the royal collection for 3,000 thaler. The *Pocal von Renoceros mit der Mohrin* (Goblet from a Rhinoceros with the Female Moor) owes its radiance to the unusually beautiful, subtly erotic horn carving. The fine-limbed female herme carries a dynamically flowing bowl reminiscent of a scallop shell on her head. The carving marvelously overcomes the coarse material of the rhinoceros' horn and is ascribed to Benjamin Thomae, master student and collaborator of Permoser's. Four small painted enamel images on the *Display Bowl*'s foot illustrate incidents from the Jason legend and the search for the golden fleece. Four other enameled medallions on the shaft contain symbols and motti referring to glory and honor. Jason and Medea appear together in an enamel picture on the reverse of the shell. Some of the latter enamels are signed on the back by Georg Friedrich Dinglinger and dated 1708 and 1709.

The *Bowl* was created on the occasion of an important state visit: At the end of May 1709, King Frederic IV of Denmark came to Dresden, in order to negotiate – during extensive festivities – future strategies concerning the Nordic War with his cousin, Augustus the Strong, The themes of Jason's adventurous, heroic act and Greece's most famous warriors, the Argonauts, refer to that warfare. This is also the reason that the squatting dragon in green enamel carries the white jewel of the Danish Order of the Elephant in its jaws. The *Female Moor-Herme* clarifies, once again, the entrepreneurial risk Dinglinger took with his works: Created without an actual commission, its acquisition was entirely left up to the mercy and liquidity of Augustus the Strong. The latter explains why this meaningful *Cabinet Piece* did not enter the royal collections until six years after its completion.

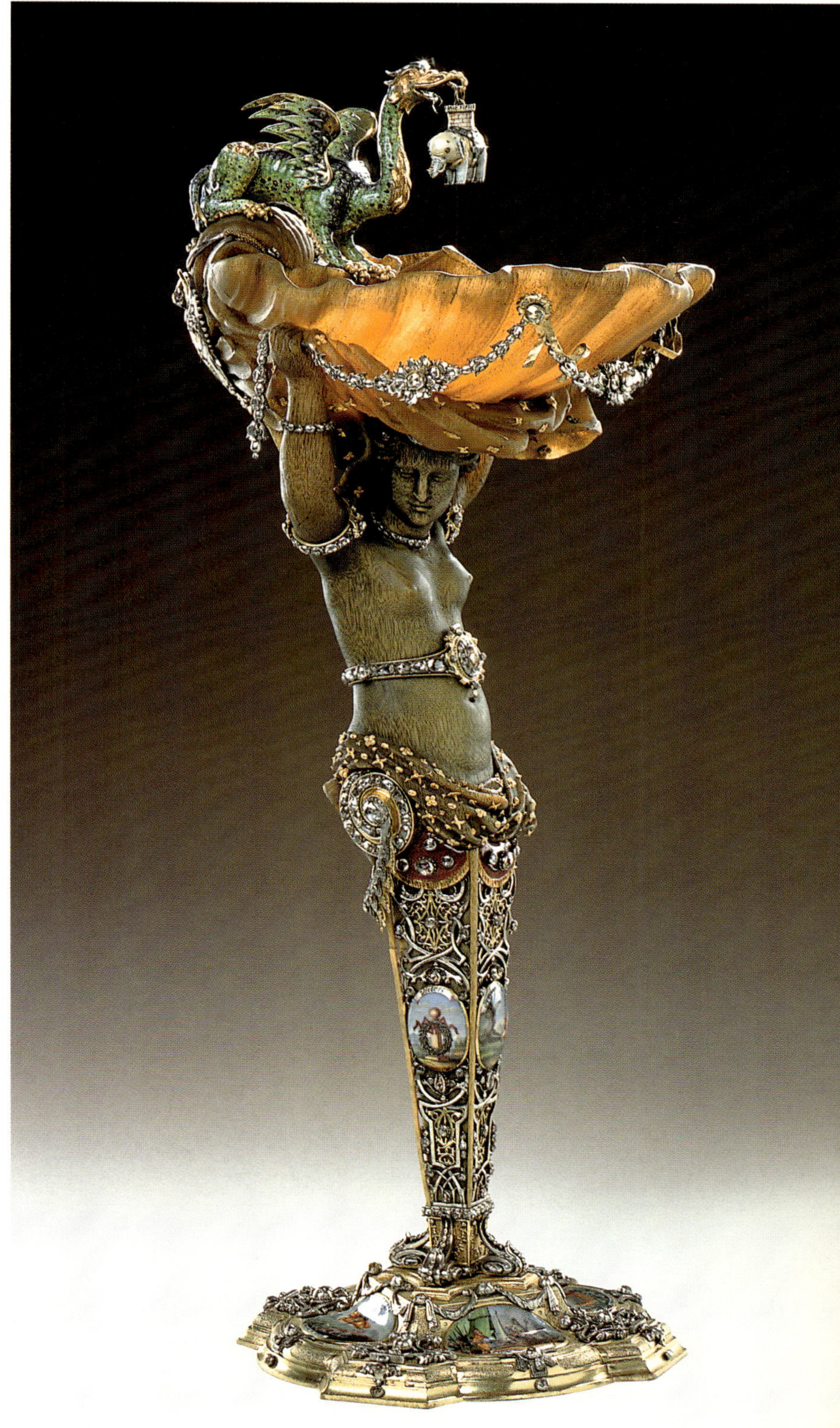

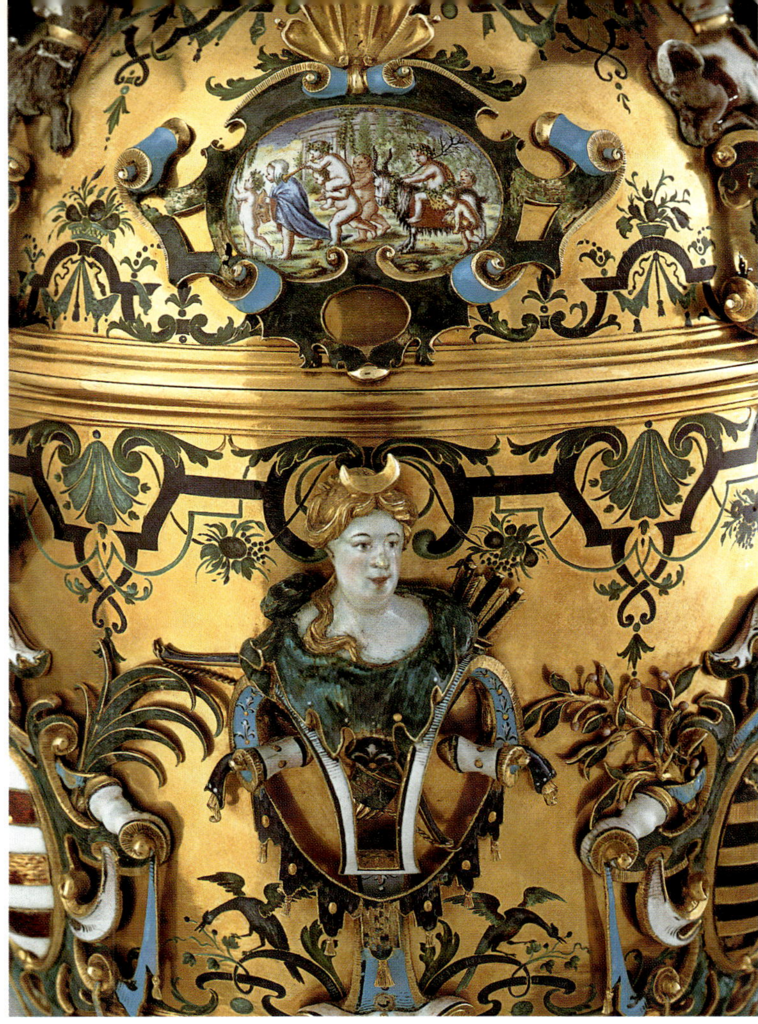

Display Bowl with Children's Bacchanal

Agate, gold, enamel, pearls, diamonds
Design and goldsmith's work: Johann Melchior Dinglinger
Enamel painting: Georg Friedrich Dinglinger
Dresden, dated 1711
H. 32,5 cm, Inv.-no. VI 98

The Weißenfels Hunting Goblet

Gold, enamel
Design and goldsmith's work: Johann Melchior and Georg Christoph Dinglinger
Enamel painting: Georg Friedrich Dinglinger
Dresden, 1712 to 1720
H. 38 cm, Inv.-no. IV 72

With the *Children's Bacchanal*, Johann Melchior Dinglinger and his brother Georg Friedrich achieved a particularly private artwork. On the almost planar lid of a quatrefoil cut agate bowl, happy, almost chaotic activity takes place. Three little boys romp around on a gold enamel forest floor. There is a remarkable degree of realism in the details presented on the stage. For instance, the growth rings can be recognized on the stump of the white beech, and the billy-goat's wavy fur is rendered most faithfully to nature. The children's bodies, however, are made from knobby, large pearls. One of the boys screams as he falls down, the drum has slips out of his hand, and a little brown dog attacks him. Another, partially nude boy tries to mount a patiently reclining goat while a second dog barks. A third child rushes onto the scene, holding a mask to his face and lifting a Thyros' staff. This figure likely gave rise to the title *Children's Bacchanal*, first documented in 1725, for the untamed children's activities. The shaft of this exquisitely worked agate *Bowl* dissolves into script and ornamentation. Placed between golden interlacing studded with diamond roses are an enameled female bust, a hobby-horse, and a fourth young fellow with his pants down. He is on the verge of taking a bird's nest. The most refined gold ornament, applied along the lid's edge, testifies to the jeweler's technical superiority.

In this piece, Dinglinger comes to terms with the humorous character of the pearl figures which Augustus the Strong venerated. In contrast to their customary use in Late Baroque jeweler's sculpture, the court jeweler inserted his pearl figures into a complex event and thereby fundamentally broadened their design potential. The artist signed the *Bowl* on the shaft of one of the collapsed hermes on the forest stage and dated it 1711. In October 1715, Augustus the Strong bought the »*Schale mit dem Ziegenbock*« (Bowl with the Billy-Goat) for 9,000 thaler.

The *Weißenfels Hunting Goblet* may have been commissioned, although this would be unusual for such works by Dinglinger. Archival information pertaining to its creation has not yet surfaced. The lidded *Goblet* is made from pure gold and did not come to the Green Vault until 1746 as a bequest. A rider in ancient garments is seated astride a horse that rears over war materials and crowns the work, whose theme clearly addresses a male owner. The sturdy shaft takes the shape of a strong stag held at bay by a dog, whereas the sculptural busts of Diana, mounted in the goblet's cup and the enamel medallions placed into the lid, as well as numerous other symbols indicate that this is a *Hunting Goblet*. This type of ceremonial drinking vessel served noble guests when drinking their libation of honor during courtly hunts. On the cup's wall, the coats-of-arms of the Saxon electoral house and of the municipality of Querfurt are arranged into appealingly designed shields. This and other initial signs allude to Duke Christian of Saxony-Weißenfels and his wife Sophie Christine von Stolberg. The duke was the head of one of the three *secundogenitures* connected with the electorate of Saxony and thereby belonged to the royal family. It is possible that Augustus the Strong commissioned the particularly valuable *Hunting Goblet* as a royal gift on the occasion of the ducal couple's wedding in 1712.

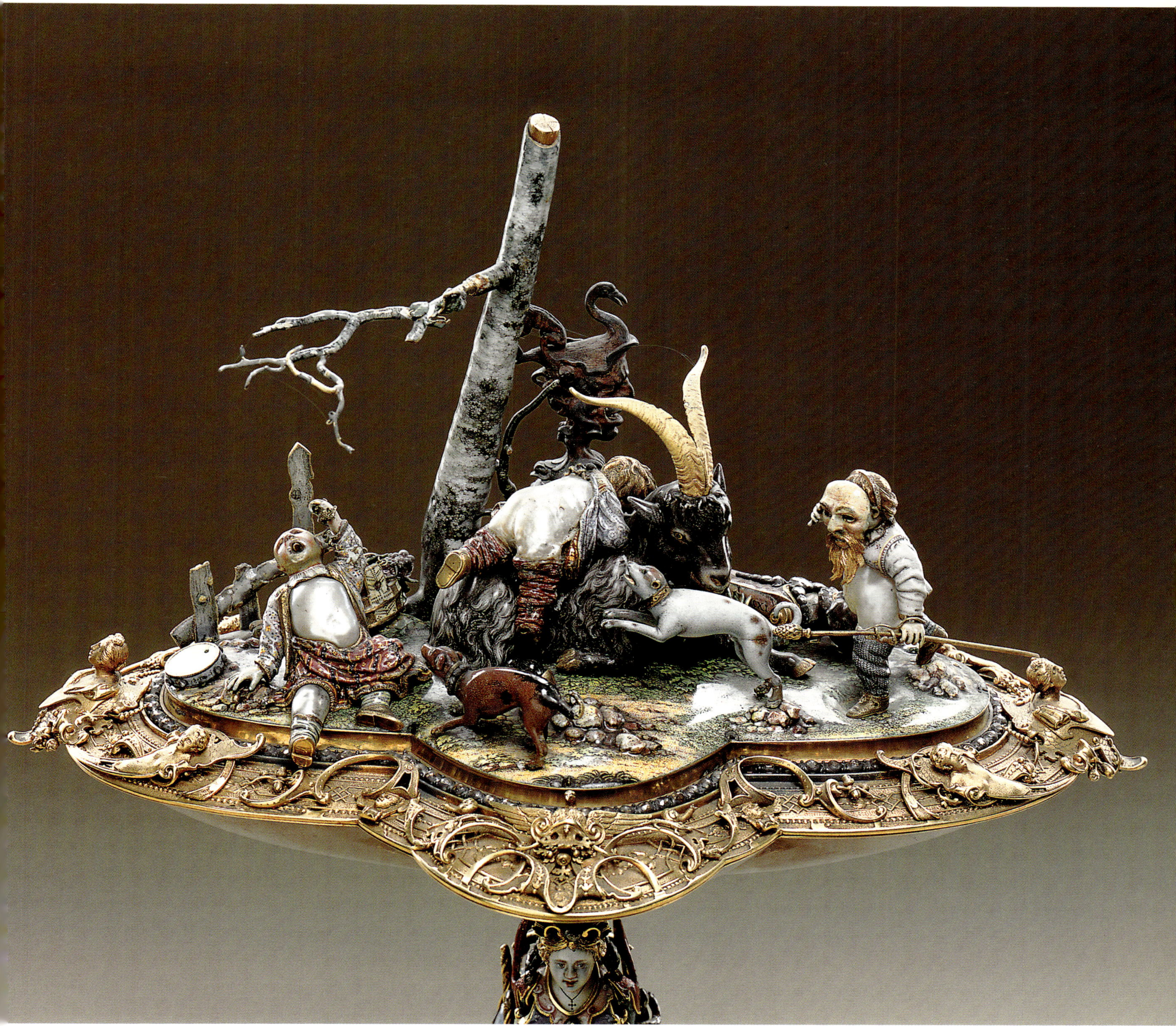

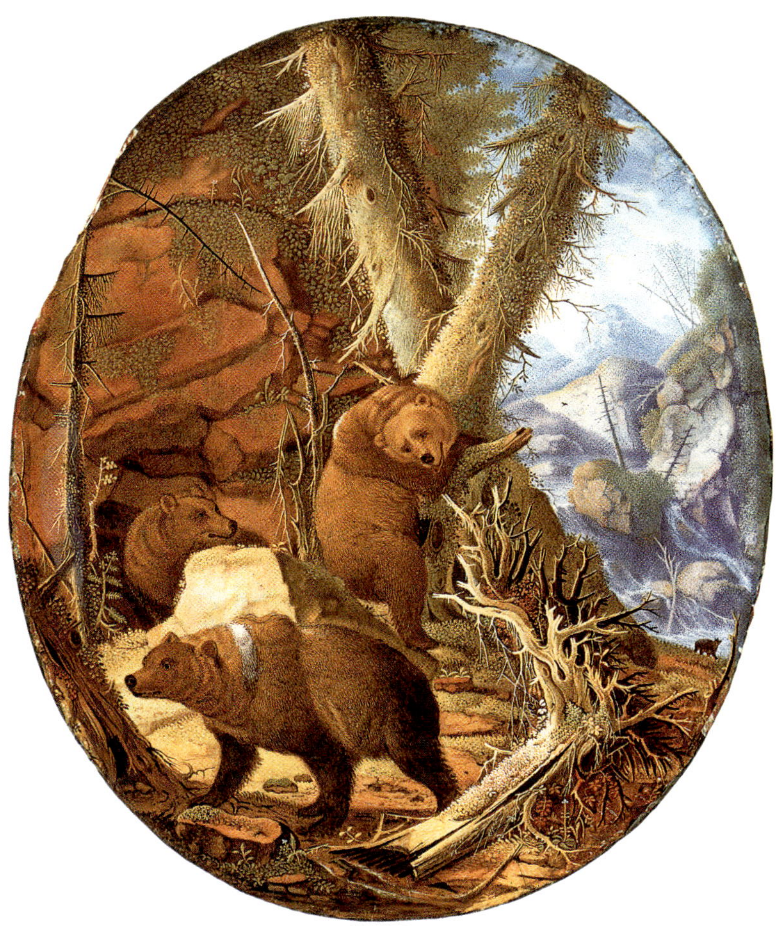

With his brother Georg Friedrich, Johann Melchior Dinglinger had a congenial artist at his side whose artistic and technical accomplishments are not sufficiently appreciated in comparison to the court jeweler. The artist, appointed court enameler in 1704, had frequently visited Dresden from the Swabian town of Biberach since 1693 to support his brother's projects. Georg Friedrich obtained his masterful enamel painting skills in an unknown place and possibly lived in Nuremberg for a while. With the firing technology available around 1700, he achieved enamel paintings that are among the best created with this technique. His profession demanded extensive experience and, most importantly, technological creativity. In addition, Georg Friedrich Dinglinger had a remarkable artistic sensibility and a particularly sure hand.

Enamel painting was not an original art form because the »fire painters« adapted pre-existing images that they transferred with the aid of pulverized glass paste onto a gold or copper ground. In an arduous procedure and with the help of numerous firings, color upon color was successively applied and individually melted onto the piece. The temperature was gradually diminished so that the most sensitive color was applied last. Fire painting required chemical knowledge as it was impossible to combine all enamel colors, and some could not be fired on top of others. Therefore, the circle of fire painters was small in circa 1700; their personal recipes and firing techniques were kept secret. Among them, Dinglinger was a particularly versatile artist. For his brother's works, he fabricated miniature portraits and paintings, a plethora of enameled vessels, and enamel sculpture incorporated into other objects.

But Georg Friedrich Dinglinger also produced picture-like enamel paintings. Since roughly 1712, the court enameler attempted large-sized enamel paintings that were especially hard to make. One of the most appealing products, dated before 1714, is a *Bear's Cave* enameled on copper. It seems that this view of nature was copied from a painting or a copperplate engraving. The colors' radiance and the mirror-like surface, as well as the finesse of the drawing and the contrasts between shadow and light illuminate the differences and the advantages between enamel and panel painting. Thanks to his court jeweler's negotiations, Augustus the Strong acquired the »große Stück mit Bären« (*Large Piece with Bears*) in 1721 for the considerable sum of 800 thaler from the estate of the court enameler who had passed away a few months earlier.

Two additional enamel paintings by Georg Friedrich are distinguished by their far larger size. They are *Cleopatra's Banquet* for the Roman general Marc Anthony and the almost life-size rendition of a half-length portrait of the *Virgin*. Augustus the Strong procured the latter in 1712 and displayed it as one of the chef d'oeuvres of his Treasury Museum in the *Pretiosensaal* of the Green Vault. *Cleopatra's Banquet* is captivating because of the garments' different colors and tonalities and the immense contrasts of shadow and light. Entitled *Banquet of the*

Bears in a Mountainous Landscape

Enamel on copper
Georg Friedrich Dinglinger
Dresden, before 1714
H. 23,2 cm, W. 18,7 cm, Inv.-no. III 42

Cleopatra's Banquet

Enamel on copper
Georg Friedrich Dinglinger
Dresden, presumably after 1712
H. 67,5 cm, W. 88,5 cm, Inv.-no. III 23

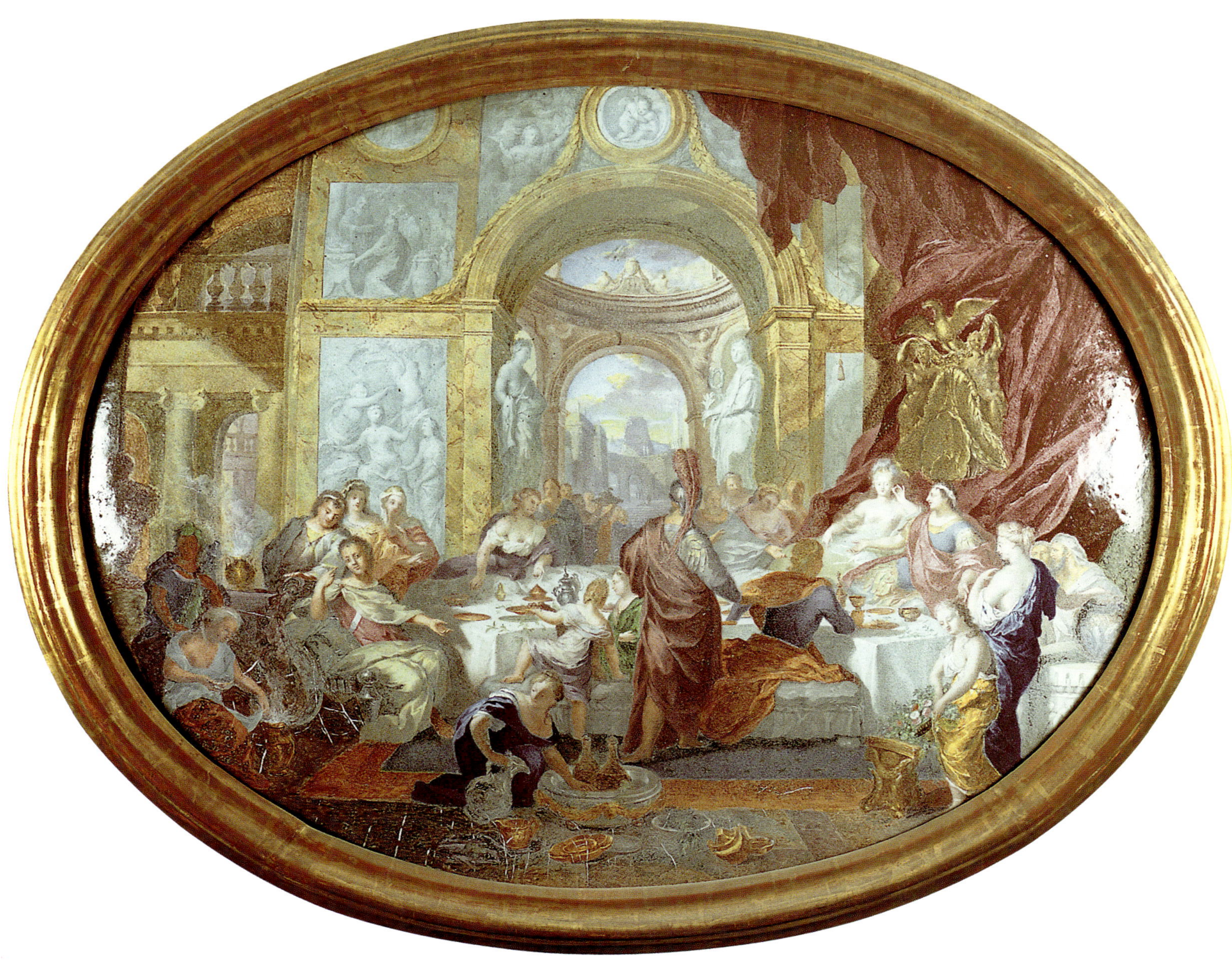

Gods, it only came to the Green Vault in 1769 as part of Count Brühl's bequest. The scene originates from an oil painting of the same topic by Ottmar Elliger the Younger. Dinglinger altered the composition of the model for his transfer into the much more challenging medium of enamel painting. He skillfully solved the problem of applying vitreous paints in a painterly fashion before they were then fired onto his copperplate. Despite all precautions, the firing process was not entirely successful, and it may be surmised that this was an experimental piece.

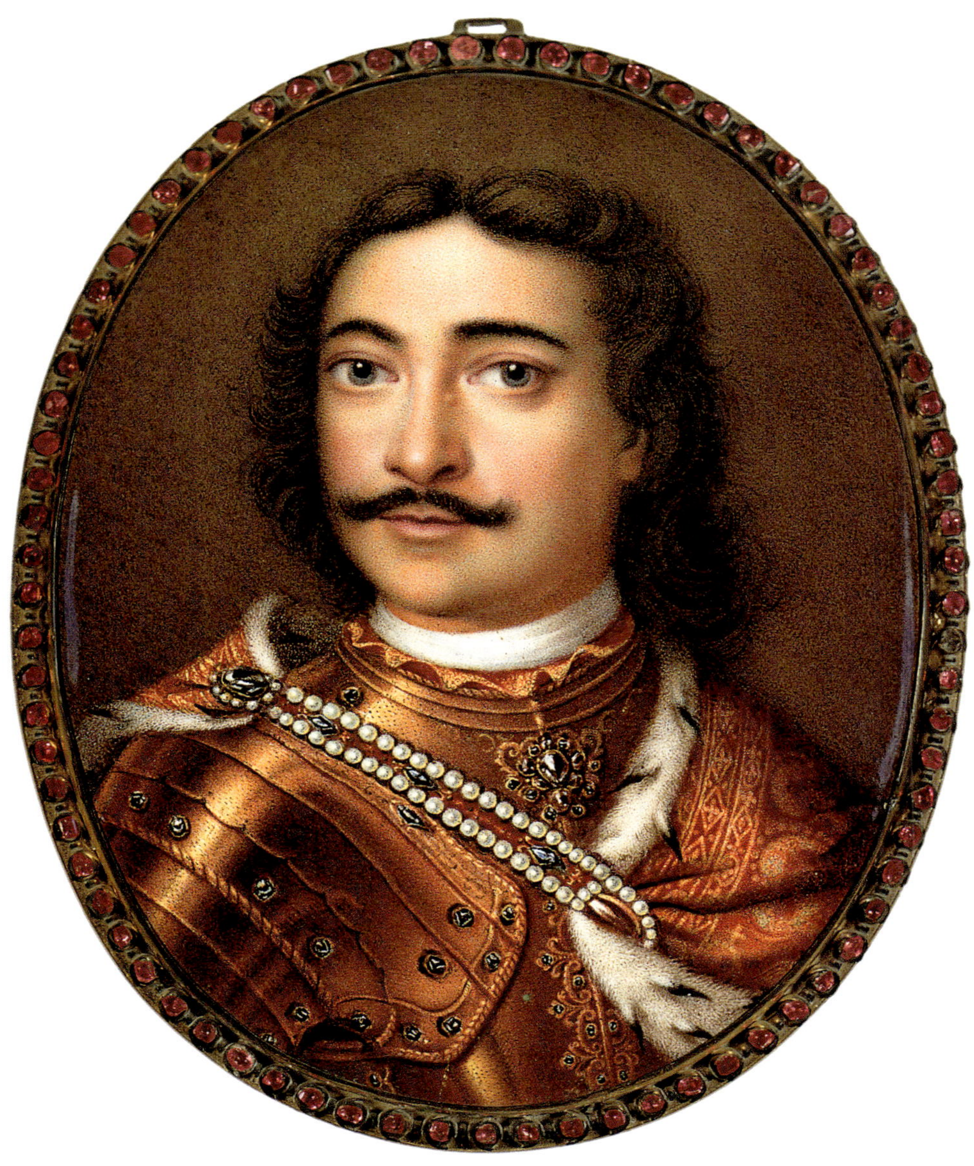

Portrait of Czar Peter I of Russia

Enamel on copper, gold, rubies
Georg Friedrich Dinglinger
Mount: Dinglinger workshop
Dresden, 1712
H. 14 cm, W. 11,4 cm, Inv.-no. III 36

Portrait of King August II of Poland

Enamel on copper
Charles Boit
presumably Dresden, 1718 to 1720
H. 12,7 cm, W. 10,1 cm, Inv.-no. III 33

Portrait miniatures represent an independent genre within enamel painting. French enamelers especially practiced this technique around 1700, seizing a topic that was vastly popular well into the 18th century. Enamel portraits have distinct advantages over the traditional gouache and watercolor techniques because of the brilliance and the durability of their colors. Large numbers of small enamel portraits have survived, as part of the trinkets and jewels of daily life. They were neither particularly susceptible to light, nor did the colors easily rub off and get damaged.

The *Portrait of Czar Peter I* was presumably made by Georg Friedrich shortly after the ruler stayed in the house of his brother, Johann Melchior Dinglinger from November 17 until 25, 1712. It is of considerable size and was intended as an independent work of art. The *Portrait*, which contemporary sources state as made from nature, shows the Russian monarch in an almost private way. Augustus the Strong purchased the ruby-studded, gold-framed portrait of his friend and

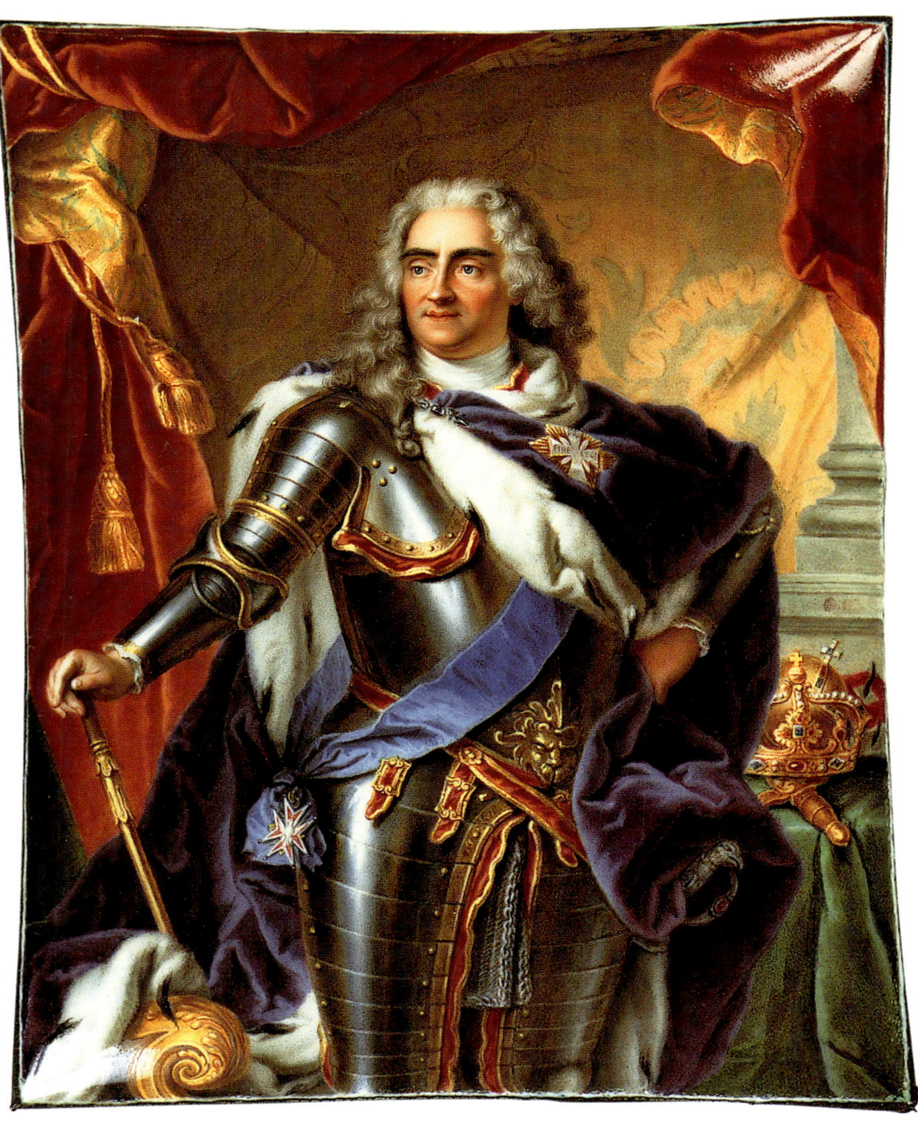

ally in 1714 for 500 thaler. Although the reference to a direct nature study would enhance its value, the complicated fabrication technique nearly rules out this possibility. The fact that an almost identical *Portrait of the Czar* by the hand of the painter Johann Kupetzky is kept in the Herzog Anton Ulrich-Museum in Brunswick makes this suggestion even more questionable.

From the vantage point of collection history, large enamel portraits are related to masterful early 17th century silver reliefs. The »fire painting« also translated the substance and the function of an image painted on canvas into a virtuoso technique and hence made it appear more appropriate to the character of a collection of treasury objects.

For Georg Friedrich Dinglinger, the creation of portraits was peripheral to his work. Yet, the highly talented enamel painter mastered them with his skillful hand. The enameler Charles Boit (1663 – 1727), on the other hand, specialized in portrait painting and was among the most accomplished French miniaturists of his time. In high demand as a »fire painter,« Boit traveled to numerous princely courts in the Holy Roman Empire, among them the imperial court in Vienna, and to European royal residences. His activities in Vienna and Dresden are documented between 1711 and 1720. During this time, he produced his *State Portrait of Augustus the Strong in Armor*. This is a largely faithful copy of the 1718 Saxon-Polish ruler's state portrait by Louis de Silvestre. An almost equally-sized miniature on parchment, kept in Dresden's Old Masters Picture Gallery, also appears to be by Charles Boit. It could have served as the model for the king's *State Portrait*, intended for the Treasury and exquisitely rendered in enamel painting technique.

Display Bowl with the Battling Hercules

Oriental jasper, gold, gilt silver, enamel, pearls, diamonds, emeralds, rubies
Design and goldsmith's work: Johann Melchior Dinglinger
Enamel painting: Georg Friedrich Dinglinger
Dresden, between 1708 and 1731
H. 59,4 cm, Inv.-no. VIII 304

Large Pendant

Five ovoid onyx discs, gilt silver, emeralds, diamonds, pearls
Johann Melchior Dinglinger
Dresden, before 1727
H. 48,8 cm, H. of the large onyx plate 15,5 cm, Inv.-no. VIII 205

The history of the creation of the *Bowl with the Battling Hercules* serves as a good example to illustrate the high financial risk Dinglinger took with his cabinet pieces, which he frequently made without direct commission. This is the largest *Display Bowl* Johann Melchior Dinglinger produced. The court jeweler seems to have begun work on the yellow-brown jasper *Bowl* – richly bedecked with diamonds, rubies, emeralds, and enamel – as early as 1708. Set within the context of daily politics, the artwork is dedicated to the superhuman deeds of Hercules. The hero who relentlessly fights the Nemean lion crowns the *Bowl*. He is in the process of fulfilling the first of his twelve classical tasks. Enamel medallions with depictions of his other heroic deeds are mounted on golden draperies along the side of the bowl's edge, and they also decorate the *Parade Vessel*'s pedestal that rises in the shape of a bell. A mighty, winged dragon, lifeless and with his head to the side, but embellished with emeralds is suspended from the extraordinarily finely executed shaft made of golden, intertwining Baroque scrollwork. Dinglinger visualizes the legend of the Greek hero – who, thanks to his superhuman struggles, is made a demi-god and admitted to the circle of gods – with the means of the jeweler's art. The mirror in front of which Hercules fights his battle, establishes a direct link with Augustus the Strong, the potential owner: On its back, he installed an idealized portrait of the prince elector-king in a dazzling disguise, and Georg Friedrich Dinglinger dated it 1712. Under the image of the sovereign squats a white eagle with widespread wings, the armorial animal of the Polish Order of the White Eagle that Augustus the Strong founded in 1705. There are further references in other places that can be politically interpreted: In a symbolic manner, the *Bowl* addresses Augustus the Strong's royal claim to power. He bitterly, and in the end successfully, defended his crown in the Nordic War and in the ensuing Polish civil war. Despite all this, the »Saxon Hercules« did not want to buy this object that alluded to his heroic accomplishments. In 1727 it stood, still not quite complete, in Dinglinger's workshop. Only after the court jeweler's demise in 1731 did the large *Display Bowl* come into the possession of the addressee.

The story of the elegantly mounted *Onyx Plate* that a visitor also spotted in Dinglinger's studio in 1727 is altogether different. Its cultural, historic and former material value are not as apparent today. For an 18th-century beholder, it was, however, a priceless marvel. Onyx belongs to the precious stone family of agate and was highly esteemed by the Late Baroque princely collectors as the »king of the stones«. Thanks to its distinctly differentiated white and brown layers, it was extremely well suited for cutting cameos. Albeit rare, large pieces of onyx were also utilized for cutting containers. Augustus the Strong frequently bought works made from this material so that in 1727, there were a total of 211 onyx objects in the Green Vault.

At approximately this time, the court jeweler managed to procure this ovoid plate that measures about eleven inches (25.5 cm) in height and four inches (9.5 cm) in width. Until well into the 18th century, it was considered the world's largest piece of onyx. With the distinctive, completely regularly formed onyx, Dinglinger ideally matched Augustus the Strong's taste as a passionate collector of large and exceptional precious stones. Thanks to his sense of fantasy and his good taste in forms, the jeweler-artist invented a type of presentation that befitted the ruler. Whereas he crowned the huge plate with three medium-sized plates of equally even finish, he had the huge *Onyx Plate* terminate in a diminutive oval, and he surrounded the precious stones with a crafty mount decorated with emeralds, pearls, and diamonds. It seems that the prince elector-king bought the *Pendant* shortly after it was finished for the immense price of 45,000 or 48,000 thaler, as contemporary travel literature cites the expense. Subsequently, the *Decorative Pendant* came to the newly finished Green Vault's Jewel Chamber (*Juwelenzimmer*) where it was displayed as an eye-catcher, suspended from the mirrored central pillar.

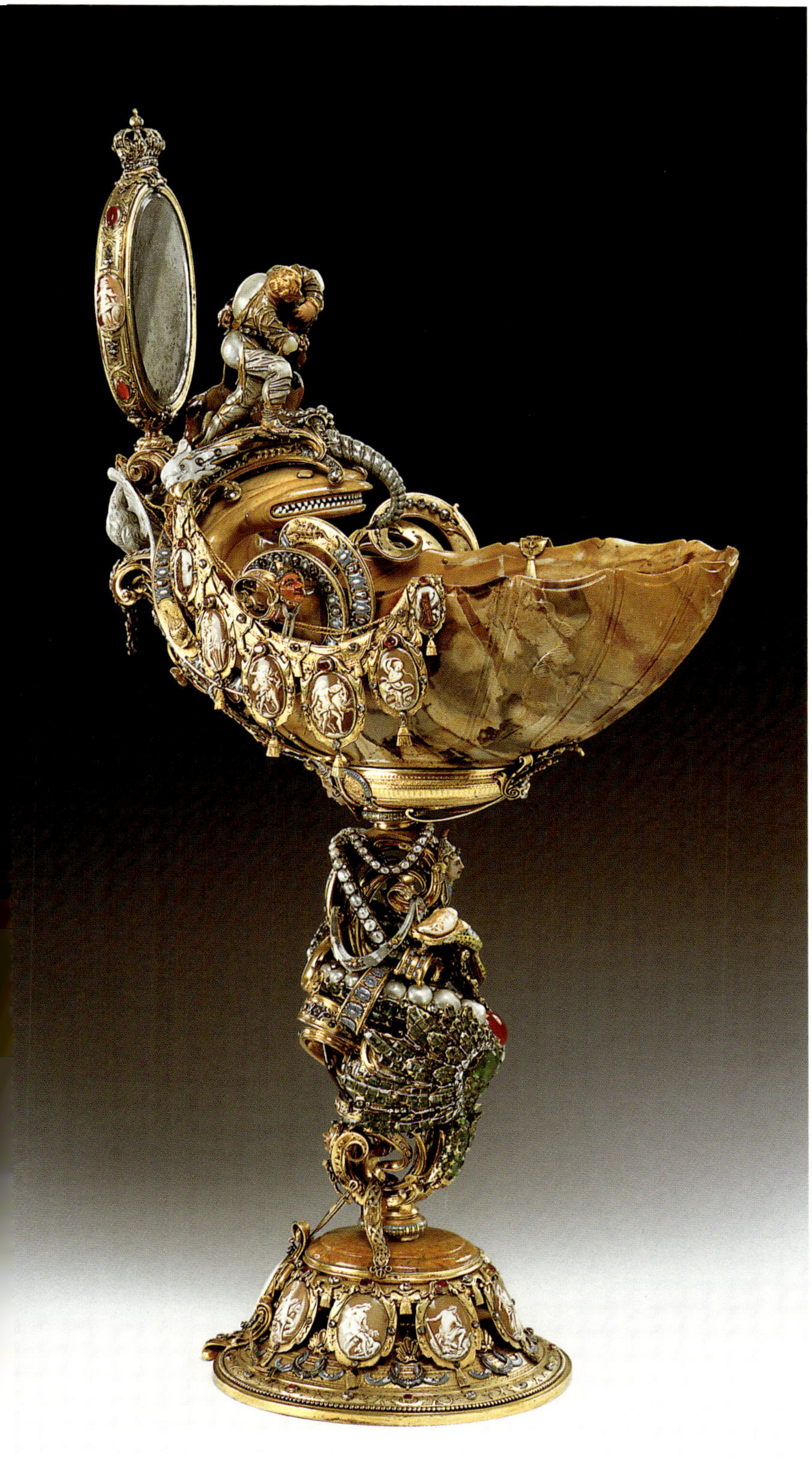

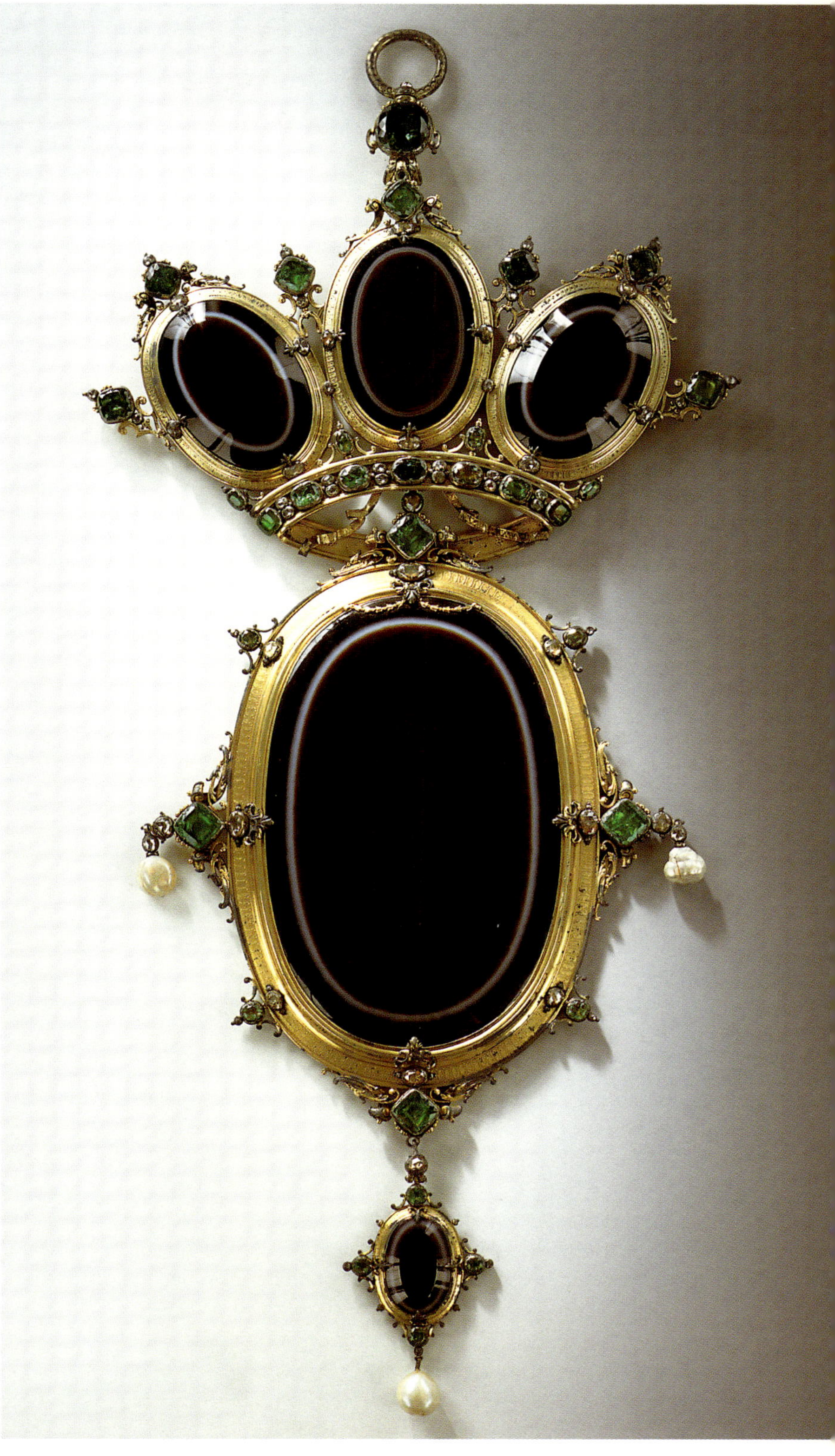

Apis-Altar

Kelheim stone, agate, gilt silver, enamel, precious stones, pearls
Design: Johann Melchior Dinglinger
Goldsmith's work: Dinglinger workshop
Stonecutter: Christoph Hübner
Sculpture: Gottlieb Kirchner
Dresden, presumably 1724 to 1731, dated 1731
H. 195 cm, Inv.-no. VIII 202

Johann Melchior Dinglinger's proficiency in processing expensive materials, along with his flawless sense of shapes and his organizational talents – all of which enabled him to collaborate with other artists and artisans – led to the making of incomparable artworks. His larger objects were only rarely works of the jeweler's art with the sole intent of pleasing the eye. Instead, the ingenious goldsmith knew how to depict present day occurrences before the backdrop of ancient history and mythology and with the ethnological knowledge of his day, to which he applied his own sensitivity and deeply-rooted intellectual insights.

The so-called *Apis-Altar* is Dinglinger's last work: he died in March 1731. Its dimensions alone classify it as extending beyond Late Baroque treasury art. As a dominant object intended to be displayed against a wall, it can only be compared with the *Obeliscus Augustalis*, dated between 1718 and 1722. The acquisition of the latter had prompted Augustus the Strong to transform his Treasury – until then strictly private – into the Green Vault, a museum with expressly designed mirrored walls.

With the *Apis-Altar*, the court jeweler formed the ultimate resume of his accomplishments at his life's end. As with his best known work, the *Grand Mogul's Throne*, Dinglinger dedicates his *Apis-Altar* to a culture entirely alien to Europe. Whereas twenty years earlier, the cultural realm of the Far East initiated the Chinoiserie fashion in Europe, thanks to missionaries but more importantly to trade exchanges, the ancient Egyptian pharaohs' universe of gods took center stage in the *Apis-Altar*. Crowned with an obelisk, the artwork thus became a singular summary of early 18th century European notions concerning the thoughts and forms that originated from this mysterious and vanished epoch.

With a plethora of figures, symbols, and ornaments, the old jeweler offered his personal interpretation of the ancient Egyptian myth of Osiris' death and resurrection. Thus, the pedestal presents engraved depictions of Osiris, the Egyptian fertility god of the underworld, reclining on a bier. In the niche above, delineated in gold enamel figures, the Apis animal (the terrestrial appearance of the god Osiris) crosses the Nile on a barge. The stonecutter Christoph Hübner created the particularly huge cameo made of red agate. It shows the veneration of the dog-headed patriarch Osiris after his death by his wife Isis and further gods derived from the Egyptian pantheon. The round enamel painting above is dedicated to the heavenly sphere of the divine couple Isis and Osiris as well as their child, Horus. Additional deities are placed on the entablature of the high obelisk. The latter is an exact copy of the ancient Egyptian monument, re-erected in front of Rome's Lateran in 1588.

The *Apis-Altar* is like a tremendous crescendo in the way it unites brilliant individual stonecutting achievements, enamel painting, and the art of the jeweler in one unique masterpiece. It was not until 1738, seven years after the death of its maker and five years after the demise of Augustus the Strong, that Augustus III bought the almost seven-foot (2 meters) high display piece of Baroque erudition for the Green Vault.

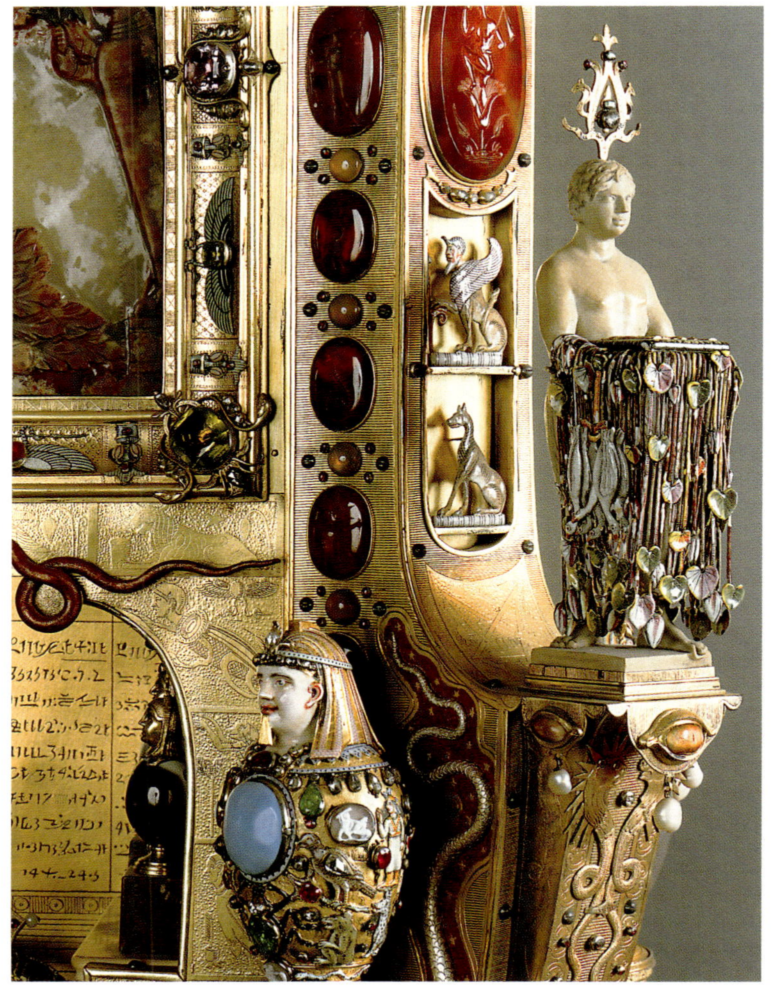

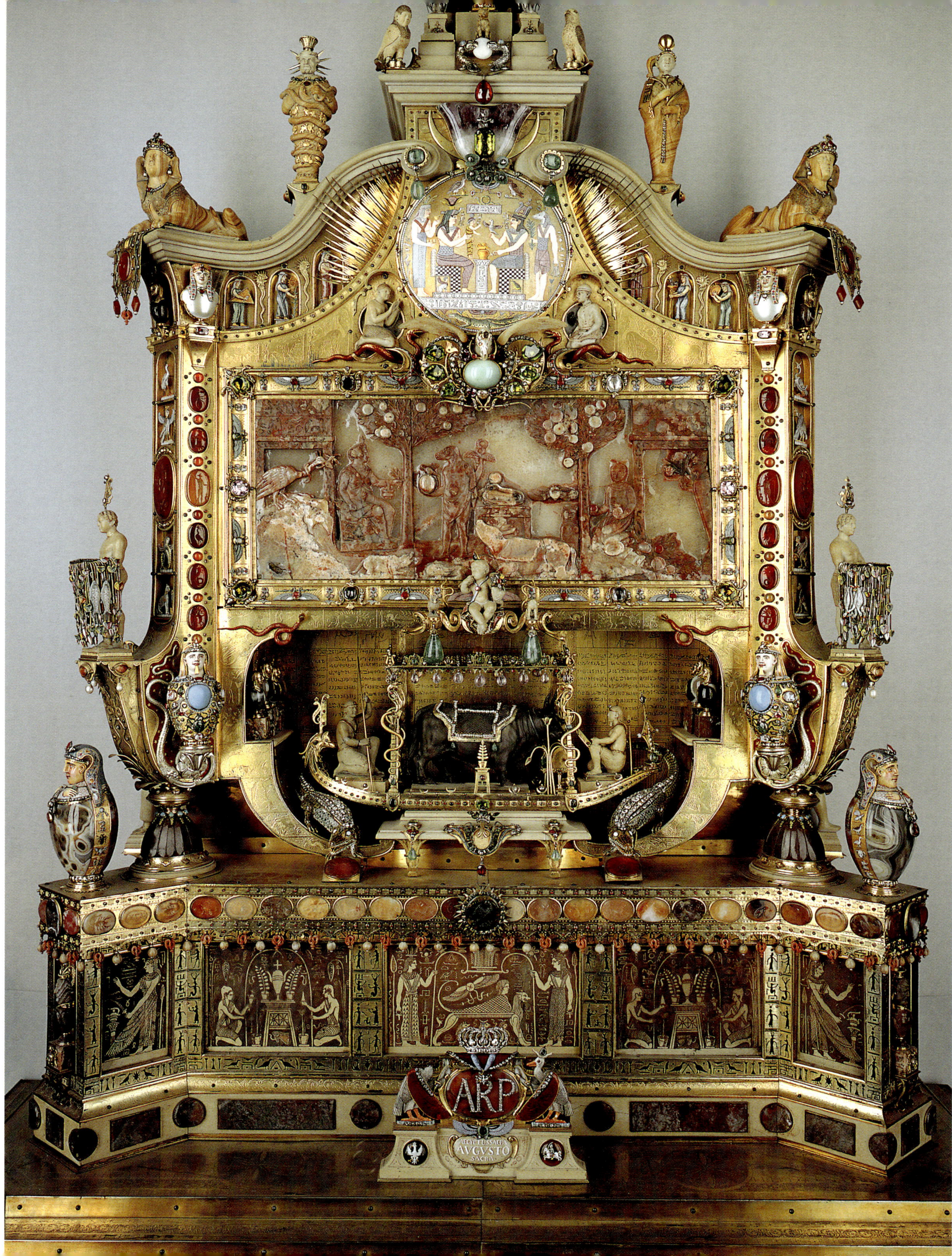
ARP
AVGVSTO
SACRA

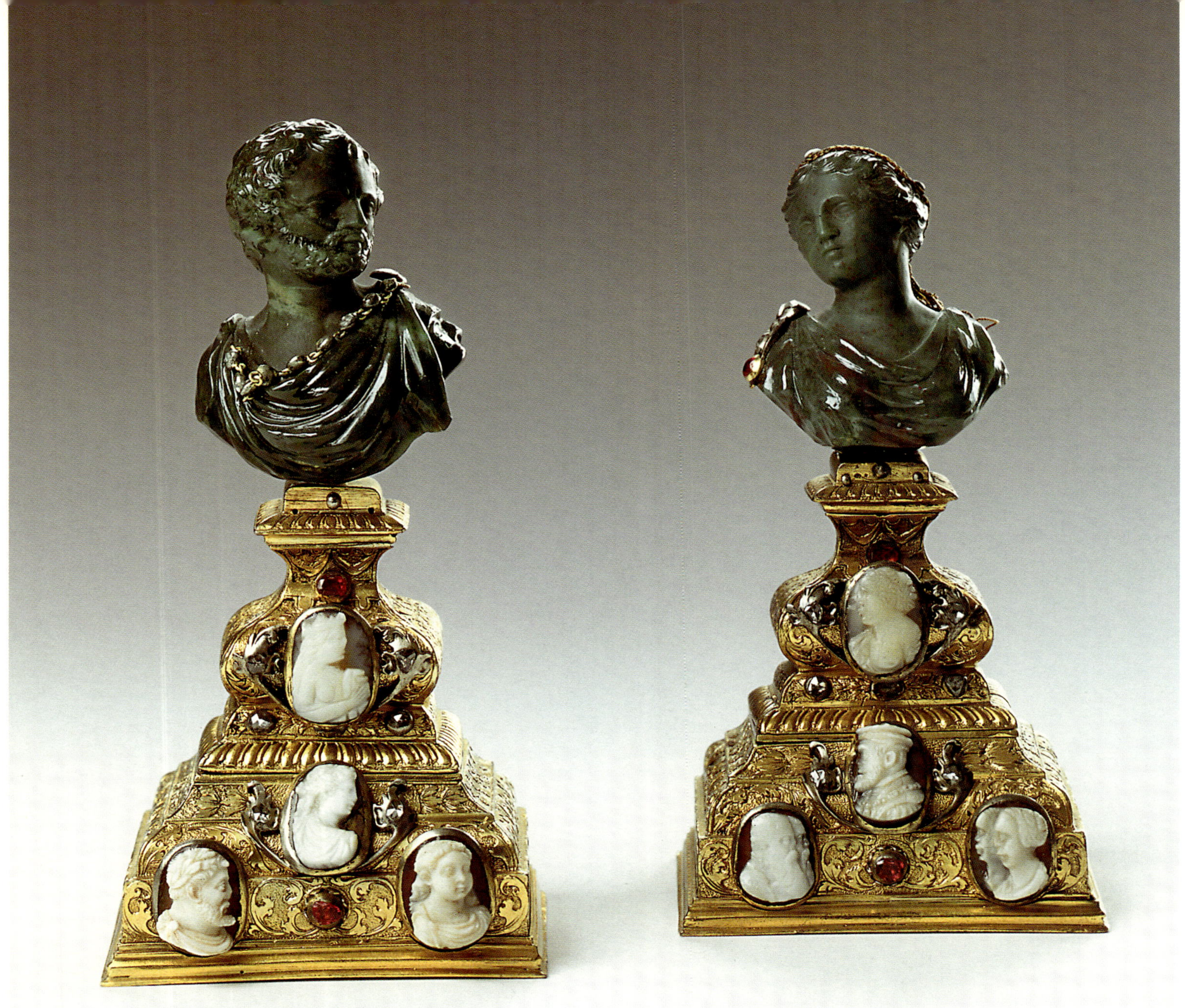

Two Busts in Antique Style

Heliotrope, gilt silver, precious stones, cameos
Unknown stonecutter
Dresden, before 1705
H. each 9,5 cm, Inv.-no. VI 110, VI 115

Cabinet Piece with Venus and Amor

Gilt silver, rock crystal, enamel, glass paste, mirror glass
Christoph Ertel
Zittau, before 1705
H. 15,6 cm, W. 9,6 cm, D. 7,9 cm, Inv.-no. VI 51

Princely collectors of the time around 1700 generally favored small precious stone busts depicting ladies and gentlemen in antique costumes. Numerous precious stone busts kept in diverse museums and private collections are testament to this today. Some of them refer to identifiable prototypes derived from ancient marble sculpture, whereas others typify male or female rulers as well as philosophers and other ancient characters. Almost three dozen of these three-dimensional busts made from cut stone have survived in the Green Vault. They differ in format as well as in quality and in style of their execution so that they can definitely be attributed to different masters and places of origin. The miniature busts from the collection of Augustus the Strong are predominantly made of green jasper, also known as blood jasper or heliotrope, and red agate. There are also some made from Saxon and other chalcedony, aventurine and emerald plasma. The portraits are mounted on different pedestals. Apart from wooden ones, there are also instances of precious stone stands, whereas some of the minuscule and finely worked stones were also attached to elaborate jeweler's works fabricated from gilt silver and garnished with stones.

The illustrated pair of *Heliotrope Busts* belongs to the earliest holdings within Augustus the Strong's *Pretiosensammlung*. Along with three others, both »Brust Bilder« (*Bust Images*) are mentioned in a 1705 listing that offers insight into the collection of treasury art already in existence. The material value of the pedestals, adorned with cameos and diamonds, is specifically mentioned. The *Heliotrope Busts*' stonecutting is of especially good quality. The stonecutter deliberately gave less polish to the faces of the heads that are turned towards one another than to hair and clothes. Their silver gilt, partly diamond embellished jewelry lends them additional splendor.

While the precious stone busts were presumably procured from independent merchants at the Leipzig Fair, the jewelry at the base bears numerous references to Dresden's jewel art. From a stylistic stance, these works are indeed close to those by the young Johann Heinrich Köhler. But Dinglinger also furnished such pedestals. For example, one of his invoices, dated January 1705, mentions the head of Julius Caesar cut from jasper and displayed on a base bedecked »mit Rubin und Diamanten« (with rubies and diamonds).

In the same year, three pieces by the Zittau-based goldsmith Christoph Ertel (um 1670 – 1719) were bought for the prince elector-king's collection at Leipzig's Easter Fair. Ertel's name is found in the 1725 inventory of Precious Objects as the source for a total of 12 small size cabinet pieces and bases for ivory statuettes, of which three reveal slight variations of Venus reposing below a columned canopy.

In one of the versions, the goddess of love, covered in white enamel, holds the Amor boy standing in front of her on a golden chain. A firm metal wall into which an ovoid mirror was installed rises behind her. Its reverse side reveals a painted landscape and an engraved ornament. The stand and the blue column, as well as the canopy – supported by the latter and dissolved into an insubstantial ornament – are decorated with enamel and small diamonds.

With his comparatively robust work, Ertel, who worked as a goldsmith in rural Saxony, approximated the prevalent court style to the degree that he caught the attention of Augustus the Strong's art agents who visited the fair. When Ertel was called to the court of the prince bishop of Breslau / Wroclaw – to fabricate »etwas Sonderbares« (something peculiar) – shortly thereafter, it was conceivably a result of his retail success.

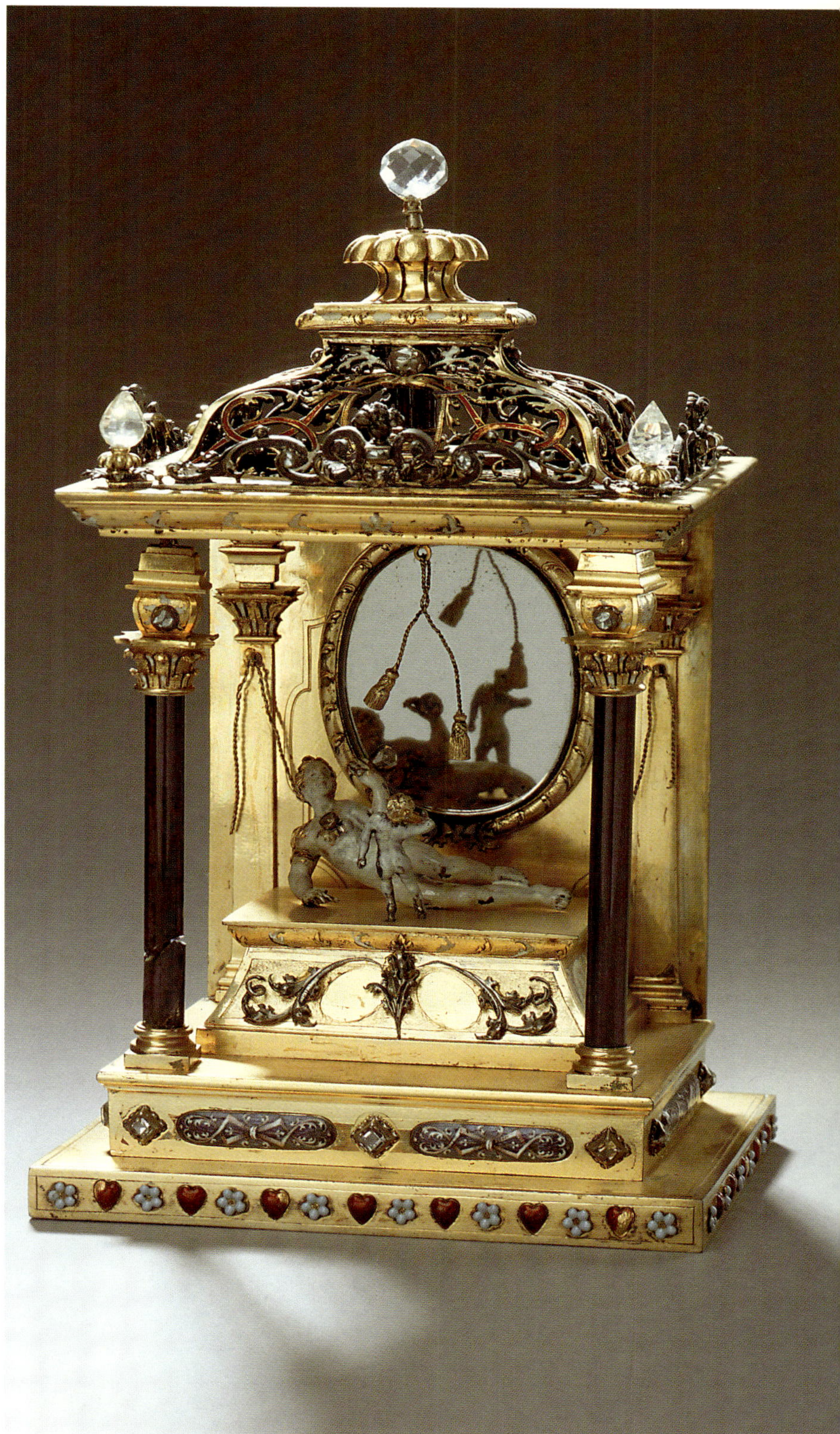

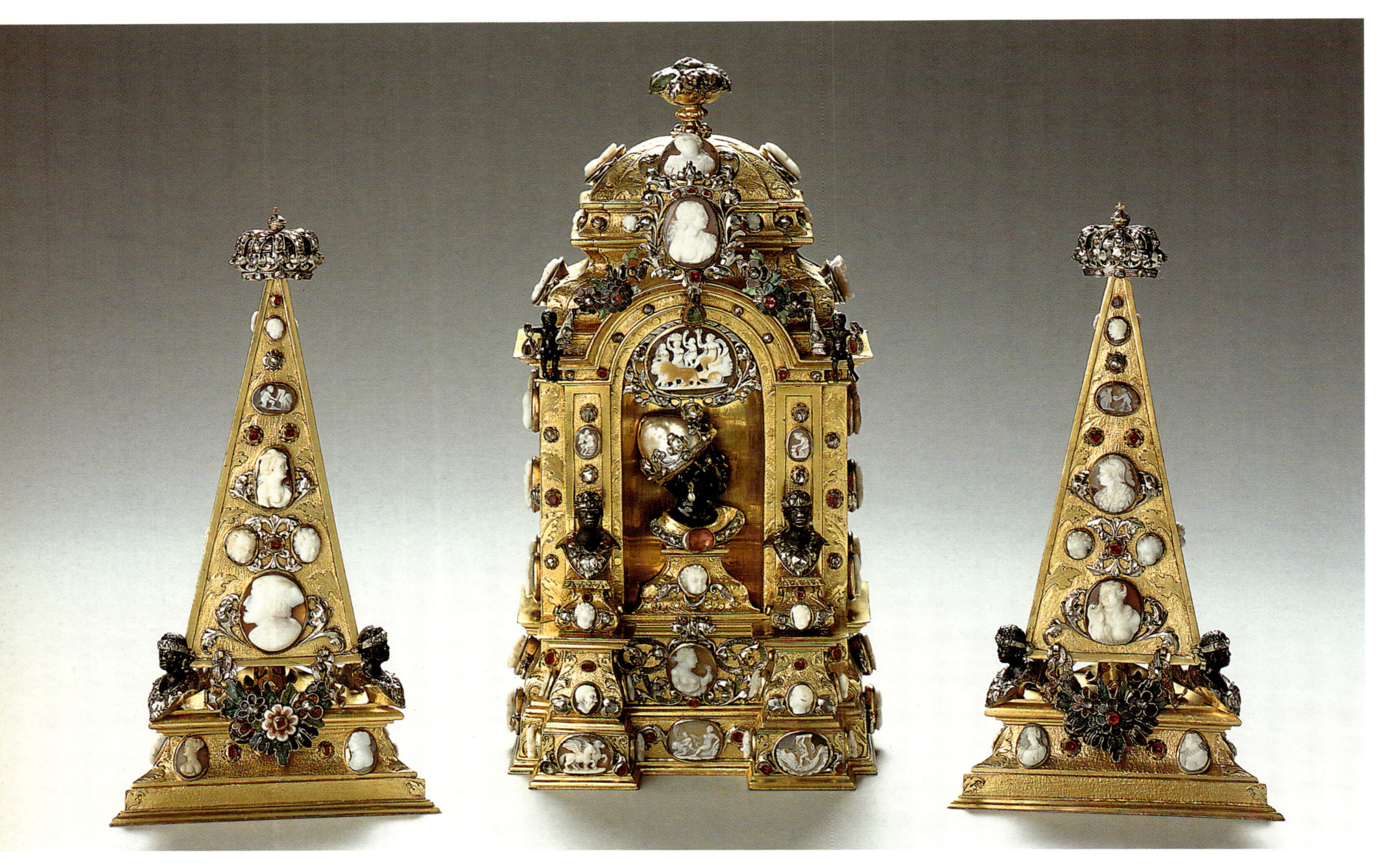

Triumphal Arch with Two Obelisks

Gilt silver, gold, enamel, cameos, precious stones
Johann Heinrich Köhler
Dresden, before 1705
H. 20 cm and 16,5 cm each, Inv.-no. VI 41, VI 40, VI 42

Display Clock with a Depiction of the Saint Hubertus Legend

Gold, gilt silver, enamel, precious stones
Johann Heinrich Köhler
Dresden, after 1720
H. 30,1 cm, Inv.-no. VI 2

When Johann Heinrich Köhler (1669 – 1736) became a master in the Dresden guild in 1701, his ascent as one of the most prolific German goldsmith-artists of the Late Baroque period began. His name first appears in 1716 in the surviving electoral files. But one of his most important works was already included on a list of pawned items drawn up in 1705. It contained items from Augustus the Strong's collection of precious objects that were to be brought to Hamburg. This extraordinary work, a three-piece cabinet ensemble, consists of two pyramidal obelisks and a »triumphal arch«. With its minute details and its bejeweled splendid fittings, Köhler executed a treasury art object geared toward the taste of Augustus the Strong. The triumphal motif prevalent in the Dresden court's festival architecture served as this ensemble's model. Built from perishable materials, it was erected for special festivities in the city or within the residential district. The inventive miniature architecture's subject is a king from black Africa whose profile image is rendered in the central field of the »triumphal arch« as »Mohren Kopff mit einer Perlen Mütze« (Moor's head with hat made of pearls.) He is flanked by additional busts of black Africans and two black putti are seated near the point of the arch's entablature. The obelisks, topped by crowns, are also supported by three more of these busts.

The iconography of African exoticism is linked to a special preference of Augustus the Strong. This is further exemplified over the decades by such works as the »Moor statuettes« by Permoser and Dinglinger in the royal collection of precious objects, but also through the disguise chosen by the prince elector-king: He appeared as a dark-skinned »chief«« of the Africans during the »Carrousel of the Four Continents,« a festive procession that took place on June 19, 1709 in Dresden. At the same time, Köhler also knew how to arouse the curiosity of the princely collector by virtue of the careful craftsmanship of the cabinet piece and thanks to the cameo trimmings in diverse shapes.

In 1718, Augustus the Strong promoted Johann Heinrich Köhler to the rank of court jeweler. At that time the maintenance of the sovereign's *Pretiosenschatz* (Treasure of Precious Objects) – of which he also furnished the first inventory in 1725 – was entrusted to Köhler. It appears that during the 1720s, his works increasingly corresponded to the desires of the ruler, so that he temporarily advanced as his favorite goldsmith. Possibly the most impressive among the artworks Köhler manufactured during this time is the *Display Clock with the Saint Hubertus Legend*, dated shortly after 1720.

Resting on a marbleized wooden stand decorated with ostentatious, bright-green chrysolite, the *Clock*'s case is adorned on all sides. At the front, its silver gilt body rests on two lions, whereas two bears support the back. Two hunting-horn players, located near the case's beveled corners, flank the dial that is surrounded with diamonds. Two music-making satyrs take their places on the reverse side. The princely hunting theme is picked up in small enamel reliefs of hunting animals that were affixed to the space between the green enameled ornaments and the emerald trimmings. Four court hunters are located on the cornice above the forest's real and mythological guardian, where they flank an adornment with hunting weapons. This is also the stage for the detailed visualization of *Saint Hubertus*' legend. In honor of the patron saint of hunters, large hunts take place each year on Saint Hubertus' day (November 3.) The prince elector-king, a hopelessly passionate huntsman himself, had such high esteem for Köhler's splendid *Saint Hubertus Clock* that he had it installed in the window niche of the Green Vault's Jewel Chamber.

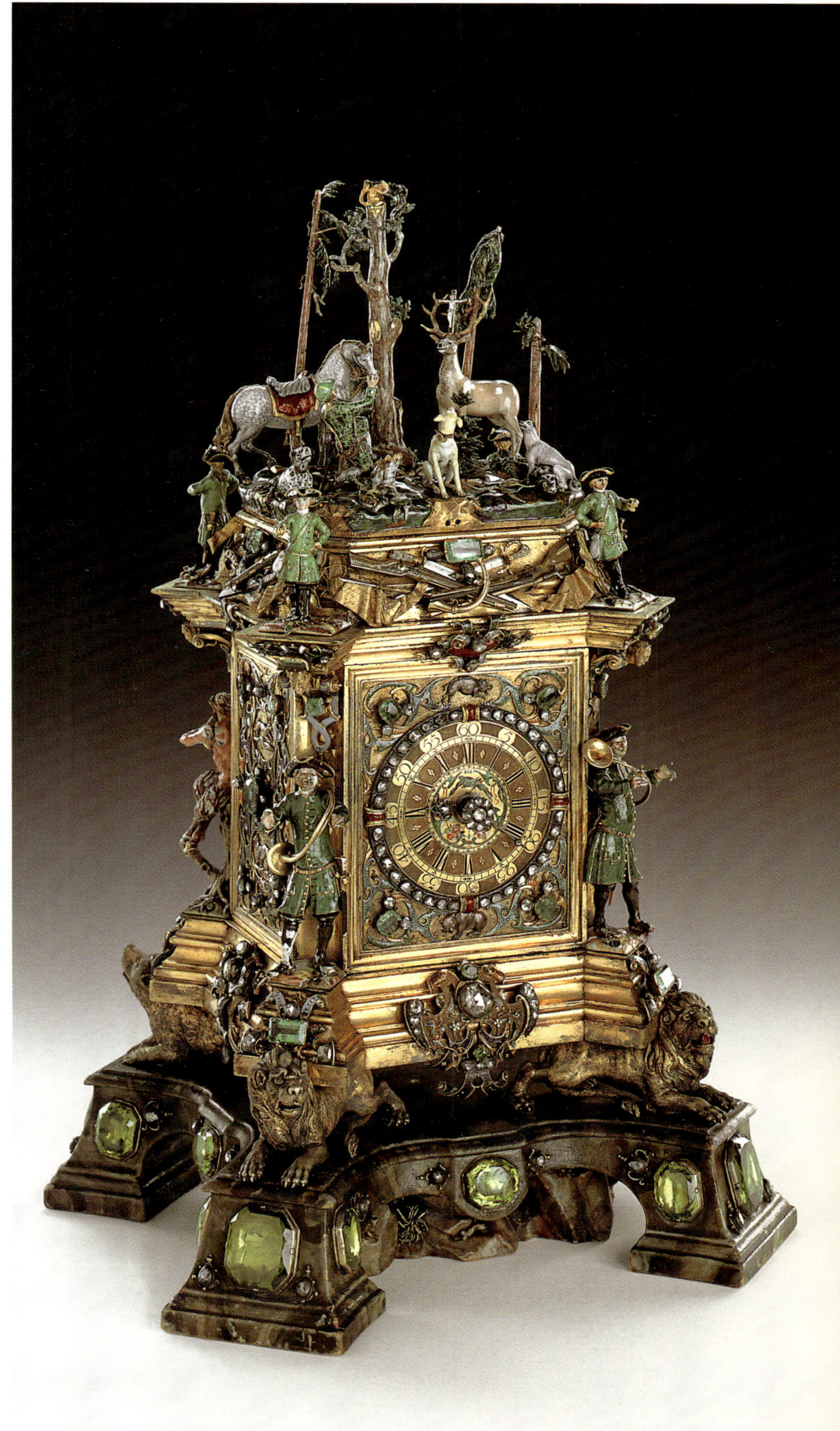

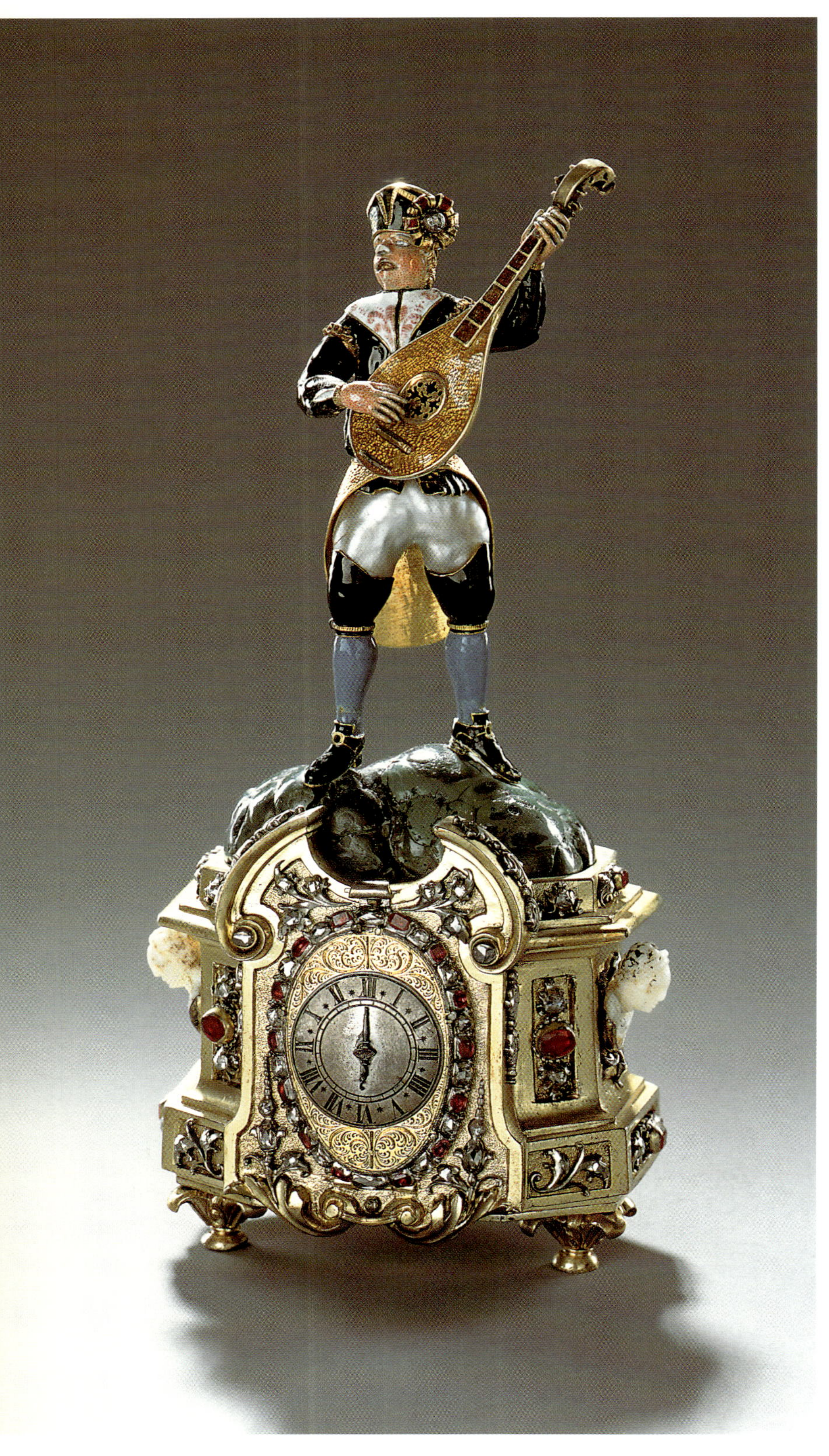

Clock Crowned by a Miner-Singer

Gilt silver, gold, enamel, Baroque pearl, mother-of-pearl, malachite, diamonds, rubies
Johann Heinrich Köhler
Dresden, before 1725
H. 15,1 cm, Inv.-no. VI 101

Potter

Ivory, gold, silver, enamel, precious stones, varnish
Design and mount: Johann Heinrich Köhler
Sculpture: presumably a member of the artists' family Lücke
Dresden, between 1710 and 1720
H. 12 cm, Inv.-no. VI 184

Knife-Grinder

Ivory, gilt silver, gold, enamel, precious stones, colored glass
Design and mount: Johann Heinrich Köhler
Dresden, beginning of the 18th century
H. 6,7 cm, Inv.-no. VI 188

In the case of the *Clock with a Miner-Singer*, Köhler subordinates the function of a time measuring device even more to the display aspect of a treasury art object than he did in the *Display Clock with the Legend of Saint Hubertus*. The jewel artist dedicated this most precious object to a specific Saxon contribution to music history. In its center stands a member of Augustus the Strong's »Churfürstliche Bergsänger« (Electoral Miner-Singers) who, as a result of empathetic observation, can be seen singing while he accompanies himself on his instrument. The musician's head is slightly lifted to the right, his mouth is open as he sings, and he is located on a naturally-grown malachite stone that appears like a costly rock under his feet. The only attributes identifying the singer as a miner are his dark green »Schachthut« (pit hat), dyed red leather on the seat of the pants, and knee pads distinctly reduced in their functionality. His festive livery connects the typical parts of the Saxon miner's costume – black shoes, pink embroidered scarf, and pants consisting of an irregularly grown Baroque pearl – to a middle-class outfit. The straddling man plays a so-called cister. This plucking instrument was especially liked by amateur musicians who, in the second half of the 17th century, began accompanying the miner-singers working at the electoral court. Augustus the Strong was very fond of this type of entertainment and also permitted his miner-singers to perform at larger festivities. The acanthus ornament dates the *Clock with a Miner-Singer* to the first few decades of the 18th century.

As revealed in his *Clock with a Miner-Singer*, Köhler was a thorough observer of daily life. Numerous little ivory groups and their

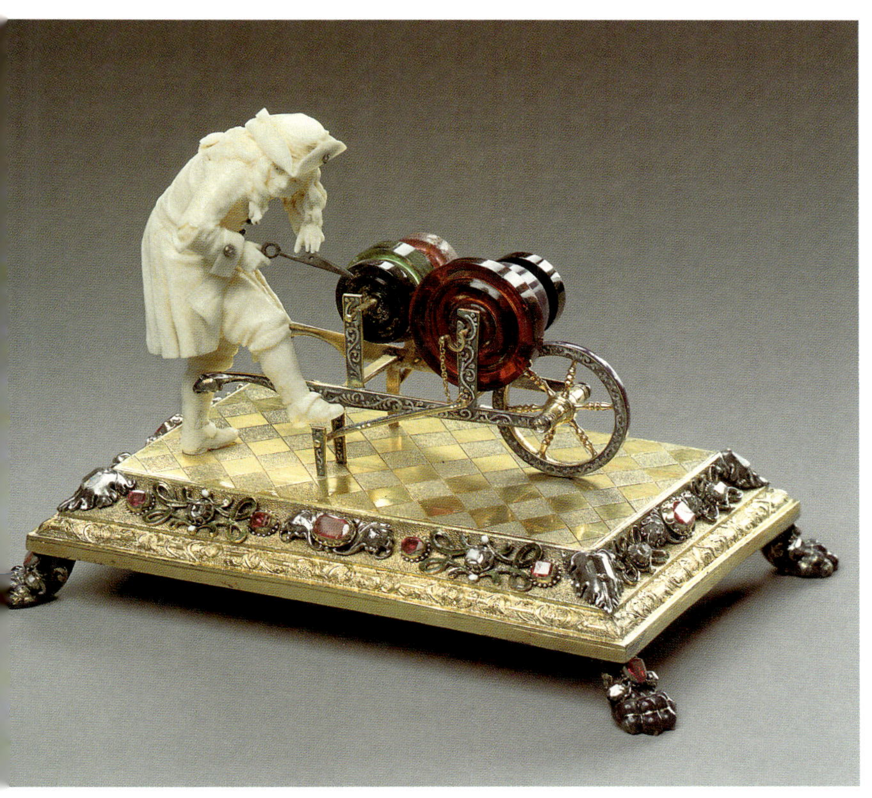

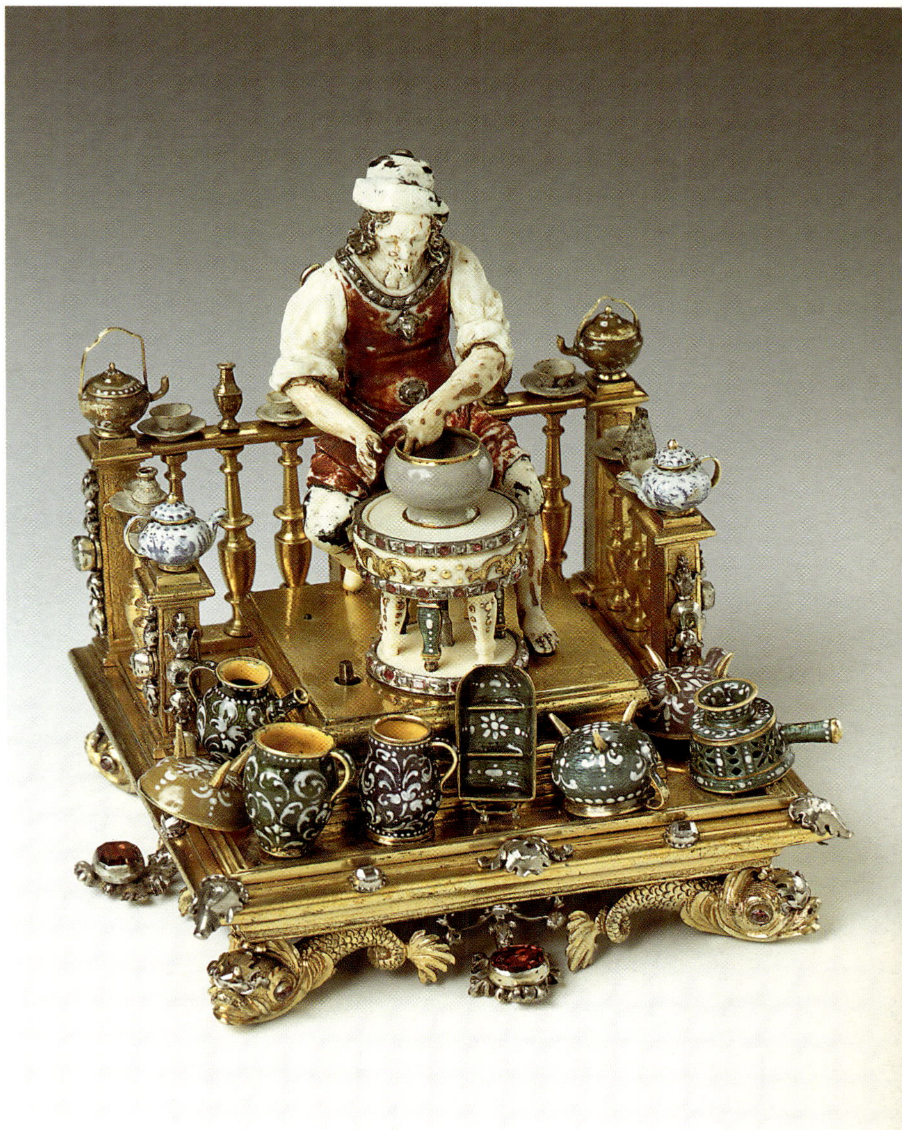

jewel-like mounts owe their existence to him. These are definitely not courtly caricatures of the third estate but rather detailed renderings of the Saxon bourgeoisie – albeit seen in somewhat more festive outfits. The seated *Potter* behind the wheel belongs to this group of objects. In order to realize his design, Köhler used a little ivory statuette. The carefully painted master *Potter* seems to have been carved by a member of the Lücke family, ivory carvers who were active in Dresden. Slightly bent, the *Potter* concentrates as he sits on a chair in front of the potter's wheel that could be put into motion by means of a gadget in the base. The *Potter* is just in the process of shaping a large receptacle. Before him, numerous jugs and pots are placed along with an ewer, a warming basin, and a baking-dish. Thanks to its strongly colored walls covered with tendrils, the latter two can clearly be identified as pieces of middle-class utilitarian ceramics. The teapots, drinking bowls, and vases arranged on the balustrade to the side and behind the master craftsman, on the other hand, reflect the production of vessels that had just begun in Meißen at this time.

Like the *Potter*, the ivory *Knife-Grinder* is also surrounded by authentically crafted and carefully enameled tools and instruments of his trade. This little figure entered Augustus the Strong's collection of precious objects in December 1709.

If compiling the works attributable to Johann Heinrich Köhler thanks to the Green Vault's inventories, a remarkable early 18th century artist's personality becomes visible, to whom we owe an unusually abundant and meticulous oeuvre.

Ice-Skating Dutchman

Gold, silver, partly gilt, enamel, Baroque pearl, rubies, emeralds, diamonds, mirror glass
Unknown goldsmith
Frankfurt / Main, before 1705
Purchased from Guillaume Verbecq
H. 12,4 cm, Inv.-no. VI 96

One-Eyed Beggar with a Wooden Foot

Baroque pearl, gold, enamel, diamonds, ivory
Jean Louis Girardet
Berlin, before 1725
H. 10,2 cm, Inv.-no. VI 94

Among the extensive holdings of pearl figures, there is an artwork of almost poetic appeal kept in the Green Vault. It is a rendering of a self-absorbed *Skater* gliding over an icy surface. The lonely man's gaze is directed towards the ice, cunningly made from mirror glass. Protecting himself from the cold, he has crossed the arms on his chest, while slightly lifting his left foot in a calm movement. This emphasizes the self-referential nature of the individual in Dutch costume. Only with the aid of the jewel sculpture's means could the goldsmith (who presumably worked in Frankfurt / Main) lend the pearl figure a nearly meditative air. The *Skater*'s pants, made from a large, irregular Baroque pearl, and his blue enamel jacket are shaped in a rather summary way, whereas the man's face and ice-skates are reproduced in great detail. A large ruby, making up the crown of his hat, further underscores the

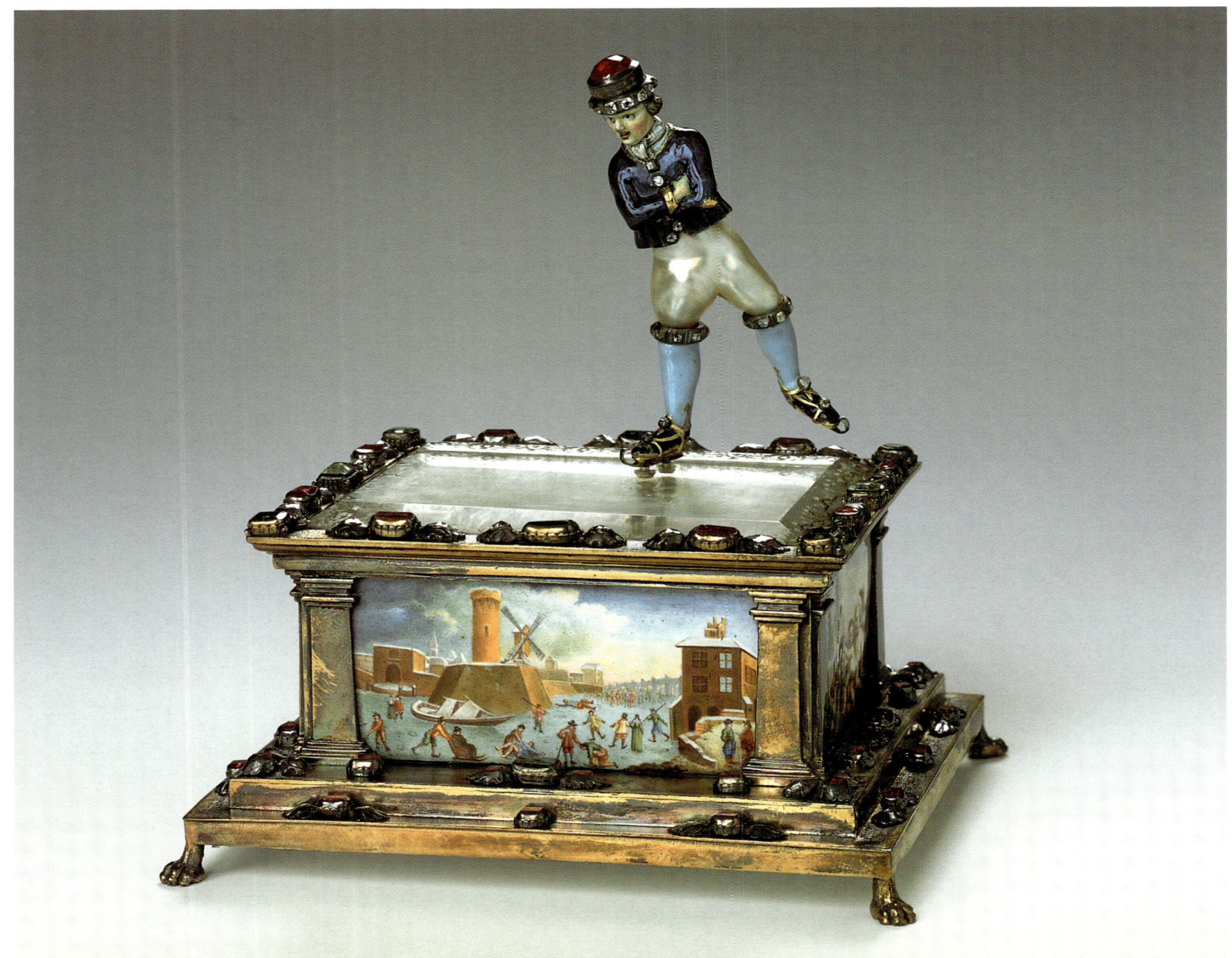

work's costliness, while a wreath of little diamonds forms the edge. Further diamonds, rubies and also emeralds surround the cover plate and the stepped support of the high pedestal on which the action takes place. The gay wintry crowd on the front of the cabinet – shown on an enamel plaque that simulates a Dutch genre scene – forms a tense contrast with the solitary pearl figure. The theme of the four seasons is nearly annihilated by the enamel plaques attached to the remaining three sides of the base; they are allegorical putti of spring, summer, and autumn. Augustus the Strong already owned the precious pearl object with the *Ice-Skating Dutchman* before 1705. He purchased it from Guillaume Verbecq, a jeweler who was active in Frankfurt / Main. The 1725 inventory mentions this source and the name Verbecq for a total of sixteen pearl figures.

In the same inventory of Precious Objects, five pearl figures are ascribed to »Gerardet aus Berlin.« The Berlin goldsmith Jean Louis Girardet is barely known in today's art historical research. He was born around 1681 in the Burgundian town of Autun and began to work in Berlin as »orfèvre en or et jouaillier« in the early 18th century. The artworks attributed to him in the Green Vault characterize Girardet as a noteworthy Late Baroque jewel artist. At the same time, his pearl figures are rare testimonies to the court art, almost entirely lost under King Frederick I of Prussia in Berlin.

Like Köhler, Girardet also shows psychological sensitivity in his works and in the treatment of his chosen themes. Positioned on the surface of his stand, the *Beggar with Crutch and Wooden Foot* is for instance clearly unstable. The man, whose body consists of one single Baroque pearl, has lost an eye. Only a stump of his left leg remains, and he is thus forced to rely on a prosthesis. As he begs, he stretches out his hat in a fleeting gesture towards an imaginary individual. This is the depiction of a person in need whom even the strictest 18th-century conditions would have counted among the »wahre Arme« (true poor.) The topboots and the short jacket, reminiscent of a uniform, as well as the satchel on the beggar's back, formed from a pearl, illustrate that this pitiful creature is a former soldier.

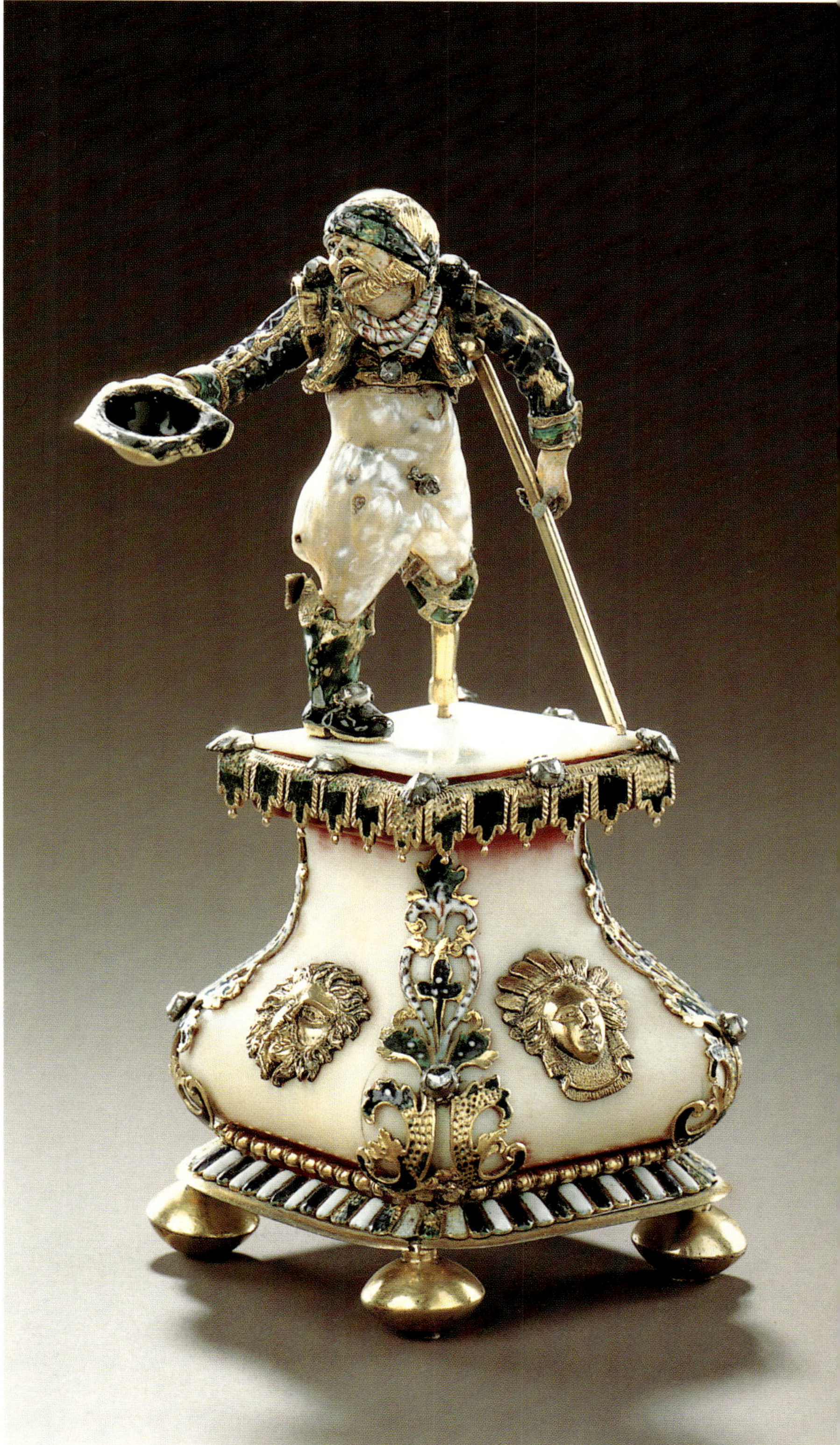

Cook Fiddling on the Gridiron

Baroque pearls, gold, enamel, gilt silver, diamonds, iron
Unknown goldsmith
Frankfurt / Main, before 1725
Purchased from Guillaume Verbecq
H. 12,0 cm, Inv.-no. VI 88

Harlequin with Mask and Wagging Head

Baroque pearl, gold, enamel, silver, diamonds, rubies, rock crystal, shell cameo
Unknown goldsmith
Frankfurt / Main, before 1725
Purchased from Guillaume Verbecq
H. 11,2 cm, Inv.-no. VI 126

The term »grotesque figures«, often used in art history to describe precious pearl objects, is borrowed from caricatured subjects such as the dwarfish *Cook*. The figure with its scurrilous features and gay smile has a distorted body resulting from growth disorders, characteristic of which are his stout, short legs, the severely protruding chest, the humpback, and the disproportionately large head. As his inspiration, the jewel artist, who presumably worked in Frankfurt / Main, used a sheet that was ultimately derived from Jacques Callot's *Varie Figure Gobbi*, published in Florence in 1616, and very popular around the year 1700. In the early 18th century, Callot's suite of engravings was the source of inspiration for numerous ivory statuettes and garden sculptures.

The *Cook* is not merely identifiable by the gracefully detailed rendering of his pearl figure and the gridiron as his extremely unusual instrument, from which the exquisitely dressed dwarf attempts to elicit sounds with the aid of a roasting-jack; further attributes include a goose with pearl body, suspended from the *Cook*'s back, as well as a flask and a carving-knife that dangle from his diamond-studded belt and are visible below his pearl-belly. During his musical presentation, the happy *Cook* dances a gracious, courtly dance that further underscores the comical aspect of his appearance. When looking at the figure, the pleasure was not to be derived from the viewer's presumably healthy measure of spite but from the memory of highly venerated dwarves who entertained at European courts. Considered a miraculous caprice of nature, they were fully integrated into Baroque society. The dwarf Hante, for example, served at Augustus the Strong's Dresden court.

The dancing pearl figure, dressed in the garments of an »arlequino« (*Harlequin*) also arose from the princely desire for »divertissement«, because the *Harlequin* figure belonged to the repertoire of Baroque comedy, where he took the role of the gay, albeit naïve and somewhat clumsy clown. From his left hand hangs a wooden sword (Prizsche) that he employed to actively accentuate his jokes. His face is covered by a black mask that is a recurring element in his roles. Part of the intimate character of this collector's item is the fact that a flick of the finger was sufficient to make the head wag.

The dwarf *Cook* and the *Harlequin* both have precious stands, typical of the object art that Verbecq delivered. They reveal features typical of Augsburg enamel painting. The base on which *Harlequin* is attached is accentuated with a carefully worked shell-cameo depicting Ovid's *Metamorphoses* story of the sculptor Pygmalion, who, by virtue of his love, brings his sculpture of Galatea to life. The carving is protected by a rock crystal cover and is surrounded by a voluminous flower bouquet. The happy and untamed *Cook*, on the other hand, stands on his pedestal, whose main side delineates a monochrome painting of putti performing a round-dance near a herme of the fertility god Priapus. Three similarly painted enamel plaques on pink ground are decorated with cornucopias and flower garlands, symbols of fertility.

Guillaume Verbecq brought both pearl figures to Dresden, from whence he received, between 1702 and 1703, considerable sums »vor allerhand Galanterien« (for numerous gallantries) as a jeweler, and he presumably also continued his business affiliation with the Dresden court until sometime later. Beside the pearl figures, the items he delivered – they were indeed heterogeneous from the viewpoint of quality and style – also encompassed ivory statuettes and other small-scale pieces. It seems adequate to assume that the jeweler, based in Frankfurt, city of fairs, worked primarily if not exclusively, as an agent for the jewelers who were active there. Verbeqc's activities during the first decades of the 18th century also brought him to other German courts.

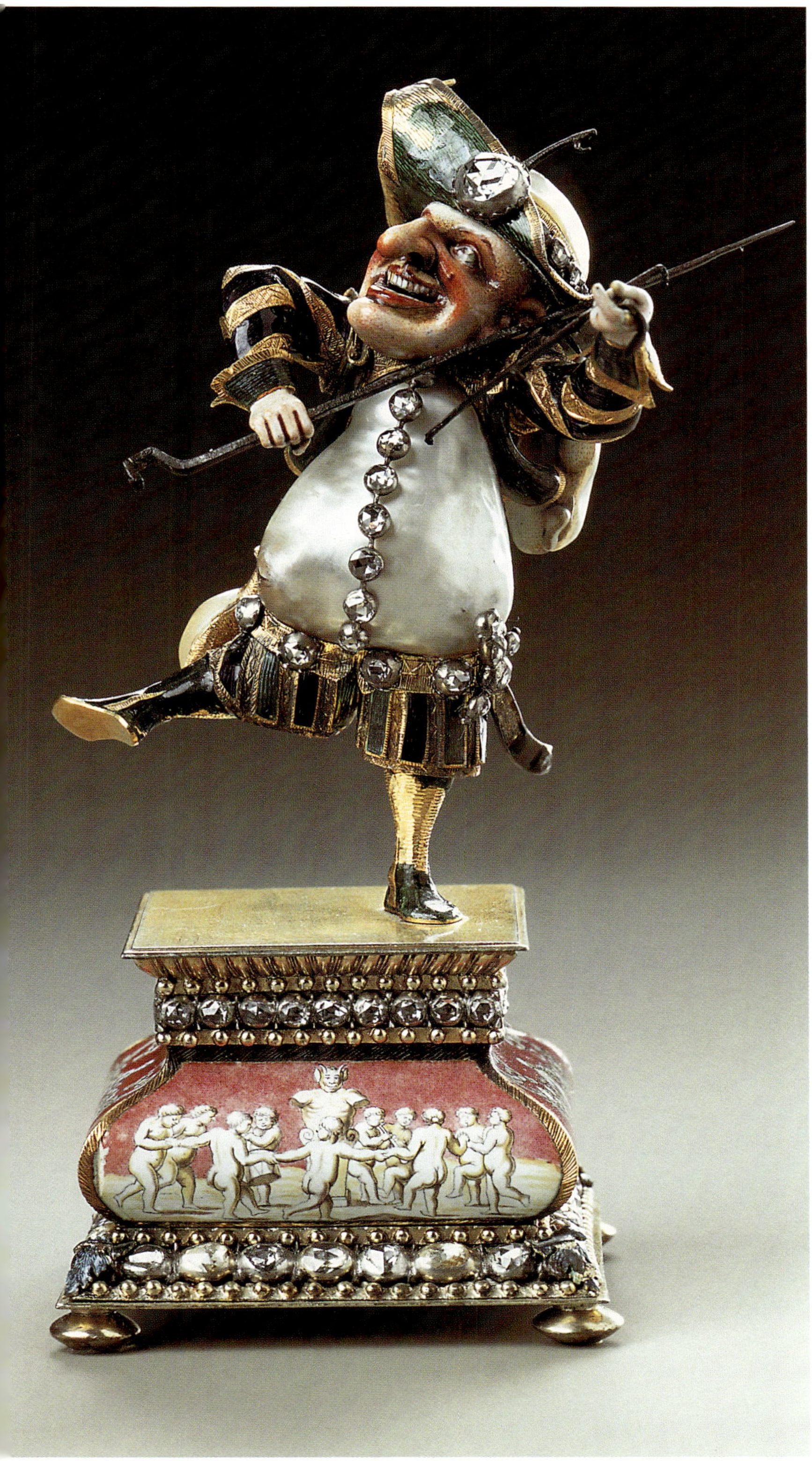

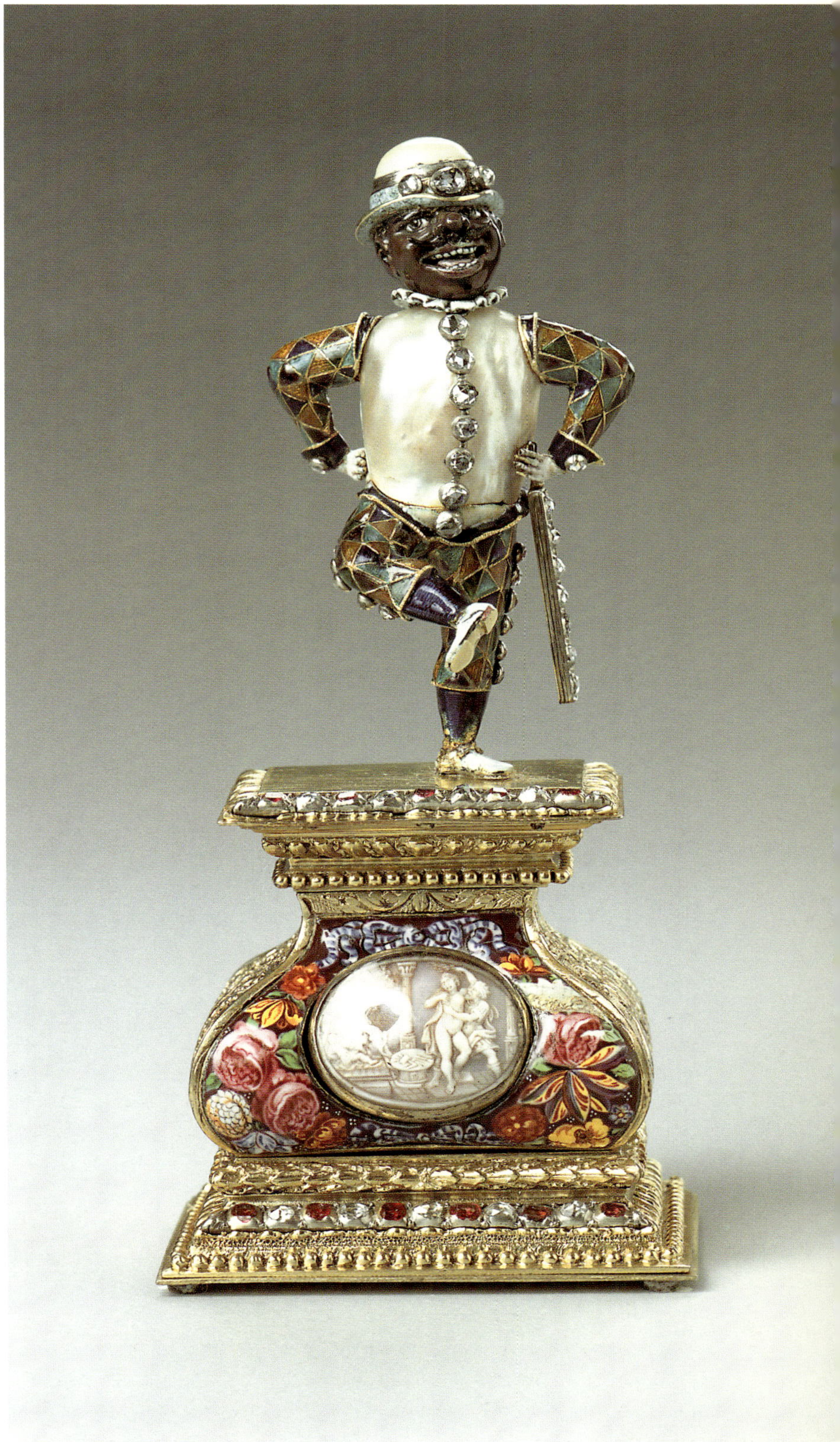

Nautilus Goblet with Satyr-Shaped Shaft

Nautilus shell, gilt silver
Design: Balthasar Permoser
Goldsmith's work: Bernhard Quippe
Berlin, circa 1707
H. 30 cm, Inv.-no. III 189

Nautilus Goblet with Coral Branches

Nautilus shell, gilt silver, coral, garnets
Nautilus carving: workshop of Cornelius van Bellekin
Amsterdam, middle of the 17th century
Foot group: presumably Nuremberg, beginning of the 17th century
New mount: Johann Heinrich Köhler
Dresden, circa 1724
H. 42 cm, Inv.-no. III 185

In the decades around 1600, goldsmiths turned the bowls of the *nautilus pompilius*, a species of squid that originated in the South Pacific, into elegant albeit fragile *Display Goblets* and *Kunstkammer* objects. The artistic peak of nautilus goblets had thus already occurred a few generations prior to the date when two masterpieces of this type were made for Augustus the Strong. The one *Goblet* grapples in a loving and detail-oriented manner with the problems of supporting the bowl that has a shimmer akin to mother-of-pearl and becomes an awkward burden to the Satyr: He painstakingly sustains the pearl boat with his neck; his head pressed to one side, while he seeks relief by putting his right goat's foot on the plain bottom of the goblet and presses his left hand under his buttocks in search of stabilization. The round area on which he sits offers him little room, making his task even more burdensome. Balthasar Permoser, who conceived of the sculptural *Display Goblet*, intelligently integrated the attributes of the sylvan deity – his Pan's pipe, ivy wreath and the animal hide clothing – into a composition that featured labor and burden. The gilt silver clasps are bedecked with acanthus and wine foliage as well as grapes – an ornament corresponding to the sensuous theme of the dionysiac fellow. The smiling face of the frenzied, rigorous Pan, deity of mountains and forests confronts the viewer from the tip of the bowl. Above him, on the *Bowl*'s crest, rests a smiling panther, symbol of the god Dionysius.

This *Goblet* is one of the rare collaborations of an eminent Late Baroque sculptor with a well-versed master goldsmith. The latter stamped the display vessel with his mark and may thus be identified as the today largely unknown Berlin-based Bernhard Quippe. Between 1698 and 1708, the Saxon court sculptor Balthasar Permoser paid numerous visits to the electoral Brandenburg residence that experienced an artistic flowering under the first Prussian king, Frederick I. Beside a number of large sculptures for Berlin's city castle and other sculptural pieces he made there, he also fabricated this unusual *Goblet* towards the end of his sojourn.

It was presumably on the occasion of the 1724 furnishing of the Green Vault's Treasury Museum, that Johann Heinrich Köhler created a very special type of »objet trouvé« for Augustus the Strong. In doing so, the court jeweler took elements from disparate artworks in the Treasury's reserve and reassembled them into original display pieces. The *Nautilus Bowl* with tendrils and grotesques inserted into the surface in relief style, was possibly – like some bowls still extant today in the Green Vault storage – originally without a mount. The refined decoration of the exotic shell was made in the workshop of Cornelius van Bellekin, who lived in Amsterdam in the second half of the 17th century. A masked figure of a grotesque with cuirass sits on a tortoise that serves as his saddle and rides on a dragon, is connected with the *Bowl*. The dragon's hindquarters and tail are made from a richly intertwined coral branch. The peculiar group on the foot was likely made in Nuremberg at the beginning of the 17th century and is first mentioned in the 1640 *Kunstkammer* inventory. With a combination of creativity and technical skill, Köhler united the parts that did not belong together with clasps and bars. On the top, he placed a lipped edge whose finely grained and heaving surface testifies to excellent goldsmith's work. A dragon, outfitted with teeth, sensitivity, and witticism crowns this imaginative new creation.

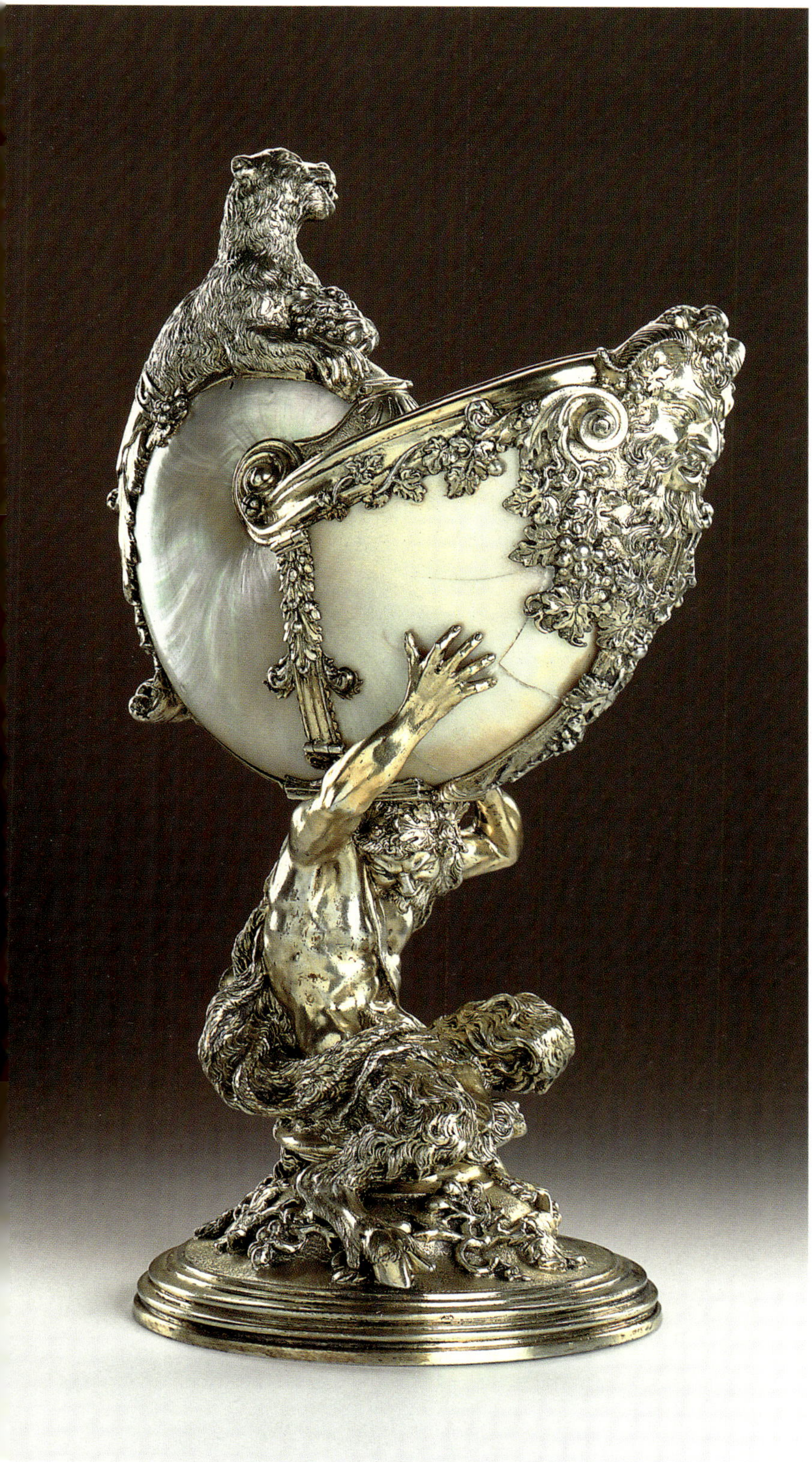

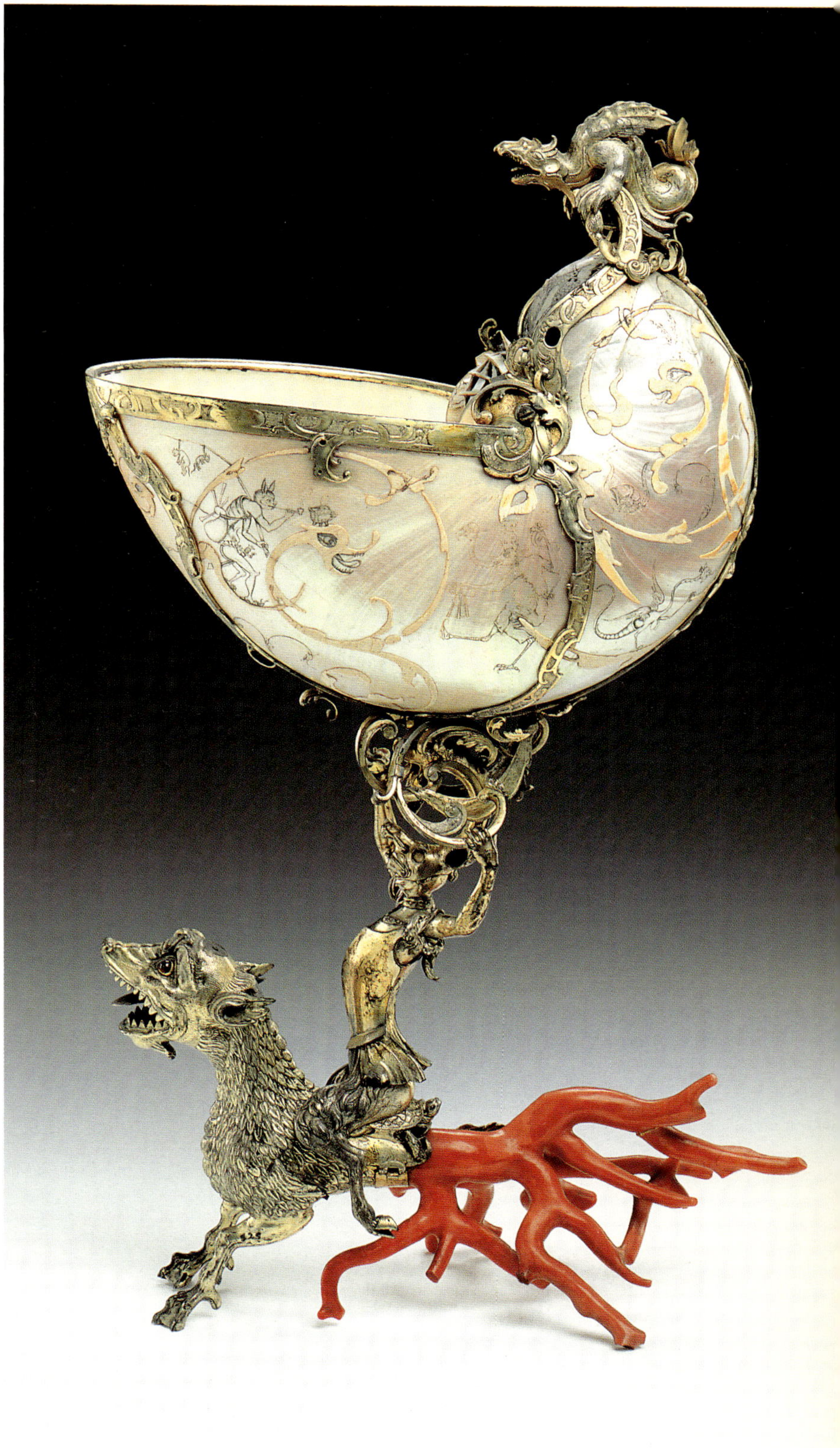

Bowl with Leaf-Shaped Handles

Chalcedony
Grinding mill of Johann Friedrich Böttger
Dresden, between 1713 and 1715
D. 13,6 cm, Inv.-no. V 544

Shell-Shaped Bowl with Dolphin

Rock crystal, gilt silver, lapis lazuli
Giovanni Battista Metellino
Milan, before 1724
H. 33 cm, Inv.-no. V 312

Today, Johann Friedrich Böttger (1682 – 1719) is primarily known as the inventor of European hard-paste porcelain, who presented his first examples to Augustus the Strong in 1709. Later, he tried to improve the technical process for creating porcelain but also worked in other innovative areas. One of the issues he tackled was the improvement of gold-ruby glass, developed by the Brandenburg alchemist Kunckel von Löwenstern. He developed a technique that facilitated the fusion of colorless glass with a shiny, ruby-red glass paste. He also concerned himself early on with stonecutting techniques that would enable one to work the hard, dark-brown Böttger stoneware.

Augustus the Strong was likewise interested in the art of traditional stonecutting, and he sought to establish the craft in Saxony. Between 1713 and 1715, his alchemist and engineer therefore founded a new grinding mill to work domestic precious stones outside the Dresden city gates. The grinding and polishing mill on the Weißeritz river was to satisfy the most advanced requirements in order to lend artistic shapes to precious stones quarried in Saxony. However, the grinding mill only operated during a test phase that lasted but a few years and was never completed.

The chef d'oeuvre of this time is an exceedingly carefully worked *Bowl* made from one piece of chalcedony and adorned with leaf-shaped handles that are only a fraction of an inch thick. An eccentric decoration based on East Asian prototypes adorns the walls of the vessel »aus einem Sächß. Kiesel Stein« (from a Saxon gravel stone). The high-qual-

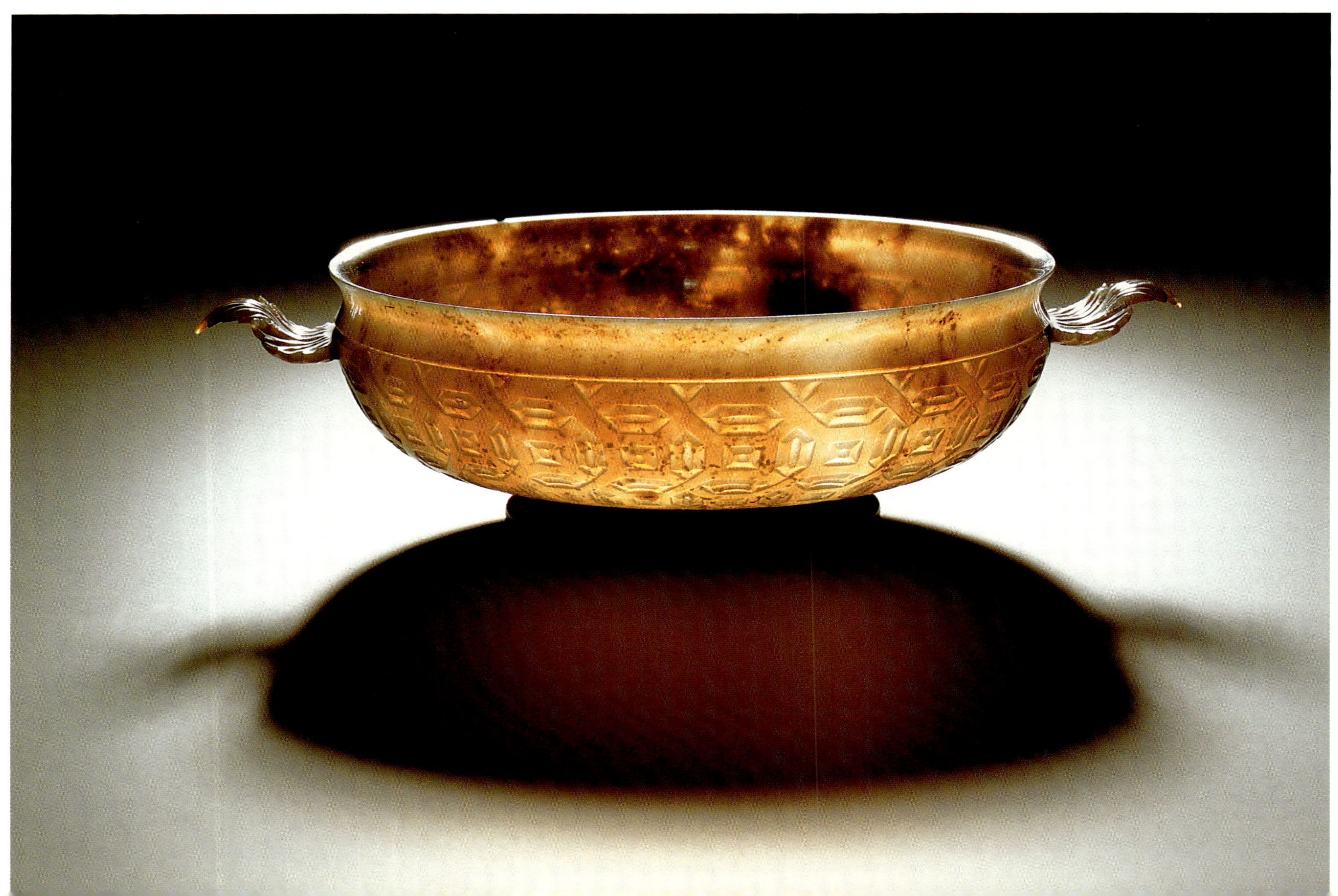

ity cutting was conceivably fabricated to demonstrate to the royal collector the level of productivity the precious stone manufactory was able to attain.

It is indicative of the Green Vault's function under Augustus the Strong that records of the most advanced Saxon technology were also integrated into his Treasury Museum. Apart from the country's inherited material wealth, the museum served – as did the artistic masterpieces of Permoser and Dinglinger – as part of the prince elector-king's self-portrayal. Beyond the discriminating *Bowl*, only very few other pieces from this Dresden-based place of production remain. In all likelihood, these stonecutting items plus Böttger stoneware and white porcelain were included in the same delivery of January 1715 and came into the possession of Augustus the Strong.

Also in 1715, the prince elector-king sent his chamberlain Alphonso to Italy. One of his tasks was to purchase modern rock crystal works, the best of which were still produced in Milan, where rock crystal cutting found its ultimate master in Giovanni Battista Metellino. Already before 1689 Louis XIV of France still counted among the latter's princely patrons. Regarding their quality and shape, Metellino's works are so indebted to the tradition of Milanese Mannerism that their creator was sometimes believed to be a master working around the year 1600. One of the typical Baroque features that distinguished them though, is that their bowls, cut in the shape of shells, are supported by three-dimensional dolphins or dragon figures. In addition, many of these vessels are adorned with a mount of silver gilt filigree and lapis lazuli trimmings. The business relationship between Augustus the Strong and the Milanese stonecutter, begun in 1716, lasted until after the death of Metellino and ended in 1724 with the acquisition of *Two Figural Rock Crystal Bowls* and a *Goblet*. The drawings used by Metellino's heirs to offer the merchandise for sale still exist.

In this context, it was possible to secure for the Green Vault, for the sum of 200 gold ducats, a *Large Shell-Shaped Bowl*. It is embraced by a dragon-like »dolphin« whose head hangs over the edge. The rock crystal object is distinguished by the perfect connection between the large bowl and its individual, sculptural parts. This is a thrilling, technically perfect work of the stonecutting art. Today, at least ten display vessels by the hand of Metellino remain in Augustus the Strong's collection of precious objects – most of them in the original boxes in which they crossed the Alps.

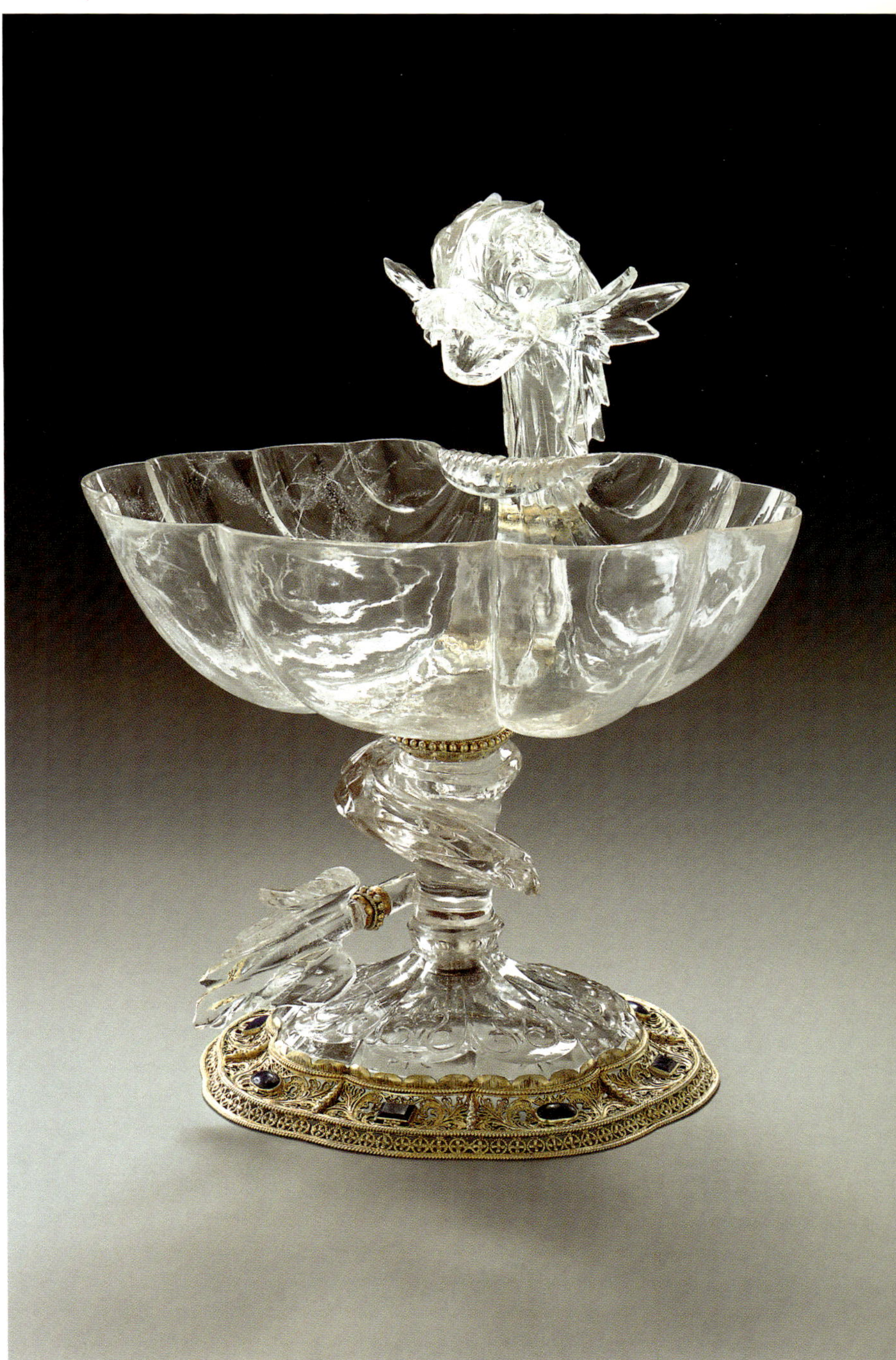

Owl

Gold, enamel, agate, diamonds
Gottfried Döring
Dresden, before 1713
H. 16,2 cm, Inv.-no. VI 17

Tortoise Shell Casket with a Camel Carrying a Perfume Phial

Wood, tortoise shell, brass, silver, gold, ivory, cold paint, silk, glass, diamonds
Presumably Augsburg, before 1727
L. 18,3 cm, H. 18,2 cm, Inv.-no. VI 240

Gottfried Döring belongs to the first generation of Dresden's Late Baroque goldsmiths. From 1686 until his death in 1718 he worked as a successful master goldsmith in the electoral residential town. Augustus the Strong even appointed him his court jeweler. However, only a few cabinet pieces in the Green Vault remain tied to Döring's name. Some of them reveal the influence of his brother-in-law Dinglinger. Döring's own creative qualities surface in a small, golden *Owl* garnished with diligently enameled plumage. The night bird's suggestively gazing eyes – in the European tradition, owls symbolize wisdom – are made from semi-spherical agate discs. The *Owl* stands on a high pedestal bedecked with emeralds, on which diamond-studded lizards also roam. The *Bird* itself has a removable head and wears a necklace made of glimmering diamonds. A gilt silver inlay in the *Owl*'s body made it possible for the collector's item to be used as a drinking vessel if needed. The prince elector-king procured this carefully conceived piece of Dresden treasury art – a naturalistic piece of goldsmith's sculpture – in 1713 and paid 1,200 thaler for it.

In 1727, the ivory statuette of a *Camel* standing on a platform of tortoise shell came to the Treasury Museum – the Green Vault had already been transformed. Along with other objects, it was part of Christiane Eberhardine's estate. The Near Eastern pack animal carries two large gilt brass suitcases and is guided by a Moor made of ivory and colored wood. The *Camel Group* with its seemingly utilitarian function (both of the high suitcases could be opened) stands in the tradition of gallantries, popular in the decades around 1700. Finely worked glass phials to store perfume were kept inside the luggage and are decorated with additional diamond trimmings and incised symbols of the four elements.

Although as a sculpture, the *Camel Group* does not reach the high artistic level of ivory carving that was possible during the first third of the 18th century, it is still a typical example of a number of South German fancy goods that are preserved in the Green Vault. In the fall of 1731, Augustus the Strong bought »von den Augspurgern« (from the Augsburgers), as the inventory notes, two works made of ivory and tortoise shell, closely related to the *Camel Group*. Little hammered-in marks may be found on the sometimes very small gold appendixes such as the edge of the bell or the camel's necklace and the suitcase hardware and reveal that they were articles of trade for the prince's requirements. Gold objects directly produced for the court do not have marks.

A comparable item is kept in the Museo degli Argenti in Florence; it takes the form of a heavily loaded *Donkey* that is ridden by a monkey while a man from the Near East holds the leash. It arrived as part of Anna Maria Ludovica de' Medici's bequest, widow of the Palatine Prince Elector Jan Willem and likely originates from their jointly held electoral Palatine collection of precious objects.

The fact that the *Camel Carrying a Perfume Phial* was originally owned by Electress Christiane Eberhardine proves once again that Augustus the Strong's collection of treasury objects was not an isolated instance within the electorate Saxony. Like this work, a considerable number of precious and fancy goods that entered the Green Vault after 1724 stem from princely inheritances.

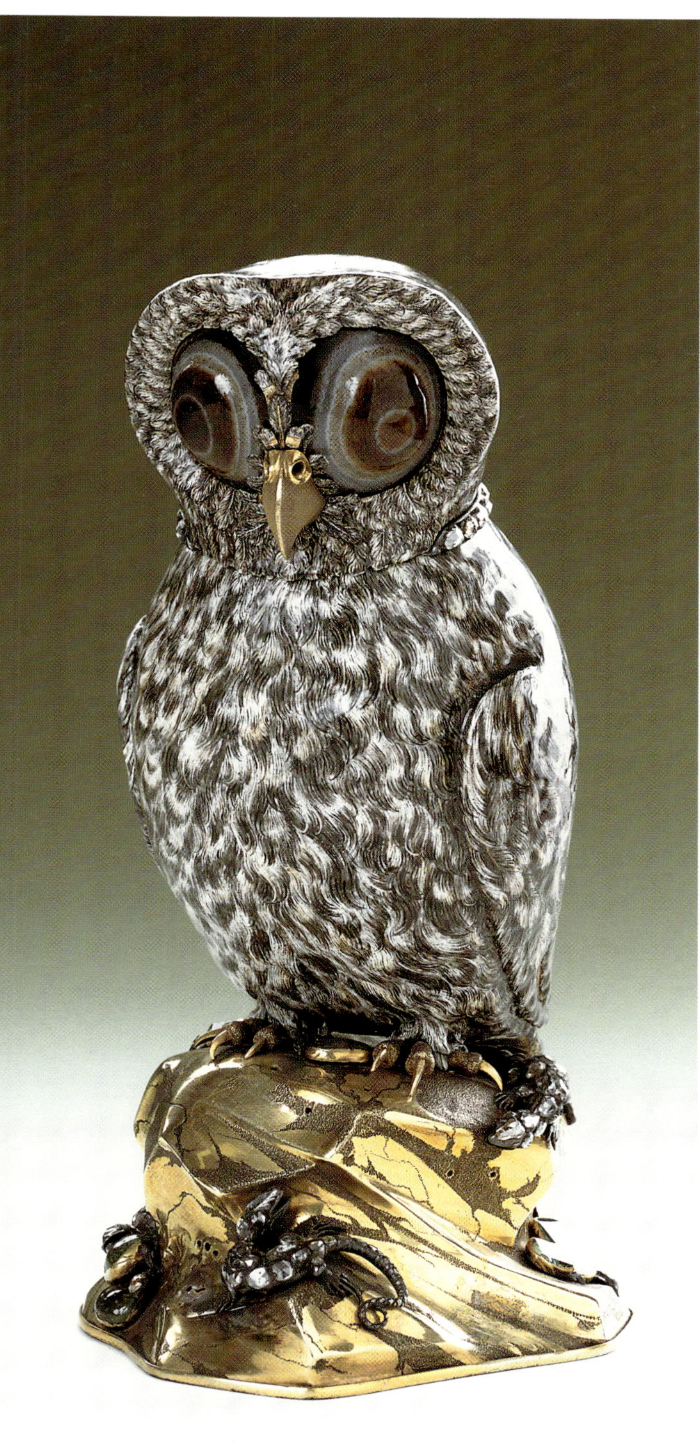

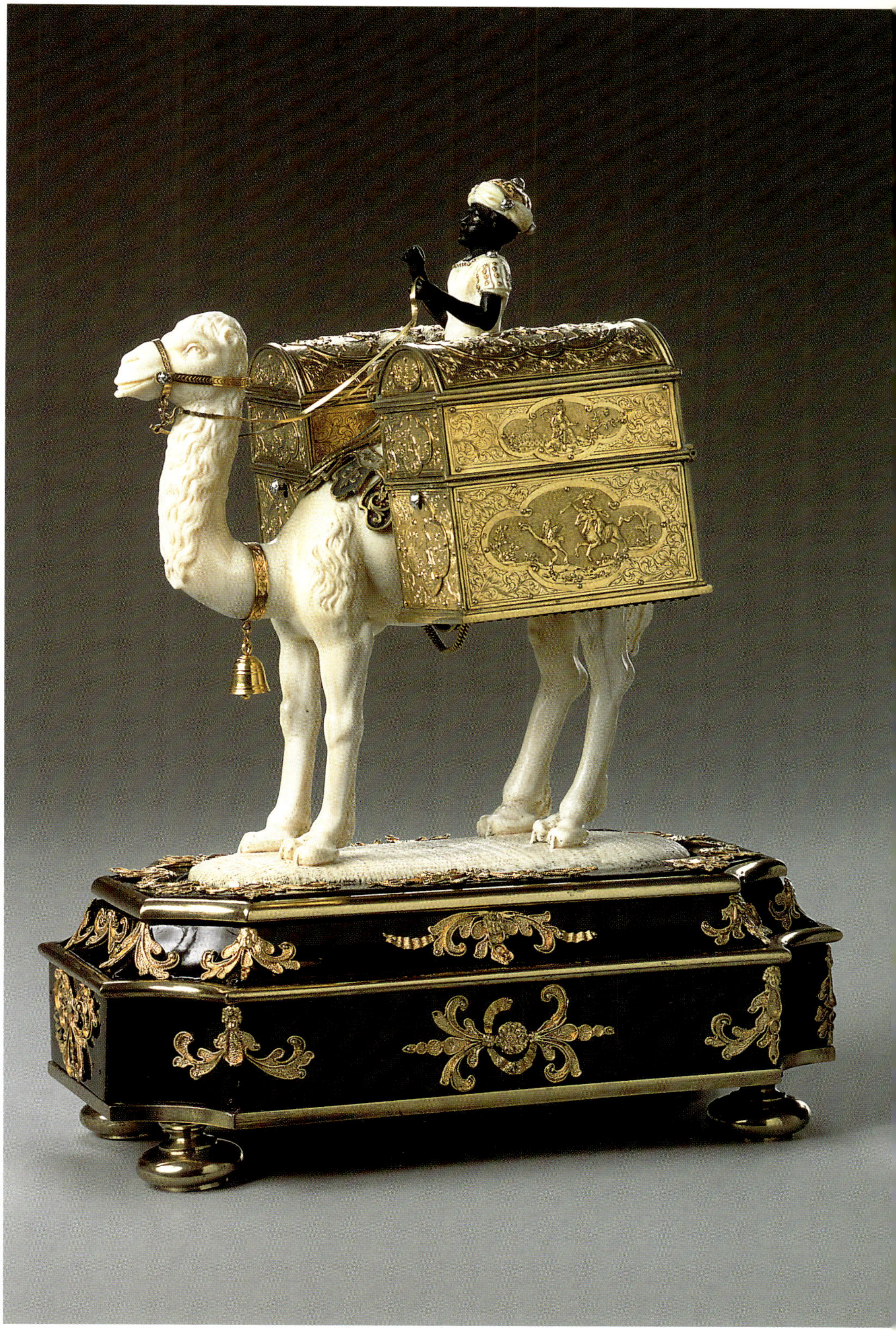

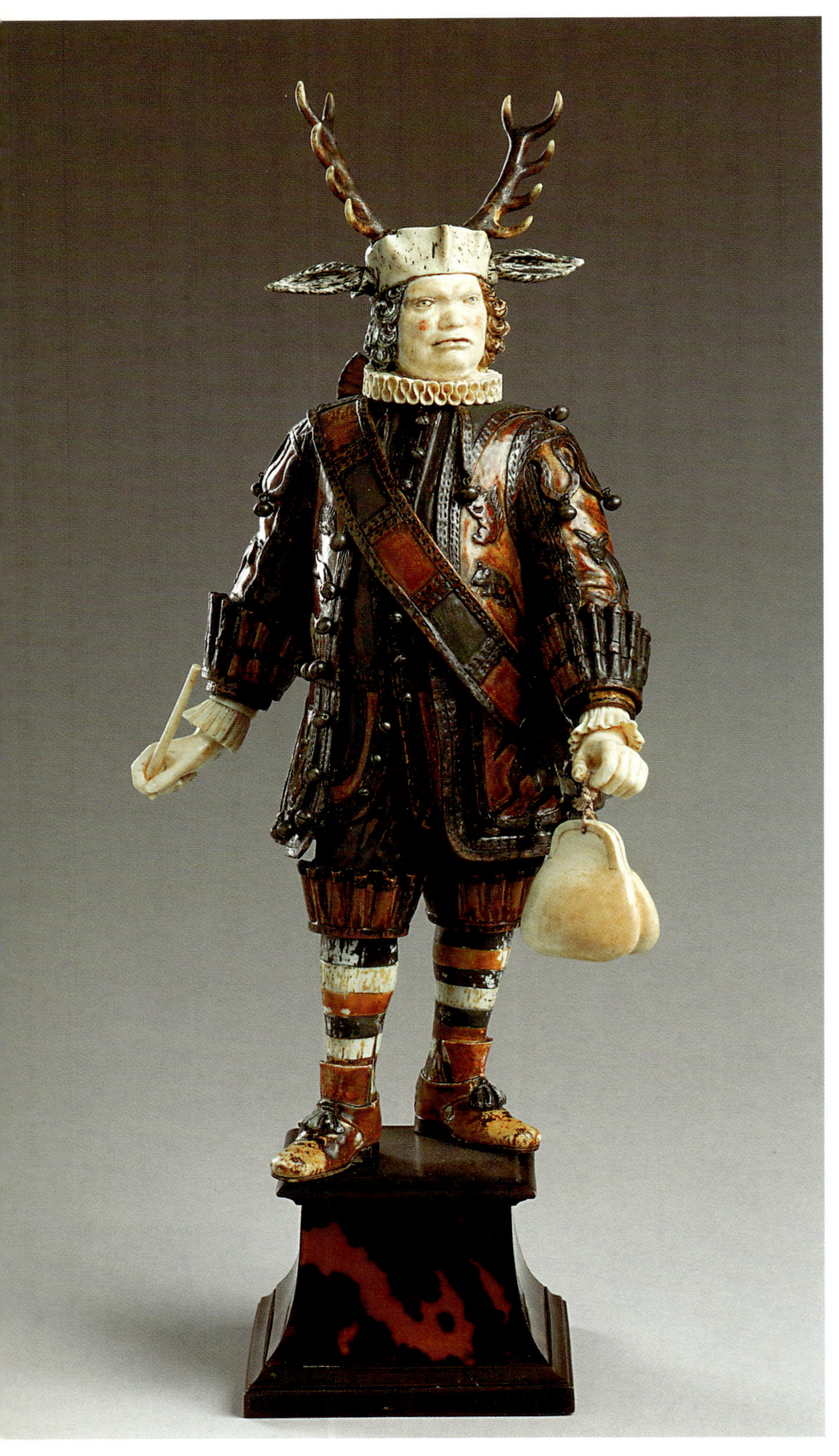

Statuette of *Hoftaschenspieler* (Court Juggler) Fröhlich with Stag's Antlers

Wood, polychromy, and ivory
Presumably Carl August Lücke the Elder
Dresden, before 1733
H. 28,5 cm, Inv.-no. 1942/1

Box for Writing Utensils with *Hoftaschenspieler* (Court Juggler) Fröhlich on a Pig-Drawn Carriage

Ivory, wood, varnish, silver, gold, precious stones
Carl August Lücke the Elder
Dresden, before 1731
H. 23,3 cm, L. 23,8 cm, Inv.-no. 1969/1

Beginning in the 1730s, the *Hoftaschenspieler* (Court Juggler) Joseph Fröhlich was a particularly popular public figure. Of those affiliated with the court, he was the second most often depicted person after members of the royal family. Born in 1694 in Alt-Aussee in the Salzkammergut, Austria, he apprenticed as a miller and first performed in front of Augustus the Strong in Dresden in 1725. By 1727, the entertainer and magician moved to the electoral royal court and was appointed court juggler. His wide array of magic tricks combined with his witty language and natural humor, as well as his tendency toward carefree presentations of coarse pranks assured him the undivided sympathy of two successive rulers until his death in 1757. His portrait in the characteristic, albeit caricatured and exaggerated costume of Styria, Austria, has survived in numerous statuettes made of porcelain, clay, faience, sand stone, and ivory, but also in copperplate engravings, etchings, paintings, and medals. Around the year 1731, a number of small size wood and ivory sculptures were added to Augustus the Strong's collection of treasury art.

The rendering of the entertainment artist in attire corresponding to courtly fashion dates to approximately this time. The jester wears a cap on his head from which grow stag's antlers and donkey's ears. In his hands, he holds a magician's staff and the juggler's satchel. Affixed and painted onto the clothes are monkey, donkey, owl, long-tailed monkey, and other animals, i.e. creatures bearing a certain iconographic reference to the jester's profession. Fröhlich's 1757 estate inventory reveals that the well-established comedian owned a large number of courtly garments, costumes, and accessories. Depending on the type of festivity, he wore the appropriate outfits and accessories. The inventory of Precious Objects lists, as an item that corresponds to the polychrome *Statuette*, the *Portrayal of Fröhlich's Wife* in a sarcastic posture and Styrian costume, today with the art trade. Both works of art, attempting to delineate faithful portraits, were presumably produced by the Dresden ivory carver Carl August Lücke the Elder.

In all likelihood, this master was also the author of »Eine Machine von schwarzen Eben Holz und Elffenbein, den Hoftaschenspieler Joseph Frölich vorstellend« (a black ebony and ivory machine depicting the Court Juggler Joseph Fröhlich,) listed on July 13, 1731 as a new acquisition in the Green Vault's inventory. The object is a *Box for Writing Utensils* whose walnut base contains a drawer to store writing tools. In an eccentrically shaped carriage situated on the plain pedestal, the »Kurzweilige Rat« (amusing counsel) Fröhlich's round head may be spotted. He wears a typical Alpine peasant's outfit including a round collar, long since unfashionable, and a pointed hat with a jester's bell. In his left hand, he sports his familiar juggler's pouch, whereas he holds the reins of the wild boars' vehicle in his right hand. A monkey is seated on one of the boars as outrider, and Fröhlich's armorial bird, the owl, is placed on the wagon shaft. The road sign lists: »NARREN DORFF. 1. Meil.« (jester's village one mile), »ZUM SAUSTAL und / GROS FLEGELS / DORF 1. MEI« (to pigsty and big hooligan town one mile), as well as »GRAETZ 80. MEILEN. / AUSEE. 4. MEI:« (border 80 miles, Aussee four miles). The precious ebony carriage with silver mounts hides a burlesque surprise: Upon opening one of the two lateral doors, one notices that the court official is seated on the wagon with his pants down. This is a practicable night-stool.

When Lücke created his *Box for Writing Utensils*, Late Baroque treasury art had reached its terminus. With the passing of Augustus the Strong in January 1733, its production decreased rapidly in Dresden, an observation that also holds true for other centers of fabrication within the Holy Roman Empire of the German Nation. With the advent of court Rococo culture, the market for comparable cabinet pieces collapsed almost completely.

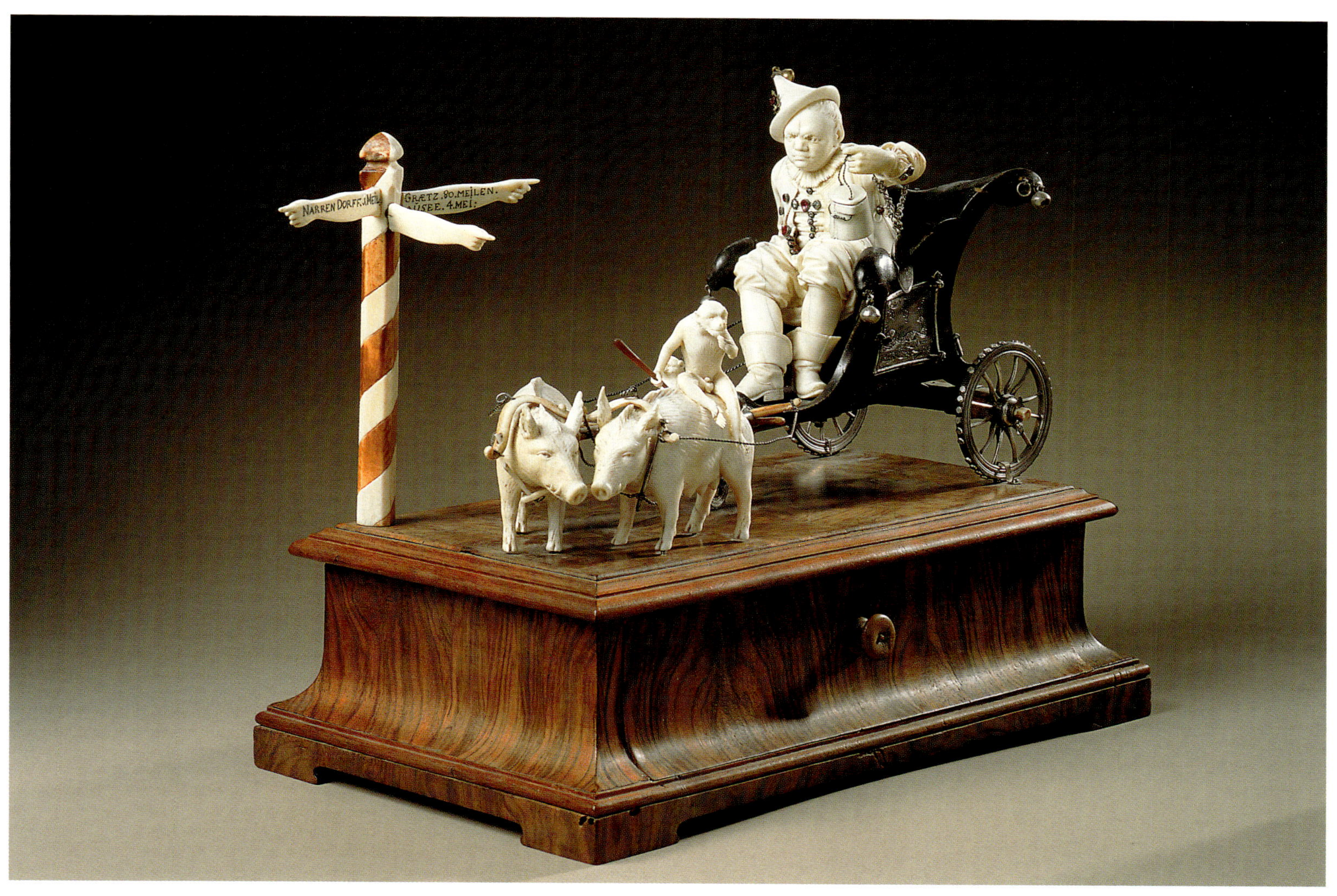

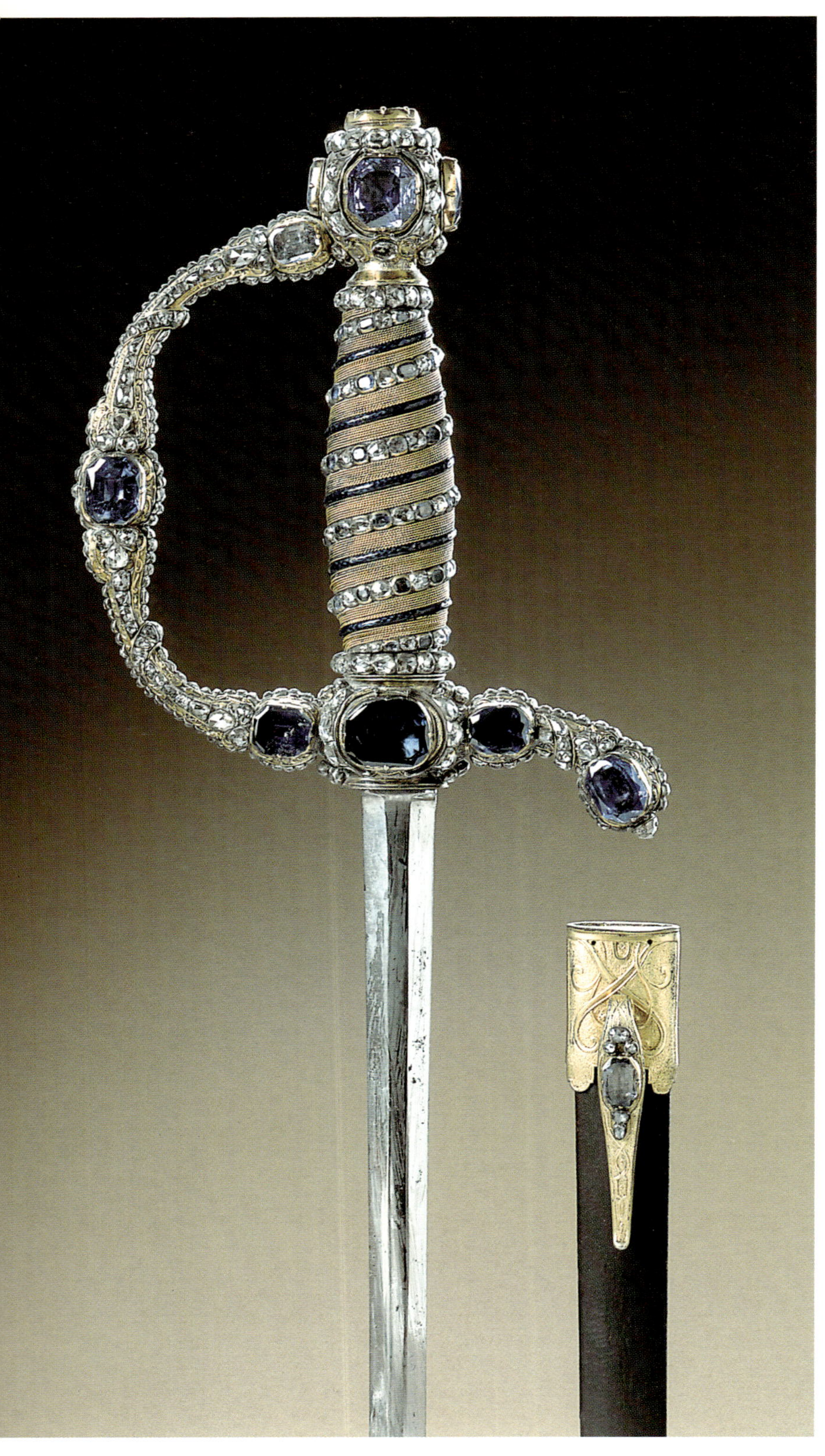

Parade Sword from the Sapphire Garniture

Gold, silver, enamel, steel, leather, sixty-five sapphires,
more than 300 diamond roses (originally 389)
Johann Melchior Dinglinger and workshop
Dresden, circa 1700, altered in 1721 and 1738
H. of the hilt 17 cm, L. of the sword 91,5 cm, Inv.-no. VIII 165

From the material standpoint, the House of Wettin's jewels represented by far the most valuable part of the Green Vault's holdings in the 18th century. As the key portion of the Saxon-Polish crown treasury, it represented an indispensable contribution to Augustus the Strong's and Augustus III's display of royal majesty. When he was a young duke, Augustus the Strong witnessed King Louis XIV of France in his gala robes at Versailles: This refined expression of royal dignity deeply impressed him. In contrast to the French model, the interest of the Saxon monarch was not concentrated on diamond garnitures alone. Augustus the Strong transferred his personal preference for colored precious stones to jewelry. During his reign, brilliant and rose cut diamond garnitures were created as well as ones bedecked with sapphires, rubies, and emeralds. Additional garnitures included those made of carnelian, one agate, one tortoise shell, as well as one golden and one silver hunting garniture. They all take their names from the most prominently represented precious stone or the dominant material. All parts of these jewel garnitures were additionally adorned with smaller diamonds. In the event that it was needed, the individual parts of an ensemble could be sewn onto selected robes or could be worn with them.

Parade weapons occupied a special position within display jewelry: Instead of serving for defensive purposes, they were meaningful symbols of the nobility, while simultaneously representing – thanks to their composition and material value – their owner's rank within the courtly society.

After 1721, Augustus the Strong commissioned Dinglinger to refurbish an old sapphire garniture with much richer stone trimmings. Although the *Sword* received its present shape in 1722, the chiseling of the »old« parade weapon's hilt guard and quillons is still recognizable. 389 medium and small size diamond roses were added to the large sapphires already in place. Typical features of parade weapons designed by Johann Melchior Dinglinger, the finely turned, ascending gold threads – placed in grooves and wound around the handle – alternate with blue enamel bands. In the first decades of the 18th century, the *Sword* was suspended from a broad band placed over the left hip and leading to the center of the chest. A large, multipart *Sword Belt* served to hold this bandoleer and was an extra piece of decoration for the garment. Also preserved as part of the sapphire garniture, it consists of three clasps, three bolts, and four prongs.

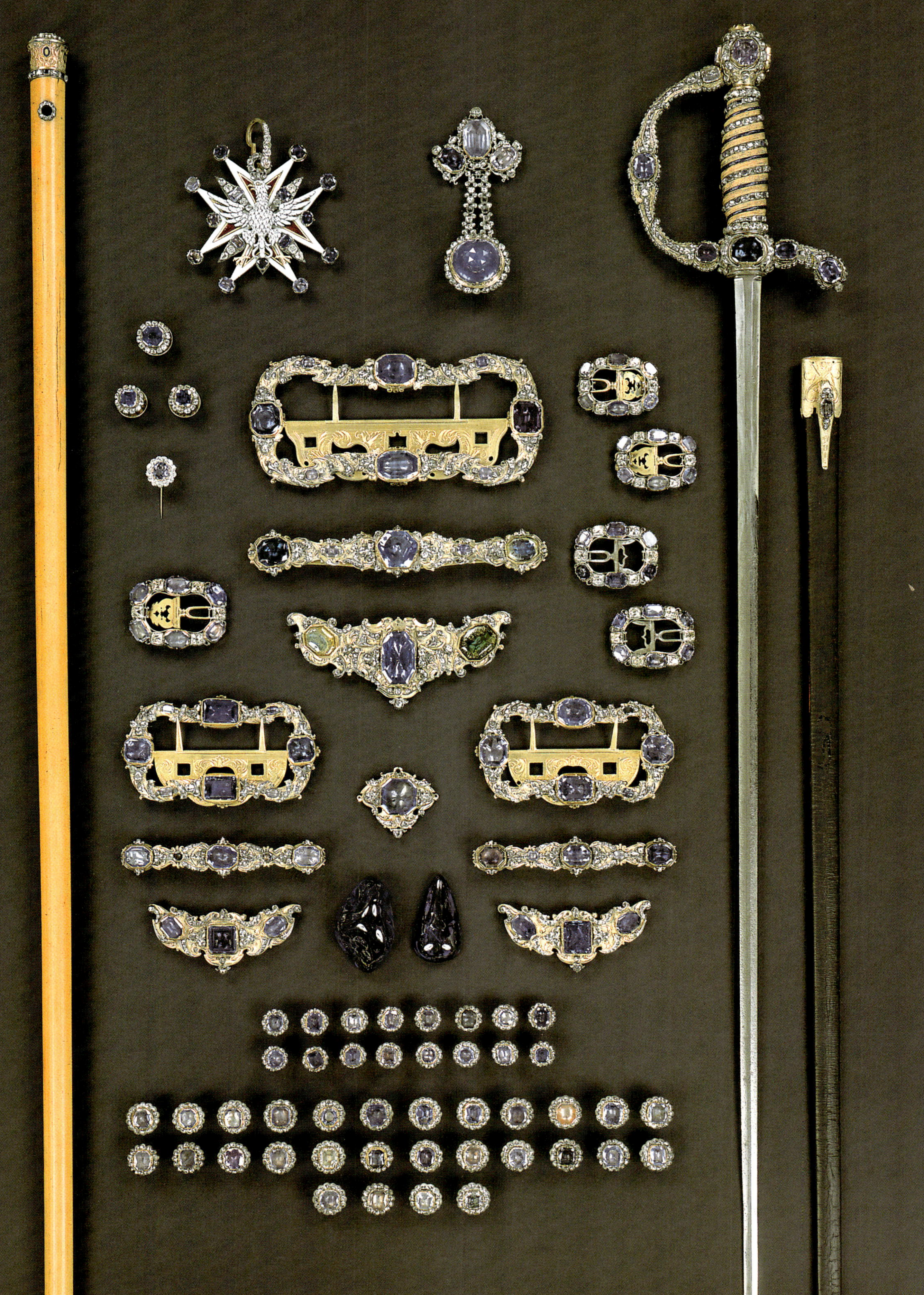

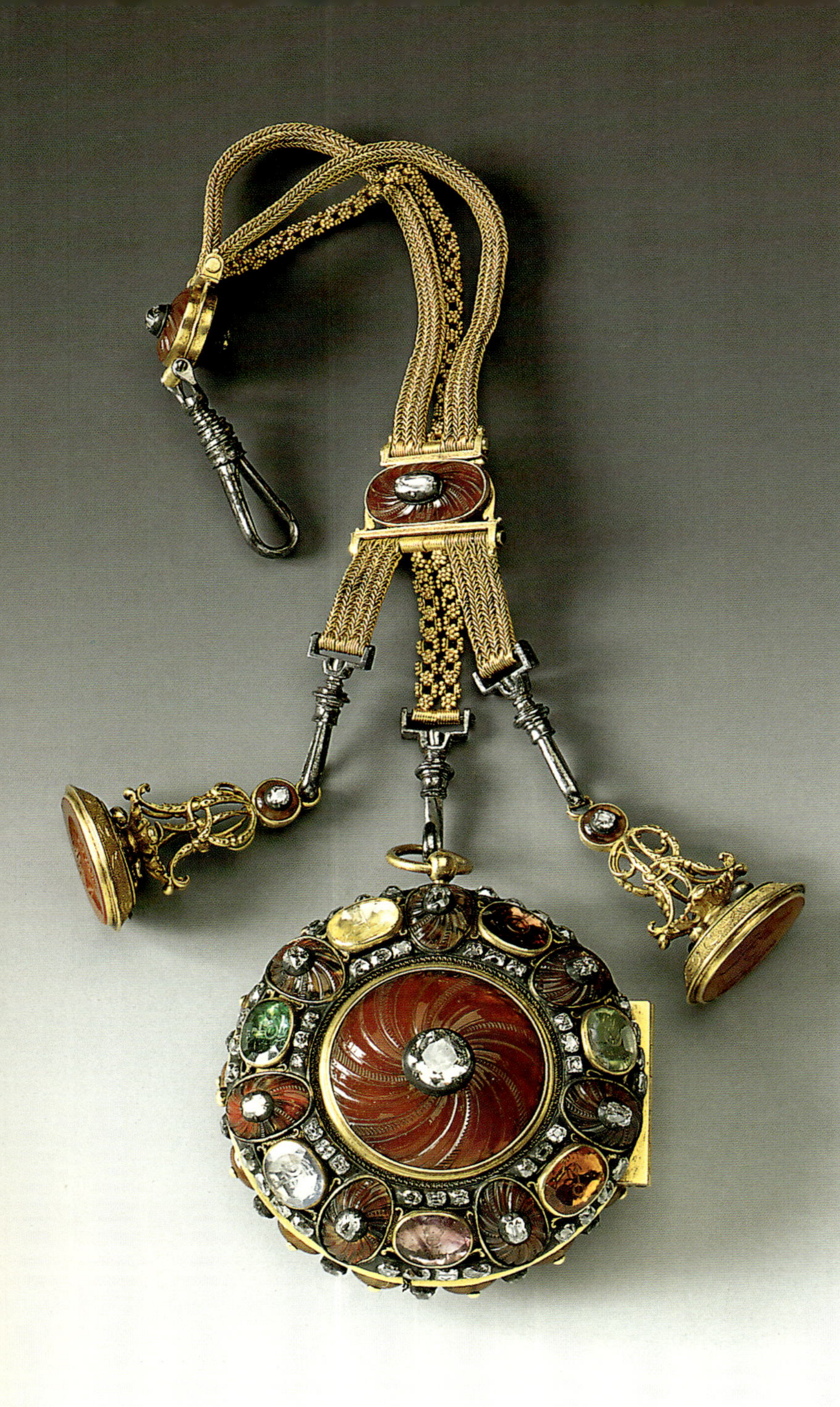

Watch with Chain from the Carnelian Garniture

Watch: carnelian, colored stones, brilliant cut diamonds, rubies, gold, silver gilt, enamel
Chain: Johann Melchior Dinglinger
Dresden, 1713
L. of the chain 22 cm
Watch-case: presumably Johann Melchior Dinglinger
Dresden, circa 1719
Diam. of the clock 5,5 cm, Inv.-no. VIII 234

Vast numbers of buttons for jackets and waistcoats – in those days at least thirty-six of each type – as well as cufflinks, shirt buttons, clasps for shoes, breeches, and hat formed part of the jewel garnitures' basic furnishings. Inseparably associated with these objects were the hat decoration in the shape of a brooch or aigrette, the parade sword, and the multipart sword belt that enabled one to carry the sword on the body. In the case of a hunting garniture, a hunting knife and whip were also obligatory. Extra items in a jewel garniture could include snuff-boxes and other receptacles, a cane, a notebook, a pocket watch, and an epaulette. The symbols of the Polish Order of the White Eagle, consisting of the eagle-shaped gem and the order's star, were crucial ingredients in the prince elector-king's clothing decoration. From 1722 onward, the decoration of the Order of the Golden Fleece was also added.

With its 127 surviving individual parts, the *Carnelian Garniture* is the largest Late Baroque jewel garniture. The ensemble likely existed in part as early as 1710 or was even mostly finished by then. The *Carnelian Garniture* was finally finished in its present state on the occasion of electoral prince Friedrich August's marriage to Maria Josepha in 1719. In the inventory of that year, the garniture's total value is estimated at 47,922 thaler, of which the production alone cost 4,680 thaler. The completely preserved stock of jacket and waistcoat buttons from this jewelry ensemble helps envision the original splendor of the other Dresden jewel garnitures. Thanks to the twenty-four drop-shaped »Hungarian« decorative buttons, the presence of two snuff-boxes, as well as one elongated carnelian case, this garniture's abundance of shapes becomes apparent.

Suspended from a finely braided, golden *Chain* with three loops at its lower end, an exquisite *Pocket Watch* also formed part of the original carnelian garniture and had already been delivered in 1713. Whereas the watch is fastened to the central loop, the lateral ones contain two of Augustus the Strong's personal seals, whose tiny golden handles take the shape of his monogram.

The watch-case, garnished with precious stones, was made for the festival of Saturn. This multi-day festivity concluded the ceremonies on the occasion of the electoral prince's wedding to Maria Josepha of Austria. A depiction of the festival edifice with its characteristic superstructure, expressly built for this state festival, is engraved onto the center of the watch's face. The precious stones on the watch-case's reverse refer to these celebrations. The signs of the planets under whose auspices the ceremonies were placed are engraved into the stones, specifically selected for symbolic reasons. Based on Ptolemeian ideas, the sun and the moon were assigned to the five planets then known. According to the view of alchemy – in which Augustus the Strong was very interested – the origin of all terrestrial metals (whose alchemical signs can also be found inside the watch-case) lay in the planets.

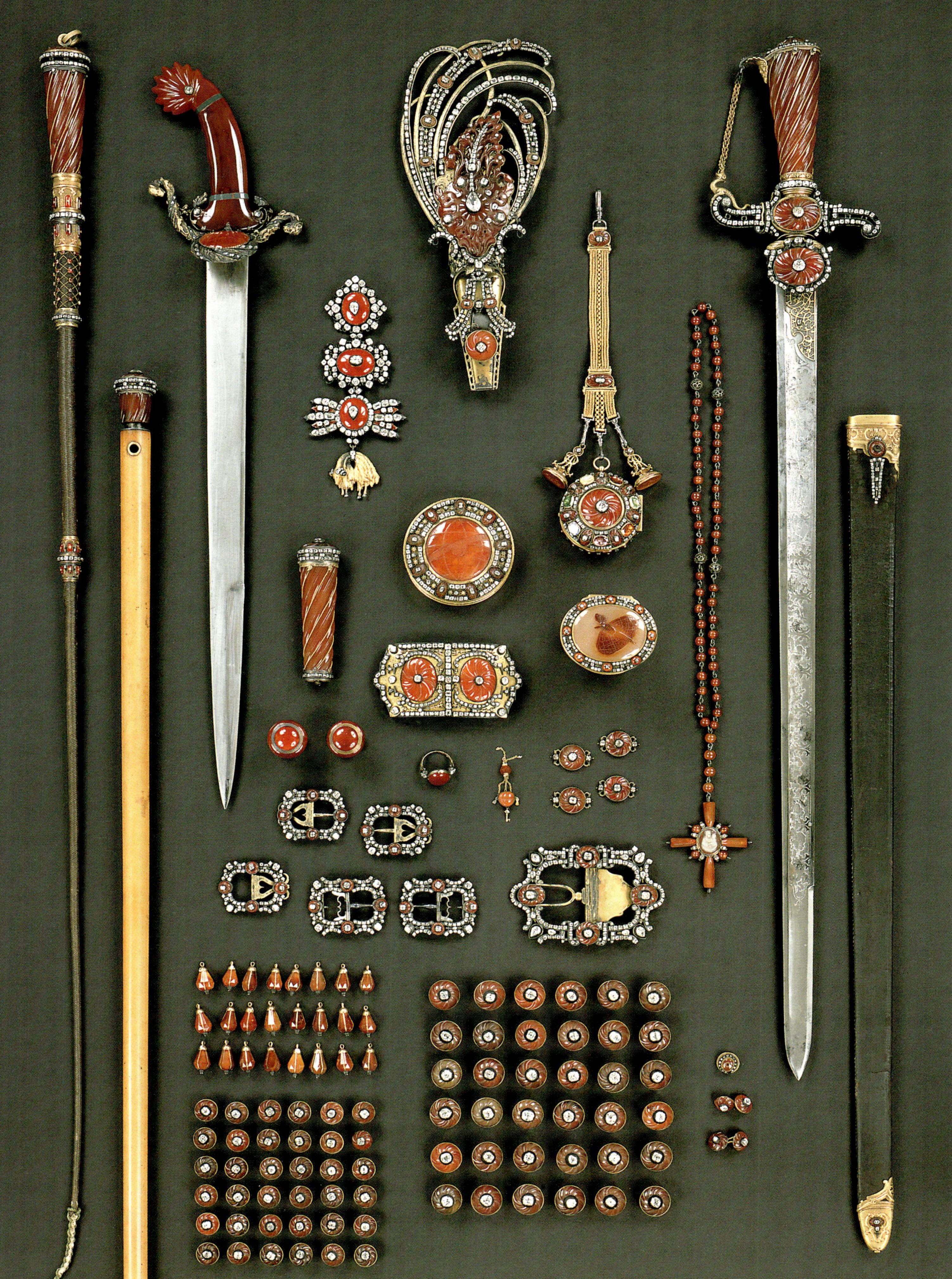

Cane from the Ruby Garniture

Gold, silver, one oval ruby, fifty-three brilliant cut diamonds, Spanish reed
Johann Heinrich Köhler
Dresden, before 1733
L. 94,2 cm, Inv.-no. VIII 12

Hunting Knife with Sheath from the Emerald Garniture

Nine emeralds, eighty-one brilliant cut diamonds, gold, silver, agate, steel, leather
Johann Melchior Dinglinger
Dresden, first decade of the 18th century
H. of the handle 15 cm, Inv.-no. VIII 144

Ceremonial and decorative staffs belong to the oldest regalia of human civilization. In almost all cultures, they symbolize strength, dignity, and power. The 18th century was, at least for members of the nobility, a century of the cane. Together with the snuff-box, it represented one of the utensils that best characterized an elegant courtier's habits. Starting in the late 17th century, great displays of extravagance were made with these two gallantry elements. As older examples preserved in the Green Vault and the Armory reveal, the thrill of promenading with walking sticks was already known to the late Renaissance prince electors. It seems that canes advanced to the echelon of luxury items under King Henry IV of France. His grandson, Louis XIV, used the jewel-studded staff as a medium for his ritualized court ceremony. The distance between the person of the king and the aristocracy is expressed by the fact that the Sun King never appeared in public without the staff, while no one else had the right – with the exception of the general controller of finances – to carry this popular and fashionable accessory in the sovereign's presence. What the French kings used for their own presentation was adapted by multiple major and minor potentates. How completely the prince elector-king internalized the French prototype of princely elegance is also illuminated by the fact that, upon his first encounter with Czar Peter I in 1698, he gave the latter a decorative cane richly adorned with diamonds as a parting gift.

With the exception of the two significantly diminished diamond garnitures, all of Augustus the Strong's jewel garnitures were equipped with at least one, sometimes numerous canes or pommels. All the surviving examples include the cane proper, made of Spanish reed. Their handles are mostly made of circular or polygonal pommels studded with precious stones appropriate to the respective garniture. Only in the tortoise shell garniture with its later date of fabrication is the handle made in the form of a bent crutch, permitting Augustus the Strong to lean on it.

The decorative ruby garniture's *Pommel* was made in the studio of a Dresden jeweler and likely already existed in 1719, although a detailed description is not found until in the 1733 Jewel Inventory. Exquisitely designed, the *Pommel* consists of a slightly convex and ovoid-cut ruby with faceted edges. A wreath of brilliant cut diamonds surrounds the large ruby, whereas an additional wreath marks the end of the golden case that is covered with abundant interlacing. The loop, inserted slightly below and intended for the hand band, is also framed by small brilliant cut diamonds.

The *Hunting Knife* was another object for princely ceremony, albeit less frequently encountered and thus surviving in fewer examples. This parade weapon goes back to the hunter's side weapon, in widespread use in the 18th century; with it, the wounded game received the fatal thrust. Within a princely hunting garniture –predominantly worn during hunting festivals – the hunting knife assumed the function of a parade sword. As a passionate lover of the hunt, Augustus the Strong owned numerous hunting garnitures. Hence, four hunting knives have survived from his jeweled ensembles.

The one originally belonging to the emerald garniture illustrates the initial character of a jewel garniture designed for hunting purposes. Its compact handle is made of light-brown agate with incised, reeling grooves. The golden threads inlaid into these grooves are typical features of Dinglinger's parade weapons. With this *Hunting Knife*, Johann Melchior Dinglinger produced a first class jeweled artwork whose meticulous details rank among the finest objects included in the treasury of Augustus the Strong. The artist varied the hunting motif: through his use of exotic and rare animals such as lions or bears, but also through the inclusion of finely delineated game living in domestic woodlands. The double-sided embellishment of the steel blade illustrates hunting scenes and was created by the copperplate engraver Moritz Bodenehr.

The *Hunting Knife* is not only a sumptuous work of art; its nine large emeralds and seventy-eight brilliant cut diamonds are priceless. In the beginning, a huge diamond, mounted over red foil, was placed on the shell of the safeguard. In 1722, Augustus the Strong had it replaced with the beautiful emerald cabochon he had brought from Warsaw.

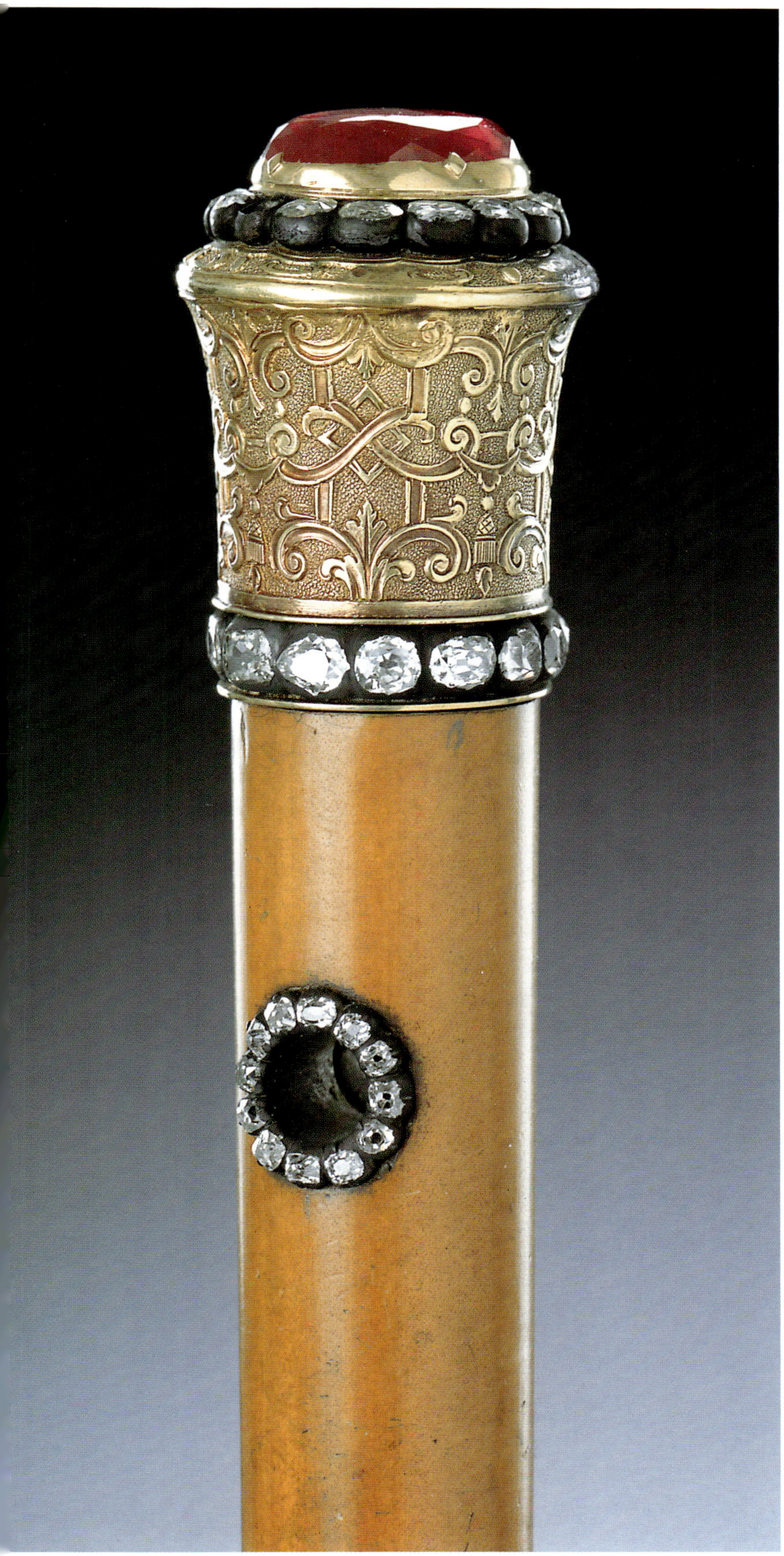

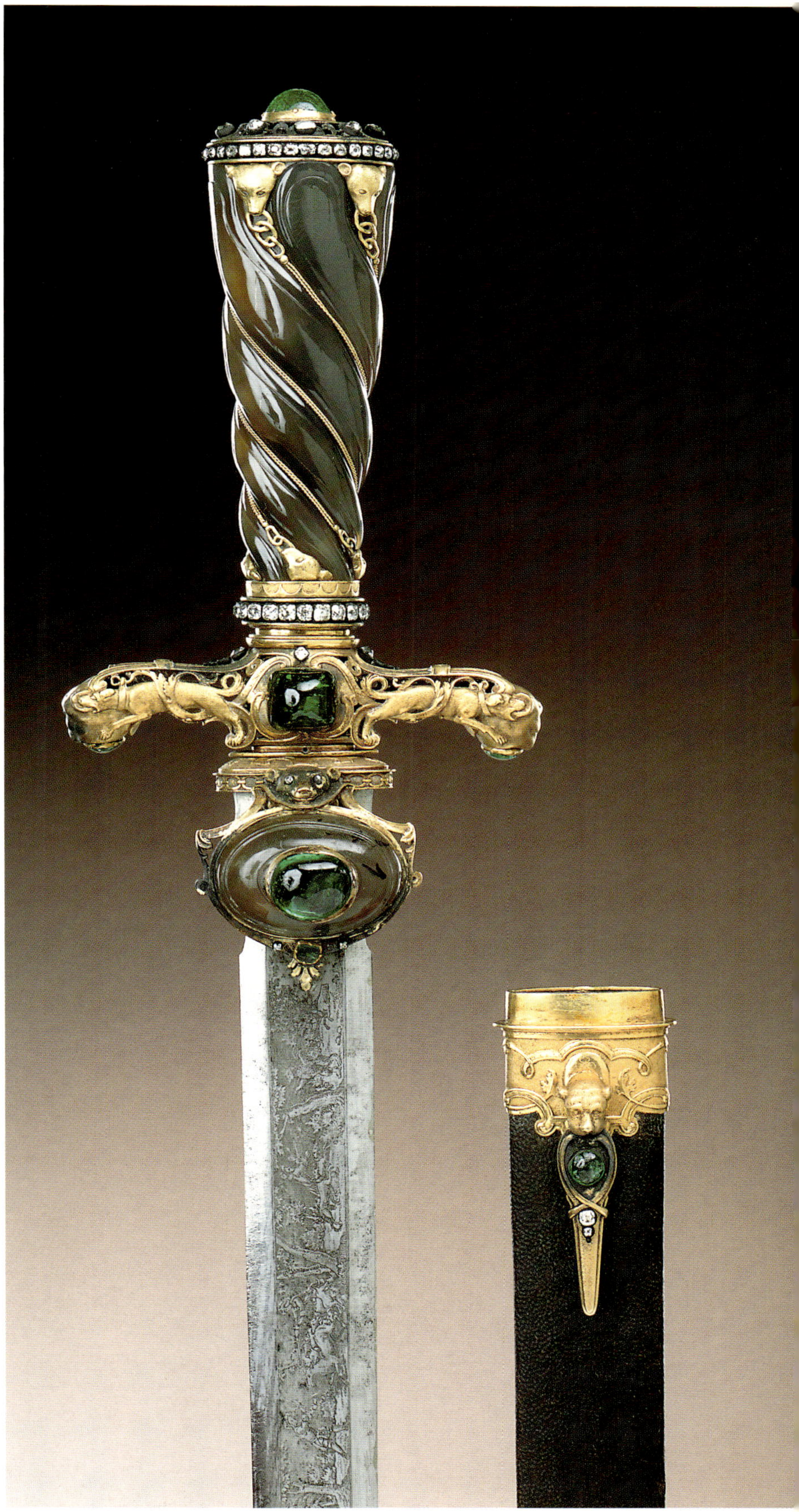

Badge of the Order of the Golden Fleece with Bohemian Garnets

Seven garnets (the largest with 46, 75 ct), 318 brilliant cut diamonds, gold, silver
Franz Diespach
Dresden or Prague, before 1749
H. in total 16,5 cm, Inv.-no. VIII 6

Badge of the Polish Order of the White Eagle from the Emerald Garniture

Sixteen emeralds, at least 342 brilliant cut diamonds, gold, silver, partly gilt
Johann August Jordan
Dresden, 1746
B. 10,4 cm, H. 7,8 cm, Inv.-no. VIII 143

The most exclusive decorative items on princely garments were the gems from secular knightly orders. One of the oldest and most respected among them was the Order of the Golden Fleece; membership was restricted to Catholic aristocrats. Founded in 1430 by the Burgundian Duke Philip the Good, the *toison d'or* became the highest order of the House of Hapsburg in the 16th century; their Burgundian heritage entitled them to hold the honorable position as sovereigns of the order. The badge of the order – tied to the person of the specific knight and bestowed upon the recipient by the sovereign of the order – was a golden pendant in the shape of a sheep's fleece suspended from a chain, the so-called collane, that consists of alternating fire steel and flint links. The sheep's fleece refers to the Greek legend of the Argonauts, relating the capture of the famous fleece by a group of Greek heroes. After the death of the last Hapsburg king of Spain, the head of the order, the succession was disputed. During the War of the Spanish Succession, both the Bourbon king of Spain and the Hapsburg emperor obtained the right to confer the order.

Starting in 1697, when he became Polish king, Augustus the Strong was the second Wettin ruler after Duke Georg (1531) to be inducted as knight of the Order of the Golden Fleece. However, it was not until 1722, contemporaneous with his son, Electoral Prince Friedrich August, that Emperor Charles VI bestowed the order's insignia upon him. The emperor granted the Saxon sovereigns the exceptional right to produce their own jeweled versions of the order for their own use. It was compulsory for the actual badge of the order to be returned to the master of the order upon the death of the respective knight. After 1722, numerous jewel-bedecked gems were fabricated of which eleven have survived. The oldest is the decorative order of the ruby garniture, made in the year the order was bestowed. The example from the tortoise shell garniture followed slightly later, as did the gem with Near Eastern topaz and the one with Near Eastern opals.

After his coronation, August III also developed an interest in the Golden Fleece jewelry and adapted it to the most current fashion. The *Badge of the Order of the Golden Fleece with Large Garnets* was made in Prague and was a new version of its predecessor. It contains the »extra große böhmische Granat« (extra large Bohemian garnets), temporarily incorporated into the king's crown in 1734. In December 1749, the *Garnet Fleece* was inventoried in the Green Vault. The three large garnet »bowls« (»Granatschalen«) are magnificently framed by four smaller garnets and 316 brilliant cut diamonds. The latter also form the elegant, richly waving »flammende Feuereisen« (flaming fire steels) from which the sheep's fleece is suspended.

When Augustus the Strong bestowed the first badges of his Polish-Lithuanian kingdom's Order of the White Eagle in the then Lithuanian town of Tykocin on November 1, 1705, he subtly referred to an earlier order that was reportedly founded in 1325 by King Vladyslav Lokietek. Early anticipation of a less-than favorable outcome of the Nordic War prompted the wise Saxon-Polish prince elector-king to order twenty-five badges of the order from Dinglinger; as the future sovereign of the order he then safeguarded them. Not only was Johann Melchior Dinglinger the authorized maker of the order's badges, but the court jeweler also developed their design in close collaboration with his sovereign. It did, however, take a number of years until the gem's final shape was determined in about 1718.

Augustus the Strong struggled to gain the favor of the Polish nobility with the aid of the order. For him and his successor, Augustus III, the Order of the White Eagle became a useful tool with which the Polish and Saxon aristocracies could be tied to the House of Wettin. The order's sign was the head of an eagle turned to the left side, with his wings outspread above an eight-pointed cross. The king's motto was »Pro Fide, Lege et Grege« (For fidelity, law, and people), while »Grege« was replaced by »Rege« (king) for the knights of the order. The motto is mounted on the gems' reverse around the royal monogram, and is visible on the matching large pectoral star's four cross bars. The *Badge from the Emerald Garniture* was made during the time of Augustus III, when the originally simple gem was altered, almost beyond recognition, by the addition of sixteen emeralds and at least 342 brilliant cut diamonds.

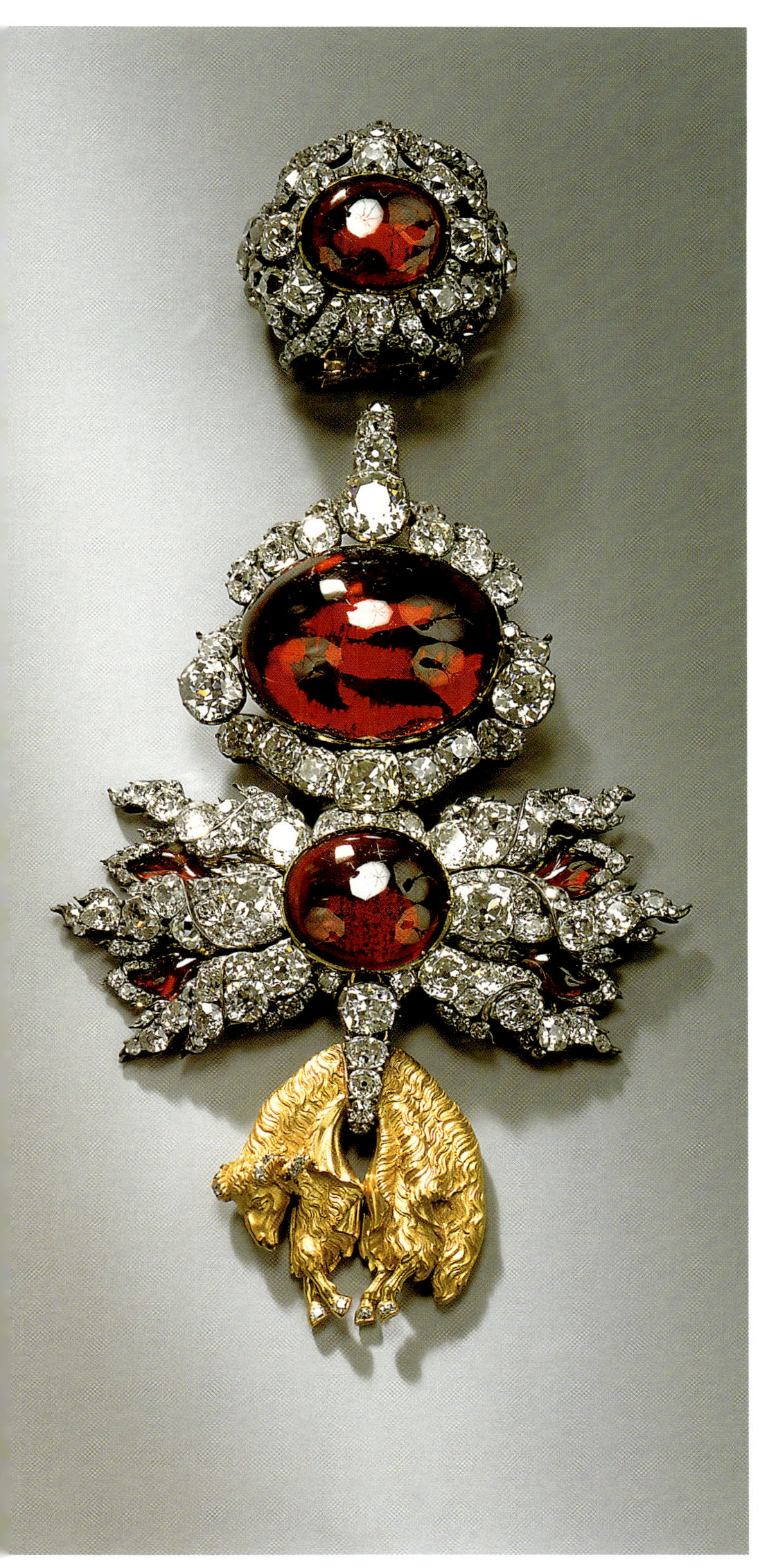

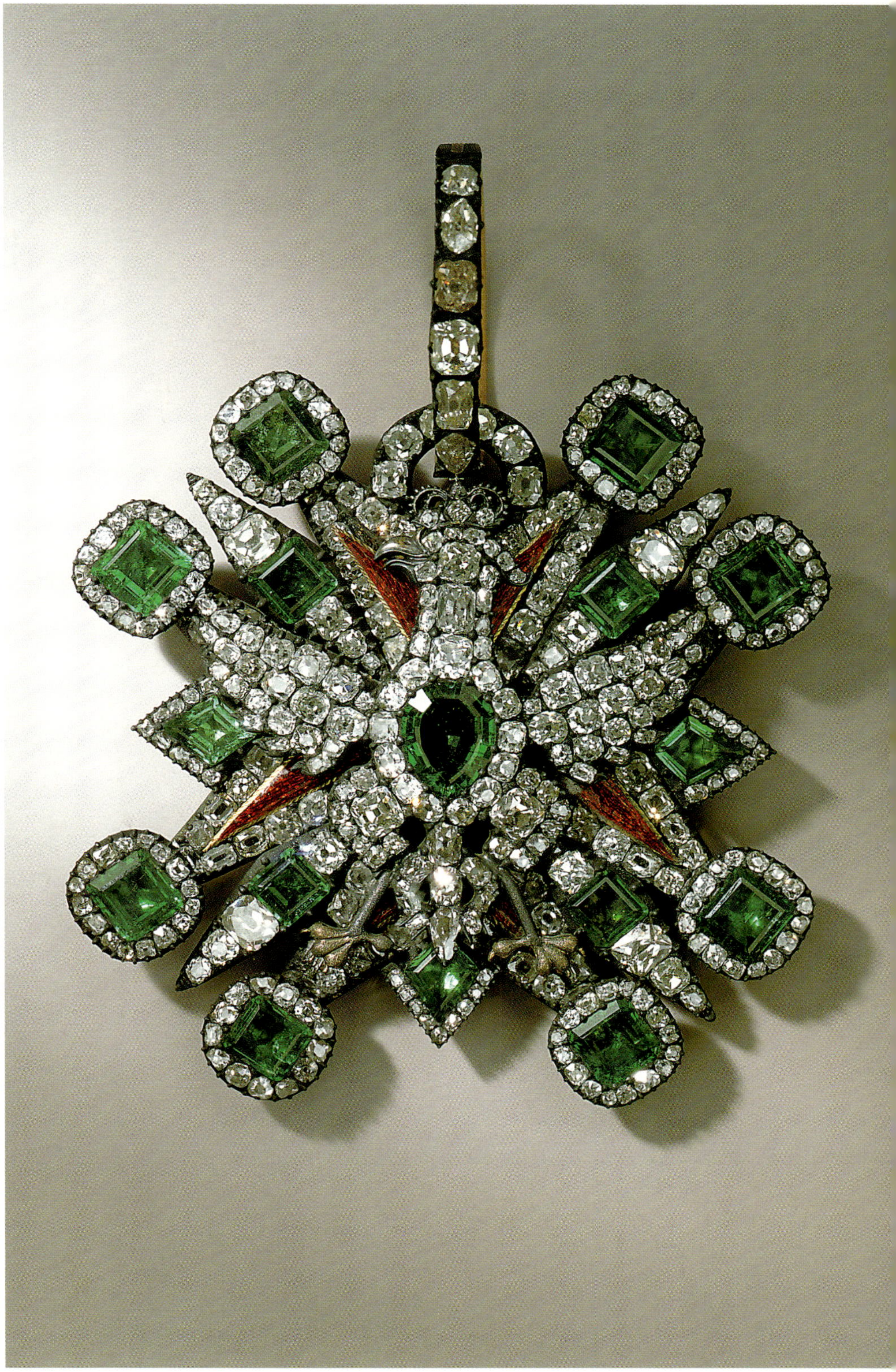

Epaulette with the »Sächsische Weiße« (Saxon White)

Large brilliant cut diamonds of 49,84 ct, 39,53 ct, and 21.01 ct, a plethora of medium size and small brilliant cut diamonds, gold, silver
Franz Diespach
Dresden or Prague, 1769
Modified by Christian August Globig
Dresden, between 1782 and 1789
H. 20,4 cm, Inv.-no. VIII 25

Hat Brooch with the »Dresden Grüne« (Dresden Green)

Almond-shaped, green brilliant cut diamond of 41 ct, round brilliant cut diamond of 6,28 ct, 411 medium size to small brilliant cut diamonds, silver, gold
Franz Diespach
Dresden or Prague, 1769
H. 14,1 cm, W. 5 cm, Inv.-no. VIII 30

Regardless of a piece of jewelry's beauty, princely grace and royal majesty gained renown in the 18th century primarily through possession of large, rare, and especially pure diamonds. Based on this standard, Augustus the Strong and his son Augustus III utilized their jewel garnitures in order to display their understanding of royal power. The material value of their jewel garnitures was enormous. The first Jewel Inventory of 1719 cites an estimated total value of almost 3.5 million thaler for all of the existing garnitures. This was far beyond the material value of all the other collections gathered in the Green Vault – including that of the treasury art in the strict sense of the word.

A look at the *Hat Brooch* and the »Achsel-Agraffe« (shoulder brooch) or *Epaulette* from the brilliant cut diamond garniture – created by Franz Diespach in 1768 and 1769 as a suite – illustrate this point. The *Epaulette* was further modified between 1782 and 1789, and its pendant appears to consist exclusively of brilliant cut diamonds. The »Sächsische Weiße« – a square brilliant cut diamond of 194,5 diamond grains (49,84 ct) and the largest diamond in the Green Vault – is inserted into the upper part of the shoulder strap. Augustus the Strong acquired the »Sächsische Weiße« on February 1, 1728 from the Hamburg jeweler Moses Abraham for 200,000 thaler »oder 2 Tonnen goldes« (or two tons of gold). Johann Georg IV, older brother of Augustus the Strong, had already purchased larger diamonds. In 1695, Augustus the Strong paid the Amsterdam jeweler Charles Le Roy the considerable price of 31,000 thaler for two diamonds. As a point of reference, it must be mentioned that the *Golden Coffee Service* completed in 1701 by Dinglinger cost 50,000 thaler. During Augustus the Strong's entire reign, substantial sums continued to be paid for the procurement of diamonds.

Together with the »Sächsische Weiße,« the crown diamond of the first prince elector-king, another diamond of 75,25 grains or 19,28 ct came into the possession of Augustus the Strong for 20,000 thaler. Today, it is set in the upper portion of the *Hat Brooch* with the »Dresden Grüne.« The sums of 120,000 and 162,000 thaler were subsequently paid to the Moses Meyer Company of Amsterdam for diamonds that cannot be identified today.

Of the two other large, circular brilliant cut diamonds from the *Epaulette*, only the price for the larger, main stone of 154,25 grains or circa 39,53 ct is known. It was bought in Vienna in 1742 for 80,000 thaler.

Augustus III's passion for diamonds went much further than his father's. With the »Dresden Grüne,« he managed to bring the most precious of all diamonds in the Green Vault into his own possession. The sea-green, very pure diamond weighs 160 grains or 41 ct and came to the Treasury in 1742 as part of a brilliant cut diamond garniture. August III bought the diamond from the Armenian merchant Delles or Telles at the Leipzig Fair. As is the case with most famous diamonds, the »Dresden Grüne« is surrounded by a riddle. No one knows how the only large, green diamond ever found made its way from the Golconda area in India to London, where it was supposedly cut, and then to Dresden, nor is its true purchase price known. It was likely 400,000 thaler. The diamond owes its unique coloration to the fact that it was exposed to natural radioactivity below the surface of the earth. It is thus a true wonder of nature.

At first, Augustus III had the new »Hausdiamant« set into the badge of the Order of the Golden Fleece and thereby obtained the most precious order insignia of any European king at the time. When his grandson Friedrich August III came of age in 1768 and assumed the Saxon reign as prince elector, he broke up the badge of the Order of the Golden Fleece and had the diamond set – together with 411 medium size and small brilliant cut diamonds – into the still extant *Hat Brooch*.

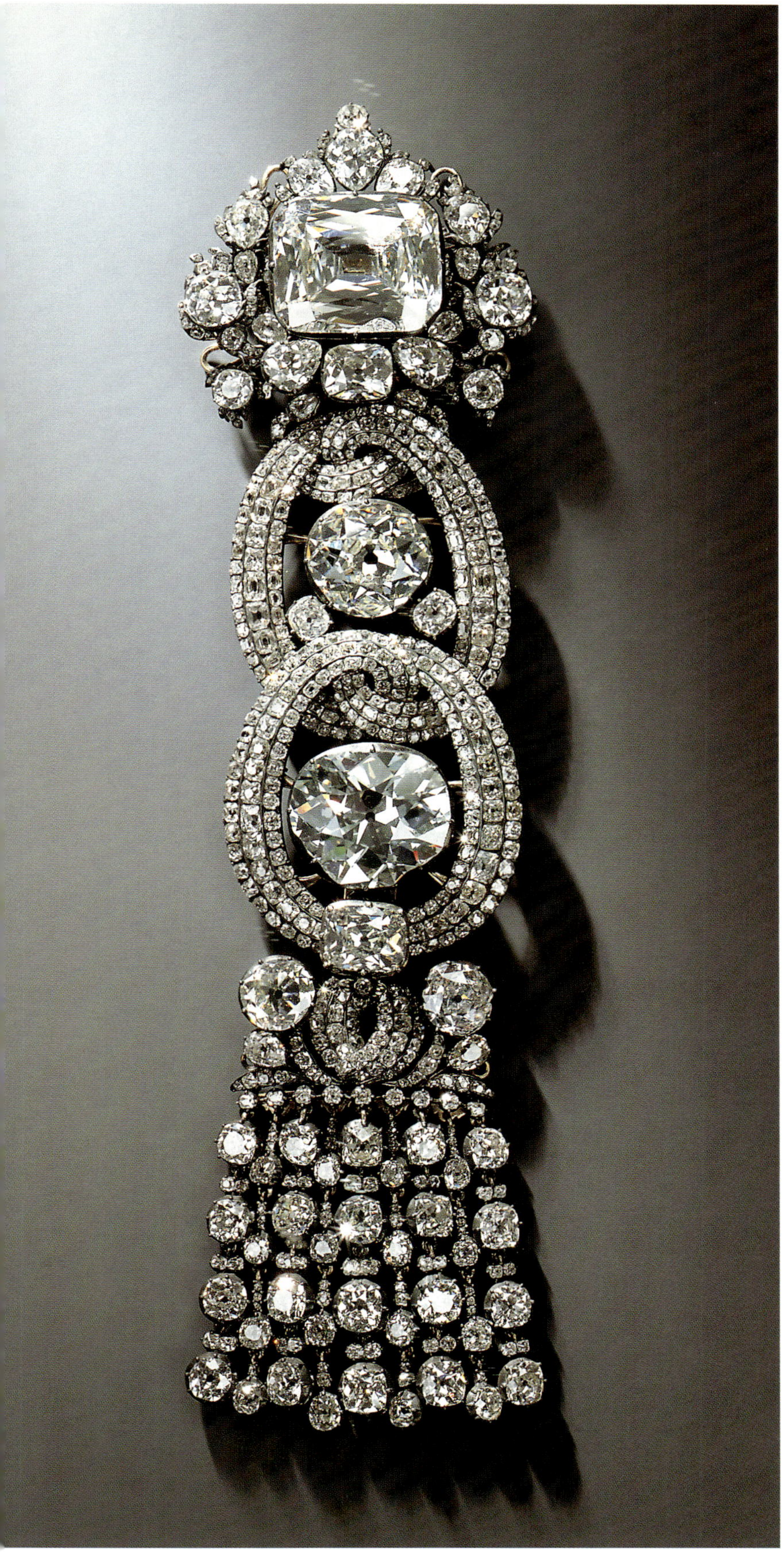

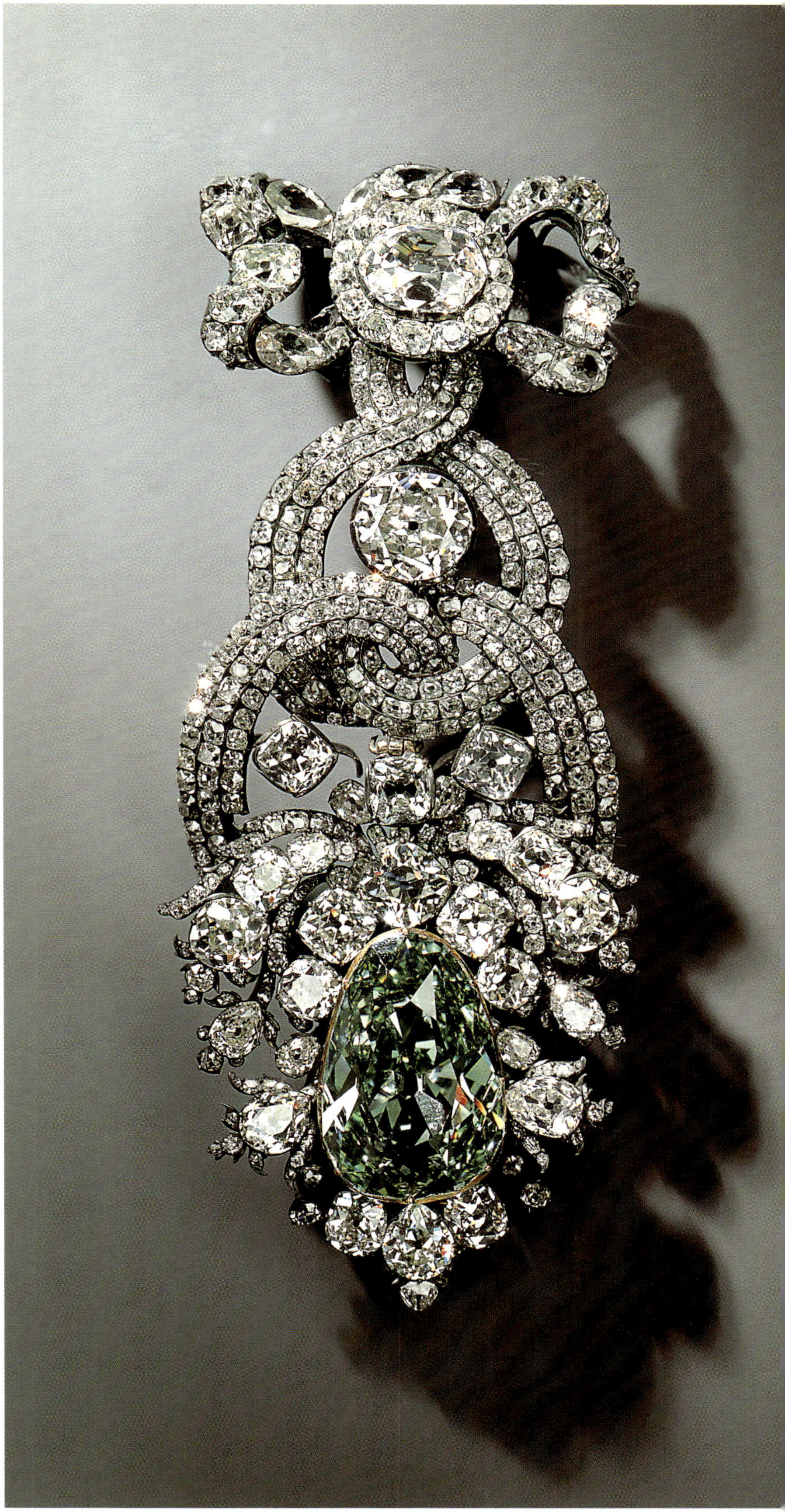

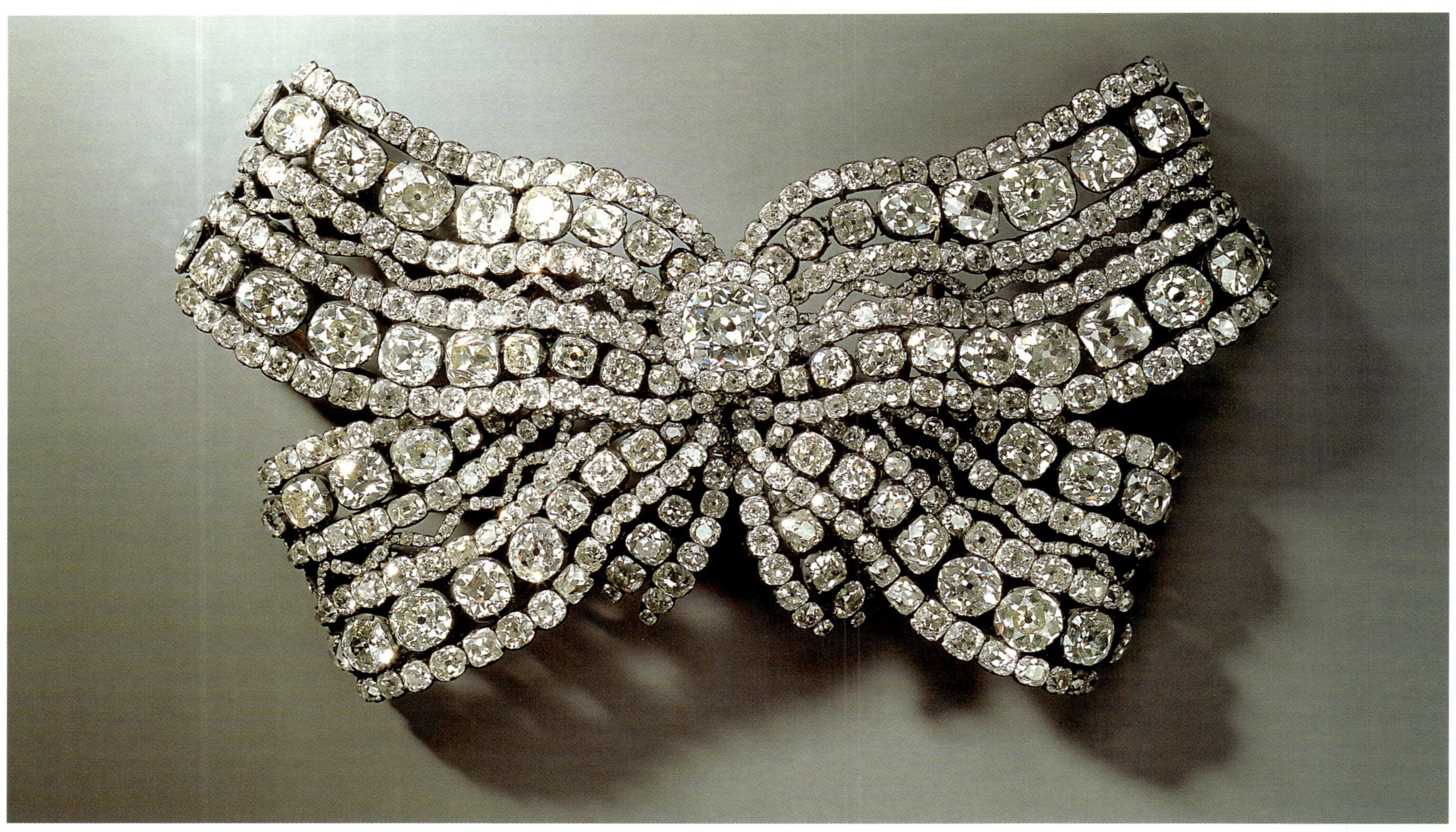

Large Chest Bow of Electress Amalie Auguste

Fifty-one large and 611 smaller brilliant cut diamonds, silver, gold
Christian August Globig
Dresden, 1782
H. 12,5 cm, W. 21,4 cm, Inv.-no. VIII 36

The Saxon jewel garnitures satisfied not only their owners' need for ostentatious display, but they also served as important, strategic financial reserves that could be easily transported if they had to be pawned in order to raise cash. This truly royal jewelry thus offered the best possibility in the 18th century for transporting considerable sums throughout Europe. Thus, King Friedrich Augustus I of Saxony, formerly Prince Elector Friedrich Augustus III, decided in 1807, one year after his proclamation as king, to mortgage nearly the entire holdings of brilliant cut jewelry to Holland for a loan of 1.4 million guilders. The *Epaulette*, all of the jacket and waistcoat buttons from the brilliant cut garniture, the star of the Polish Order of the White Eagle, and numerous of the ruler's finger rings were included in the transaction. The *Hat Brooch* with the »Dresden Grüne« and the large *Chest Bow* that Friedrich Augustus gave his wife, however, were excluded.

Up until circa 1800, similar decorative bows, worn below the neckline of a gown, were part of the popular repertory of ladies' jewelry at court. The opulent and very heavy *Chest Bow* reveals an unusually abundant diamond decoration. Made in 1782 on the occasion of the birth of the electoral couple's first child, their daughter Maria Augusta, the invaluable *Bow* was not privately owned by Amalie Auguste, unlike most of the jewelry of previous electresses. Instead, it was assigned to the collection of official state jewelry, the Wettin's »Hausschmuck« (house jewelry), and hence became part of the Green Vault's inventory. Diamonds derived from Augustus III's brilliant cut diamond garniture – out of fashion at the time – served for the fabrication of the *Bow*, among them twenty-seven jacket buttons, twelve waistcoat buttons and also other pieces of jewelry.

The *Chest Bow* is a sculptural work in the shape of a gathered band with flowing ends. The center of the wide piece is made from a shirt button that originated from Augustus III's brilliant cut diamond garniture; it remains intact in its original box setting. The total weight of the brilliant cut diamonds included amounts to approximately 614 ct which means that the magnificent *Chest Bow*, including its setting, weighs well over one pound (556 grams) – a fact that must have diminished the comfort of the wearer. But even Queen Carola of Saxony occasionally borrowed the *Chest Bow* from the Green Vault, wearing it in the 1870s and 80s during official court functions.